T0384813

# We Hold These Truths

*The Federalist* (1787–8) remains the best single account of how American democracy is supposed to work. Yet it is also incomplete. While generations of scholars from Alexis de Tocqueville to Anthony Downs have tried to fill the gaps, America's constantly changing society and political institutions continue to encounter new puzzles and challenges. *We Hold These Truths* provides a comprehensive survey of what recent scholarship adds to the Framers' vision, stressing how long-established political habits can shift as voters become more polarized, and even lead to feedbacks that amplify public anger still further. Developing a theory of American democracy for the age of the internet, Trump, and polarization, this study mixes modern social science with a detailed knowledge of history, asking where the Framers' scheme has gone wrong – and what can be done to fix it.

Stephen M. Maurer is Adjunct Emeritus Professor of Public Policy at the University of California at Berkeley. Trained as a lawyer, he has been associated with Berkeley's Goldman School of Public Policy since 1999. His books include *WMD Terrorism* (MIT Press, 2009), *On the Shoulders of Giants* (Cambridge University Press, 2017), and *Self-Governance in Science* (Cambridge University Press, 2017).

# We Hold These Truths

*Updating the Framers' Vision of
American Democracy*

## STEPHEN M. MAURER

*University of California at Berkeley*

CAMBRIDGE
UNIVERSITY PRESS

# CAMBRIDGE
## UNIVERSITY PRESS

Shaftesbury Road, Cambridge CB2 8EA, United Kingdom

One Liberty Plaza, 20th Floor, New York, NY 10006, USA

477 Williamstown Road, Port Melbourne, VIC 3207, Australia

314–321, 3rd Floor, Plot 3, Splendor Forum, Jasola District Centre, New Delhi – 110025, India

103 Penang Road, #05–06/07, Visioncrest Commercial, Singapore 238467

Cambridge University Press is part of Cambridge University Press & Assessment, a department of the University of Cambridge.

We share the University's mission to contribute to society through the pursuit of education, learning and research at the highest international levels of excellence.

www.cambridge.org
Information on this title: www.cambridge.org/9781108845700

DOI: 10.1017/9781108990646

First published 2024

Printed in the United Kingdom by TJ Books Limited, Padstow Cornwall

*A catalogue record for this publication is available from the British Library*

*Library of Congress Cataloging-in-Publication Data*
NAMES: Maurer, Stephen M., author.
TITLE: We Hold These Truths: Updating the Framers' Vision of American Democracy / Stephen M. Maurer.
DESCRIPTION: Cambridge, United Kingdom ; New York, NY : Cambridge University Press, 2024. | Includes bibliographical references and index.
IDENTIFIERS: LCCN 2023024333 | ISBN 9781108845700 (hardback) | ISBN 9781108990646 (ebook)
SUBJECTS: LCSH: United States – Politics and government. | Democracy – United States. | Founding Fathers of the United States.
CLASSIFICATION: LCC JK31 .M39 2024 | DDC 320.473–dc23/eng/20230731
LC record available at https://lccn.loc.gov/2023024333

ISBN 978-1-108-84570-0 Hardback

*To my long-ago college and law school professors,*
*who led me to these questions*

The science of politics, however, like most other sciences, has received great improvement. The efficacy of various principles is now well understood, which were either not known at all, or imperfectly known to the ancients ... these are wholly new discoveries, or have made their principal progress toward perfection in modern times.

Alexander Hamilton, *The Federalist*

It is always easy to be logical. It is almost impossible to be logical to the bitter end.

Albert Camus, *The Myth of Sisyphus*

# Contents

# Figures

# Preface

Go ahead. Ask anyone. "American politics," they will tell you, "has become more polarized."[1] Small wonder, then, that the major parties never seem to agree. But when Americans talk of polarization, they typically mean more than that. People are also angrier: 70 percent of Democrats and 62 percent of Republicans now say that they are "afraid" of the other party.[2]

And the professionals are worse. Most politicians now see nothing wrong with using congressional majorities of barely a half-dozen votes to change the country – after which, they cheerfully tell us, the average American will see how much better things are and thank them.

Well, maybe. But what happens if they're wrong?

This book takes the polarization crisis seriously and asks how America's institutions can be designed to reduce – or at least avoid adding to – citizens' resentments. This focus on institutions is unfashionable. Most recent books on polarization prefer a broader canvas, variously stressing human psychology, a decaying culture, or society at large. This is almost always followed by arguments for the author's own politics, culminating in what two leading political scientists describe as a plea for "liberals to become conservatives or *vice versa*."[3] In this telling, the Constitution and its institutions are mostly beside the point: The only real trouble is that one side refuses to see how wrong it is.

But if we accept the importance of institutions, we must also accept that today's vituperation is just as natural as bipartisan politics was fifty years ago. And this makes sense. Social scientists know that complex systems often display radically different behaviors – in the jargon, "phase changes" – from one era to the next. And indeed, the US has experienced eras of virulent partisanship before. But if American politics really does have two distinct modes, it is important to know what drives them. The dynamics of what we will call the "bipartisan" phase are reasonably clear: Despite improvements,[4] the framework that Anthony Downs laid down in *An Economic Theory of Democracy* (1957) remains definitive. At the same time, the existence of a second, "coercive" regime shows that he overlooked something vital. This book argues that the missing ingredient was legislative deadlock. This opens the door to non-Downsian strategies in which long periods of obstruction are periodically interrupted by crises in which one side tries to ride roughshod over the other.

Of course, just saying that the American system divides its time between two different regimes is only the start. Once we admit the possibility, we must equally admit that voters' beliefs and emotions can change from one era to the next. This book fills the gap with a deliberately simple account of how humans process political arguments. Our basic strategy is to capture salient facts that scientists have learned about the brain since Downs' time. Here, many readers will see large borrowings from Daniel Kahneman's pathbreaking *Thinking Fast and Slow* (2011).

The idea of reducing complex institutions such as Congress or the presidency to simple "rational man" models dates back to *The Federalist*. And this presents an opportunity. I will argue that Madison's concern with "liberty" and especially "tyrannies of the majority" anticipates our own obsession with "polarization." This connection would have been obvious to early political scientists such as John W. Burgess (1844–1931), Woodrow Wilson (1856–1924), and Frank Goodnow (1859–1933). For the most part, they simply picked up where Madison left off, writing books in which governance emerged from rule-bound institutions guided by rationally self-interested men. But that changed in the 1920s, as political scientists tried to make their subject more "scientific," embracing detailed case studies and, somewhat later, sophisticated statistical methods as their preferred tools. This was sensible at a time when Madison's approach seemed picked-over and stale. All the same, the new methods worked poorly for analyzing the system as a whole.[5] The result is that modern political scientists have done little to update *The Federalist*, even though it remains by far the most important blueprint for how the American system is supposed to work, or might be improved.

As this project matured, I realized that I was writing a love letter. In one sense, *The Federalist*, like any book, is a finished object. But it was also written by men who never once forgot that they were leading Americans to a path that had "never been trodden by man."[6] This was doubly true since social science and economic theory were still in their infancy. I think the Framers would have been delighted to see how rigorous mathematical models can extend and clarify their logic.

Then too, the Framers wrote their Constitution just one year before the French Revolution. Looking back, they could still argue for a simple historical pattern in which citizens made bad choices and then repented their mistakes within a year or so. But they could not see what was coming – a permanent Left/Right quarrel that has continued uninterrupted from their day to ours.

Finally, revisiting Madison is especially timely now. If every generation has its *annus horribilis*, ours arrived with COVID-19 and the civil unrest of 2020. The silver lining is that happy societies have little to teach us: It is only when we see institutions pushed to their limits that we learn. This makes it an especially good time to take stock.

Readers should approach this book at three levels. First and most obviously, for the pleasure of understanding. But in that case, why begin with Madison? Suffice to say that *The Federalist* has made such a good start that it only makes sense to extend and improve its arguments if we can. Moreover, our ultimate goal is not just intellectual, but also to diagnose failures and fix them. Starting from Madison's arguments keeps us focused on the Constitution we actually have. And this is prudent: As the Framers themselves pointed out, old institutions accumulate such value that we should not lightly discard them. I do not know whether Madison would have agreed with the various fixes proposed in Chapter 10, but he would certainly have understood their logic.

The second reason to read this book is political. As Ken Arrow showed in his famous "Impossibility Theorem," democracy only becomes possible *after* most of the population agrees on some minimal set of convictions.[7] This makes *The Federalist* more than just another book: It is the closest thing to an official mainstream, a blueprint for how most living Americans think their government should function. But shared beliefs must be kept in good repair: If they are false or contradictory or just widely misunderstood, we will have a hard time defending them. For example, today's politicians often complain that uneven representation in the Senate and Electoral College is undemocratic. And yet these same speakers show hardly any awareness of why the Framers adopted these rules to begin with. Before we discard Madison's various "checks" and "balances," we should at least understand what he was trying to do.

Finally, there is a narrowly legal reason. When our politics bubbles over, judges must sort things out. Yet even the strictest constructionist knows that every text contains ambiguities if you press hard enough. But if judges must choose, it is better to make the choice as impersonal as possible. This can happen only if they come to the document armed with some theory of how the American system is supposed to work. This book tries to fill that gap.

Every author owes a large debt, conscious and unconscious, to the intellectual generosity of friends and colleagues. I particularly wish to thank Gene Bardach, Jason Christopher, Mitchell Chyette, Diane Coyle, Sebastian von Engelhardt, Andreas Freytag, Sonja Garden, Roberta Hayes, Alexander Karapetyan, David Mayhew, Eric Patashnik, Martin Quitt, Ken Rosenblatt, Patrick Rey, Paul Seabright, Greg Taylor, Alex White, and attendees at the Toulouse School of Economics 13th Digital Economics Conference (January 9–10, 2020) for their insights and helpful suggestions.

## Notes

1 The evidence is all on their side. Even before Donald Trump, the median Republican was more conservative than 94 percent of Democrats, up from 70 percent two decades before. Meanwhile, the median Democrat was more liberal than 92 percent of Republicans. Kiley (2017).

2 Anon (2016b). Much has been made of polls showing that 41 percent of voters wanted to impeach President Trump before the House even started proceedings. But the numbers were not much better for Presidents Obama (33 percent), Bush (30 percent), or Clinton (29 percent). See, e.g., NBC News (2018) (Trump) and Topaz (2014) (Clinton, Bush, and Obama). Moreover, the Clinton/Obama-haters and Bush/Trump-haters were usually different people. This implies that roughly two-thirds of the electorate are happy to see Congress overturn elections they disagree with.

3 Achen and Bartels (2017) at p. 2.

4 For a recent survey see, e.g., Gehlbach (2022) at pp. 1–46.

5 See, e.g., Downs (1957) at p. 14 (noting that "relatively few studies … look at government as a whole," let alone predict "what *will* happen under certain conditions"). Public choice economists have been more faithful to the Framers' agenda, accumulating a substantial literature that applies rational actor models to US political institutions. Gehlbach (2022). That said, they almost always limit their analyses to comparatively small fragments of the overall system.

6 Stevens [1787] at p. 457.

7 Wikipedia (62).

# Introduction

This book argues that America's Constitution supports two types of politics – "bipartisan" and "coercive" – that alternate every century or so. It follows that the system's resilience is mostly a question of how well Madison's various institutions interact to stabilize bipartisan phases and destabilize coercive ones.

No book that takes Madison as its starting point can avoid making process, or rather loyalty to process, its principal civic virtue. For those who believe this, it does not matter if you are progressive or conservative, the main thing is that the country make the choice honestly according to the law and Constitution. Indeed, the Framers, Washington, and Lincoln all held that not even The People could overturn the Constitution unless they first followed its procedures.[1]

This primacy of rules also implies a certain agnosticism. Whatever we might privately believe, a procedural theory of government cannot elevate one political creed over all the others. Such logic would be anti-Copernican, reducing to the simplistic argument that the speaker knows better than every single one of the millions of voters who voted differently in the last election.[2] The deeper point is that the "will of the people" must be respected even, and perhaps especially, when we dislike the result. And this is doubly true of personalities. I have sometimes heard scholars who ought to know better blame "Donald Trump," or "Newt Gingrich," or "Nancy Pelosi" for the country's dysfunction. But the Trumps have always been with us, and Madison's checks and balances were supposed to protect us from demagogues. What went wrong that Trumpian tactics became a paying proposition?

It follows, too, that in studying history we must be more interested in whether the system worked as intended than whether it reached the same substantive results that we would today. This is unavoidable – no democracy can be any better than the people it represents. For Americans, this disconnect is most painful for slavery and the Civil War. Today, we rightly see the war to end slavery as a moral imperative. But at the time many and perhaps most voters would have preferred some other choice. The fact that they did not receive one, either from Congress or at the ballot box, must count as the Constitution's greatest failure.

Beyond philosophy, there are also practical questions. A book that claims to address Madisonian thought must first find some way to mark the main channel. Otherwise, it would be all too easy to invent and quarrel with strawmen. In what follows, I have almost always taken *The Federalist* as my starting point for the simple reason that so many past and present Americans subscribe to it. Despite selling no more than a few hundred copies when they first appeared, the essays quickly became the go-to source for lawyers and legal scholars trying to understand the Constitution, and have steadily expanded since the 1960s to include millions of lay readers as well.[3] By now, most living Americans have read some or all of the book in school, and almost everyone has heard it quoted.

At the same time, *The Federalist* is only a snapshot. On the one hand, it draws on thousands of earlier pamphlets and speeches, themselves descended from centuries of trying to extract coherent principles from England's ghostly unwritten constitution. We will sometimes turn to these when *The Federalist* is silent. On the other, its themes continue to run like a red thread through American political thought, from Washington's Farewell Address to de Tocqueville's *Democracy in America*, to Lincoln's speeches to, faintly but unmistakably, twentieth-century "rational man" theories of politics. Here, Anthony Downs' *An Economic Theory of Democracy* is, I think, inescapable. The Framers did not anticipate the rise of parties, let alone how many political questions elections would settle before Congress even had a chance to meet. But their usual habit of asking what a self-interested politician would do would almost certainly have led them to classical economics and much the same answers that Prof. Downs reached.

My choice of Richard Hofstadter's work may be less obvious. Like Madison, however, Hofstadter was mainly interested in ransacking history for evidence of what can go wrong. Other historians would no doubt quarrel with some of the lessons he drew. Suffice to say, I am less worried about the details of what *actually* happened than to discover what plausibly *might* have happened and could happen again. And of course,

Hofstadter's other virtue is that, like de Tocqueville and Downs, he never strays far from the main channel of what most Americans believe.

Each new generation finds Madisonian theory outdated and in disrepair and scarred by gaps. The result is that Americans are continually asking themselves which gaps can be filled, and what must be changed, and what remains valuable and useful. The task is still more complicated because the Constitution – having been amended twenty-seven times – is plainly a moving target. Indeed, some of these changes, like the two-term limit for presidents, run counter to *The Federalist* itself. So while it is usually a good beginning to ask "What did Madison think?" the inquiry cannot end there.

If anything, changes outside the written Constitution matter even more. Innovations like mass political parties in the nineteenth century and Big Government in the twentieth scrambled American politics. To cite just one example, Madison assumed that politicians would be loyal to, and defend, their respective institutions. But once politicians join competing parties, partisanship is bound to come first. This suggests that the Executive and Legislative branches are much more likely to cooperate than fight. This is an interesting dynamic in its own right, and may have significant virtues. But it is not at all what the Framers had in mind, and we need to rethink things for ourselves. What makes the problem urgent, of course, is that Madison was counting on separation of powers to save us from tyranny. While we can ask whether the new arrangements might somehow take over this function, the original rationale no longer serves. In the meantime, politicians who ignore this by pretending to find every answer in *The Federalist* make the Framers sound clueless. This cannot be good for democracy.

Finally, *The Federalist* was incomplete even in its own time. Faced with a bitter debate over the Constitution, the Framers understandably demoted less immediately contentious issues like the nature of The People or how to manage The Press into the background. Sometimes, this is just as well. As we will see in Chapter 4, the economics of "The Press" has changed so thoroughly since 1830 that whatever the Framers thought would not be helpful. The deeper problem concerns "The People." Though Madison repeatedly alludes to them, his comments almost always come down to the claim that we can expect their moods to oscillate between "passion" and "reason" within a year or two. Prof. Downs, writing in the 1950s, said even less, and treated voters' preferences as fixed and unchanging. This was not, as he cheerfully confessed, because he really believed this: To the contrary, changes in voter preferences were "among the most important political events possible," and he had simply "dodged the question."⁴ What mattered, though, was that the dodge worked nicely in the Eisenhower era when most issues came and went within an election or two. For Downs' theory, which never looks past the next election, that made fixed preferences an ugly but workable compromise.

The difference in the twenty-first century is that our struggles over, say, immigration and healthcare and gun control go on for decades. Rather than buying time for reflection, the Constitution's frictions have produced a permanent gridlock punctuated by violent disputes whenever one side feels strong enough to force its policies onto the other. Analyzing these extended struggles – and especially how they might end – forces us to ask very non-Downsian questions about how voters form opinions and sometimes change their minds. Fortunately, science knows much more about these issues than it did just thirty years ago.

We are used to hearing the Framers described, particularly on the Right, as geniuses inspired by God. If anything, this diminishes them. Rather, it was their all-too-human human glory to get so many things right from so little evidence⁵ and such primitive economic theory. In the meantime, they were self-aware. On the one hand, they knew they were designing a government that had "no model on the face of the globe."⁶ But on the other, they were never reckless. They had thought the problem through and knew that their arguments made sense. More than that, they saw that America's "Confederation" government was not good enough, and could not last. Above all, they had the nerve to try.

A few years later, with the new Constitution barely underway, George Washington would say only that the risk was worth taking: "Is there a doubt whether a common government can embrace so large a sphere? Let experience solve it. To listen to mere speculation in such a case were criminal ... It is well worth a fair and full experiment."⁷ The irony for us, two centuries later, is that there are still unknowns. The Constitution, despite its many patches, still has holes, some sizable. No less than Washington, we too have an obligation to say whether the chances for "happy issue" still justify "a fair and full experiment."

So much for throat-clearing. It's time to make the argument.

### Notes

1   *Federalist* No. 78 at p. 359 (Hamilton); Washington [1796] at pp. 13 and 19; Lincoln [1861(b)] at p. 441.
2   Rejecting Anti-Copernican accounts also offers the purely psychological benefit that, even if we never truly ask whether our political beliefs might

be mistaken, we at least admit the possibility. This strikes me as a small, but essential, first step toward reducing polarization.

3  *Federalist* at p. ix (Introduction by R. Raphael).

4  Downs (1957) at p. 140. Downs added that democratic government was bound to fail unless "voters can somehow be moved to the center of the scale," though he offered no suggestions on how to do this. Downs (1957) at p. 120.

5  Ricks (2020) at p. 126.

6  *Federalist* No. 14 at p. 61 (Madison).

7  Washington [1796] at pp. 9–10.

# I

# Updating the Framers

We begin this chapter by reviewing the government the Framers designed, with a special emphasis on how they expected its various components to behave and interact. This provides the baseline picture of what the Framers were trying to accomplish and, in particular, what we might want to preserve and build on.

The second part of the chapter turns to deciding which modern ideas and extensions best preserve the Framers' vision. Here, the best I can do is to offer an analogy. Today there are any number of television shows where restorers install modern equipment in, say, a seventy-year-old aircraft. The question is when this should be considered legitimate. Suffice to say, viewers seldom object to additions that implement and empower the original builders' ideas. Thus, installing modern instruments in an airplane, for example, is acceptable since the designers needed that function without much caring how it was done. But it would be different if our restorers changed the designers' ideas by, for example, trading piston engines for jets.

Staying true to the Framers, then, starts by identifying the logic, assumptions, and goals that they found persuasive. And if we can make some of these concepts more precise – for example, by asking what modern game theory adds to Madison's "rational politician" arguments – then that, too, is legitimate. The problem is harder when we come to institutions that the Framers either did not foresee, such as mass political parties, or else mostly ignored, such as newspapers. Here, all we can do is stick close to ideas that are now so widely accepted that we feel sure that the Framers would embrace them too. We end with a chapter-by-chapter guide to what follows.

## 1.1 THE FRAMERS' DESIGN

The Framers did not design the Constitution from a blank sheet of paper. Instead, they extended and made improvements to an existing tradition of political philosophers and pamphleteers, who had in turn tried to rationalize English institutions that had grown up willy-nilly through the centuries. No surprise, then, that much of the American Constitution was adopted from English practice without debate or even apparent thought.

But when topics *were* debated, the goal was nearly always stability and survival. Most previous republics, after all, had collapsed within a generation or so. The question was just what the new Constitution could do to fix this. Earlier generations, raised on Roman authors, had assumed that stability depended on citizens' "virtue."[1] But this advice was not very helpful. After all, if virtue was everything, institutional design was pointless. So Madison concentrated instead on those choices within his power, ransacking history to see how different choices had led to better or worse outcomes. This was cutting-edge stuff: As historian Thomas Ricks points out, Madison studied the problem "almost as a political scientist,"[2] systematically identifying the most likely pathologies, and designing a constitution to manage them.

In the long view, the Framers saw three problems. The first was tyranny. The basic point was that while power was necessary to government, it should also be limited to whatever was needed to achieve legitimate ends. Yet the principle of one-man-one-vote threatened this. The reason was that this formal equality ignored the fact that the costs and benefits of government were felt more intensely by some voters than others. This meant that a small bribe to 51 percent of the country, say, could quite rationally (if unethically) persuade it to endorse schemes that imposed vast suffering on the other 49 percent. This opened the door to political strategies based on buying votes cheaply from citizens who were largely indifferent and then using government power to oppress those who cared deeply. Naively, the cure for this was obvious: Replace one-man-one-vote with a system that reflects how intensely each individual feels. Of course, we know perfectly well that no real government does this.[3] But that is mostly a question of practicality: Intensity is, after all, fiendishly hard to measure. Still, there is no reason why this practical difficulty should stop us from asking whether intensity is a legitimate consideration, how an ideal democracy would accommodate intensity if we knew how to measure it, or how existing institutions can better approximate this ideal.[4] Moreover, even partial solutions are worth implementing if they improve on intensity-blind majority rule. This book argues that various features of the American system, including presidential vetoes and Senate filibusters, go some distance toward doing this.

The second problem that the Framers worried about was that The People were fallible. To be sure, determining what they wanted was easy: Elections would do this automatically, after which any representative who wanted to keep his job or reputation would know exactly how to vote.[5] But ancient history was filled with stories in which The People had made disastrous choices.[6] So the Framers imagined public opinion schizophrenically oscillating between "Reason" and "Passion." The trick, then, was to design institutions that slowed the oscillation long enough so that the Republic did not constantly swing, in Madison's phrase, between "hemlock on one day and statues on the next."[7] Judging from the history of past democracies, the Framers estimated that two to three years would normally suffice for the public to overcome its passions and to see through whatever lies the demagogues had told.[8]

For the most part, the Framers did not try to explain this oscillation, but only treated it as an observed regularity. Even so, Madison sometimes hints at two distinct mechanisms. On the one hand, some mistakes seemed to originate inside "the mob" itself, though he never explains just how this happens.[9] And on the other, he says that citizens seldom know much. This makes it easy for self-interested "factions" to hide facts and tell lies to mislead them. We argue in Chapter 2 that modern economics has fleshed out both concepts in ways that Madison would surely have welcomed.

Finally, the Framers saw a third problem. The majority might not be deluded at all – only greedy. Morality aside, there was nothing irrational about putting the majority's interests ahead of the country's or else expropriating the minority.[10] In either case, the result would be a "tyranny of the majority" in which voters tried to exploit each other instead of pursuing projects to make everyone richer. And tyranny was dangerous: After all, injustice can only be implemented by force, and government's coercive power is limited. Continue the oppression long enough, and minority's resentments could overturn the government.[11]

Having defined the threats, the Framers set up three guardrails to manage them. The first was separation of powers. Legislatures would write all laws prospectively – that is, before any violations occurred. Then the executive would enforce them.[12] And finally, the judiciary would second-guess the executive to make sure it had interpreted Congress's words correctly. This meant that no legislator could ever be sure when he voted just who the new law would be used to prosecute: They might be his enemies, his friends, or even himself. This would force him to write laws that were just, limited, and clearly defined. Meanwhile, the president could only act when one of these laws said he could.

The Framers believed that separation of powers was the only way to prevent tyranny.[13] Yet despite this they were never doctrinaire, remaining open to the possibility that shared power might sometimes be acceptable after all. Most obviously, they upheld the president's power to veto even though this formally made him a legislator. Mainly they saw this as a weapon that he could use to defend his powers so that Congress did not pile on laws until he was nothing more than a clerk. But the Framers also added the subsidiary justification that the president could use his veto to strike down bad legislation. Here was something new. *The Federalist* often rails against supermajority requirements because they let "pertinacious" minorities hold legislation hostage until the majority gives in.[14] But this was a supermajority with a difference, coming into play solely when the president chose to assert it. And when would that be? The Framers argued that two conditions would have to be met. The first was that the president had to have some reasonable chance of persuading at least one-third of one house to sustain him, since a failed veto would expose his weakness to no purpose.[15] This would deter him from acting unless his dissent was sufficiently mainstream to command "a very respectable proportion of the legislative body."[16] But second, the president would also have to gamble that voters would not punish him at the next election for having defied the majority. Together, the two conditions meant that the veto would be triggered only in the presence of large, passionate minorities where tyranny of the majority was most likely. This was very different from the traditional concept of the supermajority as a "dumb" friction that slowed good and bad legislation indiscriminately. The veto made it "smart," selectively targeting the particular pathology that Madison feared most.

The principle of divided government led naturally to Madison's second guardrail of "checks and balances." Here the Framers predicted that the House of Representatives would pose the greatest danger. On the one hand, being directly elected, it had the most influence over The People. On the other, being numerous, it was nearly as susceptible to passions as the average citizen. The danger could be contained only if some combination of the Senate, president, and Supreme Court stood in its way.[17]

The strategy was perilous not least because it assumed that The People would respect the country's elder statesmen enough to put their own judgments on hold. But even then, the scheme could work only if the Senate and president showed firmness and commanded the public's trust. The Framers wrote their Constitution to encourage both. To make senators and presidents firm, they gave them long tenures in office that helped insulate them from passing anger until the public repented.[18] As for reputation, they made the Senate and presidency so exclusive that only the most prestigious candidates could get elected.[19]

Still, checks and balances were only a holding action, and Madison understood perfectly well that a demagogue who preserved his popularity long enough could eventually replace both president and Senate. This makes it striking that he did not try to invent explicit procedural guardrails against majority tyranny. Instead, Madison relied on a simple practical estimate that politicians' virtue and, especially, their enlightened self-interest would take care of the problem.[20] Today's winners, he argued, would surely see that they could just as easily be victims tomorrow, and would therefore stop short of exploiting the minority for their own protection.[21] At one level, Madison's appeal to rationality and incentives was stunning, anticipating mid-twentieth-century game theory's "backwards induction" insight of analyzing strategy from the last countermove to the first. But at another, he must have seen that this same reasoning should have stopped the ancients from exploiting each other, which it plainly hadn't. All the same, he was on the right track: Legislators' self-interest would indeed drive them to write safeguards into Senate procedure a few years later.

It is traditional to compare the Framers' checks and balances to clockwork. But the rhetoric of "a machine that would go of itself" implies a device that senses and corrects its own errors.[22] For the Framers, that meant that when the public showed "reason," its will "ought to control and regulate the government," but when the same public showed "passion," its will had "to be controlled and regulated by the government."[23] Yet, except for the veto, checks and balances did not do that, but only slowed all legislation indiscriminately.[24] Fortunately, this friction was desirable on other grounds. Almost by definition, legislation that passes by a narrow margin can be repealed just as quickly. But laws that jitter back and forth disrupt citizens' lives and businesses, and prevent society from giving new laws a fair trial.[25] And, of course, jitter paired with tyranny would be even worse. As Washington pointed out, new governments would not just repeal abusive laws, but also become themselves more violent through a "spirit of revenge." From then on, each alternating government would escalate over the preceding one until the people finally embraced a despot to stop the chaos.[26] The lesson was that even "dumb" frictions could serve a purpose by screening out the kinds of knife-edge votes that caused jitter in the first place. At the same time, the frictions could not be too high or citizens would rightly complain that the system was undemocratic.[27]

The Framers' third and last guardrail was federalism. The basic question was how big the new nation should be. In fact, there wasn't much choice. As of 1787, the thirteen states still shared the continent with England, Spain, and France. If the US could hold together, it would remain the dominant power. But if it fractured, none of the successor entities could possibly hold its own.[28] The outcome, then, would depend on persuading citizens to embrace the new government.[29] But of course this affection had to be earned, which meant at a minimum that federal programs would have to be at least as successful as state ones. Here the Framers put their thumb on the scale by limiting the new government to issues where it enjoyed large scale economies. Examples included military power, interstate commerce, tax collection,[30] and centralizing foreign relations so that states did not fight each other instead of cooperating against outside adversaries.[31]

These rationales immediately suggested a division of labor in which the national government left most decisions close to the population. The catch was that some policies, though formally national, paired strongly positive impacts for some regions with large negatives for others. Nineteenth-century politics would revolve around two of these. The tariff made imported goods expensive in the South but generated jobs and stock dividends for the North. Conversely, the South (or at least the planter class) profited from slavery while dragooning Northerners into the ugly business of returning runaway slaves.

Finally, federalism also promised to limit the risk of faction. First, and rejecting Montesquieu's embarrassing condemnation of large democracies,[32] Madison argued that size made it *harder* for factions to assemble a majority that could seize power. The reason was that cobbling together coalitions in a large country would require so many groups to agree on common goals as to be "very improbable, if not impracticable."[33] At this point, only majorities based on "justice and the general good" could rise to power.[34] Moreover, the number of groups and goals steadily increased with distance, implying that large countries could resist tyrannical majorities more easily than small ones.[35]

Even so, the experiment was breathtaking: America was ten times larger than any previous republic.[36] Given what was known at the time, it is hard to criticize Madison's reasoning. No one could foresee how large-circulation newspapers,[37] mass political parties, and a directly elected president would make the trick steadily easier for those who came after.[38]

In a perfect world, this logic might have led the Framers to adopt a single national government. But here the politics stopped them. Instead, the best they could do was establish a federal system in which the state and national governments were coequal, each drawing legitimacy from a direct relation to the same electorate.[39] This ambiguity avoided the question of just how much national politics would set policy within each state. In the best case, democracy would take care of the problem by ensuring that the federal government expanded as far and as fast as voters wanted it to.[40] But if this did not happen, it would only be natural for citizens to place their primary loyalty in whichever government they trusted most. The Civil War ended this standoff by vastly enlarging federal responsibilities.

## 1.2 UPDATING THE FRAMERS

This book asks what contemporary economics' simplest and most basic insights add to Madison's vision. For the most part, we focus on modern theories of imperfect and impacted information (Chapters 2 and 3), oligopoly competition (Chapters 4 and 5), and game theory (Chapters 7 and 8). With one slight but unavoidable exception in Chapter 3, we almost always make the "rational man" assumption that each player knows and follows the "best strategy" for maximizing her personal utility.

Readers will immediately see that this still leaves a great deal of choice of which theories to include. All I can say is that, to the extent I have been aware of different possible choices, I have chosen on the basis of "fit," systematically favoring arguments and evidence that reinforce and extend the Framers' basic insights over those that seek to supplant them. This can easily go wrong, and anyone who has worked with coauthors can almost hear Madison crying out with frustration, "That's not what I meant at all!" Readers will see that I have tried to limit the damage by constantly recalling what the Framers actually said before trying to update it.

The deeper safeguard comes from the nature of the project itself. The Framers, after all, proceeded from very specific assumptions. But logic, as the poet says, is a machine: "You throw your money on the table and receive so much change back."[41] It follows that *anyone* who starts from the same assumptions and pursues the argument carefully will arrive at similar answers. In this sense, we really do know what the Framers would think: Even if they objected to modern economic ideas at first, we can be morally certain that they would have eventually come around in the same way that every bright graduate student does.

We begin by addressing the Framers' intellectual style. The assumption that clever institutional design could align officials' private selfishness with the public good was already a long step removed from the old Roman idea that men would do evil absent some stringent (and possibly unachievable) inner virtue.[42] At the same time, the Framers were cautious. In the first place, they knew that whatever power they derived from the Constitution's "parchment guarantees" was limited. In the long run, it was the things they could not control – primarily social norms – that would provide the most important safeguards against tyranny, sedition, insurrection,[43] and coup d'état.[44] Then, too, the Constitution could not stop citizens from making bad choices that would put the country outside "the compass of human remedies."[45] The most institutions could do was improve the odds.[46] So the Framers did what they could and left the rest to future generations.[47]

Even within this framework, reason had limits. The Framers did not need to be told that reality was always richer than theory. This meant that, in Prof. Downs' phrase, even the most thoughtful designs would sometimes be "greatly inferior to those obtained by sheer luck."[48] But what the Framers could do was consider a variety of plausible assumptions, and design institutions that made sense under all of them. The approach is perhaps most evident in the Framers' habit of offering several independent arguments for every design choice. In what follows we take this a step further: Not only do different assumptions exist, but their relative importance can change over time. This leads to the modern insight that complex systems can have radically different personalities from one era to the next. Then too, changes in one sector can propagate domino-like into others. We highlight these connections in the final "Feedbacks" section of each chapter.

Second, we will almost always limit ourselves to rational man models. Madisonian theory is a product of the Enlightenment, and trying to splice anything very foreign onto this tradition quickly leads to contradictions. This immediately rules out dark forces on the pattern of Freud's "Thanatos" argument, which holds that humankind is self-destructive because, well, it just is.[49] Beyond this, we will also honor the Copernican Principle that our theories should treat all actors symmetrically. This immediately rules out *ad hoc* assumptions that treat certain people, classes, or political parties as inherently praiseworthy or evil. Since the Copernican Principle equally implies that no group is consistently wiser than others, we will also insist that the Constitution avoids favoring particular substantive outcomes even in such fundamental matters as the choice between capitalism and socialism. It follows that any rules governing the political process should be entirely neutral and procedural. This is one of the few places where we take a harder line than the Framers, who held that some policies were so destabilizing that no democracy could tolerate them.[50] This led them to write various substantive guarantees into the Constitution. These included provisions limiting the states to republican forms of government,[51] a moratorium on any attempt to regulate the slave trade,[52] and forbidding the states to make treaties or issue paper money.[53]

Finally, *The Federalist* focused on one particular iteration of the Constitution. But the Constitution changes, and some rules that that were originally enforced by tradition, such as presidential term limits, have since crossed over into the written document. In what follows, we will therefore take the more inclusive view that any institution that decisively influences political outcomes is "constitutional." Examples include the two-party system, the Senate filibuster, winner-take-all elections, and the nine-member Supreme Court.

This filagree of institutions significantly limits democratic outcomes, at least in the short run. The justifications for this raise deep questions of when and how collective action is acceptable. Conceptually, it is best to start from the classical economics principle of "nonsatiety," that individuals always prefer more goods to fewer ones. Following Professors Buchanan and Dworkin, this implies that rational individuals, if they are honest, will always favor collective action that they expect to make them richer.[54] But this is only possible if no one dissents, which means, as Madison warned, that anyone who stands in the way must be coerced.[55] This necessarily puts enormous weight on how the list of collective projects is decided in the first place.

The principle of one-man-one-vote seems so obvious that we seldom think about it.[56] But as the US Supreme Court recently recognized, there is a "large measure of 'unfairness' in any winner-take-all system."[57] For instance, it should be obvious that in a country of 330 million people, a vote of 50 percent plus one is indistinguishable from 50 percent minus one.[58] Then too, the majority is a moving target. While elections notionally seek opinion as it stood on a particular day, opinion twelve hours later could easily go the other way. Indeed, the very existence of a majority can depend on such nonpolitical accidents as where and when it was

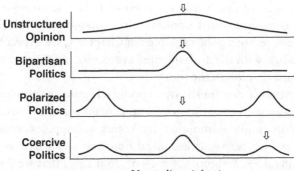

FIGURE 1.1 Voter dissatisfaction

raining on Election Day. Probably the deepest objection is that elections ignore the fact that some voters feel intensely while others barely care. This makes it possible for an apathetic majority to pass laws that make the country unhappier on net. At the most practical level, these "tyranny of the majority" outcomes set a limit on how many controversial laws the country can pass and remain stable.[59]

This book follows Madison's lead in assuming that majority tyranny outcomes present the main threat that democratic institutions should guard against. All the same, the word "tyranny" often sounds stilted to modern ears. If so, it might be better to start from the observation that what we today call "polarized politics" almost always revolves around each side's plan to win power so that it can force its policies onto the other. To the Framers, this would have strongly resembled the casual coercion that English politicians had unthinkingly practiced in the years leading up to the American Revolution. But if government's supply of coercion is limited, it follows that the best way to stabilize government is to avoid the kinds of unjust laws that had angered the colonists. Just what the Framers meant by "unjust" was no doubt vague, even to them. But in our modern parlance it would have included, at a minimum, the requirement that acceptable policies should yield a net profit to society, and that any individuals who find themselves bearing an outsized share of the costs should be compensated with side payments or offsetting transactions that systematically favor them.

Finally, Madisonian theory should be more than just descriptive: Ideally, at least, it should also help us make judgments that some institutional arrangements work better than others. For reasons that will become obvious in later chapters, we will normally focus our attention on the four distributions of public opinion depicted in Figure 1.1. We also assume that the purpose of democracy is to choose policy outcomes – shown in the figure as arrows – that implement one opinion over all the others. Note that, for reasons to be explained in Chapter 5, we expect these policies to coincide with the median voter's preference in the first three cases and extremist opinion in the fourth.

The question is how much we expect each outcome to please or displease the average voter. Cautious in our ignorance, we concentrate on the maximally simple assumption that voters' unhappiness scales linearly with the distance between their ideal outcome and what their government actually does.[60] Figure 1.1 presents four cases that we will encounter repeatedly throughout this book.

In the first sketch, "Unstructured Opinion," each voter calculates their ideal policy independently of every other voter. Provided that the political system sets policy to please the median voter (see arrow), and arbitrarily assuming that the horizontal axis is two units long, readers can confirm by inspection that average voter unhappiness is slightly less than half.[61] Our second sketch, "Bipartisan Politics," shows a more optimistic view in which people talk politics with each other, bringing their opinions closer together. In the limiting case of perfect convergence, everyone agrees with the median voter so that unhappiness shrinks to zero.

The third sketch, "Polarized Politics," shows a different possibility in which opinion is divided into two hostile camps. Here average voter unhappiness is never less than 1 no matter what policy government adopts. This is what modern Americans fear when they talk about "polarization." Fortunately, not even the Weimar Republic was ever so violently divided.[62] This book argues that the fourth sketch, "Coercive Politics," is much more likely. Readers can confirm that average voter unhappiness is also 1 no matter which segment of the electorate manages to impose its preferred policy on everyone else.

We end this section by reviewing the goals that Madison hoped to achieve, and that any reforms claiming to improve his system should be judged against. Of these, the most basic was simply physical security. The Framers had seen the British government, almost without knowing it, repeatedly anger its subjects to the point of violence. Here, the Framers hoped that time was on their side. After all, even "the wisest and freest governments," though initially unstable, could eventually hope for "that veneration which time bestows on everything."[63] Today, we would probably add that organizations whose members have successfully worked together in the past are more likely to trust each other, and that this tends to encourage more and bigger projects over time. This typically implies that long-standing institutions are more profitable than new ones, and for that reason should not be jettisoned lightly.

In the meantime, voting would play a crucial role in stabilizing (or destabilizing) the country. The first and most pragmatic reason is that voting approximates the distribution of armed force.[64] From this perspective, the Framers' constitutional protections for protecting minorities – most obviously outsized representation for small states in the Senate and Electoral College – were remarkably shrewd. This was spectacularly illustrated by the Civil War, which broke out at precisely the moment when the South no longer had enough voters to block Northern control of the government. Strikingly, this same population advantage was precisely what the North needed to win – just barely – on the battlefield. Had the Constitution given the South fewer rights, it might have seceded earlier and more successfully.

The second and perhaps deeper reason was that a suitably designed democracy could deliver policies closer to what voters wanted and felt strongly about. This rested on an implicit "Ignorant Bliss" assumption that letting voters choose for themselves would produce more happiness than the presumptively ideal policies that an all-wise, benevolent dictator would choose for them. And of course, real dictators could be reliably expected to choose nonideal policies based on their venality and self-interest. Granted that democracy did not deliver perfect policies, voters would still prefer living under it to any other system.

## 1.3 ROADMAP

We close with a look ahead. Chapters 2 and 3 begin by revisiting the social challenges that Madison's institutions were supposed to manage. Chapter 2 starts from the Framers' intuition that citizens are forever hurtling between reason and passion. Economists have since formalized the former concept within modern "limited rationality" models that explain seemingly nonrational actions as the result of "imperfect" and "impacted" information. Similarly, we will argue that the best modern understanding of "passion" starts from de Tocqueville's very different observation that citizens often hold political opinions simply because their friends do. Modern economics typically addresses this kind of conformism through network effects theories in which initially random viewpoints steadily converge until one dominates the others. This provides a natural explanation for Madison's claim that "the mob" frequently displays abrupt, violent, and even irrational passions. The chapter concludes by showing how the two theories can be reconciled within a common framework.

The main problem with these approaches is that they ignore the central role of messaging – that is, that some words and images are enormously more persuasive than others. Chapter 3 fills this gap by expanding on Downs' insight that democratic politics is almost entirely shaped by the shortcuts that voters use to extract answers from painfully limited data. We then turn to recent evidence from psychology, brain imaging, and computer science that dramatically confirm Thomas Jefferson's striking observation that political unity is nearly always unstable. In the process, we also find insights explaining why voters sometimes change their minds, and can even resolve old differences.

Chapters 4 and 5 examine how private media companies and political parties develop the issues, narratives, and ideologies that frame voters' choices on Election Day. Chapter 4 focuses on the history of for-profit journalism in America, explaining how the "invisible hand" of markets slowly grew into a plausible, if highly imperfect, mechanism for delivering accurate and unbiased news without the need for government censorship. Crucially, we also argue that rising polarization sooner or later makes business models based on slanted reporting more profitable than objective news. At this point, media companies that deliberately exacerbate polarization can make themselves still more profitable in an endless cycle. Chapter 5 turns to America's two-party system. The first part follows Downs' classic theory of bipartisan politics. The second notes that Downs deliberately ignored legislatures and the possibility of gridlock. This opens the door to a very different, coercive politics regime in which voters reward extremist politicians for the purely negative virtue of blocking their opponents.

Chapters 6–9 track the Framers' central focus on formal government. Chapter 6 examines the familiar geography of congressional districts, states, and an overarching national government. We start with the foundational puzzle of "gerrymandering," which allows seemingly arbitrary changes to congressional district borders to decide which party controls the government. We then show how algorithms based on traditional concepts of community can generate unbiased districts. (Additional technical details can be found in the Appendix.) We then turn to how the Framers designed state and federal governments to resolve conflicts across multiple communities and regions. The chapter ends by analyzing how the Framers' attempted division of state and federal responsibilities broke down in the Civil War and was rewritten to accommodate Big Government in the twentieth century.

Chapter 7 examines the internal dynamics of Congress, focusing on how arcane rules such as the filibuster and its successors have sometimes managed not only to count legislators' votes, but also to estimate their intensity. This makes them the main guardrail against Madison's "tyranny of the majority." The rub is that the same procedures also facilitate obstruction and gridlock, making it easier to tip the system into eras of coercive politics and partisanship. Chapter 8 examines how the invention of modern political parties gave presidents the power and legitimacy to challenge Congress and implement new policies on their own authority. We also examine how Big Government bureaucracies become political actors in their own right, and ask whether the arrangement is democratically defensible. We finish by discussing the president's war powers. Chapter 9 analyzes the court system's role in ensuring that legislation provides finality to political disputes that would otherwise continue indefinitely. Crucially, we argue that rule of law – though inherently probabilistic – nevertheless makes some outcomes vastly more likely than others, and that well-designed judicial institutions can increase this predictability still further. We then ask how well courts can deter abuses by Congress and the president, limit the power of private actors to slant or suppress political debate, and ensure that private bodies that perform government functions follow basic democratic procedures.

Chapter 10 summarizes how the various dynamics described in earlier chapters led to the country's current political dysfunction, and lists possible reforms for steering Madison's system back to bipartisan politics. The chapter also explains why recent disputes over COVID-19, global warming, and racial equity have proven especially challenging, and suggests reforms to manage similar debates in the future.

### Notes

1   Madison argued that virtue was, in turn, defined by conceptions of the "private good," "respect for character," and religion. Madison (1787a) at pp. 200–1.
2   Ricks (2020) at p. 22.
3   Something very like weighted voting is ubiquitous in small groups, where friends and family members nearly always give way when the minority feels the issue more intensely.
4   The task is formidable. Theorists have long debated how, and even if, intensity can be compared across humans. For a concise survey, see List (2013).

5  *Federalist* No. 10 at p. 41 (Madison); Webster [1787] at pp. 554–5.

6  Athenians' hasty decision to invade Sicily, which led to a Vietnam-like quagmire, was among the most celebrated.

7  *Federalist* No. 53 at p. 289 (Madison).

8  The Framers' decision to set a two-year term for the House implies that public opinion evolves quickly enough to open significant gaps between voters and their congressmen within a year or so. Conversely, their choice of presidential and senatorial terms suggests that four to six years provides ample time for the public to recognize bad ideas.

9  De Tocqueville would later argue that public opinion was driven by social pressures to conform. We explore this hypothesis in Chapter 2.

10  *Federalist* No. 48 (Madison) at p. 228 (citing Thomas Jefferson: The fact that despotism is "elective" does not make it any less evil).

11  *Federalist* No. 10 at pp. 38 and 41 (Madison).

12  The scheme assumed, *inter alia*, that laws have a definite meaning. We return to this issue in Chapter 9.

13  See, e.g., *Federalist* No. 47 at p. 220 (Madison); No. 71 at p. 329 and No. 78 at p. 356 (Hamilton); Jefferson [1785] at p. 7017; and Washington [1796] at pp. 18–19.

14  *Federalist* No. 10 at p. 41 (Madison) and *Federalist* No. 22 at pp. 96–7 (Hamilton). The tactic was even more destructive since the minority's leverage was greatest at moments of crisis when obstruction could "convulse society" (Hamilton).

15  *Federalist* No. 73 (Madison) at p. 338.

16  *Federalist* No. 73 (Madison) at p. 339.

17  *Federalist* No. 53 at pp. 293 and 289 and No. 47 at p. 228 (Madison).

18  *Federalist* No. 62 at p. 285 (Madison) and No. 71 at pp. 328 and 330 (Hamilton).

19  *Federalist* No. 53 at p. 293 (Madison) and No. 71 at p. 330 (Hamilton).

20  *Federalist* No. 43 at pp. 200–1 (Madison).

21  *Federalist* No. 51 at p. 240 (Madison).

22  Kennedy (1986) and Lowell (1888) at p. 4.

23  *Federalist* No. 49 at p. 233 (Madison).

24  Realizing this, Madison offered the fallback argument that indiscriminate friction was actually desirable since Congress passed more bad laws than good. *Federalist* No. 62 at pp. 284–5 and No. 73 at p. 337 (Hamilton). This claim must have sounded suspiciously *ad hoc* even in the eighteenth century, but it is hardly tenable now that roughly half the US electorate routinely votes for expanded government. Procedures that systematically disable so many voters are inherently undemocratic.

25  *Federalist* No. 44 at p. 205 and No. 62 at pp. 285–6 (Madison).

26  Washington [1796] at pp. 16–17. Downs, with his more sophisticated theory of elections, nevertheless came to much the same conclusion, arguing that a democracy dominated by extremists would experience violently unstable policies followed by "chaos" and failure. Downs (1957) at p. 120.

27  *Federalist* No. 43 at p. 202 (Madison). Popular frustration with the near-impossibility of amending the French Constitution paved the way for

Napoleon's overthrow of the Directorate in 1799. Roberts (2014) at p. 312. By comparison, the fact that the US was able to repeal Prohibition just thirteen years after passing it shows significant flexibility.

28  See, e.g., Randolph (1787) at p. 604; Pinckney (1788) at p. 590; Washington [1796] at p. 6; and Meacham (2008) at p. 321 (quoting Andrew Jackson).

29  *Federalist* No. 27 at p. 119 (Hamilton).

30  *Federalist* No. 12 at p. 9 (military power), 45 (commerce), 52–3 (taxation), and 55 (government administration); No. 4 (Jay) at p. 15 (military power); see also Washington (1796) at p. 9 (military power).

31  *Federalist* No. 4 at p. 15 and No. 5 at pp. 16–17 (Jay); No. 6 at p. 19 (Hamilton).

32  Ricks (2020) at p. 110–11.

33  *Federalist* No. 10 at p. 43 and No. 51 at p. 239 (Madison); for a modern version of the argument, see Hofstadter (1959a) at p. 810.

34  *Federalist* No. 51 at p. 240 (Madison). Madison's argument contained a crucial unvoiced assumption that factions seldom grew beyond some fixed geographic size, so that a large country would inevitably have more of them than a small one. Chapter 2 explores some possible reasons for this.

35  *Federalist* No. 53 at p. 289 (Madison); *Federalist* No. 69 at p. 315 (Hamilton).

36  Pinckney [1788] at p. 585.

37  Pielkalkiewic and Penn (1995) at p. 33 and n. 19.

38  Professor Hofstadter has argued that the Framers could not imagine *any* politics crossing state lines. Hofstadter (1959a) at p. 812.

39  The Constitution was decidedly inconsistent on this point, most obviously in letting states decide who would represent them in the US Senate. Some state legislatures even tried to tell their senators how to vote (Rehnquist 2004). The duality disappeared with the Seventeenth Amendment (1913), which provided for the direct election of senators.

40  While the Constitution tried to limit the federal government's powers, any hopes of this disappeared in the early nineteenth century, when it became apparent that the federal government's spending and regulation powers under the Constitution were not limited to the specific purposes for which they had originally been granted, but could be exercised for any goal thought to benefit the country (see Chapter 7). Later, the Civil War crusade to end slavery and the constitutional amendments that followed expressly extended federal authority to voting and civil rights, codifying the new overlap between state and federal responsibilities.

41  Shiels (2015) at p. 166 (quoting W. B. Yeats).

42  For the Framers' assumption, see Ricks (2020) at p. 22.

43  *Federalist* No. 47 at pp. 226 and 230 ("parchment" guarantees and tyranny), No. 51 at p. 239 (majority tyranny), No. 43 at p. 201 (insurrection") (Madison); No. 16 at pp. 71–2 (insurrection), No. 26 at p. 117 (coup d'état), and No. 28 at p. 121 (sedition and insurrection) (Hamilton).

44  *Federalist* No. 28 (Hamilton) at p. 121 (sedition and insurrection "will sometimes arise in all societies, however constituted"); *Federalist* No. 26 (Hamilton) at p. 117 ("If the defense of the community ... should make it necessary to have an army so numerous as to hazard its liberty, this is one of

those calamities for which there is neither preventative nor cure. It cannot be provided against by any possible form of Government").

45 *Federalist* No. 55 at pp. 257 and 263 (Madison); No. 16 at pp. 71–2 and No. 27 at p. 120 (Hamilton).

46 *Federalist* No. 43 at p. 201 (Madison).

47 *Federalist* No. 31 at pp. 137 and 142 (Hamilton).

48 Downs (1957) at p. 6.

49 In principle, we could follow the lead of behavioral economists who construct formal models around experimentally confirmed human behaviors that diverge from conventional assumptions of rationality and profit maximization. But we would then need good evidence that the supposed irrationality is sufficiently robust that humans do not eventually adjust their behaviors so that rationality reemerges. For now, this seems to me very much an open question.

50 Various writers since Beard (1918) have attacked the Constitution on the ground that it protects a particular economic system. In the twentieth century, this literature was almost always Marxist (Ollman 2017). More recently, the charge has morphed into critiques that the document is White Supremacist (Colker 2021). That said, the argument remains the same, depending almost entirely on the observation that the Framers were members of a certain group who embraced specific political views. The obvious rejoinder is that even partisans can draft neutral documents, and that credible claims of bias should be documented from the Constitution's actual text. Here, Beard and his successors say little except that attacks on private property would have been easier without checks and balances. This seems decidedly inadequate. After all, it is entirely possible to support socialism and still reject tyranny as a means for achieving it.

51 US Constitution, Art. 4, Section 4.

52 US Constitution, Art. 1, Section 9.

53 US Constitution, Art. 1, Section 10.

54 The benefits of collective action are so universally understood that in those rare cases where old governments collapse new entities immediately spring up to replace them. The history of how workers' soviets in the Russian and German revolutions morphed into governments after World War I is a particularly dramatic example.

55 Madison [1788] at p. 699.

56 The Framers' generation took it "as a first principle that the votes of the majority shall be taken as the voice of the whole." Otis. [1764] at p. 54. Since the French Revolution, this has become axiomatic to the point where even Che Guevara was willing to admit that successful revolution was impossible as long as "a government has come into power through some form of popular vote, fraudulent or not, and maintains at least an appearance of constitutional legality." Guevara (1961). We note in passing that the American winner-take-all approach is just one of many ways to implement one-man-one-vote. More complex possibilities including proportional representation and "Condorcet" schemes in which voters rank-order their preferences are described in McGinnis and Rappaport (2008). The fact that none of these methods measures intensity suggests that tyranny of the majority cannot be addressed at the level of elections but only within formal institutions.

57 *Rucho v. Common Cause*, 588 U.S. __, 139 S. Ct. 2484 (2019) at 2500.
58 Lest the example seem forced, we should remember that the 2000 presidential election was decided by just 537 votes out of some 50 million cast.
59 This is the kernel of truth behind the folk wisdom that outsized reforms such as Medicare (1961) or the Voting Rights Act (1965) should be "bipartisan." By comparison, the Affordable Care Act (2011), which passed on a narrow party line vote, sparked political controversies that continue to this day.
60 Average voter dissatisfaction can often increase nonlinearly for the important case where government policy transfers wealth from rich voters to poor ones. The reason is that we normally expect marginal utility to decline with income. This implies that expropriation makes poor recipients happy faster than it angers the rich. Cf. *Federalist* No. 36 at p. 157 (Hamilton: discussing the political benefits of progressive taxation).
61 If the curve were perfectly flat, the average voter's preferred state would be exactly half a unit distant from the median.
62 Even at the worst of times, Weimar's extremists did not significantly outnumber the center (Deutscher Bundestag 2006) (the combined Nazi/Communist vote never exceeded 52 percent).
63 *Federalist* No. 49 at p. 231 (Madison).
64 One of Madison's most revealing moments is his cold-blooded calculation that the states and their militias would always be able to outfight the federal government's regular army (*Federalist* No. 46 at p. 219 [Madison]).

# 2

# The People

## From Individuals to Communities

The Framers designed their Constitution with a relentless focus on law and institutions. But they said little about politics in the wider society. Looking back, this might have been the secret of their success. Madison's institutions were designed to stop the specific pathologies that had repeatedly sabotaged Greek and Roman democracy. But those societies had been both strongly elitist – less than a third of the Roman and Greek populations were even citizens[1] – and dominated by aristocrats. While this might have served as a very approximate description of politics in eighteenth-century Virginia,[2] universal male voting in the first decades of the nineteenth century soon erased any resemblance. Yet through it all, remarkably, Madison's institutions continued to work just as he hoped they would.

In one respect they even worked better. *The Federalist* had assumed that the people's representatives would meet in Congress to debate and decide policy. Had this happened, what the people themselves thought about the issues – supposing they thought anything at all – would not have mattered much. But the new mass parties ran on nationwide platforms which invited voters to choose between policies *before* Congress had a chance to meet. In some cases, at least, Congress did little more than formalize their decisions.

But in that case, *how* voters think about policy becomes centrally important. Following Madison, we argue for two distinct mechanisms.[3] In the first, which we will usually call "rational voting," voters strain to make reasonable decisions on limited knowledge and despite politicians' deliberate attempts to mislead them. This forms the heart of Professor Downs' "limited rationality" theory of politics. The second method builds on Madison's claim that "passions" can also emerge from the crowd itself. Following a later hint by de Tocqueville, we argue that voters often take political stances calculated to please others. We show that this dynamic can be just as important as rational voting, and in some eras more so. Finally, we present a framework for unifying the two theories and ask how they influence American politics more generally.

## 2.1 THE RATIONAL VOTER

The Framers did not foresee the rise of mass parties, and it took Americans a long time to incorporate this development into their vision of democracy. But by the end of the nineteenth century there was widespread agreement that the two-party system had taken over much and perhaps most of the moderating function originally assigned to Madison's checks and balances. Even so, the insight remained mostly intuitive until economist Harold Hotelling (1895–1973) published his theory of brand competition in 1929.[4] Hotelling immediately saw that the new theory also explained why both the American and British two-party systems were almost always moderate and centrist. Even so, voters in political "markets" behave very differently from consumers in ordinary economic ones, and it took another quarter century for these differences to come into focus. The breakthrough came with the concept of "imperfect information." Firms and consumers might be rational, post-World War II economists reasoned, but the information they needed to make intelligent decisions was costly and scarce. This forced them to invent shortcuts and workarounds to get by with what they knew. In practice these almost always empowered actors who possessed information at the expense of those who did not. It fell to a young graduate student named Anthony Downs to develop a formal theory of what these ideas implied for politics. His *Economic Theory of Democracy* (1957) remains the definitive statement of rational voter theory. In the process he also made the model more realistic, most obviously by recognizing that voting was comparatively costly so that many voters would often decide to stay home. In the process, he filled the last gaps in Hotelling's work and built a theory that neatly explained his own era's bipartisan politics.

Downs' basic idea was to extend familiar "rational man" models of buyers and sellers to politicians and voters. Like its microeconomic precursors, the new model said almost nothing about just *how* these actors reasoned. And this made sense. Economists' usual methodology, after all, is to reduce reality to a series of clear equations and solve them. They know, of course, that real manufacturers and consumers do nothing of the sort. But this does not matter so long as their actual thoughts produce answers that approximate the true one, and this is almost always true for commerce. Extending the method to politics made it similarly unnecessary to ask how voters reasoned. All the same, the argument was not obvious: Political information tends to be much more complex, and voters' budget for acquiring it far more limited, than most consumer markets. This meant that voters would often act on partial and even wrong information.

Like Madison, Downs began by specifying what each of the actors in his model wanted. For politicians, this meant making whatever promises seemed likely to gain the income, reputation, and personal power that came from winning elections.[5] And for voters, it meant supporting whichever party promised them the most benefits. At first glance, both goals might have seemed mercenary. But while Downs assumed that politicians only wanted to win elections, this was mostly a convenience. The reason was self-selection: Professionals would join whichever party best approximated their convictions, after which they would behave as vote maximizers whether they were idealists or cynics.[6] The analysis for voters was similar. Press accounts often assume that voters are moved by personal advantage in the form of identity politics or some special interest. But, in fact, Downs' formalism only says that voters maximize their utility. Since we can equally imagine voters who derive pleasure from helping others, rational voters can just as easily decide based on their estimates of what is best for the country.[7]

The question remains how rational voters go about translating their individual goals into choosing one particular party on Election Day. Here Downs insisted that voting was just as much an investment decision as buying stock. It followed that voters would choose parties based on their announced platforms, suitably discounted for each party's chances of winning and the risk that, once in power, they might not keep their promises.[8] Despite its simplicity, the assumption was already informative. We often say that voters in multiparty systems who abandon the center for extremists have become "radicalized." But in fact, the decision to switch proves nothing: If society becomes more polarized so that centrist parties have less chance of enacting their platforms, even moderates can find it rational to cast their vote for whichever extremist presents the lesser evil. Moreover, it is easy to see how this kind of strategic voting could produce an avalanche: The moment some voters abandon the center parties, those parties become less credible so that they lose even more supporters. In such cases, at least, a country's private political beliefs may change a good deal less than its election outcomes.

Downs now introduced the concept of imperfect information. In a world of perfect information and fixed political tastes, we would expect voters to make the same choice every time.[9] Elections would then be dull and predictable, changing as slowly as the US Census. But in fact, real politics is anything but predictable. Like Madison, Downs ascribed this difference to *imperfect* information, most obviously from politicians' incessant attempts to hide their deeds[10] and confuse the voters.[11]

Just how imperfect is voters' information? If we were talking about absolute knowledge, we would have to admit that there are a great many policy questions that no living human understands.[12] Thus, for example, no one really knows the right way to fight poverty, or can rigorously prove that some new version of communism might not produce goods more efficiently than capitalism.[13] In such cases, the best we can hope for is to confess ignorance and make the best estimates we can.

Still, that is not most politics. Every recession shows that even the smartest and best-paid expert stock-pickers are fallible. But this does not matter so long as they are *less* fallible than the rest of us. It follows that we should understand the term "imperfect information" as relative. One way to benchmark the difference is to note that academics who have spent years studying some particular issue probably knows as much as any living human. More to the point, they know more than any president or congressman has time to learn,[14] which in turn is far more than most voters. Just saying this makes democracy sound hopeless. The silver lining is that learning sooner or later encounters diminishing returns so that the gap is often narrower than it seems. Then too, many issues include large normative components that no amount of logic and evidence can decide. (In politics these often involve value judgments on whether the problem is important and, if so, how much society should spend to fix it.) Finally, there is a problem of statistical "noise"; that is, that the empirical evidence for and against particular policies arrives unevenly. This means, in the words of George Washington, that even good policies can be temporarily discredited by "appearances somewhat dubious" and "vicissitudes of fortune." In such cases, politicians cannot prove that they are on the right track, but only ask for the public's trust and "constancy of support."[15]

Ultimately, the size of these information gaps depends on each voter's willingness to obtain and analyze information. But since Downsian theory treats voting as an investment, this depends on the difference between what each voter expects to gain from government if their preferred agenda wins the election and the second-best benefits they will receive if it loses. This is almost always small. Worse still, it must be discounted by the even tinier chance that their vote will change the election's outcome. We therefore expect most rational voters to be poorly informed.

The available evidence supports this. For example, so-called push-question surveys tell voters facts and arguments they probably did not know before, and only then ask what positions they support. The fact that new information regularly reverses voters' preliminary opinions shows that their previous knowledge of facts they consider important must be limited.[16] Small information budgets also explain the politics of sound bites. Large claims – for example that every foreign policy intervention will be "another Vietnam" – cannot literally be true.[17] But even if voters only know one example, an anecdote may still be better than a random guess. This encourages campaigns to pick one or two persuasive facts and then advertise them over and over, hoping that voters will get the point.

In the meantime, voters' limited information budgets give public opinion a kind of inertia, making the parties and ideologies voters already know more persistent than they would be if learning cost nothing. In the bipartisan regime, this benefits the center: For rational voters, there is no reason to learn new facts and arguments unless and until extremist platforms seem likely to win. But that changes once extreme agendas become credible. Now voters must potentially learn three viewpoints – Left, Right, and Center – each advancing distinctly different facts and arguments. Yet voters' information budgets are unlikely to grow much larger than they were before. In these circumstances, rational voters will quite sensibly devote most of their effort to learning whichever set of facts and arguments initially seems most persuasive and neglect the others, and this imbalance will grow as polarization reduces the overlap between the facts supporting each viewpoint. Over time this slanted learning will make it steadily more difficult for many voters to imagine, much less be convinced by, any view besides their own.

The situation is even worse because limited budgets for learning sometimes let demonstrably wrong facts and arguments persist for generations. For example, most of the public routinely agrees that police disproportionately kill black men and that the effort to ban alcohol during Prohibition increased consumption. Yet there is overwhelming scholarly consensus that neither is true.[18] The broader point is that the public may *never* learn enough to resolve some debates *even* when clear answers demonstrably exist. This makes it perfectly rational for politicians to offer second-best solutions when voters' budget for understanding the first-best solution is hopelessly inadequate.

Finally, most of us learn more at some points in our lives than others. Usually such changes are minor, reflecting some passing enthusiasm for a particular issue or changes in our leisure time. But there is one exception: children. All of us are born very far from our desired level of knowledge and need to catch up. More than that, there are almost always parents and teachers around to help us learn, and punish us if we don't. This suggests that the importance of education to American democracy is more than just a Fourth of July platitude. If children do not learn at least some of the basic facts they need to reason about the country's political choices, it is hard to see how they will make up for this later.

But voters' limited budget for learning is not the whole story. In the long term, their budget for remembering, or more accurately forgetting, is every bit as important.[19] Hardly anyone can reel off every scandal of the past ten years. Indeed, we cull our political memories constantly. This suggests that our total store of political knowledge grows more slowly over time, even if our education never stops entirely. This explains, among other things, why presidents invariably become more moderate as reelection approaches: This gives voters who feel less intensely a chance to forget the programs they disagreed with, while still pleasing the extremists who feel strongly enough to remember the early years and feel grateful. In what follows we will usually assume, somewhat arbitrarily, that voters' estimates of the world mostly depend on facts and arguments that they learned within the past five years.[20]

In the end, of course, the events that voters know are supplied by history. But the selection is shaped by newspapers and political parties, which are constantly making editorial choices about which facts do and do not matter. Beyond this, the parties sometimes invest significant time and energy in keeping particularly useful memories alive. This was especially true in the late nineteenth century, when both parties feared that even a massive trauma like the Civil War could be forgotten. In the Jim Crow South, segregationists made a point of endlessly recalling the war, if only because they were still resisting its outcome. And in the North, Republicans constantly "waved the bloody shirt" to remind the country of what it had suffered, and that Southern Democrats were still the enemy. Needless to say, neither strategy did anything to help Americans forget their enmities.

The cost of remembering can also put widely held, "consensus" opinions at risk. The generation that saw the Berlin Wall fall had discussed the pros and cons of Communism in endless dorm room arguments. The result was not only that they rejected Communism, but also that they had thought hard enough about the issue to say why. But once the Wall fell, capitalism had no rivals and the arguments ended. The result thirty or so years later is that old-style socialists like Senator Bernie Sanders have rebranded themselves as "Progressives" and are pitching much the same theories that they did before. The difference today is that most voters have never heard the old facts and arguments, or else have died or forgotten them. Of course, it could be that the old consensus was mistaken, or that the world has changed enough since then that the old lessons no longer hold. The Millennial Generation's long flirtation with Democratic Socialism will either wastefully relearn what earlier generations knew, or else build a better society than their predecessors thought possible.

Yet forgetting is also indispensable. After all, most policy fights eventually end, and it is important that the hard feelings disappear with them. Bipartisan politics, with its transactional emphasis on passing legislation and moving on to new issues, creates a natural space for this forgetting. By comparison, coercive politics, with its deadlock and grievance, constantly rehearses old injuries so that they linger and, if anything, continue to grow.

Finally, the assumption that voters have small information budgets includes some important exceptions. Voters know most issues from press accounts and television. But some problems intrude into everyday life, and these invariably define the "third rails" of American politics. This explains why, among other things, sudden spikes in gasoline prices routinely put deep dents in incumbents' popularity. The concept of directly felt, "kitchen table" issues also includes empathy: While COVID-19 never posed much risk to the young and middle-aged, the fact that most young people had older susceptible relatives persuaded many to support stronger measures regardless.

But the logic of direct impacts is not limited to unmet social problems. It also applies to whatever programs the government launches to fix them. For example, wartime politics has traditionally been dominated by rationing and conscription,[21] while politics in peacetime religiously warns against the "third rail" of Social Security. This same logic explains a fortiori why efforts to impose mask and vaccine mandates, lockdowns, and critical race theory in public schools became flashpoints in 2021. Here the broader lesson is that ideologies that set out to change the world often contain the seeds of their own destruction. As Prof. Brinton argues, historic revolutions have almost always ended soon after elites tried to change how the great mass of humanity live their lives.[22]

Downs' image of imperfect information was elegant and parsimonious. All the same, it ignored the heart of the Framers' argument. Madison's fear, after all, was not so much that voters have limited information as that politicians work so hard to confuse them. In narrowly technical terms, Downs assumed that the cost of obtaining information was constant. But as Prof. Oliver Williamson stressed in the 1970s, this is not true. To the contrary: Politicians would almost certainly work to make information costlier by burying voters under sophistry and untruths.[23] These "information impactedness" strategies mean that almost every communication now comes freighted with spin and misdirection.[24] The result is that it is no longer enough for voters to hear what politicians tell them. Instead, they must now make a second and much larger investment in detecting misdirection and sift out whatever grains of truth they can find. In relative terms, this makes voters' information budgets even smaller than before.

The clearest example of impactedness is almost always found in conspiracy theories. These bombard the reader (and increasingly, the viewer) with rapid-fire assertions and arguments designed to bury mainstream views in doubts that audiences cannot possibly find the time and energy to think through.[25] Conventional politicians similarly try to exhaust voters' information budgets, even if their methods are less extreme. Probably the most common tactic is to "distract" or "divert" voters from recent events that might discredit the speaker. When the tactic succeeds, audiences stop listening to the first story, or listen less intently.

But in that case how much should rational politicians invest in impactedness strategies compared to broadcasting their own positive message to voters? Here, the simplest model resembles an arms race in which each side can cancel the other's weapons purchases by making equal and opposite investments of its own. This suggests that, barring some formal or informal truce, we expect the race to continue until one side exhausts its budget. When we consider that it is almost always cheaper to confuse voters than to inform them,[26] the conclusion seems even stronger.

But in fact, all is not lost. Politicians fear for their reputations, and this sets a floor for dishonesty: If their arguments are *too* dishonest, even their fellow partisans will turn on them. The question is how much this modifies our earlier argument that dishonesty is both cheap and effective. Here the most important point is that what constitutes *unacceptable* dishonesty depends on recent history. So when one political party, say, feels its back against the wall or is especially desperate to unseat the other, its spokespersons may decide that it is worth the risk to make particularly irresponsible arguments and hope that independents and their own fellow partisans won't call them out. Then, if the gamble pays off, everyone will see that the new level of dishonesty is safe after all,[27] establishing a new and lower baseline for politicians in both parties. And once most politicians descend to the new level they will be just as safe as before. On the one hand, voters can only punish dishonesty so long as they have honest alternatives to vote for. On the other, journalists' and rival politicians' limited resources mean that they can only correct the most outrageous falsehoods. This safety-in-numbers argument suggests that politicians who indulge in merely average dishonesty will seldom, if ever, be punished.

Given these difficulties, it is no surprise that voters would seek out shortcuts to decide the issues. Just how they do this – and how politicians use these same shortcuts to manipulate them – lies at the heart of Downs' theory.

First, voters can take cues from "trusted intermediaries" who know more than they do – and selectively disclose some of these facts to push their own viewpoint.[28] Recent survey research on influencers confirms that voters do indeed seek out acquaintances who seem to know more, and that this is true even when they disagree politically. The surprise is that voters seldom defer to their interlocutors' judgments because they see them as experts. Instead, influencers mostly succeed by pointing out facts that the voter did not know. Whether this improves the voter's final decision is unclear. Bias would disappear entirely if the voter talked to so many influencers that every possible slant was represented. More usually, though, voters will only have a few conversations so that the influencers they do talk to have outsized persuasiveness. But in that case, it is important to know who becomes an influencer. The answer seems to be people who have less social fear of offending,[29] either because they take especially great pleasure in talking politics, or else are so strongly partisan that they feel a duty to proselytize.[30] The result in the latter case is that voters end up receiving more slanted information and, sometimes, voting for more extreme candidates. While this can only make government more radical, it does offer the silver lining that the angriest voters have more say and, to that extent, may be partially appeased.

Meanwhile, Downs' focus on voters' limited information budgets complicates his theory. For the most part, he assumed that parties would compete based on their written platforms. But this leads to the obvious contradiction that voters with limited information budgets are unlikely to read them.[31] At this point American politics degenerates from a specific choice to, in Prof. Hofstadter's phrase, a contest between "two types of temperament, two types of style, two types of expression and character, and not between two clearly articulated philosophies."[32] In what follows we will usually refer to these approximations as "ideology."

The fact that many voters prefer ideology to a detailed platform immediately forces all parties to supply one. That, however, raises strategic questions. For instance, simple ideologies ("Democrats like to help minorities") are cheap to learn but say little about where the parties stand on specific issues. This suggests that some voters may prefer ideologies that are so detailed and logical – Marxism-Leninism is the paradigmatic example – that the party's promises are clear to everyone. Yet this too leads to problems, since highly prescriptive ideologies can straitjacket politicians into policies they know will fail. For this reason, voters who believe that their chosen candidate is competent and shares their goals will often quite rationally prefer a certain amount of ambiguity. Then too, ideology encodes more than just platforms. It also summarizes the party's main arguments about why particular promises are both virtuous and likely to work in the world as it exists. The rub, of course, is that making definite statements about how the world works also makes ideology vulnerable to counterexamples when some new event seems to falsify it. Party ideologists manage this risk by making their theories more complicated so that they can explain away these failed predictions if and when the need arises.

Polarized politics makes ideology still more tempting. The reason is that it forces voters to make large choices, which require more fact-gathering and reasoning. This encourages voters with limited information budgets to economize by replacing fact-intensive reasoning with simple ideological arguments.

The existence of ideology changes Downsian politics in several ways. First, it adds to the inertia of parties' political views. Since voters have a limited budget for learning, an ideology that changes too fast will quickly lose supporters.[33] One way for party strategists to avoid this is to invent extensions that repurpose facts and arguments that most voters already know. In Prof. Hofstadter's words, "[I]t is hardly possible for any society to carve out a completely new vocabulary for every new problem it faces."[34]

Second, the problem of teaching new ideas is especially acute for third-party challengers. Given voters' limited attention span, few will be willing to learn an entirely new ideology in a single election cycle. This, however, leads to the Catch-22 situation that challengers can never fully explain what distinguishes them from the major parties, so that voters see even less point in learning their ideologies. Here, the obvious solution is to prioritize those ideological components that seem to be simplest and most persuasive. Alternatively, third parties can seek out whatever issues voters feel most strongly about, and are therefore most willing to learn. Here, the target audiences will almost always include extremists and single-issue voters.

Finally, ideology plays a special role within parties. At the simplest level, leadership cannot constantly issue detailed instructions telling followers how they should respond to critics. Ideology fills this gap by helping members anticipate the correct answer themselves. This minimizes quarrels within the party, and helps it to assemble a unified front against outsiders more quickly. Finally, activists see mastering ideology as a sign of professionalism, since a sophisticated understanding immediately separates them from ordinary members. It even serves as a credential: Showing ideological proficiency demonstrates that the speaker is sufficiently committed to the party's ideals to have learned a complex belief system, and is therefore someone that other activists can trust. Finally, struggles over which ideological extensions should be adopted provide a natural proxy for demonstrating influence within the party. Leaders who consistently win these fights will attract followers who want to be on the winning side. For very fortunate politicians, this reputation for winning can attract still more followers and become self-fulfilling.

Still, tight information budgets are not the whole story. One of Downs' deepest insights is that voters can acquire free political information in the course of pursuing other, nonpolitical interests that they care about more. Given that the *direct* rewards from winning elections are so tiny, this *indirect* "spinoff" information can easily dominate what voters learn. Downs was primarily thinking of the entertainment value that readers receive from reading history, or showing off their knowledge.[35] But voters also learn about political causes to advertise their virtue to others and sometimes even themselves.[36] Finally, many life lessons follow more or less automatically from voters' socioeconomic status, including education,[37] gender,[38] gun ownership,[39] and computer literacy.[40] One consequence is that poor citizens almost always have worse information than rich ones, which in turn makes it hard for them to form estimates. The result is that they derive less value from voting, and so turn out in smaller numbers.[41]

Economists have learned a great deal about spinoff incentives since the 1980s, when "open source" methods for producing software showed that collateral incentives can sometimes elicit enough effort to compete with giant companies like Microsoft.[42] Probably the main lesson is that the logic of spinoff effort is subtle. For instance, volunteers typically avoid competing with each other so that each ends up colonizing a separate niche.[43] This suggests that becoming the first political expert in one's social circle is much more rewarding than being the second. The result is that the person who enjoys discussing politics the most will usually colonize the "expert" role first, after which her would-be competitors may decide that it is better to learn about cinema or wine instead. That said, social incentives will usually encourage voters to learn at least some baseline political facts. Ultimately, having an opinion, even a crazy one, gives them something to talk about, and is almost always better than confessing ignorance. Then too, most people feel embarrassed when they lose a political argument, worrying that their reputation for thoughtfulness and intelligence has been damaged. On the usual arm's race logic, this means that voters need to learn roughly as many facts and arguments as their likely adversaries do. But in that case, speakers who concentrate on learning whatever facts and arguments support their announced position have a large advantage over those who listen to all three camps. This reinforces voters' already-strong incentive to concentrate on facts and arguments that support their current views.

We usually admire markets for delivering as much or as little effort as society requires. But spinoff incentives are different. Indeed, there is no reason at all why the facts that voters learn in the course of other activities should satisfy democracy's need for informed decisionmakers, although it probably improves matters. The downside is that spinoff learning is almost always skewed by whatever nonpolitical interests produced it. Given that most voters value political news mostly as "entertainment," we should not be surprised that journalists privilege scandal over analysis. Then too, we expect the importance of spinoff incentives to change over time. Professor Grinspan has argued that the entertainment value of politics was far greater in the nineteenth century, before young people could cure their boredom by listening to the radio or buying movie tickets.[44] Conversely, the direct benefits of voting will almost always be larger in Big Government eras when politicians promise more largesse (Figure 2.1).

FIGURE 2.1    "I hear voices that tell me to vote against my own interests"

Finally – and despite its apparent completeness – the rational voter model has definite limits. Perhaps most obviously, rational decisions require articulable facts and arguments. This is plainly challenging for complex problems like global warming or COVID-19 that baffle even the experts. In these circumstances, Downs predicted that voters would simply lose faith in their estimates and abstain. But in fact, the bitter politics of COVID-19 and global warming suggest exactly the opposite.

This implies that rational voting cannot be the whole story, and that a second, comparably strong dynamic must sometimes take over. We turn to this now.

## 2.2  VOTERS IN SOCIAL NETWORKS

The Downsian idea that socioeconomic descriptors like class, race, and income determine how most people vote is compelling. And why not? Journalists remind us of this logic after every election. But if we are honest, introspection *also* tells us that this cannot be the whole story. We hesitate to talk politics with friends who might disagree, or else feel a warm glow when they validate our opinion. And we feel nervous when a boss or colleague announces their own political views at work. Whether or not we are aware of them, these constant nudges cannot help but influence how we think and vote. Besides, Downsian theory insists that most voters know relatively little, and so lack deep policy convictions. Why *wouldn't* they choose whatever politics seems most socially convenient?[45]

What's more, rational voting theory is not very predictive. Indeed, socioeconomic factors explain less than half of voters' party identification choices. Plainly, the missing predictive power points to other variables outside the theory.[46] Then too, if rational voting were all, people would vote according to their demographic status, making elections every bit as predictable as the next census. This is entirely at odds with our experience of a political world in which opinion polls change constantly, not to mention the bizarre politics of 2021 where citizens raced to adopt previously disreputable beliefs like "Defund the Police" overnight. Downsian theory, despite its usual emphasis on imperfect information and mistakes, seems wholly inadequate to explain such seismic changes. Nor does it explain why, in the words of one British scholar, "similar people vote differently in different places."[47] In the US, researchers similarly find "relatively little evidence" that voters engage in "a deliberative process based on compelling arguments." Instead, "prevailing sentiment tends to dominate"[48] so that the impact of where people live can be "just as large as class differences."[49]

All of these puzzles drop away the moment we assume that voters are not just rational but also social. Nor is this much of a reach: Practically every American has been solemnly instructed at one time or another never to discuss religion and politics in polite company.

So far as I can determine, Alexis De Tocqueville was the first to point out that Americans value social harmony at least as much as choosing the right policies.[50] But the observation remained dormant until the late 1940s, when political scientists began using surveys to probe social influences. These usually start by asking a randomly selected subject to describe her political opinions and list the (typically) five people that she most commonly discusses them with. The researchers then contact the names she provides and repeat their questions, letting the survey snowball. Sometimes the new names overlap the old and sometimes they don't. Regardless, researchers map the names and interactions to form a network; this can be done either in an abstract social space or in the familiar physical one where members live and work. The work is so hard that even the most ambitious projects seldom interview more than a thousand or so members. But this is still large enough to capture scales where most members have never heard of each other.

So what have researchers discovered? First, that most voters usually side with the majority among those they talk to. Conversely, "the socially heroic holdout is a rare event."[51] At the same time, this is not the only variable. For one thing, people who aggressively share their opinions tend to be more persuasive than other interlocutors, even if they, too, tend to be most influential when they side with the majority.[52] Then too, majoritarian effects are systematically stronger in "dense" networks where members share multiple links,[53] probably because there are more interlocutors to reinforce the dominant viewpoint.[54] Conversely, disagreements between interlocutors tend to be most durable when each hails from a different network with a different consensus.[55] Finally, indirect, friend-of-a-friend influences fall off quickly.[56] This crucially implies that chains of influence are easily interrupted, particularly in sparse networks.[57] The result is that islands of dissent can persist for long periods.

Second, members of networks that host diverse viewpoints tend to be both better informed[58] and more persuadable.[59] This seems to make partisan interlocutors more convincing.[60] At the same time, frequent contact with dissenting viewpoints also makes members less likely to dismiss opposing views as illegitimate, misguided, uninformed, or unpatriotic. The result is that opinions in diverse networks are usually less polarized,[61] and tend to harbor fewer emotional feelings for or against individual candidates running for office.[62]

Third, diverse networks are relatively common in the sense that most voters have at least one interlocutor who supports the opposite party.[63] Furthermore, this remains true even in heavily polarized elections.[64] This puts significant limits on "echo chamber effects" in which two nonoverlapping networks occupy the same physical space but refuse to talk with one another. Just why diversity persists remains mysterious. The reason seems to be that most political discussion takes place in the same networks that host conversations more generally.[65] These typically form for a wide variety of nonpolitical reasons like physical and emotional attractiveness, sports interests, or a shared passion for hiking.[66] Surveys of college and graduate students suggest that shared political views are relatively unimportant on this list even for graduate students enrolled in public policy schools.[67] Then too, people's ability to organize homogenous networks is limited since many political discussions, most notably at work, are unplanned or involuntary.[68] Moreover, even voluntary associations are significantly constrained: Unless a member is willing to reject *every* out-group interlocutor, the odds of forming at least a few diverse relationships are strong.[69] This explains, among other things, why Republicans living in Democrat neighborhoods tend to have more Democrats in their networks – and often assume that their interlocutors are Democrats even when they aren't.[70]

Finally, surveys show that social voters work hard to determine which opinions they can safely express. The catch is that they focus much more on the people they actually interact with than public opinion more generally: If one's neighbors are mostly Democrats, the fact that *their* neighbors are all Republicans hardly matters.[71] This explains, among other things, why voters are more influenced by conversations with neighbors than by national polls,[72] and also why low-technology advertising based on bumper stickers and yard signs is frequently more effective than sophisticated media campaigns.[73]

These simple results already teach some important lessons. First, most voters make their political choices based on a mix of rational and social voting, and this mix can change over time. We also expect social voting to increase in polarized eras when opinions diverge so far that many people feel strongly enough to break off ties with friends who oppose them politically.

Second, no political consensus is ever as strong as it looks. A large fraction of the population is always dissembling, implying that the country is always less mainstream than it appears. Furthermore, this fraction is greater in polarized eras as the social costs of dissent increase. The resulting silence does not, however, mean that the views have gone away, and they can easily reemerge if and when the reigning orthodoxy is challenged.

Finally, we argued in the last section that rational voters' views display significant inertia. Social voting reinforces this: Learning friends' political views, after all, usually requires several conversations. This means that voters must estimate the "weight" of opinion around them from an "ongoing stream" of interactions,[74] with older conversations suitably discounted for the possibility that the discussants may have changed their minds since. Moreover, some views have more inertia than others. Survey evidence shows that family and early social experiences often exercise a lifelong impact, particularly with respect to issues like "basic political orientations" and party identification that are "concrete, affect laden, and central."[75] Marriage partners and peer groups usually work to stabilize these views.[76] Conversely, socially mobility tends to erode parental influences by changing voters' perceived economic class interests or by exposing them to new social groups.[77]

We end this section by asking how the incentives and content of social voting change as public opinion becomes more polarized. Perhaps most obviously, we expect social voters to have roughly the same information budgets as rational ones. This limits their ability to blend, chameleon-like, with all three groups. Instead, they find themselves forced to choose whichever group offers the most social and economic benefits. Polarization also increases the need to show loyalty, which often means ostracizing dissenters.

At some point, social benefits shade into economic ones. Here the simplest strategy is to mouth popular views that show one's solidarity with like-minded coworkers and bosses. But politics can also be used to harm one's rivals. We usually think of this as a pathology associated with hysterias like the European witch hunts or Stalin's Russia, in which denunciation developed a life of its own by drawing in opportunists who invoked politics to settle personal scores against bosses and other opponents who would normally have been untouchable.[78] These, however, are only the most dramatic cases, and scholars have long known that milder versions can be found in every society.[79] In America, recent increases in polarization have dramatically heightened fears that having the wrong views can get employees fired or denied promotions.[80] Similarly, even elites who have profited from the system increasingly feel the need to forestall criticism by loudly advertising their own "politically correct" policies, or else attacking insufficient fervor in others.[81]

Strangely, these impacts are nearly always uneven. For example, while today's fears mostly affect conservatives,[82] previous "Red Scares" nearly always focused on the Left. The asymmetry is readily explainable on the assumption that many people have no deep political convictions at all, but only join whichever group they are most afraid of at the time. This leads to the usual avalanche dynamic in which the dominant group becomes still more dominant, attracting still more fellow travelers in an endless cycle. Ideology apart, it is also true that conformist pressures seem to be stronger in some industries than others. For example, recent outbreaks of "cancel culture" are overwhelmingly concentrated in elite jobs like those in higher education,[83] Hollywood,[84] media companies,[85] and internet blogging.[86]

## 2.3 MODELING SOCIAL NETWORKS

Proceeding beyond these general observations requires more explicit theories of how networks are structured. We close by considering three tentative models. Despite their simplicity, each captures phenomena that are almost certainly present in most real-world systems.

Our first model focuses on the case of "perfect mixing" where each network member is equally likely to interact with every other member. Here it helps to recall the paradigmatic example of Silicon Valley "Standards War" competitions. Suppose that consumers much prefer to use software or computers that are compatible with the ones their friends own and for that reason let them share documents.[87] Knowing this, a consumer faced with two equally attractive products will choose the one she expects her friends to buy. But which one is that? If the only thing she knows is which company has sold the most units, she will normally buy from the leader. This leads to a "rich get richer" dynamic in which even a small lead at time $t_N$ increases the leader's market share in the next period $t_{N+1}$, followed by still greater market share in period $t_{N+2}$, and so on.

Despite its simplicity, the model already offers some significant insights. First, the rule that growth in each period is proportional to the total number of units previously sold coincides with the formula for exponential growth. This means that small initial leads can quickly lead to one choice dominating all the others. (Economists often refer to such dynamics as "tipping" or a "network effect.") For politics, this same model implies that social pressure usually narrows public opinion – sometimes drastically – compared to whatever answers voters would have reached independently. This makes Congress's job enormously easier. Moreover, the consensus, once established, tends to be stable. To see this, suppose a small handful of voters were to defect from the prevailing orthodoxy. When they looked around, they would soon see that most of their neighbors disagreed. In a pure social voting model, this would immediately convince them to resume their former opinions and restore consensus.

The catch is that these simple results do not always hold for more nuanced models. For example, interactions in real social networks are known to be complicated,[88] with some pairs of members interacting far more than others. Epidemiologists studying contagious diseases have shown that modifying social networks to include knots of people who mostly interact with each other can radically delay the onset of exponential growth.[89] Then too, we have assumed every member of the network is identical to every other. But real Silicon Valley consumers often have different needs. For instance, even though most consumers use Microsoft Word, many lawyers find Corel more convenient so that both standards exist side by side in the marketplace. For politics, this suggests that voters who have different material interests can similarly form separate networks that hold equal and opposite views. But even then, social voting will continue to amplify the consensus *within* each group no matter how much it disagrees with outsiders.

We have also said that perfect mixing models tend to make initially popular choices more and more dominant over time. This, however, begs the question of just how these choices became popular in the first place. For Silicon Valley, the answer often involves small accidents like attracting "buzz" at an electronics show. This element of chance is wildly different from the usual classical economics instinct that markets reward the best product. Indeed, our Standards War example implies that almost any competitor has a chance of winning. The implication for politics follows immediately: We cannot count on the "marketplace of ideas" to select the best platforms. Instead, the most we can hope for is that systems that mix social and rational voting together will pick good solutions more often than bad ones. And even then, conformist pressures could be strong enough to truncate debate so early that the final outcome was not much better than a lottery. In the end, we might even find ourselves agreeing with eighteenth-century Americans' gloomy observation that Athenian democracy made it "a matter of contingency whether the People subjected themselves to be led blindly by one tyrant or by another."[90]

Finally, we have said that the value that Silicon Valley consumers place on software depends on how many *other* consumers eventually purchase the same product. This, however, means that challengers cannot unseat an incumbent simply by building a better product. Instead, they must (a) build something *so much* better that consumers will invest the time and energy to switch, and (b) mount an expensive sales campaign that encourages consumers to switch at the same time so that the benefits of a common standard are never interrupted. For politics we expect dominant opinions to display a similar inertia in which conformists are happy to mouth the current consensus until some large fact or hot new political argument sends them scrambling to the next idea. Since members must switch simultaneously, this automatically confers influence on party leaders and media personalities who have reliably told members when to move in the past. For "thought leaders" whose predictions enjoy strong track records, this public expectation of accuracy can become self-fulfilling.

The Standards War model is admirably simple, but it overlooks many known facts: most obviously, that the opinions that social voters care about are intensely local. As Profs. Huckfeldt and Johnson point out, the evolution of systems in which members repeatedly interact and revise their opinions can be remarkably sensitive to detailed assumptions about how those opinions are distributed to begin with and, after that, who talks to whom. Indeed, one can even imagine special configurations in which some initially tiny minority always outnumbers its immediate neighbors and converts them, so that in the end everyone agrees with it.[91] Granted that such artificial configurations are almost certainly rare, the point remains that we should expect surprises. Then too, real networks are complex. For example, surveys show that local majorities sometimes fail to persuade "holdout" dissenters; that social voters are influenced by past interactions as well recent ones; and that networks are complicated, with some members having many more ties than others.

Our second class of models – "cellular automata" – explores these effects by calculating outcomes for large numbers of otherwise identical networks in which the links between members are initially assigned at random and voters always defer to majority opinion among their immediate interlocutor(s). To date, the most ambitious simulations are due to Professors Huckfeldt and Johnson, who used computer models to simulate networks of up to 500 members interacting at varying distances across a simple checkerboard grid.[92] While they found that the great majority of starting configurations eventually settled into patterns that preserved significant diversity,[93] they also found a "powerful" tendency to homogeneity in all cases.[94] This was in radical conflict with the empirical finding that most networks host diverse opinions.

The contradiction inspired Huckfeldt and Johnson to look for simple, plausible extensions to make their models more lifelike. Surprisingly, the usual "bubble" hypothesis that voters avoid talking to people who hold different political views worked badly. So long as the bubbles were even slightly permeable – a circumstance required by the survey evidence – the networks still evolved into monocultures.[95] Fortunately, other solutions worked better. First, the models required hundreds of iterations before finally settling down into a stable pattern. Assuming that each iteration corresponds to a single interaction – something the authors called "dicey"[96] – it was hard to see how voters could complete such an extensive schedule during a single election season. Even if voter networks did have some underlying tendency toward monoculture, it might never arrive.[97] Then too, voters' opinions might be based not just on current interactions, but also some suitably discounted memory of earlier ones. Huckfeldt and Johnson found that such models naturally led to lifelike patterns in which opinion was homogenized "to a degree," but also retained substantial diversity.[98]

The foregoing models span an enormous range of complexity. On the one hand, Standards War models where everyone interacts with everyone else are simple and lead to definite predictions. On the other, cellular automata model are so general and include so many possible interactions that they are mainly useful as a hint to deciding which assumptions produce the most lifelike results. Our third and final model seeks a middle ground. Granted that real human networks are formidably complex,[99] some interactions are enormously more probable than others. In particular, face-to-face relations are heavily suppressed by travel costs. This makes it natural to consider networks where each member communicates with their immediate *physical* neighbors and no one else. While this can never be more than an approximation,[100] the predominance of face-to-face communication in everyday life suggests that geography strongly influences which networks do and don't form.

Crucially, assuming physical proximity introduces several new and potentially important phenomena. First, neighbor-to-neighbor communication implies that new ideas should spread like waves on a pond. Second, geographic networks facilitate stable bubbles where the local majority dissents from mainstream opinion. To see this, imagine that you live at the edge of a region whose members dissent from some national orthodoxy. Looking out, you see that all of your immediate neighbors hold majoritarian views, while looking inward they are all dissenters. This leaves social voters who care about majority opinion in equipoise, implying that the bubble is approximately stable.[101] Simple back-of-the-envelope arguments then suggest that stability should set in quickly once bubbles reach a hundred or so members,[102] implying a geographic scale of perhaps fifty miles on a side.[103]

We will argue in Chapter 6 that real American political systems closely resemble our geographic ideal. For now, we simply assume the result and ask how our rational and social voting models can be combined within a single unified theory.

## 2.4 PUTTING IT TOGETHER

So far we have imagined our rational and social models separately. But most real-life humans do both, simultaneously trying to figure out which political platforms are most likely to work while avoiding unpleasant arguments. We now ask how these models can be combined within a single geographically defined network.

Imagine, then, a toy geographic model in which neighbors are arranged like squares on a checkerboard. How do their opinions evolve? It turns out that solid state physicists solved this same problem in the 1920s. They knew that the atoms in metals are arranged along a repeating grid pattern, and that each generates a magnetic field that points up or down. Furthermore, the fields interact. The result is that an atom surrounded by four "up" neighbors is much more likely to be "up" itself; an atom surrounded by three "up" neighbors and a "down" feels less influence; and an atom surrounded by two "ups" and two "downs" is indeterminate.

So-called Ising models[104] calculate which patterns of "ups" and "downs" scientists are likely to see on average.[105] Unlike Prof. Huckfeldt's simulations, they do not try to calculate how particular configurations inside the metal evolve, but only estimate the probability that an atom at some particular location will be "up" or "down" at the moment when someone decides to measure it. The answer for the simplest version of the problem where the atoms only interact with each other is striking. The only stable configurations, it turns out, are 100 percent "up" and 100 percent "down." Now substitute "voters" for "atoms" and "Republican/ Democrat" for "up/down." The result seems to predict that each voter will agree with every other. This is a catastrophe, since we have seen that real voter surveys invariably find significant numbers of dissenting opinions.

But atoms do not just interact with each other: They also feel the effects of external magnetic fields and temperature. Start with external fields: When the external field is "up" at some location the atoms it influences are likely to be "up" themselves, and for very strong fields there will be no "down" atoms at all. Here the political analog is that most real voters care about more than what the neighbors think: Facts and clever arguments also matter. By comparison, conformism operates mainly to amplify whatever opinion most voters have reached already. In the limit, this can even include a consensus that particular issues have passed outside of politics and can no longer be debated in polite company.[106]

Physicists have also explored more complicated cases where the external field is "up" in one region and "down" in others. In this case the political analog might include resource endowments that vary by region, or the dominance of different media outlets across different parts of the country. This already explains why social voting does not produce identical opinions everywhere. Voters may also feel conflicted where the answers from rational and social voting disagree, and to that extent be less likely to go the polls on Election Day.

Finally, the external field might sometimes be negligible, in which case the system reverts to interactions between neighbors. For political systems, this means that we expect issues where information is scarce – whether for reasons of cost, impactedness, or simply because even experts know very little about the subject – to paralyze rational voting. Answers based on social voting motivated by social conformity, virtue signaling, and the like will then fill the vacuum and become more important.

External fields can also change strength over time. Ising models predict that metals will then display "hysteresis" or "memory."[107] To see this, suppose one system starts in a strong "up" field which later falls to some weaker intermediate value, while a second, otherwise identical system starts in a weak "up" field that later increases to the same value from below. Then the first system will always contain more "up" atoms than the second. The reason is not hard to see: Once the initially high field aligns all atoms in the "up" position, interactions between each pair stabilize their orientation even after the external field is reduced. For politics, we expect conformity to similarly preserve old opinions long after a purely rational voter would have changed them. This is yet another source of inertia in politics: Formerly dominant opinions carry more weight than those which were never popular at all.

The dynamic also works in reverse: Very strong external signals can completely erase whatever patterns existed before. The political analog is that exceptionally large events can permanently change public opinion. Isolationism and "America First" were eminently respectable opinions before the Japanese attacked Pearl Harbor. Immediately afterward, however, practically everyone jumped to the opposite, internationalist view and stayed there for years. More usually, though, we expect lesser events to only weaken the existing pattern, which may later restore itself when voters who were initially persuaded discover that prevailing opinion is not about to change after all. This logic explains, among other things, the strategy of "October Surprises" in which presidential campaigns try to incite scandals a week or two before Election Day. Campaigns that unleash a scandal too late do not give voters enough time to learn about it. But campaigns that release the same issue too early leave plenty of time for doubtful voters to resume their original views.

Finally, adding social voting changes a key prediction of the Downsian model. Rational voter models expect the public to ignore hopeless causes, so that the issue quickly passes outside politics and is forgotten. But every new cause starts with a small minority, and some causes struggle against seemingly hopeless odds for decades before prevailing.[108] This mystery disappears as soon as we expand our model to include social voters. For them, showing their friends that they share the "correct" views is much more important than what government does or might do in the future. This implies that we should be skeptical of Madison's assumption that public opinion will come to its senses: Particularly for issues that engage the emotions, hard-core social support can give conflicts indefinite staying power.

We have also said that Ising models consider temperature. In physics, this parameter summarizes the extent to which each atom randomly jostles its neighbors hard enough to flip an "up" atom to a "down" or vice versa. For low temperatures the effect is negligible and can be safely ignored. At high temperatures, on the other hand, each atom is jostled so much that its up/down status is completely random. The analogous phenomenon for voting comes from the fact that individual citizens are constantly buffeted by a host of unobserved influences. This produces a "random utility" that changes the purely material benefits they see in each party's platform.[109] Prof. Downs argued that these random influences would mostly cancel each other out, giving well-informed voters outsized power to decide elections.[110] And indeed, surveys show that while *individual* voter responses are badly informed, shallow, and fluctuating, *aggregate* opinion is often stable, coherent, consistent with the available information, and even wise.[111] More concretely, consider the 160 million people who voted in the 2020 presidential election. In the benchmark case where each voter decided purely at random – say, by tossing a coin – one candidate would still have gotten more votes than the other. But his *average* victory margin if the experiment were repeated over and over would be tiny – just 6,325 votes or about 0.004 percent of the electorate.[112] This means that a tiny minority of well-informed voters – say, 60,000 – can dominate the outcome provided that the facts on one side are sufficiently persuasive for 60 percent to favor one conclusion over the other.

In the meantime, introducing temperature adds two important intuitions to our concept of social voting. First, we have argued that people vote like their neighbors. If that were all, the chain of influence would proceed as mechanically as a row of dominoes. But that changes as soon as each voter has some modest chance of randomly disagreeing with their neighbors. This guarantees that the chain will sooner or later be interrupted so that the system does not tip over into perfect conformity after all. In this sense adding temperature – randomness – explains the stubborn diversity of real networks. Moreover, we expect this randomness to jostle voters continuously. This means that individual voters can suddenly renounce the majority's long-held beliefs. Usually this won't matter and the majority will quickly pressure the dissenter back into conformity. But in rare cases we can equally imagine new pockets of dissent growing and becoming stable.[113] Meanwhile, randomness guarantees a constant supply of dissent so that the network is at least slightly receptive when some new facts or ideological arguments encourage rational voters to revise their estimates.[114]

The question remains how much weight we should give rational voter models compared to social ones, and whether this ratio can change over time. In the short term, we know that it does. For example, one British study finds that voters' propensity to vote the way their neighbors do changes from one election to the next, and tends to be strongest when the parties are evenly matched.[115] This is unsurprising: Given that pressing friends to change their political opinions is socially costly, we expect even the most extreme partisans to avoid it in years where the outcome seems preordained.

But we also have good evidence that the balance between rational and social voting can shift over longer time periods. Prof. Grinspan has shown how the shrill and sometimes physically violent partisanship of mid to late nineteenth-century politics grew out of small towns where individuals urgently needed to join one clique or another because – quite literally – their economic and social futures depended on it.[116] This was particularly visible in the era's political rallies, which reflexively advertised political participation as a way to find friends and mentors, win adult attention,[117] advance one's career, and even find romance.[118] Small wonder, then, that politics was dominated by young adults,[119] then as now the group most in need of "networking." Yet these genteel goals were immediately submerged in the frantic need to show one's solidarity so that the rallies themselves quickly degenerated into mindless applause, shared festivities, drinking, military-style marching, and fighting with opponents.[120] These opportunities to see and be seen supporting one's friends climaxed with voters braving a gaunt-let of hecklers – secret ballots were practically unknown then – to cast their ballots on Election Day.[121] The point, of course, was that anyone willing to invest time and energy in this madness – let alone risk physical injury – was unquestionably loyal to the group.[122]

And then, suddenly, it ended. Around 1900 observers noticed what they called a "great quieting" of passion and partisanship.[123] Twenty years later, turnout had fallen to just 50 percent. One obvious cause was the rise of nonpolitical entertainments like movies that siphoned off young audiences.[124] A second cause involved tactics: Progressives now ran cam-paigns designed to educate instead of entertain, and also an increased professionalism that replaced volunteers looking for patronage with paid campaign workers. Finally, the introduction of secret ballots let dissenters lie about who they had voted for, diluting social pressure.[125] The results, in Prof. Grinspan's judgment, were mixed. While politics was indisputably "cleaner and fairer," passion and voter turnout have "never recovered."[126]

That is, until recently. Today's violently emotional politics follows the nineteenth-century's pattern far more closely than the twentieth's. Indeed, the 2020 Presidential Election saw the highest turnout (62 percent) in 120 years.[127] Meanwhile, the endless charges that this or that group is "deplorable" show just how much social forces are driving the rhetoric. The difference, this time, is that the displays of solidarity have mostly moved onto the web: Instead of attacking their neighbors, partisans can now bond with friends and attack enemies across the country. Nor does it hurt that the web's odd mix of insult and anonymity keeps mouthy "flamers," unlike their Victorian forebears, safe from physical retaliation.[128]

Finally, the Ising viewpoint invites us to reimagine the nature of politics. We have argued that network effects act as a kind of add-on to rational voting, amplifying the most common ideas on average. Philosophically, at least, the random and mindless quality of this amplification makes politics not just ignorant (the Downsian view) but nihilistic. After all, random amplification implies that *every* opinion has some chance of prevailing, and it is easy to imagine how a series of small accidents could give some outlier opinion or candidate an insurmountable lead. The hope, of course, is that there will be enough rational voters to keep the best opinions competitive. Even so, the randomness that social voting injects into politics should make us skeptical: Electoral "mandates," especially in close elections, may often reflect chance far more often than any enduring "will of the people."

Social voting's emphasis on showing solidarity also makes facts become less important. Indeed, social voters' willingness to embrace visibly dishonest or absurd positions may even be an asset, since their willingness to suffer embarrassment makes their loyalty all the more visible. Conversely, extremists often signal their power by making claims that most of their audience think absurd, but are too afraid to challenge.[129] In that case, the ensuing silence shows average people that others share their fear – and that if they do speak up, no one will support them.

In the end, social voting even changes the style of politics: For the most part, we have discussed social voting as if it was cold-blooded pandering. But this fails to capture the emotion that drives true partisans. As Martin Van Buren observed in the 1820s, "It would take longer than our lives (even if it were practicable) to create new party feelings."[130] Prof. Grinspan argues that this was natural in an era when political conflict drew its emotional energy from the failed romances, business rivalries, and social slights of small-town life. The result, in his phrase, was a politics that was "deeply felt but shallowly reasoned."[131]

## 2.5 FEEDBACKS

This chapter has asked what our rational and social voter models add to the Framers' intuitions about the behavior of crowds. We especially focus on what they say about how public opinion is likely to evolve over time.

Downs' rational voter model recognized that imperfect information is the normal condition of politics. This means, among other things, that most voters cannot adjust their estimates fast enough to keep up with new facts and arguments. This necessarily limits how fast popular opinion can change, save in rare "Pearl Harbor" moments when some very large or directly felt event eclipses all earlier evidence.

Small information budgets also force voters to slant their learning to facts and arguments that support their current political beliefs. In bipartisan eras this tends to stabilize opinion around a single dominant centrism. But during polarized eras we expect voters to disproportionately concentrate their learning on just one prevalent view (Left, Right, or center) and exclude the others. Over time, this means that the warring groups will share fewer and fewer facts in common. This is bound to produce incomprehension, anger, and still more polarization. Fortunately, the logic is reversible: If the rival ideologies should start to converge for some reason, their supporting facts and arguments will also overlap more, increasing mutual understanding and the possibility of common ground legislation.

Voters often seek shortcuts to obtain information at less cost. This frequently takes the form of "spinoffs" from activities they would do anyway. Given how little voters know, this added information almost certainly improves their decisions. That said, spinoff information is massively distorted: People who get their information from *Comedy Central* may or may not be badly informed, but they are practically certain to be less tolerant. Alternatively, voters may turn to influencers for information. But many of these are partisan, and this fraction tends to increase with polarization. Finally, rational voters often economize on information by learning ideologies. Once facts are devalued, the press sees less reward for gathering them in the first place so that any remaining pragmatists must do without.

As always, politicians see and take advantage of these behaviors. In particular, they often use "impactedness" tactics to *increase* voters' information costs. This gives content to the Framers' instinct that politicians work hard to mislead the public. The difference is that where the Framers saw humankind's dishonesty as constant, we have argued that impactedness is an equilibrium and can get better – but also worse – over time. It follows that voters' knowledge and capacity for rational voting will be greater in some eras than in others. To the extent that rational voting becomes costly, we expect a combination of social voting and apathy to fill the gap.

We have argued that social voters care mainly what their friends think. This conformism often works in the same direction as rational voting. For instance, social voters' calculation that rapid changes of opinion are unsafe means that they cannot shift to new positions unless the move is coordinated. This gives power to famous politicians, journalists, or other "thought leaders" with a history of reliably endorsing successful shifts in the past. Large events similarly facilitate coordination by providing a highly visible signal that the existing consensus might no longer hold. Given a choice, social voters prefer bipartisan politics because it minimizes conflict if they should accidentally endorse the wrong sentiment. This suggests that social voters will be among the first to return to bipartisanship if and when polarization relaxes.

By comparison, social voters in eras of coercive politics usually place a high value on learning ideology because it makes "correct" opinion that much easier to anticipate and conform to. This further deemphasizes the importance of facts and pragmatic arguments, while encouraging media outlets to substitute still more opinion content for traditional objective reporting.

Social voting also introduces new behaviors not found in rational voter models. First and foremost, it amplifies narrow majorities into larger ones. At one level, this seems terrifyingly mindless: Social voters do not care which government policies they live under so long as their friends admire their beliefs. But one could equally say that if voters value social harmony over substantive policy, then that is their business. Either way, the phenomenon of hysteresis predicts that the dominance of some beliefs and not others depends on history more than conviction. That said, this same shallowness allows for a surprisingly fluidity in times of crisis, when social voters can suddenly flock to new slogans and belief systems overnight.

Political attitudes also depend on who belongs to one's network, with diverse memberships encouraging more tolerant and informed voters. Diversity comes naturally in most eras when politics is, at best, a minor criterion for joining groups. But that could change in a hyperpolarized society. If so, it is reasonable to expect a downward spiral in which the need to avoid political arguments encouraged networks to recruit fewer dissenters as new members, after which the low social cost of ostracizing the relative handful of dissenters who remained would enforce still more homogeneity. The good news is that this process cannot happen overnight. Most social networks took years to develop, and breaking ties is socially expensive. To the extent that diversity does fade, it is mostly likely to happen gradually through the normal attrition of moving, changing jobs, and making new friends.

Finally, when polarization is very strong we expect sanctions for "incorrect" opinion to include not just social but also economic penalties. At this point, we expect members of disfavored groups to fall silent, leading to the illusion that extreme opinions have become "mainstream." It is unclear how this regime, once established, might end. Once politics becomes directly felt, however, network members may become sufficiently fed up with the dominant paradigm to reform their networks around less demanding creeds. Prof. Downs seems to have had something like this in mind when he speculated that the "violence" of ideological conflict eventually "exhausts itself," leading to a "new consensus."[132]

### Notes

1   See, e.g., Moulton (1998) at p. 366.
2   For a detailed portrait, see Guelzo (2021b) at ch. 1–2 et passim.
3   While we will often talk about "rational" and "social voters" as distinct populations, each voter actually responds to both mechanisms in a constantly changing mix.
4   Hotelling (1929). For a modern version of the argument, see Gehlbach (2022) at pp. 2–5.
5   Downs (1957) at p. 28.
6   Alternative models which assume that politicians seek to advance their personal political beliefs make similar predictions. See Gehlbach (2022) at pp. 6–7. There are, in fact, good reasons to think that politicians will join parties they agree with, if only because it saves the cost of constantly having to dissemble their actual views and avoids the potentially disastrous consequences of being found out. Then, too, joining a political party inevitably slants the news and argument one receives. This implies that even politicians who are initially skeptical of their party's beliefs will find them more and more plausible as time goes by.
7   Simon (1992) at p. 74.

8   Voters in two-party systems can safely ignore the chances that their first choice may not win the election, since they will then receive their second choice no matter what they do.

9   Downs (1957) at p. 83.

10  *Federalist* No. 16 at p. 70 (Hamilton); see also Washington [1796] at p. 6.

11  *Federalist* No. 71 at p. 328 (Hamilton).

12  There is a small caveat here for the "wisdom of crowds," which holds that the information needed to arrive at a correct answer may sometimes be spread across widely scattered individuals, who must then find each other and communicate before their knowledge can be combined to yield practical value. All the same, the required information must *already* exist *somewhere* in the crowd. If no one on earth knows some essential fact, the crowd can do no better.

13  For an economically literate fable in which the Soviet Union follows through on Khrushchev's early plans to introduce market signals and outperforms the US, see Spufford (2010).

14  Among other things, congressmen typically spend up to half their time raising money. Roemer (2015).

15  Washington [1796] at p. 4.

16  Rothenberg (2007).

17  The standard example of a successful twentieth-century counterinsurgency is the British experience in Malaysia. Burleigh (2014). Older examples date back to the Roman Empire. Luttwak (1976).

18  Fryer (2019) (police shootings); Dills and Miron (2006) and Blocker (2006) at p. 241 (Prohibition).

19  On the neurological basis for forgetting, see Small (2021). Because he deliberately focused on the next election, Downs did not need to address forgetting beyond quoting Prof. Edwards' (1927) theory that voters in the first generation find some events unforgettable, that they imperfectly hand these lessons down to the second generation, and that the memory barely exists in the third.

20  The notion of a five-year window is deliberately arbitrary. Plainly, we remember large events like 9/11 for much longer than that, while discarding most of what we read in each day's newspaper almost immediately.

21  See generally Cotton (1986). Ulysses Grant chose an unnecessarily complex plan for capturing the Confederate fortress at Vicksburg because the alternative, which required a temporary retreat, risked solidifying public opposition to the North's new draft laws and thereby losing the War. Grant [1885] at pp. 610 and 784.

22  See generally Brinton (1938).

23  See generally Williamson (1975).

24  For the history of American political spin, see generally Greenberg (2016).

25  Butter (2020) at pp. 24, 26.

26  The reason, as every academic knows, is that the first version of an argument almost always has flaws, after which it takes several more rounds to clarify it. By comparison, the point of impactedness strategies is less to persuade voters than to keep them from reaching any conclusion at all. Here a confused argument works just as well as a correct one, and sometimes better.

27  The glow of virtue that political struggle inspires in many partisans also helps to overcome the shame of embracing obviously dishonest arguments. In Hamilton's phrase, "A spirit of faction ... will often hurry the persons of whom they are composed into improprieties and excesses, for which they would blush in a private capacity." See *Federalist* No. 15 at p. 66.

28  Downs (1957) at p. 83.

29  Huckfeldt (2014) at pp. 59, 60, and 64.

30  Downs (1957) at p. 84. The suggestion that extremists often feel more intensely follows from the fact that their preferred policies are so far removed from the current one. See, e.g., Gehlbach (2022) at p. 2.

31  Downs (1957) at p. 98. Members of special interest groups and passionate single-issue voters are obvious exceptions to this rule.

32  Hofstadter (1959b) at p. 824.

33  Changes in ideology may also persuade low information voters that they no longer know what the party stands for and should stop supporting it.

34  Hofstadter (1955) at p. 276.

35  Downs (1957) at pp. 239 and 245. Recent empirical research confirms that many people do indeed "realize psychic and social rewards from engaging in political discussion. They are knowledgeable and share their information"; Huckfeldt et al. (2013) at p. 21. The more exotic possibility is that politics, being an inherently "respectable" subject, can provide cover for prurient content not normally admissible in polite society; Dyck et al. (2013) at p. 523. Such uses were particularly popular in Victorian times, when suggestive and downright pornographic versions of *The Awful Confessions of Maria Monk* attacked the Catholic Church over supposed sex abuse by priests; Butter (2020) at p. 53. Today's taboos are more likely to involve political correctness. Prof. Butter argues that some conservatives now accuse Barack Obama and Hillary Clinton of criminality because more conventional critiques would be shouted down as covertly racist or sexist. Butter (2020) at p. 89.

36  Profs. Benabou and Tirole argue that "precisely because certain self-views are more pleasant or functional to have than others, people invest substantial resources in trying to achieve, maintain and defend these beliefs. Thinking of oneself as a moral person requires spending time and money to help others, refraining from cheating or polluting, or consuming certain products." Benabou and Tirole (2006).

37  Education makes it easier to process information. For example, people who have been exposed to undergraduate economics can immediately make arguments that would never occur to them otherwise.

38  Here the most vivid recent example is the "Me-Too" movement. Most men never see and for that reason have a hard time imagining casual groping. But if it one man in twenty does it, practically every woman will have experienced it.

39  Gun control almost by definition pits groups with radically different knowledge and experience of firearms against each other.

40  People who grew up on social media are used to a world where audiences are quick to find fault and a single unwise remark can haunt the speaker for years. This makes free speech less valuable to them, and censorship more acceptable.

41 Downs (1957) at p. 264.
42 See, e.g., Maurer and Scotchmer (2006).
43 Henkel (2004).
44 Grinspan (2016) at p. 180.
45 While we will usually interpret social voting as an attempt to avoid conflict, conformity also offers psychological comfort. Churches have long understood that belief is more stable in large congregations. It follows that declining church membership undercuts the moral reassurance that congregants feel, creating room for "woke" ideology and other secular creeds.
46 Cassel (1982) at p. 278.
47 Johnston et al. (2004) at pp. 369 and 377–9.
48 Huckfeldt (2014) at p. 63.
49 Huckfeldt (2014) at p. 63. Huckfeldt's pioneering study of Buffalo, New York voters found that working-class respondents had a 0.60 probability of identifying as Democrats when they lived in working-class neighborhoods compared to 0.49 when they did not. Huckfeldt (1986) at pp. 45, 48, and 50.
50 See, e.g., de Tocqueville [1835] at p. 807 ("[A]s long as the majority is still undecided, discussion is carried on; but as soon as its decision is irrevocably pronounced, a submissive silence is observed, and the friends, as well as the opponents, of the measure unite in assenting its propriety.") Madison anticipates this idea when he explains that "The reason of man, like man himself, is timid and cautious when left alone, and acquires firmness and confidence in proportion to the number with which it is associated." *Federalist* No. 49 at p. 232.
51 Huckfeldt (2017) at pp. 8, 18.
52 Huckfeldt (2014) at p. 57.
53 Pietryka et al. (2018) at pp. 717–18. "Low-density" networks correspond to topologies in which members share links close to the simplest possible form, $a–b–c–d$…. Higher-density networks supplement this pattern with additional links of the form $c–a$, $a–d$, and $d–b$. To see why dense networks encourage more uniform opinions, first suppose that only immediate neighbors influence each other. Then for our lowest-density example, if $a$ and $c$ share the same opinion the principle of majority rule implies that $b$ must agree as well. Where $b$ is multiply connected, the chances that he or she will hear and embrace alternative views are necessarily higher.
54 Pietryka et al. (2018) at p. 721.
55 Huckfeldt (2017) at pp. 8, 18.
56 Pietryka et al. (2018) at p. 716.
57 Removing a single link stops opinion from propagating in very low-density networks. For example, removing element $c$ from the chain $a–b–c–d$ … Implies that $a$'s opinion can have no influence on $c$'s and vice versa. Where members are multiply connected, $a$ can sometimes influence $c$ indirectly even when the shortest and most direct link has been removed.
58 Pietryka et al. (2018) at p. 716.
59 Huckfeldt (2014) at pp. 64–5.
60 Huckfeldt (2014) at p. 59.
61 Huckfeldt (2014) at pp. 64–5.
62 Huckfeldt (2014) at pp. 19, 20.
63 Huckfeldt et al. (2013) at p. 16; Huckfeldt (2017) at p. 7.

64  Huckfeldt (2017) at p. 7.
65  Huckfeldt (2013) at pp. 7 and 13; Huckfeldt (2014) at p. 17; and Walsh (2004).
66  Huckfeldt (2014) at pp. 49–50; Huckfeldt (2017) at pp. 5–6.
67  Huckfeldt (2014) at p. 14.
68  Huckfeldt et al. (2013) at p. 14.
69  Huckfeldt (2014) at p. 49; Huckfeldt (2017) at p. 6.
70  Huckfeldt (2014) at p. 57. The effect is softened by the fact that many voters show a strong preference for interacting with their own class, especially when it is locally in the minority. Huckfeldt et al. (2013) at p. 16; Huckfeldt (2014) at p. 49; Huckfeldt (2017) at p. 6.
71  Huckfeldt (2014) at p. 64.
72  Huckfeldt (2014) at p. 63.
73  Professional political campaigns often use "Astroturfing" tactics to simulate the amateurism of genuine grassroots protests. Wikipedia (7).
74  Huckfeldt (2014) at pp. 18 and 63.
75  Huckfeldt (2014) at pp. 43 and 51.
76  Huckfeldt (1986) at p. 43.
77  Huckfeldt (2014) at p. 51.
78  Fitzpatrick and Gellately (1996).
79  Fitzpatrick and Gellately (1996).
80  One recent poll asks respondents, "Are you worried about losing your job or missing out on job opportunities if your political opinions became known?" Of the one-third (32 percent) who answered "yes," 28 percent were Democrats and 38 percent Republicans. Ekins (2020).
81  Fitzpatrick (1996) at pp. 844–5.
82  Democrats with graduate degrees (25 percent) are roughly as worried as high school graduates (23 percent) that their political views could harm them at work. However, the corresponding numbers for Republicans rise from 27 percent for those holding high school degrees to 40 percent for college graduates and 60 percent for those holding postgraduate degrees; Ekins (2020). The pattern is familiar from totalitarian regimes, where denunciations tend to be concentrated among elite creative workers: Fitzpatrick (1996) at pp. 853–6 (reporting denunciations of architects, physicists, and Bolshoi dancers).
83  Acevedo (2021) lists 176 cancellations in the US and Canada. Typical offenses range from dressing up as a Confederate soldier at Halloween to expressing "angst ... that a lot of my lower [performing students] are Blacks" to criticizing the 1619 Project's scholarship.
84  Couch, Siegel, and Kit (2021).
85  See, e.g., Steinberg and Moreau (2020) (ABC news executive Barbara Fedida); Kiefer (2020) (production company CEO Andrew Alexander); Anon. (2020c) (CBC Host Wendy Melsey); Elber (2021) (game show host Mike Richards); Couch et al. (2021) (movie director James Gunn and actresses Gina Carrano and Roseanne Barr); Anon. (2020b) (actor Hartley Sawyer); Breen (2020) (reality TV star Jessica Mulroney); O'Kane (2020) (reality TV stars Stassi Schroeder, Kristen Doute, Max Boyens, and Brett Caprioni); Lee (2020) (mass employee protests seeking to overrule or oust

editors at *The New York Times, The Wall Street Journal, The Philadelphia Inquirer, The Los Angeles Times, Fox News,* and *Hearst* and *Condé Nast* magazines); Helmore (2020) (*Vogue* employees criticizing editor Anna Wintour for lack of diversity though she did not step down); and Trachtenberg (2020a) (employees calling for boycott of all books by former Trump Administration officials).

86 Nolte (2021).

87 For a technical introduction, see Scotchmer (2006) at pp. 289–318.

88 Watts (2003).

89 Chowell et al. (2016); Maurer and Rutherford (2007) at p. 125.

90 Smith & Hamilton [1788] at p. 759.

91 Johnson and Huckfeldt (2005) at p. 268. The claim that certain starting configurations can generate wildly unexpected outcomes reminds us of the trope that a butterfly that bats its wings in China can (sometimes!) cause a thunderstorm in Iowa. The idea that politics is "chaotic" in this technical sense limits how well even a perfect theory could predict outcomes.

92 Johnson and Huckfeldt (2005) at p. 258. The models allowed for interactions between immediate neighbors and also, with suitable discounting, more distant ones. Johnson and Huckfeldt (2005).

93 Johnson and Huckfeldt (2005) at p. 268.

94 Johnson and Huckfeldt (2005) at p. 255.

95 Johnson and Huckfeldt (2005) at p. 257.

96 Johnson and Huckfeldt (2005) at p. 265.

97 Huckfeldt (2014) at p. 55.

98 Johnson and Huckfeldt (2005) at p. 265.

99 See generally Watts (2003).

100 For recent survey evidence profiling long-distance relationships, see Johnston and Pattie (2011) at pp. 303–5.

101 Of course, strict majority rule makes every bubble unstable since there are always slightly more people outside the bubble than inside. However, we have seen that empirical evidence for voters siding with their local majority is only approximate, and that other factors can and do enter the calculation. One natural way to accommodate this imprecision is to assume a friction term so that social voters do not change their opinions unless the ratio of majority-to-minority opinion exceeds some threshold.

102 To see this, take a sheet of graph paper and pick a square at the center. Now color the thin layer of adjacent squares that surround it. Call this "Ring 1." You will see that Ring 1 has eight members. Now draw a second "Ring 2" around Ring 1. This contains eight more cells than Ring 1, so if Ring 2 is Democrats and Ring 1 is Republicans we expect the latter to be unstable. Now draw a third ring immediately outside Ring 2, and then a fourth ring, and so on. Since each successive ring has eight more squares than the previous one, the *comparative* social pressure for voters in Ring (N) is monotone decreasing. Lacking better information, we arbitrarily estimate that the 3 : 2 ratio of Ring 5 (ninety-six members) is approximately stable.

103 Probability theory holds that a drunkard who takes steps of length $q$ in random directions will, on average, find himself at a distance $\sqrt{n} \times q$ from the

place he started. It follows that the first and last members of a twelve-member bubble will normally find themselves separated by $\sqrt{96} \times 5 \sim 10 \times 5 = 50$ miles. This naive estimate already explains the eighteenth-century observation that state-wide factions were easy to organize in Rhode Island but nearly impossible in Massachusetts. See, e.g., Pinckney [1788] at p. 586. Note, however, that 50 miles only defines the *minimum* size of factions. The *average* size presumably depends on how long most bubbles grow before finding themselves blocked by bubbles of equal and opposite opinion. All else equal, we expect this to happen sooner in political systems where new bubbles form easily.

104  Rhymes with "kissing," and named for German scientist Ernst Ising (1900–98). Wikipedia (23).

105  For mathematically rigorous papers that use Ising model techniques to explore the interactions between material incentives and peer pressure, see e.g. Fernández del Río, Korutcheva, and Del la Rubia (2012); Fernández del Río (2011); Durlauf (1999); and Galam and Moscovici (1991). I thank UC San Diego Prof. Ted Sichelman for pointing out this literature.

106  Ulysses S. Grant probably had a similar thought in mind when he wrote that he looked forward to a day when a "truthful history" of the Civil War would "do full credit" to combatants on both sides, even as "the justice" of the Union cause would "come to be acknowledged by every citizen of the land." Grant [1885] at p. 242.

107  Fernández del Río, Korutcheva, and de la Rubia (2012) at pp. 3, 10; Fernández del Río (2011) at pp. 22, 31, 89.

108  The Temperance Movement spent nine decades advocating for Prohibition before the US finally ratified the 18th Amendment in 1920; Wikipedia (56). More recently, the movement to overturn *Roe* v. *Wade* was minuscule until Reagan Republicans embraced it in the 1980s. Even then, it took another four decades to prevail. Bravin (2022).

109  Fernández del Río, Korutcheva, and de la Rubia (2012) at pp. 6, 10; Fernández del Río (2011) at pp. 21, 31.

110  Downs (1957) at p. 8.

111  Page and Shapiro (1992) at p. 17; see also Huckfeld (2017) at p. 3.

112  The result follows from the binomial distribution. Alexander Karepetyan, personal communication.

113  See, e.g., Fernández del Río (2011) at p. 31.

114  The same argument suggests that it is almost impossible for an ideology to die out entirely. Suppose the number of believers is small. Then every voter who believes or disbelieves the ideology has some modest chance of "flipping" their convictions. But since there are so many more believers, the temperature effect mostly creates nonbelievers on net. That said, a sufficiently unattractive ideology and/or strong social pressures can still swamp this contrarianism. Apologists for slavery were common in the antebellum South but are now extinct.

115  Johnston et al. (2004) at p. 396.

116  The intersection between politics and social life was so strong by the 1880s that it was "a common pastime, half jest, half earnest, for a tram full of people thus thrown together by chance to test public opinion" by asking

how each passenger planned to vote. Grinspan (2016) at p. 34. For a definitive, albeit fictional portrait of small town favor-trading and love life in early twentieth-century Pennsylvania, see O'Hara (2016).

117 Grinspan (2016) at p. 18.

118 Grinspan (2016) at pp. 18, 57–61. Since courtships often began with partisan sympathy, campaign managers routinely assured "wife-less young voters" that "all the handsome and intelligent young ladies supported their party." Grinspan (2016) at pp. 42, 59. The analogous practice today is called "wokefishing," in which males feign violent social justice opinions to bed politically correct females. Eloise (2021). Also, 71 percent of Democrats and 31 percent of Republicans say that they would "definitely" or "probably" not go out with someone who voted for a presidential candidate they opposed. Anon (2021a).

119 Grinspan (2016) at pp. 43–44.

120 Grinspan (2016) at pp. 19–20. Speeches were frequently drowned out by fireworks and roaring crowds, who openly admitted that they had "never heard a political speech to the end." Grinspan (2016). The two major parties similarly competed to see which could offer the most "free drinks and crazed parades." Grinspan (2016) at p. 14. These invariably featured wild animals, bonfires, and fireworks calculated to attract young voters [Grinspan (2016) at pp. 43–44] along with marching clubs where partisans could drink freely, smoke, practice military drills, and talk politics; Grinspan (2021) at p. 246. The nineteenth-century's political obsession with marching may seem strange to us. Still, soldiers have known for thousands of years that marching in step builds feelings of solidarity or, as we now say, "unit cohesion."

121 Grinspan (2016) at pp. 16, 94.

122 Politicians did everything they could to feed this tribal response. Rather than debate substance, they constantly appealed to supporters' emotions with nonsense and vicious slogans, false accusations, and booze. The most successful campaigners were perpetually outraged and always "ready to break their opponents' heads, or to have their own heads broken for the sake of the party." Grinspan (2021) at p. 38. The result was that political meetings routinely featured threats of violence, sarcastic songs, and schoolyard taunts, when they did not actually descend into rioting and window breaking. Some local toughs even threw bottles of acid; Grinspan (2016) at pp. 10, 34, 36, and 44. Given such insane levels of enthusiasm, it is hardly surprising that voter turnout from 1840 to 1900 almost always hovered between 70 and 80 percent – the highest rate in all of American history. Grinspan (2016) at p. 21.

123 Grinspan (2021) at pp. 11, 194–5, and 283.

124 Grinspan (2016) at p. 24.

125 Grinspan (2021) at p. 249. The fad for taking "ballot selfies" in the early 2010s has compromised this confidentiality. Wikipedia (11).

126 Grinspan (2021) at p.24.

127 Wikipedia (50).

128 This did not stop many Victorians from becoming obsessed with evils they would never see first hand. Prof. Grinspan describes "Ben," a 20-year-old

Maine resident who became passionate about the slavery issue after having dinner with a traveling lecturer. The youth immediately started devouring antislavery newspapers and spending election days haranguing everyone old enough to vote. Whatever its political impact, Ben's activism was socially useful, covering for both a natural "goofiness" – he was also obsessed with phrenology and eliminating butter from his diet – and his failure to find either romance or a job. Grinspan (2016) at pp. 51–3. Charles Dickens marveled at a similar passion for distant causes in *Bleak House* [1853], where the loudly pious Mrs. Jellyby tirelessly advocates for an African tribe while neglecting her family.

129 For example, it is hard to believe that any significant part of the population believes activist claims that acronyms are racist. Melendez (2021). This, however, only increases the intimidation value when no one dares to challenge the claim.

130 Quoted in Hofstadter (1969) at p. 237.

131 Hofstadter (1969) at p. 21.

132 Downs (1957) at pp. 120–1 and n. 3.

# 3

## Selling Policy

### *Political Narratives and Ideologies*

Chapter 2 described theories of how voters choose between issues that already exist. This is a reasonable model for individual elections in which the choices barely change from the start of campaigning to Election Day. Over the longer run, though, we know that old issues (e.g. "Prohibition") disappear, while new ones ("gender equality") grow urgent. Moreover, *which* new issues prevail can decide whether voters become still more polarized or else converge. What makes the process mysterious is that the rise of new issues can depend on innovative arguments and rhetoric even when the facts themselves have not changed. Trying to understand politics while ignoring these effects is, as the physicist Richard Feynman once remarked, like trying to construct a theory of dry water.

The failing is deliberate. Indeed, economists habitually assume that, whatever reasoning consumers use, they end by choosing whichever product offers them the greatest reward. Whether the same assumption works for politics is less clear. And certainly, the common wisdom from Ancient Athens to Ronald Reagan's "Great Communicator" is that *how* politicians say things matters just as much as their substantive proposals. Indeed, the ancient demagogues that Madison feared relied almost *entirely* on style. This distinction between policy and rhetoric is particularly important today. For the past thirty years voters have faced a threadbare choice between Ronald Reagan's *laissez faire* "Morning in America" and Lyndon Johnson's interventionist "Great Society." From this standpoint, the way forward is to find new and more attractive agendas that break the existing gridlock. But that will require fresh images and rhetoric on the scale of Bryan's Cross of Gold speech or Lincoln's Gettysburg Address. Where will it come from?

Thomas Jefferson claimed to understand the process. Where Madison imagined a politics defined by the sociology of interest groups, Jefferson championed what Prof. Hofstadter calls "a psychological conception" of parties.[1] "[I]n every free and deliberating society, he said, "there must, from the nature of man, be opposite parties, and violent dissensions and discords; and one of these, for the most part, must prevail over the other for a longer or shorter time."[2] For present purposes, Jefferson's observation offers three distinct advantages. First, it looks past the next election. This is essential if we hope to study the long-run dynamics of ideological standoffs and gridlock. Second, it is precise, identifying a specific problem in the same way that Madison warned against the passion of crowds. This gives would-be institutional reformers a definite target to plan against. Finally, Jefferson's hypothesis speaks to everyday experience: Indeed, it is nearly impossible to argue when he insists that centripetal forces sooner or later afflict every human organization "from the greatest confederacy of nations down to a town meeting or vestry."[3] There is even room for what Marxists call "the dialectic," in which each temporary victory by one side prompts an equal and opposite reaction from the other.

This chapter looks at the surprising ways in which psychology, neurology, and artificial intelligence have fleshed out Jefferson's insight, and proposes an explicit theory of how voters decide what is true. While we cannot predict the trajectory of any single belief, we can at least say something about the tendencies and what to expect on average. Our goal, then, is to say something definite about the origin and evolution of ideological conflict, how polarization accelerates, and above all how conflict can sometimes revert to consensus.

### 3.1 LOGIC AND PATTERNS

Downs never said just how his rational voters would decide which platform offered the biggest rewards. He didn't have to. The genius of classical economics lay in pretending that the world could be reduced to equations. After that, economists could simply solve the algebra to predict what rational men would do. Of course, they knew that very few human beings actually reasoned this way. But that would not matter so long as the methods they did use led to similar answers.

Yet politics is very different from markets. Unlike shoppers, voters seldom know much about what they are "buying." In this sense, the common instinct that voters are irrational is a distraction. While it could well be true, we should first see how much even rational methods can lead to wrongheaded estimates and, occasionally, wild changes of opinion.

The good news is that scholars have learned a great deal about how people decide what's true. Probably the biggest insight is that the human brain has evolved two separate methods for analyzing the world. The claim is not new. Indeed, it was already clear to the poet Percy Bysshe Shelley (1792–1822), who contrasted the mind's talent for manipulating "algebraical relations" between known thoughts with a second faculty of "imagination" that was alone capable of making new thoughts from existing ones. This second "faculty," he added, "did not depend on logic," but instead followed an aesthetic judgment of what was "beautiful and ... good."[4] Sigmund Freud's (1856–1939) subsequent reworking of this binary into a rational conscious self and an irrational "unconscious" carried this powerful intuition into the sciences.

Psychologists spent much of the twentieth century documenting both modes experimentally. In the words of 2011 Nobelist Dan Kahneman, logical thought – now typically called "Type 2" or "slow thinking" – is conscious and effortful and takes time, but once completed can be articulated to others or loaded into machines as software.[5] On the other hand, "Type 1" or "fast thinking" is unconscious, intuitive, automatic, and accompanied by hardly any sense of effort or control.[6] We look and see the answer – or at least we think we do, since "fast thinking," unlike math, is sometimes wrong. And afterward we cannot say how we produced our result, covering our embarrassment with words like "intuition" and "judgment."[7]

These psychology insights have been greatly reinforced by physical studies of the brain. Victorian scientists studying head injuries already knew that different parts of the brain have distinct functions.[8] However, these methods remained limited down to the 1990s, when new imaging technologies let scientists measure activity in specific locations while subjects performed tasks.[9] Though the technology still cannot track individual neurons in real time, it is already clear that the brain breaks problems into pieces which are then assigned to different regions for processing, followed by a final step which combines and reconciles these intermediate results in a definitive answer.[10]

This same Type1/Type 2 split also appears in our machines. Starting in the 1960s, the first engineering research into artificial intelligence or "AI" relied on humans to write down Type 2 logic, which was then translated into electronic circuits and software. The resulting machines did math problems

FIGURE 3.1 Reversing faces/the wineglass illusion
Source: johnwoodcock / DigitalVision Vectors / Getty Images

much faster than people, but were bad at spotting patterns. Newer "neural network" designs take a different approach. Like the brain, they connect large numbers of neuron-like (multiple input, nonlinear response) circuits together. The machines then constantly rewire themselves, learning by trial and error how to spot desired patterns like, for example, whether particular images contain a fire truck.[11] But they cannot do long division.[12]

One of the most intriguing results of this research is that neural net computers often spot patterns that humans cannot see even after they are pointed out.[13] This inability of two competent observers looking at the same data to agree should immediately remind us of politics. In what follows, we take this as a hint that Type 1 pattern recognition dominates political opinion. This is not to say that Type 2 logic is entirely absent. But most real-world problems are much too complex for the rigorously logical models we know how to solve. And even then, as philosophers from Aristotle to Camus have emphasized, no logical argument can prove the assumptions it relies on.[14] The upshot is that our pattern-recognizing selves are always the final arbiter of when Type 2 logical arguments do and do not convince.[15] The observation would have been no surprise to the Framers, who already knew that some truths are perceived, and "cannot be made plainer by argument or reasoning."[16]

Our purpose is to develop useful intuitions about humans' gift for pattern recognition and especially how it shapes our political judgments. We start with some examples. The first is visual: Take a long look at the "reversing illusion" in Figure 3.1. Some people see a wineglass; others two faces confronting each other. But this is not the end of the story, and people who continue to stare will see the pattern they overlooked at first.

Also, practice helps: Like the athlete who throws a football 10,000 times until it becomes second nature, the image comes quicker with repetition. Finally, people who stare for very long periods – this can take several minutes – will see the images start morphing uncontrollably into each other.[17] But even then, they never see both patterns at once.

The wineglass illusion has been carefully engineered so that both images seem equally plausible. But most real-world problems are closer to the Rorschach tests that psychologists use when they ask patients what they see in random inkblots. It turns out that, despite the randomness, people glimpse some patterns much more frequently than others. Psychologists then use unusual interpretations to detect aberrant personalities. This shows that responses are only partly about the image; what subjects see also depends on their individual life experiences.

These observations carry over naturally into politics, except that the data that supports the patterns continually grows with each day's newspaper. And since this data also includes each person's individual lived experiences, the preference for one pattern over another also changes from one person to the next. It follows that the patterns we do and do not see – and especially our estimate of their relative truth – depend on our life histories, including half-remembered and even unconscious ones. But like our wineglass example, they *also* depend on how often we have practiced spotting similar patterns in the past.

Finally, our life histories are not limited to objective events. They also include our thoughts and events that we have only imagined. These are especially influential in politics, where almost everything we know comes from reading or else daydreaming about what might happen if this or that law is enacted. But in that case, it follows that our estimates of whether particular party platforms will be effective is also influenced by having imagined them succeed or fail hundreds of times in the past. Finally, the concept of pattern recognition encourages us to see Professor Williamson's "information impactedness" in a new light. If we superposed random spots on the image in Figure 3.1, both the wineglass and the faces would be that much harder to make out. This explains why politicians spend so much time adding inconsistencies or just irrelevancies to their opponents' patterns, while constantly repeating their own preferred facts.

Because we seek to understand politics, the patterns we care most about are narratives. But the simplest narrative is a short story, and the simplest short story is a joke. Consider, then, the famous sketch in which a mugger approaches comedian Jack Benny and shouts, "Your money or your life." What follows is the longest silence in vaudeville. Almost a full minute later, the robber repeats his demand. And Benny petulantly delivers his punch line: "I'm thinking, I'm thinking." The skit includes just fourteen words from beginning to end. All the same, a lot is going on. The joke begins by reminding us of a pattern we already know. We have seen hundreds of robberies in the movies, and our first reaction is to imagine Benny's terror. But then comes the long pause and Benny's exasperation. And suddenly, with a gentle push from the punch line, we see that the facts fit a very different but equally familiar pattern: Benny's legendary cheapness. The unexpectedness of this new pattern delights us. And yet, like the wineglass illusion, the old pattern remains: We see that Benny should give up the money and know that he never will. There is a dissonance here, and we deal with it the way we always do, with laughter.

It is easy to see a similar dynamic at work in political narratives. Consider the politics that surrounded George Floyd's murder in 2021. The traditional narrative – call it American Calvinist – would have framed Floyd's death as the downward spiral of a broken family, drugs, and crime. The alternative counternarrative – call it Progressive – was to see a Black man killed by a white police officer and call it racism. But the known facts left plenty of room for one, both, or neither interpretation. So in the end, what voters actually felt depended on a blend of their own accumulated life experiences and the reported facts. And somehow, the Floyd story, coming when it did, contained just the right elements to make the Progressive pattern plausible to Americans who had mostly seen the Calvinist one before. And having seen it, they felt themselves (for a time at least) sufficiently changed to see the racism narrative in still more cases going forward.

The tension between competing patterns also drives politics on longer scales. During the Cold War every American knew the long and inconclusive debate between Communism and Capitalism, even if their life experiences slanted most people to favor the latter. Yet there were always dissenters who would happily argue for Communism, and when they did people who normally opposed the disfavored view would sometimes, however briefly, see it in a new light that seemed plausible. And for a few people the new vision would replace the old so that the conversion was permanent.[18]

For now, most of what we know about the human passion for confirming and sometimes reversing dominant narratives comes from scholars who study literature. Prof. Armstrong thinks that the joy we feel in seeing new patterns is hereditary: Humankind, he argues, evolved in environments where spotting danger meant the difference between life and death. But since learning never ends, it is equally important to go on noticing when each successive event either confirms a known pattern or else suggests a new one. Then too, patterns are scarce: In our world, most experience is just unintelligible noise.[19] So when we do finally glimpse one, the brain's pleasure centers respond.[20]

The idea that humans delight in pattern reversals also explains Hegel's otherwise bizarre concept of "the dialectic"; that is, the claim that every idea calls forth its opposite. On the face of it, the notion seems absurd. After all, "the opposite" of, say, feudalism could be a great many things. But the history is suggestive: It is hard to imagine more successful institutions than the medieval Catholic Church, absolutism in eighteenth-century France and Tsarist Russia, or America's absurdly enthusiastic tradition of flag-waving patriotism. Yet despite this, the medieval Church was repeatedly challenged by heresies, the French and Russian Revolutions introduced weirdly millennial societies, and corporate America abruptly embraced the rabidly anti-American "1619 Project." In each of these cases the new creeds were built around the same historical events and even symbolism as the old ones. Their only novelty was that the heroes and villains had changed places. Note too that the more unquestioned the original paradigm was, the more surprise (and, potentially, pleasure) we feel at its reversal. And this is where Hegel and Jefferson meet: Every dominant ideology makes its potential replacement that much stronger.

This, however, leads to a distinctly postmodern question: Does the fact that one pattern replaces another show that one or possibly both choices were arbitrary to begin with? Certainly, Madison viewed the crowd's "passions" with contempt. But the whole goal of rational man theories is to make definite predictions, whereas invoking "passion" can "explain" literally any behavior. And indeed, Madison's theory becomes much less predictive the moment it departs from rationality.

This makes it important to ask whether The People can come to bad ideas for entirely rational reasons. We start by looking at the completely logical, Type 2 methods that economists and engineers use to analyze patterns. We will argue that where data is scarce, a single new fact or insight can often shift and even reverse our previous estimates.

Our minds evolved to solve some very specific problems. Our hunter-gatherer ancestors were not like other creatures. A buffalo crops the long grass, safe in its herd, all summer long. A whale cruises the ocean endlessly, straining plankton from the blue water. For these animals nothing much changes so that the need to make choices barely comes up. But

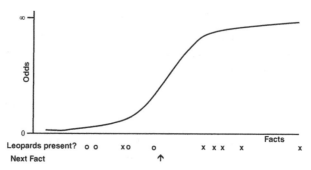

FIGURE 3.2  "Logit" methods for threat estimation

hunter-gatherers are forever choosing. How fresh is that deer print? We
need the meat badly, but wasting time and energy on an animal that's
long gone will likely be fatal. Is that a leopard in the shadows? And if so,
is the animal stalking us, or can we safely ignore it?

Stripped to their essentials, each of these choices required humans to
reduce everything that they had ever experienced in the past to a pattern and then compare it against their current situation. The difference
today is that – sometimes – we deploy better methods. Ask an economist
or engineer how to solve such problems and she will usually suggest a
mathematical technique called "Logit." To see how this works, suppose
we possess a detailed record of just when the variables we see today –
say, color, odor, motion, and terrain – coincided with a leopard in the
past. The Logit prediction then draws an S-shaped curve (technically,
the "logistic regression function") which estimates the odds of a leopard
being present for all possible combinations of fact (Figure 3.2). Now consider how our hunter-gatherers might use this estimate. On the left side
of the diagram they would immediately see that there almost certainly
is no leopard present (odds near zero) and feel safe. Conversely, if they
found themselves on the far right of the diagram (odds near 100 percent)
they would almost certainly flee. That said, the middle part of the curve
remains mysterious. In Newton's clockwork universe where humans
understand the world perfectly, this region would be very small so that
the rising part of the S was nearly vertical. But for real problems the
region is often substantial. Political issues, which are uncertain almost by
definition, nearly always display large zones of uncertainty.

Still, this is not the end of the story. Real hunter-gatherers are forever
trying to improve their estimates. This requires them to add data after
each new event and recalculate their S-curve all over again. Usually, the

new estimate won't be very different from the old one. Confirming that a leopard was absent when the previous estimate was close to zero isn't very informative. But the relative handful of cases where the variables fall in the rising branch of the S are another story. Returning to Figure 3.2, suppose that previous observations in this central region found a leopard present once and absent twice. Now consider a new observation at the location labeled "Next Fact." If the leopard turns out to be present, that confirms the existing estimate. But if it doesn't, the estimate will shift the whole S-curve to the right so that our estimate has a larger safe region than it did before. Because of its position, the new event exerts an outsized influence on the final estimate – in the jargon, it supplies an "influential point." Among other things, this gives content to our intuitive notion that some facts are immensely more important than others.

For voters with limited knowledge the rising part of the S is often gradual and the region of uncertainty substantial. But the same intuition holds. Most of the time, new events will more or less confirm, or at least fail to refute, the old ones. However, a few events will either clearly contradict the old estimate or fill in gaps where facts used to be scarce. When that happens, a single isolated fact can cause voters to change their minds. This observation should give us hope. Voters may well be irrational, and we will duly explore the possibility in Section 3.2. But even in the fully rational Downsian model, large shifts in voters' opinions are to be expected.

We finish this section by asking how our pattern-recognizing habits affect our interactions with others. So far, we have considered hunter-gatherers as individuals. But we know that they lived in communities that included a great many life histories. It follows that each individual would have possessed different data and to that extent different Logit estimates. This makes it sensible to ask what would have happened when a *group* came upon some possible danger and asked themselves what to do next.

Many situations, of course, would not have been controversial: In those cases at least, everyone's leopard estimate would have fallen comfortably in one zone or the other. Instead debate, when it did break out, would have focused on situations that most group members placed in the rising part of the S. When that happened most members – call them "centrists" – could not have decided whether a leopard was present or not. But there would also be minorities (the "extremists") whose unusual life histories told them that the situation was plainly dangerous, or else plainly safe. Finally, none of our hunter-gatherers would know what the others had experienced, or why they believed what they did. This might sometimes

FIGURE 3.3  "I swear to tell my own truth"

have persuaded them to defer to elders who possessed more life experience. On the other hand, they might equally have concluded that people who disagreed with them were either stupid or lying (Figure 3.3).

To this point the lessons for our own day seem clear enough: Given that there is no political advantage to be gained from policy proposals that most people see as obviously wrong, the issues that people really do agree on are invariably nonpolitical. But for controversial issues, voters' budgets for information and remembering will normally be so thin that all but the largest facts disappear within a few years, and almost nothing remains after a generation or two. The result for most voters is that the rising section of the "S" almost always has a shallow slope and is thinly populated. This makes it reasonable to think that events that are important and surprising on, say, a twenty-year time scale can become influential points that hit voters with the force of revelation.

The fact that we all have different life experiences also poses deep problems for politicians. It would be one thing if we could articulate the evidence that leads us to disagree with our neighbors. More usually, though, most of it is half-remembered or unconscious. The result is what Hollywood producers call the "nobody knows anything" problem. Creating a winning movie or book, it turns out, only partly depends on the artists. Instead, the experiences the audience brings to the work matter just as much. The result is that even highly paid publishers and studios often guess wrong, routinely investing in money-losing "turkeys" and "bombs."[21] The point is that none of us is ever entirely sure what most of our fellow humans will find persuasive. And this is especially true for political messages. Yes, the professionals almost certainly make better guesses than your next-door neighbor. But that never stops them from nervously trying out new catch phrases with every audience they see. "Running for President is like doing standup," the experts tell us: "You try bits, see what sticks."[22] This is a strong hint that creating ideology is beyond the powers of any single human, no matter how gifted. Instead, producing messages that work requires a constant cycle of audience interactions, messaging adjustments, and still more interactions.

## 3.2 DISTORTIONS

So far, we have limited ourselves to the hypothesis that voters make purely rational estimates, albeit using incomplete data and imperfect methods. And that is a reasonable guess: In general, we expect evolution to push our Type 1 selves toward greater and greater accuracy. But it is also true that our brains evolved in environments that were vastly different from the modern world. So it is entirely possible that methods evolved to survive in the Serengeti could mislead voters trying to understand an industrial society. This section examines various lines of evidence suggesting that evolution may predispose us to over- or underreact to large classes of events.

Our first candidate follows from Professor Armstrong's claim that narrative craves novelty. The observation is more radical than it sounds. We normally expect our analytical methods to be symmetric; that is, to produce similarly sized corrections whether they confirm or refute our previous estimates. If, on the other hand, evolution encourages us to *prefer* new patterns, we could be too willing to discard old ones even when they are valid. Politicians and voters would then suffer from a psychological restlessness that seeks out novelty even when the events themselves offer no particular reason to change their existing policies.

Moreover, this restlessness is not confined to audiences: It also infects politicians themselves each time they try to invent a new argument. The reason is that creativity has a well-known peculiarity. Literature scholars like Prof. Harold Bloom have long pointed out that no first-rank author can imitate his predecessors.[23] The psychological reason, presumably, is that since imitation is an inherently conscious (Type 2) activity, any deliberate attempt to copy earlier works unavoidably undercuts the unconscious (Type 1) thought that creative work requires. But this difficulty has a well-known cure. The trick is to inject enough variation in one's own writing for it to feel new again or, in Prof. Bloom's phrase, escape "the shadow" of earlier authors.[24] It follows that great politicians cannot imitate, but must instead dwell on how their new message differs from earlier ones. Moreover, great politicians do not just benefit themselves. Once the new pattern has been glimpsed, it (like all literary genres) can inspire lesser politicians, be they allies or opponents, to be creative, adding still further threads to the tapestry.

But this brings us back to Jefferson's hypothesis: It is easy to see how an attractive new pattern could make bipartisan voters more polarized. But it must also be possible for the pendulum to swing back in the other direction. How else to explain eras like the early twentieth century when American politics became markedly *less* partisan than it was before? Prof. Armstrong's emphasis on novelty neatly supplies this element: Indeed, in an age of polarization, what could be more surprising than a return to the center?[25]

Our second source of distortion involves imagination. Hunter-gatherers based their estimates on what they could see. But the "facts" that modern voters rely on are almost entirely imagined from the printed page, or delivered at second hand through television.[26] Furthermore, imagination enters into political reasoning not once but twice: First, voters must decide that a problem they have never seen at first hand actually exists and is worth solving. And second, they must "see" the proposed solution succeeding in their mind's eye. As usual, both steps come down to recognizing patterns, but in this case the "evidence" for the second step is mostly imagined. Nor is this necessarily a bad thing. Imagination is, after all, an attempt to simulate what we have never seen in life.[27]

Relying on imagination nevertheless raises new difficulties for voters, who must now keep track of what they know first hand and what they have only visualized. This is particularly hard since imagined events can sometimes raise one's blood pressure just as much as real ones. Indeed, imaging data shows that reading about a character doing something triggers exactly the same parts of test subjects' brains that they would use to do the act themselves.[28] It follows that voters rely on everything from direct perception to the running soundtrack of their thoughts and feelings as raw material for their estimates. We have argued that Downsian reasoning will often be sensitive to "influential points." Sometimes, these will be real events in the same way that school shootings often lead to new gun control legislation. But history offers no shortage of examples where the "influential point" was fictional, as when *Uncle Tom's Cabin* helped mobilize Northern opposition to slavery,[29] or the nuclear war movie *The Day After* persuaded President Reagan to prioritize ending the Cold War.[30]

Psychologists have worked hard to trace how imagination changes our estimates of risk for political issues. At first blush, the results seem to prove that voters are irrational: As Prof. Slovic and his coauthors show, people rank-order risks in ways that bear almost no relation to the actuarial risk of dying. But when researchers ask how people feel about each risk separately, it turns out that easily imagined risks are systematically overestimated compared to the others.[31] This is, of course, exactly what we expect from our argument that imagined events are life experiences in their own right. Moreover, imaginability depends on the politics and culture we inhabit. Indeed, for some policy issues like nuclear power the fictional disasters greatly outnumber real ones.[32] When this happens, end-of-the-world fiction is bound to carry more weight than experience.[33]

Once people experience disaster directly, on the other hand, imagined data becomes less important. Wars and epidemics typically cross this threshold once large numbers of voters know someone who has died. On the numbers, this should happen when deaths exceed roughly one in a thousand citizens.[34] In such cases, the public's revised reaction to casualties can be more but also less frightening than the imagined one.[35]

Our third set of distortions depend on emotion. Not all memories, it turns out, have equal weight. Instead, we are much more likely to remember events when they are paired with strong emotions, especially when they involve survival.[36] But in that case, memories that frighten us will almost always be more common than reassuring ones, systematically inflating our sense of risk. This is confirmed by Prof. Slovic's findings that humans routinely rate "dread" risks that produce a "gut reaction" or are likely to kill large numbers of people far above their actuarial value.[37]

Our fourth set of possible distortions is not so much irrational as nonrational. We have said that politics depends on value judgments that stand outside the objective world. Probably the most important of these originate in the brain circuits that neurophysiologists call "theory of the mind," which help us imagine what other humans are thinking and feeling.

But theory of the mind is more than just a cold-blooded estimate of what others feel. When we imagine the feelings of others, our own emotions take on a similar tinge. In politics, this leads to the well-known fallacy that people who feel their victimhood passionately are more likely to convince others that they really have been wronged. Our empathy also supplies most of the normative judgments that our logical (Type 2) thought nearly always lacks. In the extreme version where we value others equally with ourselves, this leads to egalitarian doctrines like the Golden Rule. More commonly, weaker values of empathy explain Prof. Simon's comment that rational voters often include the (estimated) happiness of others in deciding among political platforms. But since political empathy almost always focuses on people we have never met, it also tempts us to imagine grievances that they may not actually feel. Marxism's insistence that the proletariat *ought* to feel angry but does not because it suffers from "false consciousness" is a particularly well-known example of this disconnect.[38]

We have said that deciding which pattern – and even which logical argument – is most convincing is itself a Type 1 judgment. This prompts us to ask whether, given enough time, most voters would ultimately converge on similar judgments.[39] Here, the wineglass illusion seems to tell us that people who stare at the facts long enough should come to see both patterns and, beyond that, decide that one is more persuasive than the other. This is, among other things, reassuringly close to the traditional academic advice that repeated comparisons between theory and evidence ultimately refines both, as when an historian reads original sources, constructs a theory, reads more original sources, sees that they disagree, and revises her argument.[40]

   Whether the universe is indeed structured so that this interaction leads to consensus and truth is forever unknowable. But we should be encouraged that different humans' Type 1 selves really do seem to converge for physical truths. Moreover, this convergence is independent of culture. For example, thirteen of the nineteen standard Rorschach test inkblots are known to be universal across North America, Europe, Japan, and Latin America.[41] In these cases, at least, "[t]he boundaries between realistic and unrealistic perception are universal and not culture bound."[42] More surprisingly, our aesthetic perception of "beauty" similarly turns out to be a reliable guide to truth in mathematics[43] and physics.[44]

   The question is harder once we ask whether our aesthetic sense similarly points to the moral truths that politics depends on. For now, all we know is that humans reliably agree on at least some subjective truths outside the physical world. Scholars first began studying an underlying unity in humans' emotional response to "beauty" in literature, music, and their "sister arts" in the eighteenth century.[45] At first this seemed to be cultural since, it turned out, the opinions of *average* people differ widely from country to country.[46] The surprise came in the mid-twentieth century, when Prof. Child and his coauthors showed that artists and critics who contemplate art for long periods make the same aesthetic choices roughly two-thirds of the time – and this is true regardless of the specific cultures and educations that shaped them.[47]

The fact that this universality only applies to experts shows that learning is important. Child argued that we learn by contemplation, independently discovering "similar facts about the adequacy of particular works for satisfying aesthetic interests."[48] However, this still leaves the question of where these underlying "aesthetic interests" come from. This was unanswerable in the 1960s. Today, however, we know that the brain's pleasure centers reward us for forming new neural connections and using old ones.[49] In this view, art is a form of play designed to question our established views of the world and try out new ones. Presumably our aesthetic responses converge because the processing regions that perform them have been repurposed from brain circuits that have been programmed by basic experiences that every human shares, or else inherited from the evolved physical structure of our brains.

Finally, we might worry that our pattern-recognizing selves have simply been miswired, in the same way that certain commercial microchips sometimes fail to multiply numbers correctly.[50] Here the best evidence that this might be happening comes from the observation that our Type 2 logical selves sometimes scoff at the answers that convince our Type 1 pattern-recognizing selves. For example, statistics show that the people who worry about global warming also fear heart attacks more.[51] While it is hard to say much more than that, the existence of such disconnects suggests that we should be open to the possibility that evolution has made us error-prone.

What does seem clear, though, is that each voter's conviction of being right about some issue can never be more than the proposition that "I belong to an ensemble of people whose life histories support the same conclusion" or, at best, that "I am part of a *majority* ensemble." In either case, our judgments can never be more than probabilities. This teaches, or at least should teach, a certain humility. As Hamilton says in *The Federalist*, "we, upon many occasions, see wise and good men on the wrong as well as on the right side of questions of the first magnitude to society. This circumstance, if duly attended to, would furnish a lesson of moderation to those who are ever so much persuaded of their being in the right in any controversy."[52] The realization that we might, after all, be wrong also reminds us to respect other people's life experiences. Whatever its defects, one-man-one-vote is an essential step in this direction.

### 3.3 HEURISTICS

We have argued that political reasoning is divided between Type 1 pattern recognition and Type 2 logical thought. But the simplest and most common reasoning often invokes rules of thumb ("heuristics") that speak to both, and to that extent are potentially more convincing than either. These form the simplest possible elements of any political argument: Indeed, pollsters have found that just mentioning them makes political speeches more convincing.[53] Moreover, the fact that they are simple makes them easy to learn and use. At the same time, their persuasiveness depends on their perceived "fit" to recent events. Since this track record changes constantly, the same heuristic can sometimes be compelling in one era, yet roundly mocked in the next.

By far the simplest heuristic is pragmatism: If a policy experiment seems to work, government should try similar but more ambitious versions in the future. Conversely, failed policies should be avoided.[54] At this point the only remaining problem is the pattern-recognition question of how far successful precedents should be extended before they become reckless.

Substantively, pragmatism often leads to an attractive politics: Incremental improvements can, and probably will, make the status quo better. Then too, pragmatism is tolerant, acknowledging that ideas that look good on paper will often fail in practice. It follows that not every failure is blameworthy, and that people who oppose the next experiment are not necessarily immoral but only cautious. At the same time, pragmatism is inherently limited. There is, after all, no guarantee that some other, radically different approach might not work better.

The fact that election experts routinely turn to "Is the Country Going in the Right Direction?" polls for insight suggests that pragmatism is alive and well in today's politics. But it is also much reduced from the 1960s, when debate featured a ferocious appetite for facts.[55] This is an advantage to the extent that we no longer debate whether poverty and civil rights problems matter, and can immediately proceed to the next step of debating how to fix them. At the same time, trading concrete evidence for abstractions makes this consensus fragile. Thinking about criminals in abstract categories like the "oppressed" or "structural racism" encourages voters to forget whatever underlying facts originally supported these estimates, making it easier to change their minds if and when some new viewpoint challenges the consensus.

Pragmatism is particularly attractive for issues that even the best scholars cannot answer with any degree of rigor. These include such questions as whether government is too big, taxes too high, or wartime casualties too great. Yet another form of pragmatism is simply to blame the guy in charge. Here the definitive example is Herbert Hoover, who was universally blamed for the Depression despite having been lionized as the supremely competent "Great Engineer" just two years before.

Finally, pragmatism does not always lead to gradualism. Rather, the public's tolerance for risk is linked to how good (or bad) things are. Thus, Populism grew out of the searing Depression of 1893–7,[56] while the New Deal's "chaos of experimentation" reacted to the catastrophe of the 1930s. "It is common sense to take a method and try it," Franklin D. Roosevelt explained. "If it fails, admit it frankly and try another. But above all, try something."[57] Nor was that the end of the story, because even FDR's willingness to experiment did not extend far enough to include John Maynard Keynes' proposals for fighting the Depression, "except in war conditions."[58] When war did come, it taught Americans that government could permanently engineer higher living standards, putting the federal government at the center of economic policy in a way that earlier generations had never imagined.[59]

Some of the most important heuristics involve intuitions about what is fixable; that is, the limits of government. Optimists assume that many if not most morally desirable goals must also be feasible. Thus, the populist William Jennings Bryan argued that "the great political questions are in the final analysis moral questions concerning which the intuitions of the people are as good as almost any degree of experience."[60] If anything, Radical Republicans took an even more extreme position during the Civil War, when they jeered that generals' knowledge of strategy was "cowardly and unmanly," and that "rank amateurs were as qualified as experienced officers" if only the Army would decide to fight.[61]

On the other hand, such views were and are outliers. For every optimist there has usually been a skeptic like H. L. Mencken ready to drily observe that "it is difficult for a certain type of mind to grasp the concept of insolubility."[62] And indeed, voters in every era have agreed that certain issues are beyond government control: As Mencken said, citizens never think to hold politicians responsible for "colds in the head, marriage, the noises of the city, bad cooking, and the certainty of death."[63] Instead, these cease to be political questions entirely. The remarkable thing, though, is that this boundary can and does change over time. Populism was the first political movement to insist that the federal government had some responsibility for the common good.[64] Today's Progressives seek to extend the consensus still further, so that practically all unequal racial outcomes, for example, are attributed to "systemic racism" without ever bothering to explain just where and how this supposed bias entered the system.

Probably the most important contemporary heuristic addresses the choice between socialism and capitalism. Conservatives see government as inefficient, while liberals see it as a bulwark against private greed. It should be obvious that both of these things can be, and to some extent must be, true. But voters who believe one of these things more than the other can immediately simplify most political judgments. If you are a conservative, the "fact" that government is incapable of implementing reform means that the existing system's bias toward Wall Street does not matter since there is really no alternative. But if you are a liberal and believe that reform is possible, evidence that government has been incompetent in particular instances only shows some lack of will. What matters is to win the political fight so that your side can finally implement its agenda going forward.

It is easy to imagine a kind of oscillation here, in which reasonably successful governance encourages overreach, followed by an equal and opposite prejudice against fresh interventions.[65] Here the best recent example was Congress's decision to pass roughly $5.7 trillion in COVID-19 relief in 2020–1. When this caused no obvious ill effect, Progressives successfully pushed for another $2.5 trillion,[66] arguing, in the words of one prominent commentator, that the pandemic had been a "teachable moment" and that "being nervous about our debt 30 years from now … [was] not a smart way to think about our economics."[67] Here the politics was all the easier because the traditional argument for sound money, Weimar Germany's hyperinflation, was 100 years in the past, while the last major American inflation dated from the 1970s. Even so, this newfound equanimity seemed to melt when inflation rose in 2022, alarming voters and through them politicians who had previously ignored the risk. Whether this new attitude will endure is an open question.

There are many other heuristics, but a few stand out as more significant than the rest. One of the most common is the Manichean argument that one party is motivated by selfishness and the other by hope. This cannot be strictly true: It is the worst kind of anti-Copernicanism to insist that every single Democrat, say, has lower morals than every Republican.[68] If the heuristic persists, therefore, it is because voters need a tie-breaker when they have no other information to go on. In the limit, Manichean arguments dispense with facts altogether: We are now awash in claims that seemingly anodyne statements are "dog whistles" for hidden racist meanings, or else betray an "unconscious bias" that even the speaker is unaware of. At this point, the assertion becomes so circular that no amount of logic or facts can refute it – the literal definition of hysteria. In extreme cases this allows true believers to launch large policy initiatives on little more than indignation.[69]

The purest examples of the Manichean heuristic are almost always found in conspiracy theories. As Hofstadter famously emphasized, the idea that a handful of humans can dictate world history is the clinical definition of paranoia. But in a deeper sense, it follows from Manicheism's need to ascribe moral content to every event. Grievance, after all, resists the impersonal. If a meteor were to extinguish all human life tomorrow, we would feel sorrow but no anger. Harm only evokes emotion when it feels deliberate, which in turn requires some human villain behind it.[70]

As usual, conspiracy theories provide the most dramatic examples. Conventional politicians frequently invoke Manichean arguments because they let voters replace complicated factual problems with moral judgments. This is particularly true in foreign policy, where most voters' information budgets are especially limited. Faced with some obscure conflict in, say, the Balkans or the Middle East, apologists frequently seek justification in some centuries-old outrage by one contestant against the other. But this sort of argument is itself uncomfortably fact intensive, and in any case only leads recursively to further arguments based on still earlier offenses by the other side, and so on ad infinitum. The simpler approach then comes down to favoring the current underdog on the theory that weak groups are unlikely to do much evil. This is, of course, trivially true, though it ignores what would happen if the situation were reversed.

Voters also prefer politicians who seem admirable, and sometimes just personable. At the most basic level this stems from the fact that competence is hard to observe, so that success in past ventures promises still more good results in the future. Sometimes this logic is strong enough to eclipse issue-based platforms entirely: Voters elected Washington, Jackson, Taylor, Harrison, Grant, and Eisenhower on their military reputations with very little discussion of their domestic priorities.[71] The rub comes later when voters who assumed that their heroes agreed with them are sooner or later disappointed. But in that case, charismatic leaders have every incentive to hide their policies as long as possible. This leads to a politics in which presidents let their followers fight out the issues themselves, only intervening when one side seems to be winning.

Eisenhower's Fabian strategy of delaying his final showdown with Joseph McCarthy as long as possible owes a great deal to this dynamic.[72]

The inference of competence does not, however, explain why voters also respond favorably to politicians who are merely personable or, in the jargon, "someone you would like to have a beer with." Possibly this is rooted in the everyday experience that casually nasty people often cause trouble for themselves. Regardless, the heuristic is undeniably cheap to use: Most of us make the judgment automatically with every human face we see, and it is no stretch to think we can do the same thing watching politicians on television.

Finally, heuristics change with each generation's life experience. The rise of monopoly in twenty-first-century America has significantly eroded the price signal, allowing wages to diverge ever farther from what each worker produces. Small wonder, then, if younger voters treat the old saw that "it's not what you know, but who you know" as if it were some species of revealed truth, and see unequal outcomes as deliberate malice. Life in the Information Economy has only deepened this skepticism. Freshman economics classes teach that markets can deliver products more cheaply than any human planner. But this is almost entirely beside the point for software firms, whose products (after the first copy) can be duplicated endlessly at *zero* cost. This gives Silicon Valley engineers a very different view of the world than, say, factory workers.

Unsurprisingly, these changing attitudes increasingly shape college curricula. Twentieth-century social science typically stressed how economic outcomes were driven by markets and other, similarly blind social forces. Today, however, these ideas have increasingly given way to simplistic but more easily taught concepts like "systemic racism" that locate human malice at the root of every problem. But if bad humans cause problems, it follows that well-intentioned ones can fix them. The result is that college-educated Americans are increasingly receptive to solutions by government fiat. This, in turn, has encouraged politicians to show a new casualness in imposing mandates – formerly limited almost entirely to conscription – in everything from Obamacare to masks to vaccines. Yet these directly felt interventions still cause as much resentment as ever, sowing rising anger among those targeted.

## 3.4 NARRATIVES AND IDEOLOGY

Downs understood that many voters never read and compare party platforms directly, but only rely on party ideologies as a kind of shorthand.

At the same time, he also acknowledged that parties trying to justify their platforms normally had "a wide range of possible ideologies ... to choose from."[73] But in that case it is only natural to assume that some choices are better than others, and that good politicians beat poor ones by finding the right words and images to convince voters.[74]

The importance of ideology has also increased over time. Looking back to Greek and Roman history, the Framers assumed that citizens' "passions" would be temporary but also pragmatic; that is, that they would recognize and correct errors when they saw them. But pragmatism had been easy in the Ancient world: When Athenians decided to, say, order Socrates' suicide or invade Sicily, the resulting disasters followed almost immediately. That, however, was before Big Government made public interventions so complex that it is hard to tell when they fail, let alone why. Now too, the sheer number of programs greatly exceeds voters' information budgets, or for that matter the media's willingness to research and write stories about them. Finally, there is information impactedness: No matter how bad the program, the politicians and clients who benefit will invariably insist it was successful.

All this disables the kind of pragmatism that Madison assumed voters would exercise. But in that case, voters must find some way to simplify the analysis. Narratives and ideology do this by abstracting away from detailed facts. Because these are necessarily broader than any single problem, however, this immediately bundles a great many issues together. To the extent that individual government programs are discussed at all, they are repurposed as lessons that validate or, more often, falsify whatever narratives and ideologies inspired them. And since every narrative and ideology can claim a long list of successes and failures, this too is indeterminate. The result is that our narratives and ideologies become more and more decoupled from facts, evolving in whatever psychological directions promise to keep their rhetoric fresh.

Once evidence is disabled in this way, our political reasoning has nothing to constrain it. Instead, its trajectory is set by neurological factors. So far, at least, no researcher seems to have imaged voters' brains as they listen to and argue about political narratives. There is, however, a substantial scholarship on how the brain processes art and literature.[75] In what follows we will usually assume that the two activities are essentially identical. Here the best proof is subjective: Our emotional response to the images and associations that language elicits *feels* the same. As G. K. Chesterton said, the Declaration of Independence is not just "practical politics" but "great literature."[76] The point has been made so many times as to be a commonplace. Thus, former President Obama insists that "Politics is not just about policies. It's not just about numbers. It's about the stories that are being told."[77] And even Richard Nixon, a man of famously limited oratory, used to tell associates that "Politics is not prose, it's poetry."[78] From the other side of the fence, political rhetoric resembles nothing so much as what Orwell called a "good bad poem," summoning and pounding home mundane ideas and feelings that every human can share, and on which all political mobilization depends.[79]

No surprise, then, if poets and politicians often trade places. On the one hand, many of history's strongest authors have sooner or later written political creeds. Examples include the Roman poet Virgil, who created his masterpiece the *Aeneid* for the express purpose of giving Imperial Rome a new founding myth to supplant nostalgia for the Republic;[80] Shakespeare's long cycle of history plays with their glorification of Tudor rule; Herder's invention of "Das Volk" as a new and (thanks to Hitler) disastrous centerpiece for German identity;[81] Kipling's innumerable hymns to Empire; Yeats' deliberate reworking of traditional peasant folklore into a modern Irish identity myth; and Nikolai Gumilyov's mystic visions of a post-Soviet Russian nationalism.[82] On the other, the process works equally in the other direction, so that great politicians often write first-rate prose. Here the best-known examples are probably Benjamin Disraeli, who churned out seventeen bestselling novels before and after serving as Britain's prime minister,[83] and Winston Churchill, who often lived by his pen and won a Nobel Prize in Literature for his graceful *History of the English-Speaking Peoples*. On the American side and in our own time, William F. Buckley and Bill Clinton have both written thrillers, though Clinton had a coauthor.[84]

We process narrative, which appeals to our pattern-recognizing (Type 1) selves, without conscious effort. For this reason, our political beliefs almost always begin with storytelling.[85] After that, the most successful stories proliferate in near-copies until visible patterns emerge in the facts they emphasize, the facts they ignore, and the relations they see. But the patterns also give political narratives a kind of inertia. Politicians cannot bend them in any direction they choose: At any given moment, only a handful of choices will be consistent with what has come before. Even when the extensions surprise, the audience must immediately realize that the new development fits what came before.

While we will normally treat facts and new narratives as distinct, relevance is itself a Type 1 judgment. Thus, a surprising new fact can help audiences to see narratives that they might never have accepted otherwise. And a new narrative can encourage journalists to report facts that might have gone unnoticed before. Associations also matter. Narrative transfers feelings aroused by much larger patterns to particular people, events, and symbols, which can then be repurposed for new messages.[86] But none of this can happen if the symbols change too fast for audiences to keep up.[87]

There is also a path dependency at work. Every great political narrative reworks familiar elements in some new and surprising way. On the one hand, working with an established genre helps evade the "nobody knows anything" problem by identifying storylines that have succeeded in the past. It also offers important economies for voters with limited information budgets who lack the patience to learn new arguments month after month. This is more or less what happens in movies like *The Wild Bunch* or *The Godfather*, which never need to explain their central conceits because audiences arrive at the theater already knowing what to expect from a Western or a gangster film. On the other hand, politicians who hew too closely to previous examples risk boring voters who crave novelty. The trick is to balance these imperatives so that the audience arrives effortlessly at the punch line, only to feel surprise and delight when the narrative cleverly departs from convention.[88]

By comparison, ideology starts with the deep handicap that it requires conscious effort to invent, learn, and use. It must therefore offer some countervailing advantage. At the margin, voters must decide whether to spend their limited budget learning more ideology or more facts. In general, we expect voters to choose whatever mix gives them the best understanding of the country's problems within their overall budget for learning. Here ideology's biggest advantage is prestige: The answers it generates are always, within their assumptions, true.[89] But this credibility comes with the large caveat that, as Prof. Popper said, all genuine theories must be "falsifiable,"[90] even if real ideologies hedge their bets by adding extra assumptions and epicycles that let them "explain" almost any outcome.[91] "We laid the foundation for this success in the last Administration," the pundits say, or "Things would be worse if we had not taken the measures we did."

Social voters, on the other hand, prefer ideology not because it is true but only because it is predictive, telling them what it is safe to say with a minimum of risk.[92] For them, the fact that an ideology recommends policies that fail or that most voters see as crazy is a small price to pay.

Indeed, an ideology that requires a few crazy positions may even be desirable. This is partly because supporting a crazy position shows that the speaker places loyalty to his group over any momentary embarrassment. Then too, counterintuitive results are hard to mimic for people who have never studied the ideology in detail. This makes it easier to screen out opportunists who only pretend loyalty to the group.

Ideology also adds inertia to politics. Leaders must respect the internal norms left over from previous iterations of their beliefs,[93] or else risk undermining their own legitimacy.[94] While ideologies can usually adapt to slow, sustained pressure, their response to sharp, sudden blows is always awkward and, if the blows are heavy enough, brittle. Finally, because ideology ultimately depends on judgments about which facts are and are not important, it shares the Hegelian tendency to breed its opposite. Thus "progress" breeds "backlash," "nationalism" leads to "internationalism," "liberalism" invites "reaction," and "communism" ends in "fascism."

In the end, of course, no real political creed is ever purely narrative or ideology. Despite this, we will almost always assume in what follows that Type 1 pattern recognition and narrative is vastly more powerful. Partly the prejudice is historical: Compared to Europe and especially Russia, Anglo-American political thought has seldom been systematic.

But at a deeper level, logical thought often finds itself incapable of addressing the questions most central to politics. First and most obviously, logic cannot supply its own assumptions. Instead, the pivotal decision of which facts matter is almost entirely left to Type 1, narrative thought.[95] This is especially true in ideology's choice of goals, starting with voters' sense of identity. Where Americans have traditionally identified themselves as individuals, ideology can equally turn on membership in a particular race, national origin, gender or sexual preference, or any number of alternatives. Yet logic is powerless to prove that any of these is more "correct" than the others. Then too, logic cannot speak to moral and spiritual matters – the nature of the Good, say, or the existence of God. This is a large drawback for political argument, which almost always mixes normative and positive arguments. Finally, logic is unemotional. Only our Type 1 selves can get angry or sentimental.

But if political thought is dominated by Type 1 pattern recognition, we should also expect certain rare and important facts to act as "influential points" that cause voters to abruptly revise their estimates. In the way of Type 1 thought, this is even more true when the same events are also strongly emotive.[96]

This kind of sudden reversal is especially noticeable in Americans' attitudes toward war and peace, most likely because voters know even less about foreign policy than about domestic issues. Certainly, the basic logic of when the country should be willing to fight changed little over the twentieth century.[97] But that has not kept voters from switching back and forth. Though Americans enthusiastically supported President Wilson's decision to intervene in World War I, the adventure ended with nearly 120,000 US soldiers killed, seemingly endless violence across Europe, and Bolshevik Russia promising World Revolution within a year or two. This produced a violent shift against the Democrats, whose presidential candidate received just over one-third (34.2 percent) of the vote – an even worse showing than Herbert Hoover's 39.7 percent score twelve years later.

If this history seems unfamiliar, it is because the next generation suppressed it after Pearl Harbor.[98] The resulting internationalism was still the dominant narrative in the late 1960s, when Vietnam made talk of "quagmires" conventional. Since then, the balance has remained unsettled. Despite loud opposition, the US has since fought in Iraq (twice) and Afghanistan: These yielded bad press, but also much lower casualties than Vietnam or Korea. Later, as the Afghan War dragged on, President Obama would sometimes claim that the public was "war weary," a mood continued in President Trump's scorn for "Endless Wars" and President Biden's casual exit from Afghanistan. Yet the quagmire concept also seemed hollowed out, consistently low on the public's list of concerns. Partisans invariably called each of these turning points a lesson, by which they meant a kind of one-word argument for or against intervening. But like most political narratives, the logic always "proved" the speaker's preferred result: "No appeasement" or "No more Vietnams." Like the proverbial stopped clock, each argument was always right except when it was wrong.

Finally, we have said that ideologies are scarce and take time to develop. It follows that an ideology that springs up suddenly can go unopposed for months and even years. Something like this seems to have happened for 2020's lockdowns. However shoddy, the public health narrative that ignored everything but COVID-19 deaths at least had the advantage of having been road-tested in universities, and for a time there were no coherent replies on offer.[99] This was hardly surprisingly given that no mainstream political party had thought about communicable disease for nearly a century. So politicians ended up invoking "The Science," which in practice meant passing authority (and hopefully also responsibility) to a host of previously obscure public health officers who then locked down whole states with seemingly negligible opposition.[100] The deeper problem was that the epidemic was not *just* about science but also about how much risk to tolerate. This value judgment was inherently political. In the event it took months to find a narrative that was simultaneously convincing and sufficiently indirect to avoid the inevitable accusations of heartlessness. When the counterattack finally did come, the critics barely mentioned economic factors. Instead they stressed that the lockdowns caused their own health problems like depression, drug abuse, and suicide. Republican politicians finally had slogans they could say out loud.

The question remains whether ideas can ever die entirely. Eugenics was mainstream before World War II, when polls showed that 73 percent of all Americans favored forced sterilization for habitual criminals and the hopelessly insane. But that was before the world discovered Hitler's extermination programs. Today's percentage is so small that pollsters no longer even bother to ask the question.[101]

But even the deepest memories fade, or at least lose their novelty and with it their emotional content. Meanwhile, the fact that ideologies are scarce means that it is often easier to rehabilitate old ideologies than to invent new ones. This often depends on how long an ideology has suffered eclipse, draining it of the foot soldiers it needs to proselytize. When socialism made its astonishing comeback after the Great Recession of 2007, it helped that there were still politicians like Bernie Sanders (b. 1941) and Bill de Blasio (b. 1961) who had flirted with Communism the last time it was fashionable. Their success was no accident: Being born or, like Pete Buttigieg (b. 1982), raised in the socialist tradition gave them an edge that politicians from more mainstream backgrounds could seldom match.

We close this section by considering what Prof. Hofstadter called "The Paranoid Style in American Politics." Conspiracy theories represent an intermediate phenomenon that, while it seldom if ever persuades the majority, still attracts enough adherents to dominate the country's politics, at least for a time.[102]

Excepting only slavery and Jim Crow, America's closest approaches to majority tyranny have usually involved conspiracy theories. We have said that new ideologies are rare. A partial list includes the supposed Federalist plot to discredit the Articles of Confederation (1780s);[103] claims that leading American politicians were conspiring with France (1790s);[104] Jefferson's fears that his vice president was plotting to lead

Western states out of the Union;[105] Federalist claims that their opponents hoped to establish a monarchy[106] and topple Christianity (1810s);[107] claims that the Pope and Europe's Catholic powers were sending immigrants to destroy the USA (1830s and 1840s);[108] claims that Southern aristocrats had fomented the war with Mexico (1840s) and were trying to extend slavery across the country (1850s);[109] claims that the English "Gold Power" was plotting to destroy Free Silver (1890s);[110]; a post-World War I "Red Scare" (1920s); claims that munition makers had secretly instigated World War I (1930s);[111] and a second, post- World War II "Red Scare" (1940s and 1950s).[112] Perhaps the only good news about the list is that the outbreaks nearly always dissipated after a decade or so. The fact that this was not much longer than the public fevers that the Framers had planned for may explain why the Constitution was able to absorb these shocks with so little damage.

Like other heuristics, voters' willingness to believe in conspiracies is constantly evolving. Taking the long view, Prof. Popper argued that the decline of religion encouraged people to replace Homer's gods with powerful men. The Enlightenment then reinvigorated the image by emphasizing that wise leaders could reengineer society.[113] Given their ubiquity in Western culture, the fact that conspiracy theories went into a temporary eclipse after 1960 is puzzling. Part of the explanation was the deep post-war revulsion against Naziism's endless claims that its enemies, and particularly the Jews, were constantly conspiring against Germany. For Americans, this lesson was promptly reinforced by the experience of McCarthyism in the 1950s.[114] A second factor was increased college enrollment after World War II, which taught unprecedented numbers of Americans to appreciate the intellectual elegance of theories that attributed events to markets and similarly anonymous institutions. This made conspiratorial explanations sound vulgar by comparison.[115] This instinct was quickly cemented by the timely appearance of widely read polemics by Karl Popper and Richard Hofstadter that linked conspiracy theories to mental illness.[116]

That said, this marginalization of conspiratorial explanations was only temporary. By the early 2010s, memories of the Final Solution had faded. Meanwhile, increased market concentration from the 2000s onward made faith in impersonal markets less tenable even to sophisticates.[117] This created significant space for conspiracy theories to make a comeback. In 2016 pollsters invented an entirely fictitious "North Dakota Crash" and asked a large group of respondents whether the government was trying to suppress the story.[118] Roughly one-third agreed that it was, suggesting that they were prepared to accept almost any conspiracy.[119] From there, the explosive growth of shabby hoaxes from the Steele Dossier to QAnon during the Trump Administration should have been predictable.

Still, credulity is not enough. To be politically relevant a conspiracy theory must also arouse passion and ideally anger. Historically, this usually occurs when economic or social changes make large and previously secure groups feel inexplicably powerless. Additionally, most conspiracy theories have historically brought two previously distinct groups together. The first is the reliably hard-Left or hard-Right extremists who almost always feel aggrieved.[120] But the second is some group – in a dynamic society there is never any shortage of these – who see themselves in some unfair or unfathomable decline. From there it is a short jump to conclude that their misfortunes have been engineered by human enemies, and to that extent are both personal and moral injuries. Here the most prominent examples include Protestant clergy in the 1840s, agrarian populists in the 1890s, and Trump voters today.[121]

### 3.5 FEEDBACKS

The rational and social voter theories described in Chapter 2 were mostly static. Given perfect information, voters would find an equilibrium and stay there. For rational voters, new facts could sometimes change opinions, and impacted information could cause them to miscalculate. But the size of these effects was not obvious, and in any case Downs' theory had little to say about them. Moreover, social voting was still more static: Having found some narrative or ideology that everyone could agree on, conformists had no reason to change it.

This chapter has extended Downs' rational voter model by peeking inside the black box of how real voters reason about politics. The simplest and often the most reliable reasoning involves heuristic "rules of thumb." By far the most important of these is pragmatism; that is, the idea that extensions of previously successful programs are themselves likely to succeed. As we have seen, Prof. Hofstadter saw most of American history as a grand oscillation in which rigid pragmatism left many problems unaddressed, only to be progressively loosened until some especially large failure restored voters' risk aversion.[122]

But this cannot be the whole story. Once we admit the possibility of polarization – which by definition requires large departures from existing practice – pragmatism itself becomes impractical. This is particularly true for agendas ("abolish capitalism") that seek to replace existing institutions root and branch, or raise goals that depend more on normative judgments than on objective experience. In these cases, at least, voters must rely on narratives and ideology.

Narrative relies on the brain's talent for seeing and extending patterns. But we have argued that seeing patterns gets easier with practice. This opens the possibility that voters who constantly listen to a particular political party or cable news network, say, will find it makes their preferred patterns more and more persuasive.[123] Conversely, groups that spend their time looking at one particular pattern will find other groups' estimates unconvincing and even dishonest. The fact that pattern recognition – unlike logical thought – also engages our emotional and moral selves means that narrative can lead us to question our values and goals, along with the policies built to achieve them. Lastly, the fact that our pattern-recognizing selves crave novelty and surprise makes narrative restless. This explains Jefferson's observation that unity cannot last: Sooner or later, someone will invent some twist on the dominant orthodoxy to create a split. Here the good news is that this same restlessness can also bring previously estranged patterns back together.

Finally, ideology reflects our craving for Type 2 logical thought. We argued in Chapter 2 that both rational and social voters find ideology attractive. Here we add that the intellectual elegance of any specific ideology, how well it fits known facts, and indeed which facts should be considered relevant in the first place are all pattern-recognizing, Type 1 judgments. This means that ideology is also restless: On the one hand, today's dominant ideologies are constantly changing and improving and trying to stay fresh and attractive to the average person. On the other, their victory is never final, and some brilliantly surprising theory is always just around the corner ready to change them. In the most extreme cases, ideologies can become so decoupled from fact that adherents' quest to find new extensions and surprising reversals stimulates still more ideological innovation in an endless chain. This is the polar opposite of pragmatism, and provides the social analog to hysteria in individuals.

### Notes

1 Hofstadter (1969) at p. 205.
2 Hofstadter (1969) at p. 115.
3 Hofstadter (1969) at p. 116.
4 Shelley [1821] at p. 480.

5   See Kahneman (2011) at p. 20. Cf. Wikipedia (59).
6   See Kahneman (2011) at p. 20. Cf. Shelley [1821] at p. 506 (the poetic imagination "differs from logic, that it is not subject to the controul of the active
    powers of the mind, and that its birth and recurrence have no necessary connexion with the consciousness or will").
7   Kahneman (2011) at pp. 236–7.
8   Wikipedia (41).
9   Yeo et al. (2015).
10  Yeo et al. (2015).
11  Anderson (1995) explains that artificial intelligence networks typically combine three elements: Sensors (S) which detect signals from the external world,
    Associative Cells (A) that are wired to multiple sensors to detect simple patterns (e.g., lines, triangles), and Relational Cells (R) that are wired to multiple
    "A" cells to detect higher-order patterns like houses or fire trucks. Crucially,
    the "A" and "R" cells exhibit "threshold," which means that they only fire
    when incoming signals exceed some predetermined value. The machine then
    evolves to maximize the probability that one and only one "R" cell will fire
    when the desired pattern appears. This is done by rewiring the connections
    between the "A" and "R" cells each time detection fails. Specifically, "A" cells
    that sent out a positive signal are adjusted to produce a higher output the
    next time, while "A" cells that sent out a negative signal have their strength
    reduced. This makes it more likely that the relevant "R" cell will guess right
    the next time. Anderson (1995) at 220.
12  See, e.g., Ciucci (2017) (schizophrenia symptoms); Perez (2018) at p. 96
    (long division).
13  See, e.g., Kessler (2017); Thompson (2008); Ciucci (2017); and Captain
    (2016).
14  The problem is that every attempt to "prove" basic assumptions requires
    still further ones. As Dostoevsky says, "I am constantly exercising my powers of thought and, consequently, every primary cause with me at once
    draws another one after itself, one still more primary, and so *ad infinitum.*"
    Dostoevsky [1864] at p. 114.
15  Conspiracy theories provide a nice illustration of this. We are used to the
    claim that science is settled by experiment. But every experiment generates
    "errant data" that do not fit, and whether they can be safely ignored is ultimately unprovable. Conspiracy theories stress these inconsistencies instead
    of ignoring them. Butter (2020) at p. 61.
16  *Federalist* No. 23 (Hamilton) at p. 101.
17  Brann (2016) at pp. 368–9.
18  Strangely, the most thorough conversions often involve zealots, who sometimes channel the emotion formerly invested in one creed into an equal and
    opposite passion for its nemesis.
19  Armstrong (2013) at p. 15.
20  Armstrong (2013) at p. 50.
21  See, e.g., Goetzmann, Ravid, and Sverdlove (2013) at p. 297; Waldvogel
    (2017).
22  Giridharas (2019) at p. 22; King (2020).

23 This explains why national literatures are almost always dominated by first-comers such as Shakespeare, Milton, Racine, and Cervantes. As T. S. Eliot observed, "That every great work of poetry tends to make impossible the production of equally great works of the same kind is indisputable." Eliot [1944] at p. 66.

24 See, e.g., Bloom (1978) at p. 6 et passim. William Butler Yeats makes much the same point when he complained that his fellow poets had "lost the old nonchalance of the hand" and were "but critics, or but half create." Yeats [1919a]. Raymond Chandler similarly has his fictional novelist Roger Wade declare, "You know how a writer can tell when he's washed up? ... When he starts reading his old stuff for inspiration. That's absolute." Chandler [1953] at p. 619.

25 Bill Clinton's 1996 State of the Union announcing that "the Era of Big Government is over" was one such turning. Anon (1996).

26 The Romantics were especially insistent about imagination's role in politics. Prominent examples include Keats ("I am certain of nothing but of the holiness of the Heart's affections and the truth of the Imagination – What the imagination seizes as Beauty must be truth"), Schiller ("If man is ever to solve the problem of politics in practice, he will have to approach it through the problem of the aesthetic, because it is only through Beauty that man makes his way to freedom"), and Goethe ("I return to myself, and find a world.") Blanning (2012) at pp. 21, 44, and 53.

27 Fernández-Armesto (2019).

28 Speer et al. (2009).

29 Gordon-Reed (2011). Lincoln would famously greet Harriet Beecher Stowe with the words, "So you are the little woman who wrote the book that started this great war." Gordon-Reed (2011).

30 Wikipedia (57).

31 Slovic, Fischhoff, and Lichtenstein [1979] at p. 105.

32 The fictional disasters also include politicians' and media personalities' constant predictions that a nuclear reactor meltdown, say, is likely to occur at any moment.

33 For full-length histories of plague and nuclear contamination narratives in Western culture, see Wald (2009) and Weart (1998), respectively.

34 By comparison, only about one in four Americans reached this point a year into the COVID-19 pandemic; Galvin (2021). During World War II American combat deaths averaged 6,600 per month. At this rate it would have taken twenty months to reach the one in a thousand mark. Anon (2010a).

35 In the twentieth century the advent of strategic bombing often *reduced* public anxiety compared to what citizens had imagined beforehand. Maurer and O'Hare (2007) at pp. 446–7.

36 See, e.g., Small (2020) at p. 57; Heshmat (2015); and Wikipedia (22).

37 Fischhoff et al. [1978] at pp. 87–8, 91.

38 Wikipedia (24).

39 Of course, the idea that repeated confrontations between theory and experiment can lead real voters to truth is only a thought experiment. In life, events come so thick and fast – and politicians confuse voters so thoroughly – that voters cannot possibly glimpse the underlying pattern before it changes.

40    Historian Hugh Trevor-Roper argued that theories that repeatedly failed such tests had to be discarded:

> [I]n studying history, I believe that while we must always appreciate its extent and variety, we must always study one part of it in detail ... We cannot penetrate below the surface all the time, or we shall never come up for air, never rise above the subject to survey and compare. But if we do not, at some point, penetrate below the surface, we shall fall into the opposite error. We shall be obliged to take all our evidence at secondhand and shall end by believing, without testing, the fashionable orthodoxy of our time or place. Every age has its orthodoxy and no orthodoxy is ever right. It is changed, in due course, by those who approach the subject, whatever it is, with a certain humility and above all, independence of mind. But those intellectual gifts need material on which to work, and that material, in history, must be raw material. (Trevor-Roper 1969 at pp. 15–16)

   The subtext of Trevor-Roper's essay was that the same logic applied to political reasoning, especially including Marxist theories that tried to make history fit a predefined ideology: "Every age has its own social context," he wrote, "its own intellectual climate, and takes it for granted, as we take ours ... To neglect it – to use terms like 'rational,' 'superstitious,' 'progressive,' 'reactionary,' as if only that was rational which obeyed our rules of reason, only that progressive which is pointed to us – is worse than wrong, it is vulgar." Trevor-Roper (1969) at p. 15.

41    See, e.g., Andronikov-Sanglade (2000) (France); Vinet (2000) (Spain, Portugal, Chile, Brazil, and Venezuela); Weiner (2003) (Japan).

42    Weiner (2003) at p. 53.

43    Russell (1910) at p. 60.

44    Dirac (1939).

45    See Starr (2013) at pp. xii–xiii and 4.

46    Child and Siroto (1965).

47    In the 1960s, Prof. Irwin Child conducted a series of experiments in which Western art critics and non-Western folk artists were shown the same pairs of closely similar paintings and asked to pick the most aesthetic one. Child and Siroto (1965) at p. 165. In his best-known study, Japanese potters in small rural villages agreed with Yale experts 63 percent of the time. While this agreement may seem modest, the odds of it happening by chance were less than 1 percent. Iwao and Child (1966) at p. 30. By comparison, the same Ivy League experts agreed with Connecticut high school students just 47 percent of the time – indistinguishable from a simple coin toss. Iwao and Child (1966) at p. 32. Child and his coauthors went on to document similar results from around the globe. Ford, Prothro, and Child (1966) at p. 26 (Fiji); Child and Siroto (1965) at p. 351 (West Africa); Child (1983) (Latin America). More recent studies continue to find similar results. Renoult (2016) at p. 282.

48    Child and Siroto (1965).

49    See Armstrong (2013) at pp. 48–9.

50    Wikipedia (59).

51    Viscusi and Zeckhauser (2005). Other examples of seemingly inexplicable judgments include the fact that people who enjoy classical music

disproportionately enjoy the Beatles, that moviegoers who enjoy the family drama *Pay It Forward* likewise enthuse over the sci-fi movie *I, Robot* (Thompson 2008), and that people who like "curly fries" score higher on intelligence tests. Kosinski, Stillwell, and Graepel (2013) at p. 5804.

52 *Federalist* No. 1 at p. 3 (Hamilton).

53 Williams (2004) lists various poll-tested phrases including "personal injury lawyer," "tax relief," "climate change," and "working poor."

54 The same instinct appears in the Framers' argument that the president should hold power long enough to see whether the policies he was elected on actually work. *Federalist* No. 72 at p. 331 (Hamilton).

55 Viewers in the 1960s were routinely flooded with documentaries like CBS News' "Harvest of Shame" and "Christmas in Appalachia" (CBS News 1960, 1964) that showed problems close up and in intensely human terms. Lyndon Johnson's "Poverty Tour" similarly brought what we now call presidential "photo ops" to the poorest places in the country. LBJ Library [1964].

56 Hofstadter (1955) at p. 150.

57 Hofstadter (1955) at p. 279.

58 Hofstadter (1955) at p. 280.

59 Hofstadter (1955) at p. 281.

60 Hofstadter (1955) at p. 239.

61 Tap (2002) at pp. 1 and 3–5.

62 Mencken [1920] at pp. 276-77.

63 Mencken [1920] at p. 279.

64 Hofstadter (1955) at p. 58.

65 Prof. Hofstadter argued that American political thought oscillated between conservatives stressing "institutional continuities, hard facts, and the limits of possibility" and reformers who "arouse moral sentiments, denounce injustices, and rally the indignation of the community against intolerable abuses." Hofstadter (1955) at p. 286.

66 Committee for a Responsible Budget (2022).

67 Klein (2021). For a mainstream critique of such views, see, e.g., Mankiw (2020).

68 Similar heuristics can also define particular voting blocs. The fact that Democrats led in passing the 1965 Civil Rights Act turned Black voters away from their traditional support for Republicans as the "party of Lincoln" overnight. White and Laird (2020). Similarly, California Republicans' support for Proposition 187, which denied state services to illegal immigrants, alienated large numbers of Hispanic voters. The state has been solidly Democratic ever since. Nowrasteh (2016).

69 Woodrow Wilson led America into World War I on the same thumpingly moral terms that the era's Progressives invoked to justify everything they supported. Hofstadter (1955) at pp. 256, 257, 260, 261. Then, eight months after entering the war, he decided that the country needed war aims. The president and his chief of staff stayed up past midnight turning ideas solicited from a journalist, a philosopher, and various Europe experts into Wilson's

Fourteen Points. As House later remarked, "I never knew a man who did things so casually." Beschloss (2018) at p. 343. This set the stage for endless fights at the victors' conference in Versailles and the disastrous League of Nations politics that followed.

70  Hofstadter (1955) at pp. 68 and 254.

71  Hofstadter (1955) at p. 254.

72  Nichols (2017).

73  Downs (1957) at p. 100.

74  This fits naturally with the Framers' endlessly repeated instinct that talented demagogues can make even bad policies sound good.

75  See, e.g., Armstrong (2013).

76  Ricks (2020) at p. 143.

77  Key (2020).

78  Williams (2004).

79  Orwell [1942].

80  Mendelsohn (2018).

81  Wikipedia (30).

82  Vladimir Putin's allies routinely treat the works of Gumilyov and his intellectual successor Alexander Dugin as a semi-official ideology. See, generally, Clover (2016).

83  Wikipedia (13).

84  Clinton and Patterson (2018, 2021); Anon (n.d. (h)).

85  In what follows we will take "narrative" to mean arguments that recite facts in ways that our pattern-recognizing (Type 1) selves respond to. Conversely, "ideology" will mean systems like Marxism-Leninism or, less coherently, American Progressivism that speak to our logical (Type 2) selves by promising to derive policy recommendations from first principles. In practice, real political messaging almost always mixes the two.

86  Americans began singing the national anthem in 1917 to show the world (and each other) that there was a limit to our internal arguments, and that even those who had opposed America's entry into World War I would support the war effort. A quarter century (and another World War) later the custom was so ingrained that people even stood for the anthem watching televised games in their homes. Brown (2022). But standing as a collective action set up the opposite symbolism. While Colin Kaepernick is the most visible current practitioner, he did not invent the tactic. Black athletes had done much the same thing by raising their fists at the Mexico City Olympics in 1968 while Black soldiers had refused to stand for the anthem as far back as 1919 (Ottley [1942] at pp. 435 and 443). Such protests exploit the fact that symbolic meanings, being imaginary, are inherently arbitrary and changeable. The power of Kaepernick's protest plainly came from trolling traditional audiences who wanted to advertise the nation's solidarity. But if kneeling "really" meant that Black lives matter, then patriotism and collective action were no longer an issue and there was nothing to stop others from joining his protest.

87  Pielkalkiewic and Penn (1995) at p. 67.

88 Successful genres are also scarce enough for both parties to steal and adapt each other's tropes. Thus, the long-running claim that President Obama was a narcissist was later repurposed as an attack on President Trump. In the same vein, years of conservative rhetoric about the "left-wing outrage machine" morphed into equal and opposite attacks on the "right-wing outrage machine."

89 Of course, this is only the ideal, and real calculations often have errors. Even so, if two people argue long enough – possibly for a very long time – they will finally come to agree that one (or neither) was right. This is, or should be, the defining feature of university knowledge.

90 Popper (1963). Popper lists Marxism among the theories which were "rescued" from falsifiability by vagueness and indeterminacy.

91 The evasions are costly since each new epicycle makes the ideology harder for rational voters to learn and less predictive for social voters trying to anticipate their friends' opinions. Epicycles also dilute the aesthetic argument that the ideology is intellectually elegant and therefore true.

92 Ideology also offers a certain social cachet. Being difficult to acquire, it shows evidence of learning. This is still more true given the prestige that formal logic has enjoyed in Western culture since Isaac Newton showed that the paths of planets could be deduced from a handful of equations.

93 Pielkalkiewic and Penn (1995) at p. 61.

94 Pielkalkiewic and Penn (1995) at p. 64.

95 The one small exception is that logic can sometimes identify inconsistencies and new arguments that point our Type 1 selves to narratives we had not previously considered.

96 National events can sometimes be more traumatic than personal ones. It is easy to find internet images of ordinary people weeping after the fall of France (1940), the Kennedy assassination (1963), and the *Challenger* disaster (1986). Our emotional selves also respond to emotion in others. The unhappiness communicated by civil unrest from the 1960s to Antifa to the January 6 Capitol riots spoke far more loudly than any politician.

97 It is true, of course, that the list of international threats changed continuously. But the hard isolationism of the 1930s occurred despite the rise of fascism, while the Soviet threat in the 1970s was not noticeably less than it had been in the 1960s. If America's posture changed, it reflected internal psychological truths far more than the outside world.

98 As one war correspondent sneered, "Their generation had been told in the all-important first ten years, in its teens, and at the voting age that it was not necessary to fight." Sherrod (1995 [1944]) at 684. We can still hear echoes in the era's movies like *Casablanca* (1942) or *From Here to Eternity* (1951), which invariably start from America's selfishness in staying out of the war as long as it did. This mid-century trope fits oddly with the equal and opposite view that noninvolvement erases guilt. Thus, many abolitionists would have been happy to see the South secede because it would have ended the North's participation in slavery. Catton [1961] at p. 200.

99 The situation was reminiscent of the Russian Revolution when the Tsar and the mainstream parties that opposed him had all been discredited by the

catastrophe of World War I. Wikipedia (51). That left the Bolsheviks, who numbered just 24,000 members in early 1917, as the leading contender to form a government. In Lenin's words, "power was lying in the street; we picked it up." Parry (1969).

100 The obvious answer from freshman economics should have been to calculate net social welfare by assigning a dollar value to human life so that the costs of lockdowns, say, could be compared against lives saved. But this had always been a notoriously hard sell even for college students. The fact that similar cost–benefit arguments had opened the Obama Administration to charges of heartlessness or, in Sarah Palin's phrase, "death panels" further underscored the danger.

101 Rosenthiel (2010).

102 The Anti-Masons won 7.8 percent of the popular vote and carried Vermont in 1832.

103 Smith & Hamilton [1788] at p. 772.

104 Hofstadter (1969) at p. 120.

105 Brands (2018) at p. 17.

106 Hofstadter (1969) at pp. 85, 123, and 126–7.

107 Hofstadter (1969) at pp. 68 and 129.

108 Butter (2020) at pp. 27 and 120.

109 Hofstadter (1955) at p. 68. As Tap (2002) emphasizes, "Many Republicans had come to prominence in the 1850s utilizing harsh, anti-Southern rhetoric that emphasized a 'Slave Power' conspiracy" by Southern elites. The rhetoric included Lincoln's own 1858 "House Divided" speech, in which he "linked all the leading Democrats, North and South, in a gigantic conspiracy to expand slavery into the western territories." Describing what he called "the machinery" of the plot, Lincoln admitted that he had no proof but then immediately added:

> [W]hen we see a lot of framed timbers, different portions of which we know have been gotten out at different times and places and by different workmen – Stephen, Franklin, Roger, and James, for instance – and when we see these timbers joined together, and see they exactly make the frame of a house or a mill, all the tenons and mortices exactly fitting, and all the lengths and proportions of the different pieces exactly adapted to their respective places, and not a piece too many or too few – not omitting even scaffolding – or, if a single piece be lacking, we can see the place in the frame exactly fitted and prepared to yet bring such piece in – in *such* a case, we find it impossible not to believe that Stephen and Franklin and Roger and James all understood one another from the beginning, and all worked upon a common *plan* or *draft* drawn up before the first lick was struck. (Lincoln 1858; emphasis original)

Anyone mouthing similar accusations in the late twentieth century would have been immediately labeled paranoid.

110 Hofstadter (1955) at p. 79.

111 Hofstadter (1955) at p. 68.

112 Hofstadter (1969) at p. 129.

113 Butter (2020) at pp. 115, 119.

114 Butter (2020) at pp. 121, 123.

115 Butter (2020) at p. 125. Prof. Butter argues that the social sciences' recent return to anthropomorphic labels like "capitalism" and "institutional racism" has made college students significantly more open to conspiracy theories than they were fifty years ago. Butter (2020) at pp. 125–6.

116 Butter (2020) at p. 36.

117 Markets became steadily more concentrated in the US after 2000. This was most visible in industry profits, which rose from 7 percent in 12,000 to 9.5 percent today. Covarrubias, Gutiérrez, and Philippon (2019).

118 Anon (2016c).

119 The fact that respondents answer this way based on literally no information at all suggests extreme credulity. Still, things might not be as bad as they seem. Respondents who already believe at least one crashed UFO story might be welcoming news of a second, "North Dakota Crash" as confirmatory.

120 Butter (2020) at p. 92. Extremists on both Left and Right are much more likely to believe conspiracy theories than those in the center, with the Left nearly as credulous as the Right. Butter (2020).

121 Butter (2020) at p. 92; Hofstadter (1955) at p. 67.

122 Hofstadter saw the public's faith in government alternating in a kind of grand cycle. The fact that "Americans do not abide very quietly the evils of life," he argued, produced a valuable "restlessness" but also lacked "sufficient sense of the limits of … the human condition." The result of this restlessness was that political reform "often wanders over the border between reality and impossibility." Hofstadter (1955) at pp. 18–19.

123 The idea that repetition convinces also accounts for the enduring belief that a president who spends eight years preaching from his bully pulpit can permanently change the country's views. Here the leading examples are the Roosevelt New Deal and Reagan–Bush presidency. But for Donald Trump's election, the Obama presidency might have been similarly transformative.

# 4

# The Public Forum

## *Mass Media and the Web*

We have argued that persuasive political narratives are scarce, and that finding them requires effort. These, however, are not just psychological facts: Scarcity and effort are also economic attributes. Suppose, then, that some new political idea occurs to one or even several people. To be useful, it must still be repeatedly tweaked, developed, and audience tested before being disseminated. It follows that an ideology, like a medieval cathedral, is the work of many hands. More than that, it also implies that the rate at which society identifies and develops new political ideas depends on more than just its citizens' natural inventiveness. Things will go faster if there are strong institutions to reward and coordinate the work. In practice, Americans have almost always relied on markets to organize these tasks.

Just saying this already takes us takes well beyond the Framers. Indeed, *The Federalist* barely mentions newspapers,[1] probably because the Framers found it hard to imagine interventions that did not involve government censorship.[2] Yet by the middle of the nineteenth century, Americans had begun to see a better way. Mass markets, they realized, are anonymous. Each day they give millions of consumers exactly what they want without putting any single human, let alone a government, in charge.[3] But in that case, why couldn't a well-functioning market give readers the news and opinion they want? If so, all government had to do was administer whatever antitrust and intellectual property laws were needed to keep the market competitive. And government would never have to regulate political content at all.

This chapter begins by reviewing the evolution of commercial news organizations from the 1790s to the present. It then analyzes the system's shortcomings, which too often let publishers, advertisers, and powerful politicians influence and even suppress news and opinion. Finally, it explores how political polarization helps increase media companies' market power and profitability, rewarding them for content that increases extremism still further.

## 4.1 JOURNALISM EVOLVING

The Framers could not have anticipated, still less solved, the problems of managing an independent commercial press. How could they? The news business has reinvented itself a half-dozen times since their day. The trouble, as we will see, is that none of these incarnations has remotely resembled economists' ideal of a perfectly competitive market, leaving plenty of power to slant or suppress news for politicians,[4] publishers, and advertisers to fight over. This section reviews the history of journalism to identify recurring problems that reforms should target.

The country's first national newspaper, the *United States Gazette*, was founded in 1789 for the express purpose of supporting the Federalist Party. Two years later, then Secretary of State Thomas Jefferson diverted government funds to establish its rival, the rabidly anti-Federalist *National Gazette*.[5] By 1800, more than 250 party-funded newspapers were operating across the country. Together they invented a new vocabulary that helped Americans discuss their politics.[6]

For the next half-century, hardly any newspapers could survive without political patronage. The payments typically took the form of government printing contracts[7] supplemented by party leaders' endless demands that rank-and-file members purchase subscriptions to show their loyalty.[8] Partisan newspapers also received better access to party officials, legislative hearings, and party caucuses. Editors then returned these favors by backing their party's candidates and principles. The business model was sufficiently successful for the total number of US newspapers to reach 1,200 by the early 1830s.[9]

Naively, the system should have produced the worst kind of propaganda. But even though party bosses demanded complete party discipline from editors,[10] they also realized that this was worthless if readers did not trust those editors to begin with. The result was that newspapers with reputations for honesty could command higher subsidies. Knowing this, editors were careful to publish enough nonpartisan news and opinion to maintain their credibility.[11]

The era of party newspapers might have gone on forever if not for technology. Instead, newsprint prices fell steadily in the century after 1820,[12] while advances in high-speed printing made new scale economies possible. The trouble was that taking advantage of these technologies required large print runs. This meant replacing six-penny newspapers which catered to the middle class with one-cent papers targeting the poor. Serving this new audience, in turn, forced deep changes in content, notably including a vast increase in crime stories and lurid material.[13] It also made newspapers at least slightly more independent. The key was that a few large-circulation newspapers could now earn more by selling ads and subscriptions than by begging political subsidies.[14] Just why this was true remains obscure. One might have thought that political parties, with effectively unlimited access to government money, would have outbid the new business model. Perhaps politicians' budgets were tighter than they appeared, or the benefits of slanted coverage may have encountered diminishing returns as circulation increased.[15] Then too, some newspaper owners plainly cared about power at least as much as profit. Thurlow Weed's *Albany Evening Journal* and Horace Greely's *New York Tribune* are two obvious examples of newspapers that took an independent line because they preferred to seek political influence for themselves rather than sell it to others.[16]

Editors could now be more independent, and even tout their objectivity as a selling point to drive their circulations still higher.[17] Even so, change came slowly. In 1850, 85 percent of newspapers still had a party affiliation[18] and 80 percent were still openly partisan ten years later.[19] Yet percentages do not tell the whole story: For most readers, having even one independent newspaper in town was a big improvement over none at all.

In the meantime, scale economies also made news production more professional. Once a story was written and typeset, the per capita cost of providing it to additional readers fell steeply.[20] This meant that large-circulation papers could now hire professionals. Full-time reporters had been rare in the first half of the nineteenth century. But by the 1870s, the average big-city daily had a chief editor, a managing editor in charge of news, a telegraph editor who sorted through wire service stories, and a city editor who supervised two dozen or so reporters.[21] Newspapers also began experimenting with news-sharing. The invention of the telegraph led to the first news-gathering cooperative (Associated Press) in 1848. Soon the AP and imitators like United Press International (1907–) and the International News Service (1909–58) were conducting operations that no single paper could possibly afford on its own. The system worked because members could share costs at the national level and still monopolize news in the particular markets they served. Suddenly, "national" news was vastly cheaper and more plentiful than the local kind, undermining the Framers' assumption that voters would always know and care about their own state governments more than the federal one.

The technology that drove these changes accelerated after the Civil War.[22] This led to even cheaper newspapers serving readerships in the rapidly expanding cities. In 1870 the country had 574 dailies with a total circulation of 2.8 million readers; by 1909 the number had grown to 2,600 dailies with a circulation of 24.2 million.[23] Larger audiences, in turn, boosted ad revenues from 50 percent of newspapers' total income in 1880 to 64 percent in 1910.[24] Predictably, this allowed more newspapers to become independent. Prof. Gentzkow and coauthors report that only 11 percent of daily newspapers (26 percent by circulation) were independent in 1870, while the rest were openly partisan. Meanwhile one-quarter of all American cities were served by a single partisan newspaper, while fully half (53 percent) had competing Democrat and Republican papers but no independent one. The result was that editors usually ignored information that conflicted with their newspaper's official viewpoint, or else dismissed it as sophistry.[25] By 1920 the fraction had reversed, with 73 percent of all big-city circulation supplied by independents.[26]

Once again, the need for ever-greater circulation drove changes in content. Beginning in the 1880s, journalists began to seek out previously unreported stories,[27] including human interest items and attacks on special interests. The result was that the press's political influence began shifting from writing editorials to teaching new facts.[28]

These developments reached a climax in the "muckraking" magazines. The earliest magazines had appeared just before the Civil War, serving genteel audiences of 130,000 or so. Beginning in the 1890s, however, new cost-cutting technologies meant that publishers needed to sell anywhere from 400,000 to one million copies to turn a profit.[29] Scholars have shown that this second generation of magazines had immense political influence.[30] At the same time, thin margins made magazines and newspapers painfully dependent on advertising and credit. Big Business routinely used these levers to coerce them,[31] leading to, in H. L. Mencken's phrase, "dreadful little rags, venal, vulnerable, and vile."[32]

The situation improved after World War I when newspapers themselves became Big Business. Suddenly, publishers had the economic clout to resist outside pressure. At the same time, newsrooms grew bigger, more professional, and better paid. This made it harder for editors to insert their own slant into articles[33] and led to a new "objective journalism," which held that reporters should anticipate and deliver whatever facts any substantial group of readers might want to know.[34]

Per capita newspaper circulation peaked in the 1940s[35] and has declined ever since.[36] The silver lining, for a time, was that increasing concentration cushioned the surviving papers' revenue losses. The result into the 1980s was that most big papers remained sufficiently well funded to put teams onto investigative stories for long periods. This is very different from the current situation, where bureaucrats who hide stories can be reasonably sure that the press will lose interest after two or three days of digging.[37]

By then, print newspapers were competing against new kinds of media. The first nationwide radio networks (NBC and CBS) date from 1926, and were joined by a third competitor (Mutual) in 1934.[38] By the end of World War II they had become more important than print for fast-breaking stories.[39] Whether radio increased the country's total supply of news is less clear. On the one hand, the new outlets drained revenue from established newspapers, leaving fewer resources to support their newsrooms. On the other, increased competition probably goaded publishers to provide more content despite their thinning margins. Given that the newspaper business was so highly concentrated, even a small increase in competition would have been significant.

Meanwhile, radio was also concentrated. In 1943, the New Deal's antitrust authorities effected a modest improvement by forcing NBC to spin off part of its holdings as the now-independent American Broadcasting Co.[40] This confirmed that the market was big enough to support at least three independent broadcasters. By the late 1940s, CBS, NBC, and ABC began moving into television.[41] TV news soon displaced radio and continued to expand well into the 1970s, After that, competition from tabloids and cable TV forced network news organizations to downsize and take on gossip and soft news content they had formerly disdained.[42]

Print journalism's decline accelerated in the late 1990s, when sites like Craigslist started offering low-cost online postings[43] that slashed demand for the classified ads that had helped support newspapers since the 1830s. Meanwhile, Google's market power limited the advertising fees that newspapers could charge for their own online articles. This accelerated the decline of traditional print newspapers, though the effect was partly offset by the rise of digital outlets like *Huffington Post* and *Daily Beast* that could sell their content nationwide. Declining profitability also made it easier for billionaires to buy big-city newspapers like *The Washington Post*, *The Philadelphia Inquirer*, *The Boston Globe*, and the San Diego *Union Tribune*. Like Hearst before them, they were more interested in political clout than money.[44]

Meanwhile cable television entered the news business with the launch of CNN (1980), followed by MSNBC (1993) and Fox (1996). At first, CNN, which had the biggest news staff, dominated ratings by emphasizing news over any particular viewpoint. The turning point came in 2005, when MSNBC – originally a mostly centrist network[45] – shifted left after Keith Olbermann's attacks on then President Bush's Hurricane Katrina response produced unexpectedly large audiences. It has remained a reliably liberal brand ever since.[46] Soon after in 2010, Fox became the nation's most watched cable news channel by adopting the mirror-image strategy of stressing right-wing commentary compared to a news staff that was just one-third the size of CNN's. Watching these developments, CNN revised its own format to become more partisan in 2013. Despite this, it remains firmly stuck in third place.[47]

Fox's big advantage, of course, was that it had conservative viewers – half the country – all to itself. But this required an exquisite balancing act. By the early 2010s, a swarm of smaller outlets like The Blaze, One America News Network, Breitbart News, and CRTV were marketing themselves as more conservative than Fox. At the same time, the leftward drift of CNN and MSNBC hinted that Fox could pick up more viewers by shifting toward the center. In 2014 Fox tried to become modestly more centrist, only to move right again after the election of Donald Trump. Suffice to say, the honeymoon was temporary, so that by mid-2019 President Trump had turned to hyping Fox's conservative rivals because, he said, Fox wasn't working for "us" anymore.[48] Meanwhile, Trump allies explored the possibility of funding small companies like Newsmax TV to the point where they could become full-blown rivals to Fox.[49] For its part, Fox's decision to fire its most popular personality, Tucker Carlson, in 2023 is best understood as an attempt to retake control of the network's perceived political slant from a generally pro-Trump host who had dragged it steadily to the right.

The web also created new business models. One early innovation was to let outsiders compete with traditional editors in recommending stories to the public. Historically, editors had been tied to large news organizations. But now entrepreneurs like Matt Drudge could put up web pages that pointed readers to stories culled from hundreds of outlets.[50] This let small players to find stories that the big media companies had overlooked or ignored.

Social media like Twitter and Facebook similarly became news providers, replacing human editors with algorithms that targeted users with individualized newsfeeds. For the most part the algorithms – which mostly followed the simple logic of "People who liked ____ also liked ____" – were much less discriminating than human editors.[51] But that was enough for most Twitter users, who were usually less informed than people who read newspapers or watched network television.[52] The paradoxical result was that many less-educated and lower-income users relied on social media for their news even though nearly two-thirds (59 percent) of them considered it "largely inaccurate."[53] This made them the most manipulable segment of the population, giving social media giants the power to swing millions of votes to whichever politicians they favored.[54]

Looking back, the history of American media reveals some enduring patterns. First, news media have almost always possessed significant market power. The basic reason is size: Big outlets that can spread their news-gathering costs over vast audiences are inherently more profitable than small ones.[55] It follows that Americans' traditional "invisible hand" argument for letting markets enforce press neutrality comes with significant caveats. We normally think of industries with so-called Herfindahl indexes above 2500 as "highly concentrated."[56] But nineteenth-century local newspapers typically scored above 6000, while today's media still hover near 3500.[57] And of course, the advertisers that tried to dictate content were nearly always similarly concentrated.[58]

Yet despite these market imperfections, the profit motive almost always made coverage fuller and fairer down to the late twentieth century. Even so, there was always a tension. On the one hand, business models based on advertising tended to generate larger newsroom budgets[59] while subscription models were more likely to reduce bias so long as most readers preferred objective coverage[60] and publishers faced significant competition.[61] This made classical newspaper models that blended advertising and subscription an attractive compromise, trading modest bias for lower subscription prices and bigger readerships.[62] From this standpoint the fact that broadcast and electronic media depended entirely on advertising probably represented a step backward, even if the perennial struggle between publishers, newsroom employees, and outside advertisers kept any single group from fully wielding this power.

## 4.2 TODAY'S ECOSYSTEM

So far, we have concentrated on the big media outlets. We now turn to the intricate network of small entities and freelancers that invent, find, and steadily refine new fact and opinion content until the mainstream media embrace it. We have already said that the "nobody knows anything problem" makes it hard for publishers to tell when some fresh innovation in news and opinion will interest the public. Over the centuries, commercial book publishers met this challenge by funding elaborate ecosystems of independent entrepreneurs to find promising new titles and match them with readers.[63] Until recently, however, print newspapers gathered most news in-house.[64] The rise of the web changed that. Sometimes the outside effort is individual, with politicians and pundits producing content in the same way that authors write books. But it can also be collective, as when novel arguments and slogans emerge from anonymous online forums and posts. In practice, the distinction hardly matters. Even genius requires some starting material, and successful novelists often take their best ideas from "oral tradition," "folklore," and "urban legends." For political content, the best ideas similarly percolate upward from groups debating issues around watercoolers and backyard barbecues.[65] This is not surprising: Scholars have long studied this process, noting how small groups that regularly meet for breakfast, say, tend to be intensely creative. While they often take cues from the morning newspaper, their comments go beyond simple echoes to inject their own preconceptions and framing to make sense of what they read.[66]

The difference on the web is that millions of readers now share their thoughts. Of course, only a small percentage of these remarks contain anything innovative, and of these still fewer will be noticed. But those that are will be reworked through hundreds if not thousands of additional conversations until they become narratives that no single participant could ever have invented on her own.[67]

Folklore scholars have long known that audiences are exceptionally responsive to narratives polished in this way.[68] So it is no surprise that many folkloric political creeds and beliefs are also exceptionally durable. Probably the best-known example is German Antisemitism, whose regional patterns remained almost entirely unchanged between the fourteenth century and the rise of Hitler.[69] Similar examples of word-of-mouth political traditions in America include the persistence of Civil War enmities along the Kansas–Missouri border,[70] radical labor traditions in the Pacific Northwest,[71] and Black American conspiracy theories that AIDS and more recently COVID-19 vaccines were deliberately engineered to commit genocide.[72]

The downside is that word of mouth is also capricious, randomly elevating some ideas even as it suppresses other, equally promising candidates.[73] This effect has long been known in publishing, where authors of self-published or poorly advertised books typically sell perhaps a dozen copies per week. These titles are always in danger of dying out, depending on whether each new tranche of readers happens to be sympathetic. The upshot is that sales of a book that is lucky enough to find early fans grow geometrically until the Law of Large Numbers takes over. But the same title could just as easily encounter hostile audiences early on and never recover. Scholars have confirmed that this capriciousness is a major determinant of which titles do and do not succeed in both computer simulations and experiments using artificial online markets.[74] The obvious cure for this, as in publishing, is organization. Large media companies hire human editors who constantly search for content that might please their readers, and then publicize the most promising titles to ensure a fair hearing.[75]

Word of mouth's other drawback comes when the potential audience for a particular title is geographically dispersed so that face-to-face interactions are hard to arrange. The problem is particularly important for extremist ideologies that are unlikely to attract many adherents in any case. For literature, society has evolved several institutions to overcome this difficulty. The simplest and most traditional is to collect audience suggestions over time through a single itinerant speaker. Like the Homeric bards that preceded them, the politicians and ideologists who tour modern speaking circuits have a built-in incentive to notice, incorporate, and try out the best improvements at their next speaking engagement.[76] A second way is to host meetings where enthusiasts can get together to read and comment on draft texts. Since the Enlightenment, elites have routinely used salons to polish political arguments. While this offers smaller audiences than a conventional lecture tour, those who do participate tend to bring more talent and energy to suggesting improvements.

In many ways, universities provide the best of both worlds by offering a permanent physical site where like-thinking ideologues – typically though not always extremists – can spend years studying and debating each other. The model also offers the added advantage that college students are often young males, whose penchant for brawling can be used to publicize otherwise forgettable views. This nursery for new political faiths has been dramatically rejuvenated since the 1960s, when American universities introduced special curricula to appease campus radicals. The new faculty have been particularly friendly to student activism.[77]

Finally, the internet has made casual word of mouth enormously easier. To the extent that creativity benefits from group discussion, we expect ideological innovation to scale with the number of interactions. Fifty years ago, most fringe ideologies developed slowly, clinging to obscure (*The Turner Diaries*), outdated (nineteenth-century Celtic nostalgia), or despised (Nazism) content for decades. The great innovation on the web is that geographic density no longer matters. Like the print conspiracists who preceded them, QAnon's anonymous author(s) are profoundly unoriginal, recycling and reworking familiar tropes. The difference is that the pace of these inventions has vastly increased. This is directly traceable to their newfound ability to road-test narratives on virtual audiences who could never meet in person.[78]

To this point we have imagined an atomistic network of individuals interacting bilaterally or very occasionally in groups. But if word of mouth were all, most tropes and ingenious new narratives would remain forever obscure. What saves them is a well-funded ecosystem for finding, repeating, and sometimes improving the best ones until some big media outlet broadcasts them to the wider society.

The system is not confined to any single platform, or even to the web as a whole. Even so, we can get a good sense of how the it works by looking at large individual platforms. Figure 4.1 lists the number of Facebook "Fans" for the 1,000 or so most popular politics pages in 2017.[79] Strikingly, the graph shows the same "long tail" pattern that has long defined commercial publishing. Reading from left to right, a tiny handful of very prominent authors quickly gives way to a much larger and mostly anonymous population on the right. Thus, the very largest pages (1 million to 17 million Fans) are dominated by household names: A-list politicians, vocal celebrities, and nationwide media outlets.[80] This is followed by a second population of slightly smaller sites with 100,000 or more Fans, which includes regional media outlets ranging from *The Chicago Sun-Times* and *Boston Globe* to *The Palm Beach Post*, with a smattering of enterprising individuals near the lower end. These last sites seem to be at or near the cutoff where commercial earnings are big enough to support staff beyond the authors themselves.[81] Finally, a third tranche extends down to 10,000 or so Fans and is almost entirely populated by current and recent office holders.

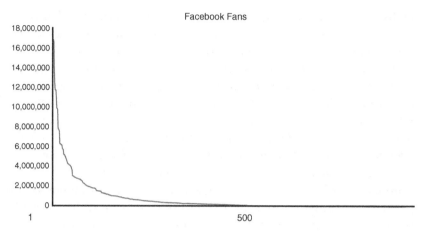

FIGURE 4.1  Facebook fans: the top 1,000 sites

But that leaves the mysterious right-hand part of the graph. So far, no one seems to have studied sites with fewer than 10,000 Fans in any detail. Anecdotally, however, we expect to find a mix of volunteer enthusiasts and entrepreneurs promoting various sideline businesses, with the latter group including everyone from college professors writing blogs in hopes of promotion to conspiracy theorists looking to sell their next video.[82] Probably the most intriguing category of sites involves small discussion forums, which often form around specialty interests before migrating to politics more generally. These typically act as digital focus groups where new narratives can be endlessly revised and road-tested against sympathetic audiences.[83]

Tracing the evolution of large ideologies in detail would be a mammoth task. But it is already clear that few, if any, ideologies are completely original. Indeed, even socialism built on Christianity's most distinctive themes, with a millenarian End of History standing in for Heaven and believers being rewarded for their proletarian virtues.[84] This inspired multiple competing socialisms in the early nineteenth century. Marx's achievement was then to merge them by adding the distinctively compelling subthemes of "class struggle" and a "science of history."[85] The result was so politically attractive that even his bitterest enemies have picked up the framing, most notably in Hitler's claims for a "National Socialist" alternative.

This constant reworking of values and tropes is equally visible in the evolution of American political rhetoric. To take just one example, nineteenth-century Americans were taught that rural life and farming were sacred. This agrarian myth had started in the eighteenth century when the country's educated classes adopted it from Roman literature. It then gained a class tinge after Jefferson's followers repurposed the image of virtuous yeoman farmers to attack the Federalists. This new twist was so successful that by 1840 even conservative Whigs were claiming that their candidate had been raised in a log cabin.[86] Later still, the rhetoric had merged with the xenophobic belief that the US was a kind of non-Europe or anti-Europe. This led to the Populists' mistrust of all people who were physically remote and alien, including Americans who lived in cities.[87] By then the idea of middle-class virtue had outdistanced its original agrarian roots, so that the "general theme" of Progressivism became the attempt to restore a type of economic individualism and political democracy against the country's great corporations and political machines.[88] This would still be visible a century later in Bill Clinton's encomiums to common people who "played by the rules" and deserved the government's protection.

The balance between the inertia of an established theme and restless innovation is most visible in conspiracy theories. Here no author ever breaks entirely new ground: That would require massive research on her part, and far more effort from readers than repurposing facts and ideas they already know. Worst of all, it would almost certainly fail since, according to our "nobody knows anything" principle, authors almost always do better by presenting ideas that audiences have warmed to in the past. The result is that conspiracy genres are strongly path dependent, with the success of a single book sometimes serving to revive an entire genre, while simultaneously enriching it with new themes and wrinkles that then become standard.[89]

This is spectacularly illustrated by the modern family of Globalist/New World Order theories, all of which descend from eighteenth-century reactionary authors who claimed that the French Revolution was so unlikely that it could only have been the work of conspirators. The earliest villains in these accounts were variously identified as Catholics, Socialists, Illuminati, and Freemasons. Then, in 1795, Jews joined the list. Looking back, this essentially chance event formed the starting point for all modern Antisemitism.[90] But this was not at all obvious at the time, and by the second half of the nineteenth century the narrative seemed to have run its course. Instead, an obscure author named Nesta Webster published *The French Revolution: A Study in Democracy* (1919). Though forgotten today, the book seized the imagination of conservatives including Winston Churchill, and prompted a tidal wave of imitators.[91] A century later, Webster's book still provides the basic template for conspiracy theories across the internet, though in the usual mix-and-match way only some of these are antisemitic.

A more recent example illustrates how chance accidents still decide which tropes succeed. French writer Renaud Camus had published more than 100 books, but only achieved fame when he invented his catchphrase "The Great Replacement" to describe his theory that African immigrants were supplanting the native population of Europe. No doubt Camus' label showed a certain literary talent. All the same, it would have promptly died out if *The New York Times* had not noticed and reprinted the phrase. From that initial boost it soon spread to, and received additional publicity from, Neo-Nazi marchers in Charlottesville, a mass murderer in Christchurch, New Zealand, Yellow Vest protesters in France, and – perhaps most remarkably – radical Islamists. The final step came when prominent journalist Eric Zemmour made himself Camus' herald, crisscrossing France to share the vision at meetings. The eye-catching theme caused just enough controversy to make Zemmour one of the country's leading presidential candidates. Meanwhile, the slogan's international appeal continues to surprise even its author.[92]

These dynamics are of course timeless. But the internet has accelerated and in some ways distorted traditional mechanisms. Most obviously, digital technologies have made self-publishing dramatically cheaper for authors and video makers, while simultaneously helping audiences learn about and obtain copies of their work far more easily than before.[93] This makes it easier for enthusiasts to circulate their ideas, and for small entrepreneurs to earn a profit. Commercial incentives have reinforced the revolution, with large media and internet platforms providing technical support to the most popular content producers[94] to attract users to their own sites, and connecting small entrepreneurs to companies interested in placing online ads. The downside is that we expect today's dominant platforms, like every monopolist, to provide less support than a competitive market would. After all, web users who find today's content inadequate have nowhere else to turn.[95] This suggests that the best way to promote small upstream political voices is to make the big internet search and social media companies more competitive.

The question remains how much any single large actor can do to monitor and shape the narratives that word-of-mouth networks are constantly inventing. In the old days when most interactions proceeded through physical meetings, the task would have been overwhelming. However, digitization has made the tangle of relationships far easier to trace. For instance, Facebook engineers now use artificial intelligence to map the online networks that create, amplify, and eventually distribute right-wing content to hundreds of thousands of users. Starting in 2021, they began to remove or limit players responsible for what they saw as problematic content, eliminate phrases like "Patriot Party" when they showed early signs of popularity, demote selected content from newsfeeds, and block notifications when such content was posted. Crucially, Facebook claims that these interventions were both effective and also invisible to everyone except those removed.[96]

In principle, Facebook could also create its own messaging and then shepherd it through user networks to refine and isolate the best versions. For now, the problem is how to generate an acceptable first draft. The genius of folkloric methods, after all, is that they select the best content from many millions of proposals. So while platforms could pay professionals to create a message, the results might not be especially persuasive or seed further refinements. In the long run, the most promising solution is for artificial intelligence to identify the words, phrases, and content that web users already find compelling.[97]

## 4.3 SPINNING THE NEWS

History encourages Americans to think that market forces will limit, though probably not eliminate, private power to control what voters know. The challenge is to distinguish fixable flaws from the defects inherent in any system based on free enterprise. This section takes a closer look at the mechanics of slanting and suppressing content.

Many types of spin reflect nothing more than simple business judgments. These include first and foremost the desire to give readers what they want. Many readers are fastidious, and this has historically encouraged newspapers and advertisers to kill scandalous stories that might alienate subscribers.[98] Moreover, this logic is particularly strong for political stories. As Downs pointed out, voters with limited information budgets want newspapers to prescreen which facts are reported.[99] This requires editors to guess which stories readers will find informative. Catering to social voters is even simpler: By definition, they would rather read "respectable" facts and opinion than informative ones. This means that editors do not have to guess which stories readers *might* like, but need only perform the *service* of telling them which stories they *should* like.

Publishers are happy to go along with this, if only because it is wasteful to provide more news than readers want to consume.[100] But of course, this drastically limits what is printed. On any reasonable estimate there must be tens if not hundreds of thousands of greater and lesser injustices across the US each day. Yet the front section of each day's *Wall Street Journal* only contains about thirty national news stories, most of which are devoted to updating previously reported topics. By comparison, trying to document every Washington graft or sex scandal would fill the newspaper many times over. Then too, outlets choose stories that rational voters find helpful in understanding the world. Since those audiences vary from one outlet to the next, there is no real surprise that Fox's coverage of Russia collusion stories came later and less plentifully than other channels, while its coverage of Hillary Clinton's putative scandals was just the opposite.[101]

Finally, competition forces editors to give the public what it wants. In the maximally simple case where every outlet competes with every other, we expect media companies that suppress stories that readers care about to lose money and eventually disappear. For journalism, where outlets almost always compete on quality rather than price,[102] profitability mostly depends on market share. In the short run this tends to be fairly stable. The reason is that, except for inveterate channel-surfers, most viewers settle on what looks like the best channel for them and stay there. In the longer run, however, scoops matter. This is because they provide scarce information that viewers would not otherwise have about the relative quality of each network's newsroom and how often they suppress stories that viewers would want to see. More immediately, scoops give news organizations the chance to show their wares to viewers who normally watch other networks. This exposure usually lasts several days, during which some viewers will inevitably decide to stay, permanently improving the outlet's market share.

All of this assumes a simple model where each outlet competes with every other. But of course no outlet wants to compete in this way, and will escape this dynamic the moment it can. Economist Harold Hotelling was the first to work out when and how firms are able to do this. Hotelling's key insight is that consumers have different tastes, so that they often go on buying their preferred product even when competitors offer a lower price. Of course, this can't go on forever, and customers will sooner or later defect if the price difference is high enough. But so long as firms are careful to stay safely below this threshold, each can exercise the same power over its customers that a monopolist would.[103]

The question remains how these strategies change the choices available to consumers. In practice, Hotelling's predictions depend sensitively on how many firms compete in the market. Where there are three or more firms, the most profitable strategy is for firms to space themselves evenly across the whole spectrum of preferences so that each serves the same number of consumers. To see why, imagine that one of the firms moves closer to one of its competitors. Then competition will increase so that both firms become less profitable. This persuades each firm to stay where it is.

The story is different in the two-firm case. Here Hotelling predicted that competitors would offer near-identical products.[104] To see why, imagine that both firms start out clustered near the midpoint of consumer tastes, with Firm A slightly to the left of Firm B. Then consumers to the left of Firm A will prefer its product to Firm B's, while consumers sandwiched between the two firms will choose whichever product is closer to their preferences. But in that case if Firm A moves to the left, Firm B can follow it to capture still more market share while keeping all of the existing customers to its right. Since this logic is reciprocal, the correct advice for both firms is to position their products as close to the center as possible.[105]

Hotelling's logic has sinister implications for media markets. On the one hand, each fresh increase in polarization makes product differentiation more profitable.[106] This encourages media outlets to increase their slant even more, giving viewers still more practice in seeing the patterns that led them to favor those outlets in the first place. That, in turn, makes audiences more polarized (Figure 4.2), so that slant becomes steadily more profitable in an endless cycle, limited only by diminishing returns in how much each repetition can influence viewers' beliefs.

Today's big three cable television empires are polarized much as Hotelling predicted.[107] Perhaps the most important question is whether there might be room for a fourth competitor to enter. Certainly, the history is suggestive: We have seen that radio flirted with a fourth network and that television news very nearly inherited the pattern. Given that cable TV has thus far added a major outlet every decade or so, a fourth competitor might be just over the horizon (Figure 4.2).[108]

And indeed, there are hints that this is happening. For the past decade, right-wing Fox has drawn roughly as many viewers as left-leaning CNN and MSNBC combined. This makes it practically certain that a new entrant would target conservatives. Moreover, Fox seems

FIGURE 4.2   "Then we agree. Ten minutes of your news, then ten minutes of mine"

to know this. Beginning in 2020, the widening gap between pro- and anti-Trump Republicans forced it to choose. But as soon as Fox's coverage began favoring anti-Trump conservatives, pro-Trump outlets like One American News Network ("OAN") and Newsmax showed rapidly expanding market shares. If pro-Trump investors were to bankroll them, the usual Hotelling analysis would predict that a somewhat shrunken Fox would move closer to center-left CNN. This would make it easier for viewers to cross over between stations, reinvigorating competition and making today's polarization strategies dramatically less profitable.

In the meantime, media companies have a vested interest in having their reporters deliver slanted coverage. In principle, their power to do this is limited. After all, trying to monitor and control what employees write and say is costly. In practice, though, the task is made easier by journalists' habit of self-selecting into outlets whose views they find congenial. The rise of "advocacy journalism,"[109] which argues that reporters should present stories in a way that advances specific social and political agendas, has made Hotelling strategies still more feasible by freeing newsrooms from older "objective journalism" norms that considered slanted coverage unethical.

Hotelling strategies also deprive centrist viewers of the news they want. This is very different from the mid-twentieth-century case where ABC, NBC, and CBS competed head to head for a single audience.[110] Rational voter theory predicts that this will sometimes stop centrists from reaching any conclusions at all, depressing turnout.[111]

A biased press becomes even more dangerous when government encourages it. The modern high-water mark for this sort of synergy occurred during World War I.[112] Rejecting the old-fashioned coercive censorship then being practiced in Europe, the Wilson Administration realized that it could achieve better results by offering the press more carrots than sticks.[113] The resulting policy aimed not just to suppress news, but also to persuade the press to actively cheerlead the war.[114] For the most part, the Administration got its wish. The new federal Committee on Public Information ("CPI") started by exploiting Progressivism's weakness for moral crusades. The tactic worked particularly well in newsrooms. Then as now dominated by upper middle-class Progressives, they had long been habituated to seeing politics as an exercise in virtue to rid the country of corrupt (and not incidentally foreign born) urban political machines.[115] Progressives now repurposed this moral zeal and xenophobia in a new crusade to defeat German militarism and "make the world safe for democracy."[116] The centerpiece of this creed was an "almost messianic" message that defined "Americanism" as being "a responsible citizen, supporting the community and the government, exercising restraint in criticizing or opposing the government."[117] The pitch became all the more persuasive when CPI pandered to Progressive bias by hiring more than 200 college professors along with prominent muckrakers like Ida Tarbell, Jane Addams, and S. S. McClure to produce its bulletins.[118]

Editors who wanted to promote the war effort – or simply avoid charges of what Progressives called "slacking" – also received detailed guidelines on how to write their stories.[119] When newspapers did depart from CPI releases, it was almost always to make their coverage still more patriotic.[120] On those rare occasions when the journalists attacked the government, CPI admitted that it might sometimes delay articles "pending efforts at rectification."[121] For friendly editors, the government's most important carrot was content. With access to the battlefields practically nonexistent, CPI prepared its own readymade copy. In California, the dispatches added up to a 6 lb bundle every day.[122] By one estimate, enthusiastic editors turned the handouts into 20,000 newspaper columns per week.[123]

There were also sanctions, although most were only threats: CPI routinely said that "reckless journalism" was the same as treason.[124] But the Administration also knew that its unspoken cartel to slant and suppress news would unravel unless small defections were punished. This made it important to sanction those few who defied official policy. Some of the Administration's weapons were economic: The CPI controlled newsprint allotments and could stop publishers who were not "reliable" from

selling books overseas. Others involved straightforward censorship: All
magazines had to submit articles several weeks before publication[125] and
the Espionage Act of 1917 authorized the postmaster to refuse any publication that willfully obstructed the war or the draft. In the end seventeen major publications, mostly socialist, were suppressed outright, while
postal inspectors punished lesser violations by tearing out the offending
pages before delivery.[126] None of this posed much risk to mainstream
journalists. But the prevailing rhetoric made it reasonable to think that,
if further repression did become necessary, the Administration would be
able to find enough defenders to make it stick.[127]

## 4.4 SUPPRESSING FACTS

Down to the mid-twentieth century most newspapers knew many more
scandals than they printed. This was not all bad, since newspapers often used
their power to suppress character assassination premised on fake news,[128]
allegations of homosexuality,[129] or Communist Party membership.[130]
While the suppression was seldom complete, what coverage did occur was
often exiled to a fringe of underground scandal sheets sold in plain brown
wrappers.[131] In the case of politicians, editors' sense of decency was further
reinforced by partisan calculations that there was no telling where a policy
of tit-for-tat revelations would end. Some of the better-known examples
include Harding's mistresses Nan Brinton and Carrie Fulton Phillips, FDR's
Lucy Mercer, Eisenhower's Kay Summersby, and JFK's assignations with
an East German prostitute.[132] Still other acts of suppression were motivated
by a sense of the national interest. This almost certainly included ignoring
Lee Harvey Oswald's obvious ties to the Soviet Union in favor of fanciful
right-wing connections and "grassy knoll" theories following the Kennedy
assassination.[133] Indeed, this was probably the most responsible thing
they could have done: Both politicians and ordinary citizens would have
reviled editors who ran stories prodding the country into a no-win nuclear
confrontation with the Soviet Union. More recently, similar scruples may
have helped to motivate the media's year-long refusal to report claims that
COVID-19 came from a Chinese government laboratory.

It seems obvious that no single mechanism can explain all suppression.
Some facts would not have been discovered even in a competitive market;
others were ignored because imperfect markets make it profitable to do
so; and still others were suppressed because the big outlets could safely
ignore what readers wanted. Probably the simplest way to untangle these
cases is to start with the baseline case of perfect competition.

Developing a new investigative lead is fundamentally an investment decision. In the simplest case where leads are scarce, each newspaper decides whether or not to investigate on the assumption that it is the only one that knows about them. For their part, politicians can be reasonably sure that a story quashed at one outlet will not spring up later somewhere else. This makes killing stories affordable: Some of the most common methods include offering or else threatening to withhold other, more positive stories;[134] threats of political retaliation;[135] withholding advertising; pressuring distributors to drop offending publications; buying up and destroying offending newsstand copies;[136] and encouraging friendly newspapers to pay witnesses for stories that will never be published.[137] Once publication occurs, libeled individuals can also sue for defamation.[138] In some cases, a successful jury verdict can also encourage more victims to bring suit and even bankrupt defendants.[139] Finally, targets can simply live with unfavorable coverage from tabloids whose circulation may be small in any case.[140]

The case is different when stories are widely known. Probably the most common scenario is when one outlet discovers that rivals have come across the same lead and decided to investigate.[141] Sometimes editors take this as evidence that the story is a good investment. But they may equally decide that, on the most naive estimate, they have a 50 percent probability of publishing second and losing the scoop.[142] This will be especially discouraging if the story is only moderately interesting or the other paper has a large head start. Finally, newspapers that find out that their competitors have *stopped* investigating a story may decide that the topic is a dead end and drop their own investigations. This can lead to a false signal in which each side abandons the project simply because the other has.[143] This outcome is especially likely in the modern era of tight journalism budgets.

The dynamics by which leads do or do not become mainstream stories is neatly illustrated by the media's year-long refusal to report claims that COVID-19 originated in a Chinese laboratory. At the very latest, the lead should have been clear to everyone by March 2020, when *The Bulletin of the Atomic Scientists'* editor-in-chief ordered his staff to follow the issue.[144] Despite this, no major outlet reported the story for another fourteen months. This was almost certainly due to early denials by prominent researchers writing in two prestigious science journals (*The Lancet* and *Nature*) coupled with silence from a virology community reluctant to

anger members who wanted to continue controversial experiments.[145] This
was disabling for media companies that depended on academic experts to
decide whether such claims were sufficiently plausible to be newsworthy.
In the end, prominent freelancer Nicholas Wade, who had been following
the story, wrote an article "to get it out of my system." Even then Wade
had to self-publish after receiving rejections "left, right, and center." That
might have been that, except that *The Bulletin* noticed Wade's article and
published the piece. This triggered a further letter by leading virologists to
*Science* saying that the lab story should be taken seriously after all. At this
point, the media embargo suddenly collapsed. The logic for large outlets
seemed obvious: If MSNBC, say, refused to run the biggest story of the
year *after* prominent scientists vouched for it, CNN could take part of its
market share for years to come. Nor did it help that Fox had been covering the story for months and was sure to pile on.[146]

Suppression is vastly harder when outlets try to ignore a story that their
rivals have already published. Indeed, this would be impossible in an
Adam Smith world where thousands of outlets compete: Offenders that
refuse to give readers the news they wanted would simply go out of business. The problem is more difficult in Hotelling markets where most
viewers strongly prefer one outlet to all the others.[147] But if the suppressed story is big enough, viewers may still switch networks at least
temporarily. And if they find the new network more congenial, the shift
can become permanent.

News embargos are also unstable. The reason is that each member is
tempted to gain market share by providing slightly more news than its
rivals. This encourages stories that skirt the edges of the embargo. If the
other outlets then retaliate, the cartel will sooner or later unravel. That
said, the dynamic tends to be damped for network news, where violations can be immediately detected so that rivals catch up within a day or
so. For this reason, only very large scoops can attract enough viewers to
make breaking the embargo profitable.

Today's publishers show a worrying capacity to suppress newsworthy
stories. Just before the 2020 presidential election, the *New York Post*
ran a story suggesting that the Biden family had been selling access to
the then presidential candidate for years. CNBC, CNN, and most newspapers silently refused to cover the story. Among major outlets only Fox
ignored the cartel, while NPR elegantly sniffed that "We don't want to
waste our time on stories that are not really stories, and we don't want
to waste our listeners' and readers' time on stories that are just pure

distractions."[148] Taken as a whole, the efforts were successful, reducing the story's audience by at least 50 percent.[149] In fact, there is no real question that the *Post* story was true.[150] This almost certainly mattered in an election where the final margin was just 44,000 votes spread across six states.[151] Despite their market power, it is not clear that any of the outlets could have unilaterally ignored the story. The cartel was greatly facilitated by the fact that any violation would be immediately obvious, ensuring that none of the participants could gain a lasting advantage by breaking its (presumably unspoken[152]) promise not to publish the story before the others did. Additionally, mainstream journalists' refusal to report *The Post*'s allegations further reduced the chances that the broadcasters would be criticized for their silence, or lack defenders if they were.

For Fox, of course, hosting the anti-Biden story had no downside. The situation for MSNBC and CNN was more nuanced. On the one hand, the risk of losing viewers to Fox, even temporarily, was negligible. On the other, the barriers between left-leaning MSNBC and center-left CNN were much lower, so that whichever outlet broke the embargo first was likely to take viewers from the other. Despite this, CNN and MSNBC both held to the embargo until well after the election. The task was made easier by business considerations that had nothing to do with market share, most obviously that the Trump Administration was angry with the mainstream outlets and would likely pursue new antitrust legislation and perhaps even prosecutions against them in a second term.

But being able to suppress news is not the end of the story. The question remains who controls it. On the one hand, the rise of newspaper chains in the early twentieth century gave publishers the market power and deep pockets to be independent.[153] On the other, their owners were often vulnerable to pressure from politicians and political parties,[154] and even their own employees. This last group was particularly hard to resist because creative workers are inherently hard to manage: Publishers could either regulate reporters so tightly that quality suffered or decide it was better to tolerate a certain amount of evasion. As in Wilson's time, the fact that most newsrooms overwhelmingly reflected the same upper-middle-class social and educational backgrounds meant that these views usually trended liberal.

Moreover, mid-century publishers were not the only ones who held market power. Large companies could also demand restrictions and withhold advertising from media outlets that violated them.[155] Moreover, companies sometimes coordinated these pressure campaigns by withdrawing all of their ads simultaneously.[156] As one corporate spokesperson put it after General Motors (GM) cut ties to the *Los Angeles Times*: "We recognize and support the news media's freedom to report and editorialize as they see fit. Likewise, GM and its retailers are free to spend our advertising dollars where we see fit."[157] The silver lining was that such pressure was only effective to the extent companies could plausibly threaten to withhold future ad purchases, at least for a time. This required near-monopoly power, since firms competing in concentrated industries could not refuse to buy ads without losing market share. Perhaps less intuitively, threats of retaliation also required market power on the newspaper side: Otherwise, competition would drive down ad prices to the point where newspapers barely covered their costs, at which point slanted journalism would be no more profitable than the honest kind.[158]

In the twentieth century, this complex economics usually produced benign results, encouraging publishers to push back against advertisers trying to hide scandals that might injure their brands. The result was that most reporters were given broad discretion to cover stories as they saw fit.[159] And why not? Publishers knew that objective journalism was good for circulation and the bottom line. That said, many owners happily "boosted" friends and allies. Here William Randolph Hearst's outsized political influence is the best-known example,[160] followed closely by Colonel McCormick of *The Chicago Tribune* and Harrison Gray Otis and his descendants at *The Los Angeles Times*.[161]

In a perfect world, antitrust law would have ended the power struggle by eliminating both sides' market power. This was unachievable, however. On the one hand, our natural monopoly argument suggests that media markets will always be at least mildly concentrated no matter what government regulators decide. Then too, many local and especially national advertisers are large enough to ignore market signals, at least for a time. These structural facts suggest that modern regulators will do well to keep market power within something like its historical limits, while also leaving a rough balance between publishers and advertisers in whatever power remains. While the results are bound to be imperfect, we can take heart from the many moderately concentrated media markets that managed to supply a reliable stream of plentiful and mostly unbiased content throughout the twentieth century.

Meanwhile, the rise of the internet has opened new possibilities for private censorship. In the nineteenth century, the existence of a half-dozen or so competitors in each city practically guaranteed at least one dissenter. This made it nearly impossible for the dominant outlet to suppress scandals entirely. The difference on the web is that most news and opinion now passes through a few big social media platforms. This gives owners the power to suppress *every* voice they disagree with using tools that range from "deindexing" pages so that they turn up less frequently in web searches to outright bans. Alternatively, Google's dominance of online ad markets gives it the power to "demonetize" offending web pages by blocking their ability to sell space to advertisers.

The question remains how far this sort of behavior can go before the platforms undercut their own dominance. Here, banning individuals seems fairly safe.[162] After all, consumers prefer big platforms like Facebook because they offer the most content, and the loss of a few obscure extremists cannot change this. The case would be different, though, if customers stopped trusting the site's editorial judgments because they saw it using its power capriciously or with a partisan slant. In that case, they might well be open to changing providers. Even then, however, the newcomer would need to offer roughly as much content as the old one, which for a social media site means that users would have to switch simultaneously. Coordinating this would require an expensive marketing campaign. Even so, the fact that Twitter eventually withdrew its ban on *The New York Post*'s Hunter Biden story suggests that social media platforms' confidence in what they can get away with is shaky, and that their monopolies may be more fragile than most people assume.[163]

Meanwhile acts of slant and suppression, even if they succeed in the short term, are almost certain to be exposed over time. When that happens, rational voters will become more skeptical of the next story, requiring larger and more flagrant lies the next time. Eventually, their credibility will be no better than citizens' ability to cross-check coverage against whatever independent outlets remain and word of mouth from friends who know the facts directly.[164] Disfavored groups will also quite rationally look for more information on their own, making them more vulnerable to "fake news" purveyors.[165]

## 4.5 FEEDBACKS

We argued in Chapter 3 that our physiological craving for novelty guarantees that narratives and ideology are restless and will evolve at some basal rate whether or not society encourages them. But this is only a lower limit, and they can evolve faster where institutions organize the effort. For Americans, these institutions have almost always been private companies operating in highly concentrated markets.

The distinctive economics of commercial media balances the massive scale economies in newsgathering against individual voters' Downsian desire for outlets that deliver the facts and analysis they find most helpful in understanding the world. These facts immediately imply several consequences that are likely to persist as long as news is funded through markets.

First, the combination of scale economies in newsgathering and steeply falling distribution costs gives incumbents market power approaching that of natural monopolies. We therefore expect news markets to be dominated by a few large firms, as indeed they have been throughout US history. This is especially true for national news, whose costs can be spread over enormous audiences. The result is that – contrary to the Framers' expectations – voters can now track national politics far more easily than their own state's. Next to the Civil War, this is probably the biggest reason that Americans came to see themselves as citizens of the US far more than any individual state.

Second, market power gives publishers and newsrooms significant discretion to slant and sometimes ignore important news stories. The ability of social media and legacy outlets to suppress news ahead of the 2020 election shows a worrying capacity to manipulate voters in numbers large enough to swing close elections.

Third, publishers' market power provides a powerful counterweight to the influence of politicians and advertisers. The fact that outlets that slant or suppress news reliably lose market share is especially salutary since it reminds publishers to resist outside demands and to use their own power sparingly.

Fourth, the foregoing market arguments are hostage to consumer taste. If readers and viewers prefer invective and scandal to objective reporting, publishers will happily supply it. Worse, rising polarization opens up new business models. We expect slant and suppression to increase abruptly once Hotelling-style market segmentation becomes more profitable than objective journalism. Here, the good news is that the same feedback should work in reverse if audiences become more moderate.[166] The bad news is that the Hotelling dynamic is self-reinforcing: As broadcasting becomes more slanted, audiences will become still more polarized so that Hotelling strategies earn even higher profits in an endless loop.

Meanwhile, the saving grace of a polarized media is that humans' hardwired desire for novelty guarantees that readers and viewers will eventually tire of familiar facts and arguments. It follows that today's dominant narratives and ideologies will sooner or later be replaced. The only question is how quickly this happens. We have argued that efficient media markets are the best way to accelerate the turnover. Ideally, the new narratives and ideologies will be more unifying. But even if they aren't, increasing the rate at which issues come and go will make it easier for the losing side to forget its anger.

Finally, the damage from slanted news will spread to the broader society. According to our rational voter model we expect press accounts to be more heavily discounted, reducing available information so that voters either abstain, or vote at random,[167] or practice social voting instead. In the longer term, viewpoint suppression will also make it difficult for the majority to understand just how many people disagree with the supposed mainstream, or how passionately. If organized mass violence should ever return to America, it will not be because one side has cold-bloodedly decided to attack the other. Instead, it will come the way it did before, with outlets on both sides insisting that they represent the vast majority and cheerfully ignoring the other side's passion. And just as in 1861, people will not see through the illusion until the fighting starts and there is no way to turn back.

### Notes

1  But see *Federalist* No. 84 (Hamilton) at p. 396 (arguing that citizens learn about pending legislation from "public prints").
2  The Framers avoided the topic of censorship less because they opposed it than because they thought it raised issues too complex for any Constitution to resolve. This is most visible in Hamilton's argument that laws guaranteeing "liberty of the press" can never be more than "fine declarations." *Federalist* No. 84 at p. 395.
3  In Prof. Hofstadter's paraphrase,

> One of the glories of the competitive model had been that it purported to solve the question of market power by denying that such power had any particular location. The decisions of the market were beautifully impersonal, since they were only the averagings of the decisions of thousands of individuals, none of whom enjoyed any decisive power. The market mechanisms suggested that power was not really exercised by anyone. With the perfect impersonality of Adam Smith's 'invisible hand,' the market made decisions that ought not be vested in the hands of any particular man or body of men. Hence, the market mechanism met the desire for the diffusion of power and seemed to be the perfect economic counterpart of American democratic pluralism. (Hofstadter 1964a at p. 674)

4  Although the current chapter focuses on market forces, readers should bear in mind that American politics has occasionally spilled over into outright coercion. The most spectacular example of censorship dates from 1798–1800, when the Federalist Party charged its opponents in Congress with being "a conspiracy, a faction leagued with a foreign Power to effect a revolution or subjugation of this country." They then passed a Sedition Act that made any criticism of the government or its leaders a crime. Federalist prosecutors ultimately brought seventeen indictments against the country's biggest partisan newspapers in hopes of silencing the many smaller newspapers that reprinted their articles. The trials were also timed to coincide with the climax of the presidential campaign. In the end, one editor was jailed for six months and fined $400. The attempted intimidation failed owing to the US Army's weakness and widespread public support for the opposition. See Hofstadter (1955) at pp. 107–9.

 Censorship in the country's most dangerous moment, the Civil War, was surprisingly mild, with many Northern editors virulently attacking the Lincoln Administration and voicing pro-Southern views throughout the conflict. Hofstadter (1955). The Administration did, however, shutter the *Chicago Times* and arrest anti-War congressman Clement Vallandigham for denouncing the war when the Union seemed headed for defeat in 1863. Guelzo (2013) at pp. 49, 94.

 The high-water mark for modern censorship occurred after America entered World War I. The campaign continued after the war when Attorney General A. Mitchell Palmer ran for president promising to extend wartime sedition laws against the country's large foreign-language press and radicals' efforts to stir up trouble in Black communities. Wikipedia (53). Voters rejected him in favor of a "return to normalcy."

 State and federal governments continued to exercise milder forms of censorship into the 1960s. The most common was to deny postal privileges to offending publishers, forcing them into marginal business models based on newsstand sales and seedy advertisers. Barbas (2018) at pp. 44, 169. Prosecutors also brought criminal libel prosecutions which could be ruinously expensive to those targeted. Barbas (2018) at pp. 18, 29. California's action against the scandal sheet *Confidential* in the 1950s cost the publisher $400,000 in legal fees and only ended when he agreed to stop publishing Hollywood exposés. Barbas (2018) at p. 312. The Supreme Court declared criminal libel unconstitutional in *Garrison* v. *Louisiana* (1964).

5  Ricks (2020) at p. 241; Bulla (n.d.); Gentzkow, Glaeser, and Goldin (2006) at p. 207.

6  Ricks (2020) at p. 250.

7  Gentzkow, Glaeser, and Goldin (2006) at p. 189; Petrova (2012) at p. 18.

8  Petrova (2011) at p. 793; Petrova (2012) at p. 26.

9  Bulla (n.d.)

10  Hofstadter (1969) at p. 245.

11  Jenkins (2021a). Credibility was also needed to persuade readers to part with the papers' comparatively high, six-cent price.

12  Gentzkow, Glaeser, and Goldin (2006). Prices began falling with the invention of the Fourdrinier process for rag paper in the 1830s. The discovery

of a process for making paper from wood pulp caused prices to plummet from 1867 onward. Gentzkow, Glaeser, and Goldin (2006) at p.210 and Figure 6.5.

13  Norman (n.d.); Wikipedia (44).

14  Gentzkow, Glaeser, and Goldin (2006) at p. 189; Petrova (2012) at p. 18.

15  Petrova (2012) at p. 18. Prof. Petrova argues that this might have occurred because bigger audiences are less homogenous and include more skeptics. These larger audiences are normally less persuadable, so that partisan messaging delivers less value.

16  Gentzkow, Glaeser, and Goldin (2006) at p. 207.

17  Bulla (n.d.)

18  Gentzkow, Glaeser, and Goldin (2006) at p. 188 and n. 1.

19  Bulla (n.d.)

20  This is the defining feature of "natural monopolies" (e.g. hydroelectric dams), which require a large initial investment to serve the first customer but can then be expanded to serve large numbers of additional customers at little or no cost. Industries that fit this criterion are almost always dominated by a single large supplier.

21  Gentzkow, Glaeser, and Goldin (2006) at p. 213.

22  The fixed costs of printing fell fifteen-fold from 1870 to 1890. Gentzkow, Glaeser, and Goldin (2006) at p. 215.

23  Hofstadter (1955) at p. 173.

24  Gentzkow, Glaeser, and Goldin (2006) at pp. 211–15.

25  Gentzkow, Glaeser, and Goldin (2006) at p. 188.

26  Gentzkow, Glaeser, and Goldin (2006) at pp. 190, 192, and 216.

27  Hofstadter (1955) at p. 174. Hearst's coverage of Spanish atrocities in Cuba famously helped win his circulation war with Joseph Pulitzer, while vastly increasing the pressure on President McKinley to declare war. Wikipedia (48); Beschloss at pp. 262–64.

28  Hofstadter (1955) at p. 175.

29  Hofstadter (1955) at pp. 173, 176; Dyck et al. (2013) at p. 549.

30  Dyck et al. (2013) show that a 1 standard deviation increase in the circulation of *McClure's* within a particular congressional district increased the chances of electing pro-consumer candidates by 4 percent, implying that roughly half of all readers were persuaded to change their votes. Dyck et al (2013) at pp. 537–8.

31  Hofstadter (1955) at p. 197.

32  Mencken [1927] at pp. 363–4, 373.

33  Hofstadter (1955) at p. 175; Gentzkow, Glaeser, and Goldin (2006) at p. 219.

34  Beyond its obvious democratic virtues, the new doctrine also offered the commercial benefit of appealing to the widest possible readership while reassuring advertisers that "their side" of the story would always be covered. Wikipedia (33). The doctrine was often paired with professional codes that taught reporters to avoid certain types of prurient stories. Barbas (2018) at pp. 18, 29, and 38.

35  Gentzkow, Glaeser, and Goldin (2006) at p. 196 and Figure 6.2.

36  There were 1,772 daily papers in 1950 but only 1,480 in 2000. Total circulation plateaued at just over 62 million (0.3 per capita) in 1970, falling to 55.8 million (0.17 per capita) thirty years later. This made two-newspaper towns a thing of the past in most big cities. Wikipedia (36).

37  Jenkins (2021b).

38  Wikipedia (16). Mutual lagged far behind its rivals, with the two NBC networks earning eleven times more ad revenue in 1940. Wikipedia (39).

39  McDonough (1994).

40  Wikipedia (15).

41  Wikipedia (15). Mutual considered launching a network but decided that it was too financially weak to succeed. Wikipedia (39).

42  For examples, see Barbas (2018) at pp. 326, 328, 330, and 331.

43  Wikipedia (36).

44  Jenkins (2021a).

45  It is easy to forget that conservative icons Laura Ingraham, Ann Coulter, and Tucker Carlson got their start as CNN hosts.

46  Savage (2019).

47  Pasley (2019).

48  Pasley (2019).

49  Mullin et al. (2020).

50  Lysiak (2020).

51  See, e.g., Maurer (2018) at pp. 683–6.

52  Shearer and Mitchell (2021).

53  Shearer and Mitchell (2021). Citizens who score lowest in political knowledge supply 23 percent of the audience for news websites compared to 31 percent for print media, 35 percent for cable news, 36 percent for network TV, 57 percent for social media, and 69 percent for local TV. Mitchell et al. (2020) at pp. 5 and 9. Conversely, 81 percent of users who get their news from social media have heard conspiracy theories about COVID-19 compared to 62 percent on cable TV and 63 percent in print. Mitchell et al. (2020) at p. 6.

54  One in five (18 percent) of Americans gets their political news primarily through social media compared to 16 percent for cable TV, 25 percent for news websites, 13 percent for network TV, and 16 percent for local TV. Just 3 percent rely on print media. Mitchell et al. (2020) at p. 3.

55  The situation is further aggravated by substantial barriers to entry including fixed plant and equipment costs for print newspapers and various regulatory and technology ("bandwidth") constraints for over-the-air broadcasters. There are also more subtle issues. News is an experience good whose quality cannot be estimated until it has been consumed. But in that case, viewers who are happy with their existing provider may not take the time to sample competitors' choice of news stories. Worse, it is almost impossible for audiences to judge news outlets' quality, except on those rare occasions when one of them "breaks" a story ahead of its competitors. New entrants lack this track record and can often take years to build one.

56  Herfindahl indexes reduce market concentration to a single number defined by the formula (Market Share of Largest Competitor)$^2$ + (Market Share of

2nd Largest Competitor)$^2$ + (Market Share of 3rd Largest Competitor)$^2$ + etc. This formula has the useful property that markets dominated by one large firm have bigger indexes than markets shared between two firms, let alone markets where most demand is supplied by multiple small firms. While higher indexes imply more concentration and (presumably) market power, firms' economic power has no obvious relationship with any specific score. See US Department of Justice (2010) at §5.3.

57 Based on market shares reported by Gentzkow, Glaeser, and Goldin (2006) at p. 216 (nineteenth- and twentieth-century newspapers), Johnson (2021) (cable and network television), and Shearer and Mitchell (2021) at p. 5 (social media).

58 This was practically inevitable since economic theory predicts that firms in highly competitive markets have such thin profit margins that they cannot afford ad purchases in the first place.

59 Ellman and Germano (2009) at p. 681.

60 Dyck et al. (2013) at p. 549; Ellman (2009) at p. 681; Petrova (2011) at p. 18.

61 Ellman and Germano (2009) at p. 681; Petrova (2012) at p. 26.

62 Petrova (2012) at p. 18.

63 The earliest and simplest model was folklore, in which the tellers and the audience are essentially identical. In the way of Adam Smith's pin factory, progress since then has relied on specialization. The rise of itinerant bards in Homer's time emphasized repeat interactions between a talented author and thousands of successive audiences. Later developments included elite literary salons that helped authors polish their works, and publishers who constantly sought out what they hoped would be popular titles. Print technologies and copyright further expanded the list of specialists to include bookstores, libraries, newspaper critics, and literary agents. See generally Maurer (2014).

64 There were exceptions. Newspapers routinely paid outside freelancers or "stringers" to provide additional content, copied each other's stories, and subscribed to wire services. Gossip journalists also supported enormous networks of paid tipsters and private detectives whose tactics regularly included bribing celebrities' servants, wiretapping their telephones, and paying Western Union employees to copy private telegrams. The practice continued with the *National Enquirer*'s paid network of over 5,000 tipsters in the 1980s and TMC, which operated a similar network in the early 2000s. Barbas (2018) at pp. 82, 102, 326, and 330.

65 These networks are almost certainly subsets of the social networks we described in Chapter 2. The difference in this chapter is to see them less as passive recipients than as the active inventors and improvers of new political arguments.

66 Huckfeldt et al. (2013) at p. 9.

67 Conservative firebrand Ann Coulter, a long-time denizen of the system, writes that "Twitter is where the NYT, Politico and Fox News etc. get their stories and find their guests," usually after a delay of twelve to thirty-six hours. Mainstream outlets also mine the service for its often-powerful video, investigative reporting, and memes. Coulter (2022).

68   Scholars have long argued that the apparent perfection of European folklore
     from *The Odyssey* to Grimms' *Fairy Tales* reflects the accumulated polish-
     ing of incremental improvements suggested by live audiences over countless
     retellings. See Sale (1977) at pp. 375–6 and 379–80.
69   Voigtlander and Voth (2012). Hawes (2019) makes the still more ambitious
     case that oral traditions explain why Germany's politics change abruptly at
     the Elbe – and have since Roman times.
70   Thompson (2007).
71   Anon (n.d.) (m).
72   Heller (2015); Hargett (2020).
73   In the predigital era, *Divine Secrets of the Ya-Ya Sisterhood* (1996) bounced
     around reader networks for two years before becoming an unexpected best-
     seller. Deschatres and Sornette (2005) at p. 26. Such stories have become
     increasingly common as the web enables ever larger word-of-mouth net-
     works across readers. Here, the first example was *Fifty Shades of Grey*
     (2011), which became wildly successful on the web after several mainstream
     publishers had turned it down. Since then the Big Five publishers have rou-
     tinely monitored self-published titles and offered the strongest ones book
     contracts. Today this path accounts for roughly 10 percent of all "top ten"
     bestsellers. Waldvogel and Reimers (2015) at p. 47.
74   For computer simulations, see, e.g., Deschatres and Sornette (2005) at p. 5;
     Watts and Dodds (2007) at pp. 442–3. The leading experimental evidence
     comes from Professor Salgalnik and coauthors, who constructed a private
     online music market and asked tens of thousands of real consumers to rank
     forty-eight songs. After running the experiment multiple times, they found
     that the popularity of each "hit" depended partly on its quality, but also
     varied significantly from one iteration to the next.
75   The catch, according to our "nobody knows anything" principle, is that even
     highly skilled editors often guess badly. As one Disney executive put it, "You
     can buy an opening weekend," but if the product is bad "It will be disappoint-
     ing for you and for them"; Elberse (2013) at p. 69. Barnes & Noble typically
     returns about one-fourth of the books on its shelves to the publisher unsold.
     The figure for new titles is often closer to one-half. Trachtenberg (2020b).
76   Giridharas (2019).
77   Wood and Pierre (2019).
78   Butter (2020) at p. 88.
79   Facebook "Fan pages" were once the only way in which celebrities and polit-
     ical figures could represent themselves on Facebook. George (2012).
80   The bracket from 4 to 17 million Fans includes various political celebrities
     ranging from Barack Obama (17 m) and Donald Trump (11.9 m) down to
     Paul Ryan (5 m) and Sarah Palin (4 m), along with national media outlets
     like Fox News (17 m), *The New York Times* (17 m), and *The Wall Street
     Journal* (6 m). Online and print newspapers like the *Huffington Post* (10 m),
     *Breitbart News* (4 m), MSNBC (2.3 m), *The New York Daily News* (3.1 m),
     and *Esquire* (1.3 m) boast somewhat smaller audiences. Finally, politicians
     with national name recognition, entrepreneurial TV personalities, online
     journalist sites, and special interest groups round out the list. Examples

included Elizabeth Warren (3.1 m), Rick Perry (1.1 m), Conan O'Brien (3 m), Rachel Maddow (2 m), MoveOn.org's *Democracy in Action* blog (1.1 m), *Politico* (1.8 m), and *The Daily Beast* (2.2 m). It is worth remembering that nonpolitician celebrities like Ellen DeGeneres (29.6 m) swamp all of these players. While audiences presumably understand that such people are not policy experts, this hardly matters to social voters who care more for conformity than substance. Moreover, politics is about more than expertise. A celebrity's normative view that society ought to help certain people and causes is just as good as anyone else's.

81 The Indianapolis-based "Four Chicks on the Right" page was founded by two friends who parleyed their idea for a conservative talk show into a local radio program. At its height, the page claimed just over one million fans, supporting two full-time writers in addition to the owners. Anon (n.d. (e)). The group specializes in combing the internet for content that makes prominent Democrats look foolish. Its most famous coup was finding Nancy Pelosi's "We'll have to pass the bill to see what's in it" comment on Obamacare. Maguill (2017). This was quickly picked up by Fox News and has circulated widely ever since. Capehart (2012).

82 Even sites with fewer than 10,000 followers can be influential. Brooklyn real estate seller Chaya Raichik created her "Libs of Tik Tok" Twitter page to repost progressive political videos which she treats as unintentional satire. Raichik, in turn, crowdsources much of her content from followers. Her influence derives mostly from the many Fox News personalities and conservative politicians who monitor and selectively republish her videos. Lorenz (2022).

83 Tara Burton describes how teenaged admirers repurposed the *Harry Potter* books' simple good-vs.-evil cosmology for social justice advocacy. Burton (2020) at pp. 76–7. A less mainstream example involves the quarrel between white male gamers and feminists who wanted game designers to create more diverse characters. While the gamers' attacks started on the radical "4chan" platform, they were sufficiently innovative to be picked up by aspiring alt-right journalists who spread them to wider audiences. Burton (2020) at pp. 95–6.

84 Maier (2022).

85 Revision World (n.d.)

86 Hofstadter (1955) at pp. 10 and 27.

87 Hofstadter (1955) at pp. 74, 79, and 260.

88 Hofstadter (1955) at pp. 9 and 13.

89 Conspiracy books share this characteristic with most literary genres, notably including crime and espionage novels. Here a comparatively small number of titles, such as Joseph Wambaugh's police stories and John le Carré's spy novels, have focused on stories that seem true to life. What is striking, though, is how many reject this, choosing instead to keep alive the wholly fictional worlds invented by Ian Fleming and Raymond Chandler in the 1940s. The advantage seems obvious. On the one hand, exposition is simplified since authors can reasonably expect a certain amount of background knowledge from readers. On the other, readers know what to expect: To some extent, at least, they really can judge a book by its cover.

90 Butter (2020) at p. 130.
91 Butter (2020) at p. 26.
92 Décugis, Guéna, and Leplongeon (2021) at pp. 73–81.
93 Butter (2020) at pp. 154–5.
94 Wikipedia (55).
95 For a discussion of this logic in the context of open source software production, see Maurer (2012) at pp. 282–4.
96 Horwitz and Scheck (2021).
97 Publishers already use artificial intelligence to find out what children like and commission human authors to write books that incorporate these elements. Gammerman (2021).
98 Barbas (2018) at p. 18, 29, and 38–9; Farrow (2019) at p. 41.
99 Downs (1957) at pp. 207–8.
100 The effect is amplified when newspapers target average readers so that voters with large information budgets are never offered as much information as they would like.
101 Chang (2018); Smart (2018).
102 Media rivals almost always charge the same price for their products – five cents for old-time newspapers, zero for TV news.
103 Technically, the "customers" for cable news are advertisers rather than viewers. But that hardly matters so long as Fox viewers refuse to watch MSNBC and vice versa. This makes Fox and MSNBC "monopolies" for any advertiser trying to reach their respective audiences.
104 Ahlin and Ahlin (2013) at pp. 1752–3; Hotelling (1929).
105 Economists have long debated whether Hotelling's solution is stable. D'Aspremont, Gabszewicz, and Thisse (1979) argue that firms offering similar products will each try to undercut the monopoly price by just enough to attract the entire mass of customers between them and their rival(s). The resulting competition destabilizes Hotelling's result where (a) there are only two competitors, or else (b) there are many firms sharing a crowded field. On the other hand, Prof. Economides has shown that price stability returns where consumers have low willingness to pay, so that they buy no product at all instead of switching to a competing one. Economides (1993) at p. 305. Ahlin and Ahlin similarly find that firms can evade conflict by randomly offering better terms to some consumers and not others. Hotelling's result can also be stabilized by a wide variety of market imperfections including congestion in the most popular product, brand snobbery benefiting less popular products, and high transportation costs. Ahlin and Ahlin (2013) at pp. 1752–3.
106 Opinion-heavy news also cuts costs by replacing expensive investigative journalism with invective and ideology. This is particularly visible in Fox's model of funding opinion pieces at the expense of a smaller newsroom.
107 One might wonder why over-the-air broadcasters have not adopted their own Hotelling strategy by imitating cable's Left–Right positioning. One possibility is that the broadcast audience is bigger and therefore less polarized than the cable one, delaying the onset of Hotelling-style segmentation.

108 Meanwhile we are left with a puzzle. Hotelling logic predicts that a three-firm industry should be equally spaced with firms occupying the Left, Right, and center. Why then are there two on the Left? One possibility is that the middle does not lend itself to segmentation because centrists are more willing to sample equally from the Left and Right. Then too, CNN appears to be having second thoughts. Since 2022, its new leadership has sporadically pushed the network's on-air hosts to be less partisan. Ecarma (2022); Fischer (2022).

109 Wikipedia (5).

110 While viewers can theoretically assemble this information by repeatedly sampling Left- and Right-leaning outlets, limited information budgets make this prohibitive.

111 Downs (1957) at p. 235.

112 Free speech was far more restricted under the Wilson Administration than it had been during the Civil War – when Lincoln was routinely vilified – or would be in World War II or the McCarthy era. The restrictions were also incredibly broad, identifying threats to the war effort with anything that sapped morale. Barry (2005) at p. 206.

113 The carrots were reserved for the bulk of the population who were sympathetic or neutral. But the Wilson Administration did not shrink from coercion. Eugene Debs, who had received nearly one million votes in the 1912 election, was sentenced to ten years for opposing the war, while, nearly 200 union members were convicted in mass trials in Illinois, California, and Oregon. Local authorities also turned a blind eye when vigilantes locked 1,200 Industrial Workers of the World (IWW) members in boxcars and dragged union organizer Frank Little to his death behind an automobile. Barry (2005) at pp. 206–7. In all, the government prosecuted 2,200 protesters on charges of sedition of whom 1,055 were convicted. Vaughn (1980) at p. 230. Many states also passed their own sedition laws and arrested dissenters. Trickey (2018).

114 Vaughn (1980) at p. 35.

115 As President Wilson told followers, "Any man who carries a hyphen about with him carries a dagger that he is ready to plunge into the vitals of this Republic whenever he gets ready; Wikipedia (27). Fellow Progressive Theodore Roosevelt, still hoping for a triumphant return to the White House, agreed:

> There is no room in this country for hyphenated Americanism ... The one absolutely certain way of bringing this nation to ruin ... would be to permit it to become a tangle of squabbling nationalities ... each preserving its separate nationality, each at heart feeling more sympathy with Europeans of that nationality ... The only man who is a good American is the man who is an American and nothing else. (Wikipedia (27))

116 Daly (2017).

117 Morrison (1980) at p. 150.

118 Vaughn (1980) at pp. 37–51.

119 Vaughn (1980) at p. 250.

120 Vaughn (1980) at p. 250. Notable exceptions included *The San Francisco Examiner, The Washington Post,* and *New York Evening Post.* Vaughn (1980) at p. 345.

121 Vaughn (1980) at p. 32. The habit of protecting the government quickly spread to other subjects, most notably claims that the mounting 1918 influenza pandemic wasn't serious. These proved massively short-sighted: Once citizens saw the disease kill people, they stopped believing government and press alike. Barry (2005) at pp. 340–1.

122 Vaughn (1980) at p. 208.

123 Daly (2017).

124 Vaughn (1980) at p. 233.

125 Vaughn (1980) at pp. 236, 238.

126 Vaughn (1980) at pp. 47, 52, 235; Johnson (1962) at pp. 46–58.

127 This was an era when even *The New York Times* called members of radical unions "treasonable conspirators" and urged the government to make "short work" of them. Barry (2005).

128 Tabloids routinely invented news and doctored photographs into the 1940s. Barbas (2018) at pp. 18 and 48.

129 Barbas (2018) at p. 42. Similar racist and misogynistic formulas drove their immensely popular successor, *Confidential* magazine, in the 1950s. Barbas (2018) at p. 46.

130 Barbas (2018) at p. 55.

131 Barbas (2018) at p. 120. The archetypal example, *Broadway Brevities*, ran from 1916 to 1932 and mainly existed to support an extortion racket which suppressed salacious stories in exchange for advertising. Barbas (2018) at p. 121. Two successor papers lasted into the 1940s. Barbas (2018) at pp. 124–5.

132 Rosen (2011).

133 Jenkins (2019). The cartel is even stronger when it is organized by government. President Kennedy had little trouble persuading *The New York Times* and *The Washington Post* not to publish confidential information that would have revealed the then still secret Cuban Missile Crisis in 1962. Plokhy (2021) at p. 171. Suppression plainly works best for unfolding national security crises where readers are overwhelmingly likely to condemn any editor who defies secrecy. By comparison, the Nixon Administration famously failed to stop *The New York Times* from publishing the "Pentagon Papers" exposé of government duplicity in Vietnam. The difference, presumably, was that the material was historical at the time of release, and for that reason could not put ongoing military operations or American lives in jeopardy.

134 *National Enquirer* owner AMI routinely suppressed damaging stories in exchange for tips and exclusives. Farrow (2019) at pp. 30–1.

135 Then governor Andrew Cuomo promised one outlet an exclusive interview if it killed its story, while threatening to retaliate against another if it published. Pehme (2021).

136 Barbas (2018) at pp. 18, 29, 80–3, 87, and 156. The strategy was not as quixotic as it seems. Not only did it immediately negate advertisers' investment in the current issue, but it showed that the same thing would happen again if future issues offended. Hearst followed essentially the same strategy when he lobbied MGM to buy and destroy all copies of *Citizen Kane*. Anon (2016b).

137 The strategy is particularly effective for sex scandals, which typically depend on the testimony of a single witness. *Enquirer* publisher David Pecker is said to have killed perhaps ten fully reported stories about President Trump. Farrow (2019) at p. 31. Staffers were told not only to ignore leads but also to seek out and suppress whatever new information they came across. Farrow (2019) at p. 32; Swaine (2018).

138 High-profile lawsuits by Robert Mitchum, Carol Burnett, and Jesse Ventura killed several well-known scandal magazines in the second half of the twentieth century. Barbas (2018) at pp. 327 and 331. The deterrent was dramatically reinvigorated when Dominion Voting settled its defamation suit against Fox News for an astonishing $787 million in 2023. The size of the recovery almost certainly reflected politics: Many jurors would already have known and strongly disliked reporting that supported former President's Trump's claim that the 2020 election had been "stolen."

139 The phenomenon is similar to mass tort litigation: When plaintiffs win a case, law firms often file dozens more. Later, when plaintiffs lose, many of these same cases settle. Maurer and Scotchmer (unpublished research).

140 Barbas (2018) at p. 164.

141 *The New Yorker* and *The New York Times* published independent investigations into sexual harassment claims against Hollywood mogul Harvey Weinstein within five days of each other in 2017. Kantor and Twohey (2017); Farrow (2017).

142 Farrow (2019) at p. 246 ("Now, finally, I had [persuaded] *The New Yorker* [to run the Weinstein story], but it might be too late. I had no idea what the *Times* had. For all I knew, if it published first, our work at the magazine would be rendered moot.")

143 For a rigorous description of this logic in the context of patent races, see Scotchmer (2006) at pp. 112–14 and 120–3.

144 Green (2021). There was ample reason to investigate. Chinese whistleblowers, former US Secretary of State Mike Pompeo, and former MI6 intelligence chief Sir Richard Dearlove had all publicly endorsed the theory. Despite this, a top *New York Times* editor twice refused senior staffers' requests to investigate, telling them that such a story was "dangerous" and "untouchable." Among other things, publication would have alienated the *Times'* readership by supporting President Trump's claims of Chinese guilt in an election year. It would also have angered Chinese-controlled companies that were paying *The Times* millions in advertising. Green (2021).

145 Academic scientists often face strong peer pressure not to make controversial statements that might "split the community." See generally, Maurer (2017b).

146 Wade, Mecklin, and Bronson (2021).

147 Unreliable reporting also hurts ratings. CNN and MSNBC lost significant market share after the Mueller investigation failed to confirm their earlier claims that President Trump had colluded with Russia.

148 Baker (2020).

149 1.94 million people read the *Post*'s Hunter Biden story in the first twenty-four hours compared to 3.69 million who read an *Atlantic* article accusing President

Trump of calling fallen soldiers "losers and suckers," and 4.12 million people who read a *New York Times* story describing a single year of Trump's tax returns. Twitter also locked *The Post*'s entire account for two days. Unlike Twitter, Facebook didn't block users from linking to the *Post* story. It did however flag it for third-party fact-checkers who immediately called it "false," a tag that normally suppresses views by 80 percent. Bond (2020).

150  Jenkins (2021d).

151  Swasey and Jin (2020).

152  At least one US Senator has charged that Facebook's censorship teams communicate with their opposite numbers at Twitter and Google to ensure that all three companies maintain a united front. CEO Mark Zuckerberg has denied coordination, but admits that it is "pretty normal" for Facebook employees to communicate with their peers at other companies. Anon (2020f).

153  Mencken [1927] at pp. 373–4.

154  Gentzkow, Glaeser, and Goldin (2006) at p. 207.

155  Businesses have been forming coalitions to punish newspapers and magazines since the "muckraking" era of the early 1900s. More recently, Procter & Gamble refused to advertise in any issue of a magazine that included stories about gun control, abortion, the occult or cults, disparaged religion, or portrayed business "as cold [or] ruthless" into the 1960s. Coca-Cola similarly punished NBC for criticizing the company's working conditions in the 1980s. Ellman and Germano (2009) at p. 682 and n. 5.

156  US tobacco companies withdrew all ads from *Mother Jones* and *Reader's Digest* after the magazines ran articles describing the medical evidence against smoking. Ellman and Germano (2009) at p. 682 and n. 5. This made other outlets visibly more cautious. Industry has since mounted similar pushbacks over climate change and automobile safety. Ellman and Germano (2009) at pp. 681–2.

157  Petrova (2012) at p. 26.

158  Petrova (2012) at p. 18.

159  Mencken [1927] at pp. 374–5. Whether modern publishers use their power as benignly is unclear. The "Twitter Files" revelations show that Twitter worked closely with the White House and other political organizations to suppress what used to be considered "everyday views"; Wade (2022). That said, Twitter's gatekeepers did resist Congressman Adam Schiff's request to suspend journalist Paul Sperry's account, at least for a time, for revealing the name of a Trump whistleblower. Golding (2023).

160  Hearst made an unknown preacher named Billy Graham into the country's leading evangelist by instructing his editors to "Puff Graham" in 1949. Buntin (2010) at p. 151. Hearst also blackballed Hollywood *Wunderkind* Orson Welles for making *Citizen Kane*. Hearst immediately banned all ads and even mentions of the film from his newspapers and threatened to sue RKO if it dared to release the picture. Anon (2016a). When RKO went ahead anyway, Hearst pressured Fox, Paramount, and Loews to refuse distribution. In the end, RKO forced out Welles and the studio head who had overseen the project. Welles' best years as an artist were already behind him; Anon (n.d. (b)).

161 The argument assumes that the public judges the honesty of each media company separately. If it lumps them together individual outlets have no incentive to be honest since they will be punished regardless.

162 It is much harder to ban entire communities. Commercial hosting sites typically become viable once they approach a million online members, half of whom visit daily. Wells and Lovett (2018).

163 Anon (2020a).

164 The ability of even totalitarian regimes to whitewash reality is limited. Nazi propaganda minister Josef Goebbels never even tried to suppress the regime's biggest disasters, like the loss of 500,000 soldiers at Stalingrad or 40,000 civilians in the bombing of Hamburg. Too many people knew the stories at first hand. Given that German news outlets needed at least some credibility to influence the public, telling such outsized lies would have ended their usefulness to the regime.

165 Academic studies find that conservatives consume more fake news than liberals. Guess, Nyhan, and Reifler (2018). But that is not because conservatives are stupid: Indeed, tests show that liberals are roughly as credulous. Alcott and Gentzkow (2017). Rather, the problem is that conservatives are underserved; i.e. that the big media outlets publish few stories that interest them.

166 The rise of objective journalism following the "Great Quieting" of partisanship in the early 1900s may be an example of this.

167 This statement refers mostly to centrists. Convinced partisans are unlikely to change their minds and therefore care less about the truth; indeed, they might *prefer* press dishonesty as a weapon against "the other side." Social voters similarly care relatively little about facts so long as outlets reliably identify the "right" opinions.

# 5

# Mass Democracy

## Political Parties and Elections

Every four years, American democracy narrows 330 million opinions down to a single plan of action. Yet Madison's formal institutions play almost no role in the first and largest step in this process – reducing the debate to just two distinct choices. Instead, this is mostly left to the country's political parties. The development would have horrified Madison. To him, parties were something to be resisted: The only reason to tolerate them, he insisted, was that the only known cure – tyranny – was even worse.[1]

For once, Madison was wrong. The mass parties which began to spring up in the 1790s vastly improved his system. The key was competition. On the one hand, it forced parties to invent the most attractive bundle of promises they could possibly find, and then try to follow through if elected. On the other, nineteenth-century Americans quickly found that two-party competition usually made politics more centrist, even if the precise reasons for this would not be clearly understood until the work of Hotelling and Downs a century later. Sections 5.1 and 5.2 review these results.

Today, though, there is more to say. First, the politics of polarization and gridlock show that not all voters reason the way Downs thought they would, and this fraction changes over time. Section 5.3 asks how this changes Downs' results. Then too, the Downsian model assumes that there are always clear winners and ignores the possibility of deadlock.[2] But legislatures *do* deadlock, and Madison's checks and balances deliberately *encourage* these frictions. Section 5.4 explains how this opens political strategies beyond Downs' model. Finally, Downs assumed that politicians would rationally choose whatever platforms and candidates seem most likely to win elections. Section 5.5 asks how the parties' actual methods fall short of this ideal.

## 5.1 DEMOCRACY EVOLVING

The Framers loathed political parties. Where we see parties offering – however cynically – policy choices to voters, the Framers imagined gangs or "factions" that were merely interested in enriching themselves.[3] The results, Madison said, could only be "injustice," "instability," and "confusion." Worse still, factions had often proven fatal to past democracies and were now spreading across America too.[4]

Yet the Framers' solution, "separation of powers," did little to contain these dangers. At most, it put sand in the gears so that election winners could not change the country too quickly. It is hard, more than two centuries later, to appreciate just how gloomy this remedy was. The US would stumble from one bad law to the next, barely avoiding disaster. And in the end its luck would run out, and some especially disastrous policy would overwhelm it entirely.

What happened instead was a kind of miracle. By the 1820s, the country had two mass parties. These held each other in check, providing most of the moderation that Madison had originally looked for in the Senate and the president. Separation of powers was now just a second line of defense. In Prof. Hofstadter's memorable verdict, "Without the two-party system, it was dubious that their constitutional system for all its ingenuity could have been made operative."[5]

We should not blame the Framers for hating parties. Parties from the Roman Republic to the English Tudors had been structured like mafia gangs, with a handful of bosses telling followers how to vote and the latter unquestioningly obeying.[6] The outcome was a politics less about issues than the enmities of the rich and powerful;[7] corrupt politicians who used the people's trust to advance their own personal interests;[8] and the pursuit of goals "adverse to the rights of other citizens, or to the permanent and aggregate interests of the community."[9]

The pattern was little better in eighteenth-century Britain or its colonies. England's parties had consisted almost entirely of Members of Parliament "held together primarily by hopes of obtaining office," supplemented by blood relations and friendship. The result was a politics based on party leaders' "greed and whims," in which transient coalitions would form during crises and disappear afterward.[10] While politicians had begun to call themselves "Whigs" and "Tories," the labels mostly described "broad stylistic and ideological characteristics" instead of organized bodies,[11] and many legislators claimed no affiliation to either beyond their membership in one of Parliament's endlessly shifting factions.[12] Kings exploited this formlessness by organizing "Court Parties" whose loyalty was purchased with government funds.[13]

Meanwhile in America, colonial politics had been similarly rooted in governor-supported court parties and the "personal factionalism of magnates and notables."[14] This meant that even in the Framers' day New York politics, for example, proceeded through family cliques in "a dense tangle of Livingstonians and DeLanceyites, of Lewisites, Burrites, and Clintonians," while citizens outside the Assembly had essentially no influence. And when significant economic and social issues did reach legislatures, they were almost always resolved by *ad hoc* personal alliances rather than stable political groups.[15]

The good news was that a more democratic, bottom-up version of politics had begun to emerge. For the first half of the eighteenth century, the Whig Party had dominated Parliament in the traditionally corrupt and policy-free way. But the rising power of middle-class voters made the Whigs vulnerable, with especially controversial and directly felt issues sometimes inciting waves of public meetings and petitions. The South Sea financial bubble (1721) and new wine and tobacco taxes (1733) sparked particularly memorable outcries that, for a time at least, seemed to offer the Tories a path back to the majority.[16] But it was the king's war against Frederick the Great (1742–5) that threatened to make Parliament ungovernable. Desperate, the prime minister demanded that the king invite William Pitt into the government. The king agreed, even though he hated Pitt for having spoken out against the war. But this was precisely why the people trusted the man, and Pitt's performance in office – astonishingly for the time he refused to collect a penny more than his official salary – quickly won "the admiration and confidence of the middle classes, the City, and the rising mercantile towns, and the country freeholders."[17] Where earlier politicians had relied on their connections in Parliament to reach high office, Pitt would pioneer the radically new strategy of leveraging his "weight in the country." Now dubbed the "Great Commoner," he became prime minister in 1756. As Dr. Johnson observed, Horace Walpole had become prime minister in 1721 as "a Minister given by the Crown to the people." Pitt, on the other hand, "was a Minister given by the people to the Crown."[18]

Henceforth, successful politicians would have to anticipate and offer what voters wanted.

The Framers' Constitution soon unleashed a similar mass politics in America. The reason was the country's rapidly expanding suffrage. This started when new states like Kentucky liberalized eligibility to vote to attract desperately needed settlers.[19] Soon even the original thirteen states found that they had to expand their own voter rolls to keep citizens from emigrating.[20] The experience of mass voting also undercut conservative resistance by showing that the lower classes could be trusted to cast thoughtful votes after all.[21] The result, by 1824, was that nearly all white males outside Virginia, Rhode Island, and Louisiana could vote.[22] In 1840 90 percent of the country's white male population was eligible,[23] and twenty years after that essentially all of them could vote.[24]

Modern political parties grew up to persuade and mobilize this flood of new voters. Probably the first stirrings were thirty-five "Democratic Societies" founded in 1793. These proto-parties – part fraternal organizations, part political discussion groups – also urged citizens to vote for their favored candidates.[25] Then in 1800, Jefferson used his party's superior campaign machinery to drive the Federalists from power.[26] Soon both parties had permanent organizations to deliver their messages in every community.[27] By the 1820s these had grown into armies of rank-and-file campaigners who turned up at each election to make sure supporters got to the polls. The implication was nothing short of revolutionary: Politics had become a middle-class profession, displacing the elites who had long "shape[d] how the broad mass of Americans would think and speak."[28] By the 1840 election the system had reached its definitive form, with such still-familiar features as traveling orators, mass meetings numbering in the tens of thousands, and occasional violence. Former President Adams, elected just sixteen years before, saw in these developments "a revolution in the habits and manners of the people" – and warned that the "natural progress" of such a system was to become increasingly "antagonistical" with a "manifest tendency to civil war."[29]

Strangely, the biggest political development of all was inadvertent. The idea of proportional representation did not reach the US until the early twentieth century, and would remain limited even then.[30] Instead, America practiced a winner-take-all system which gave small parties hardly any chance of sending representatives to Congress.[31] This meant that a vote for any party other than the two frontrunners was almost certainly wasted.[32] The advantage was further reinforced by the fact that voters hardly ever knew much about politicians' platforms, so that party endorsements became crucial in deciding between candidates. Finally, there was a kind of Catch-22: Given that third parties had no track record, voters could not be sure that they would actually be able to govern, much less keep their promises. And this same skepticism kept the major parties on top.

Of course, third parties could still win if one of the major parties was split by internal conflict and collapsed.[33] But otherwise the dominant parties were indestructible so long as they were willing to abandon outworn orthodoxies and, when necessary, adopt third-party issues as their own.[34] Indeed, stealing issues was positively good for democracy, since any party that remained truly faithful to its founding principles would sooner or later fall out of step with the public. Much better for both parties to become empty vessels, competing to find and offer whatever agendas Americans might like best at the time.

Political philosophers spent years catching up to these developments. Indeed, none of them seems to have had anything good to say about parties before 1770, when Burke repurposed the familiar idea of checks and balances to argue that a multiparty system would select whichever platform best served the voters.[35] Yet twenty years later, Thomas Jefferson still spoke for most when he declared, "If I could not go to heaven but with a party, I would not go there at all."[36] In the end, theorizing did less to settle the issue than practical experience. This led Madison to qualify his hatred of "faction" as early as 1792.[37] Nine years later he even allowed that "party division," instead of being regrettable, might actually be "necessary to induce each to watch and relate to the people the proceedings of the other."[38]

Still, Madison remained the exception. Down to the 1820s, most partisans preferred to believe that, given time, the vast majority of Americans would come to their side, after which party competition would wither away.[39] The prediction seemed to come true when the Federalist Party, which had doggedly opposed the War of 1812, suddenly collapsed after Andrew Jackson won a large and almost entirely unexpected victory at the Battle of New Orleans.[40] All the same, the wildly misnamed "Era of Good Feelings" that followed was a deep disappointment. The immediate reason was that voters still wanted a choice. With just one party left, this meant seeking alternatives to whichever presidential candidate the Jefferson-Republican establishment endorsed. The result was a series of free-for-all elections among the party's various factions, culminating in a scandalous four-way split in 1824 that let congressional insider John

Quincy Adams prevail even though Andrew Jackson had won the popular vote.[41] Meanwhile, the absence of a coherent opposition made party
discipline less important to voters, who were then less likely to punish
congressmen who defied the president. This deprived Presidents Madison
and Monroe of the political leverage they needed to influence the House,
which now seized unprecedented power.[42]

Above all, widespread suffrage introduced a new style of mass politics
starting with Andrew Jackson's victory over John Quincy Adams in the
landslide election of 1828. The innovations that year included the first
national nominating convention, a public speaking tour, and a powerful local campaign organization. These arguably helped rational voters
by improving transparency and making information easier to come by.
Other innovations, however, were only comprehensible in terms of social
voting. These included emphasizing Jackson's charisma, establishing
local "Hickory clubs," and holding barbecues and parades.[43] Minimally
informative, each existed mainly to provide a reason for partisans to display their solidarity in public.

Jackson also introduced the enduring American narrative of a man of
the people taking his country back from Washington elites.[44]Above all, he
understood the uses of controversy. To enemies, Jackson's claim that elites
had stolen the election of 1824 and were using the Bank of the United
States to take over the country[45] made him a demagogue; to his friends,
he was a champion of the common man. But either way, polarization
encouraged people to vote. Added to all the campaign's superior organization and ballyhoo, Jackson's rhetoric boosted turnout from 27 percent
in his unsuccessful 1824 bid to an astonishing 57 percent in 1828.[46]

Jackson's tactics were equally innovative between elections, stressing his
ties to the people and claiming mandates when he won elections.[47] The
result encouraged Americans to reimagine Madison's institutions to include
Jackson's insistence that the president, unlike Congress, had been elected
by all the people – and should therefore claim the true center of power.[48]

By 1828, former Jefferson-Republicans who supported Jackson were
calling themselves "The Democracy," soon to become the Democratic
Party. Six years later, those who opposed Jackson's supposedly monar-
chical ambitions founded the competing "American Whig Party."[49] By
1842 they were strong enough to eject Democrat Martin Van Buren from
the White House.[50] By then most Americans had come to see two-party
competition with its occasional alternations of power as the best – if

still highly imperfect – way to implement democracy.[51] The consensus was more practical than philosophical. As Prof. Wallace emphasizes, the new mass parties had many virtues: They were popular, democratically run, and gave ordinary people a role in government.[52] Still, acceptance was grudging: While van Buren granted that the other party might sometimes contribute useful ideas, he insisted that his own party was best and should hold office most of the time.[53]

Even so, the important thing was to avoid repeating the Era of Good Feelings when, "In the place of two great parties arrayed against one another in a fair and open contest for the establishment of principles, ... the country [had been] overrun with personal factions."[54] Whatever its defects, the party system had replaced the chaotic and largely hidden politics of faction with open debates.[55] In the meanwhile, the growing expectation that the two major parties would alternate in power introduced a certain sportsmanlike tolerance,[56] even if no one could quite give up the idea that their own party was wiser and more virtuous.[57]

### 5.2 DOWNSIAN POLITICS

Voters make their choices in a great many ways, all of which can broadly be called "rational." Nevertheless, the conventional assumption since Prof. Downs' work in the 1950s is that they choose between party platforms, supplemented by occasional stand-ins like ideology or recommendations from trusted intermediaries.[58] Here we trace the main results of this model, deferring alternative hypotheses to the next section.

Downsian politicians seek bundles of issues that a majority of voters will prefer to all others. Nineteenth-century Americans quickly noticed that these winning bundles almost always favored centrist causes and candidates. Even so, the insight remained mostly intuitive until 1929, when Harold Hotelling's landmark paper showed that the problem of maximizing votes was identical to the one manufacturers faced in deciding which features new consumer products should have.[59] For reasons already discussed in Chapter 4, he found that the answer depended on the number of competing players, "N." Hotelling then went on to show that, for the American two-party (N = 2) case, the correct solution was for both parties to target the median voter. In other words, politicians would imagine the country's voters lined up along the usual Left–Right spectrum and aim their platforms squarely at the middle. Since this was the winning strategy for both parties, the system would then converge on the (hopefully moderate) middle no matter who won the election.[60] It followed that both sides would have a similar chance of winning and that most elections would be close.

Of course, that oversimplifies matters. Since new facts and ideologies are forever arising, parties cannot simply repeat the same campaign promises season after season. This implies that whichever side comes across a new winning platform before the other can sometimes win so-called realigning elections by landslide margins. Alternatively, a sufficiently nimble opponent may sometimes develop its own countermessage fast enough that the realignment happens *between* elections without giving either side any lasting advantage.[61] In either case, as soon as one party's ideology proves effective, the other must "revise [its] ideologies to attract votes from the same group."[62] Finally, the fact that both politicians and voters have limited information makes errors inevitable. This implies that the eventual winner will often be decided by small accidents and misunderstandings.

The empirical evidence for Hotelling's prediction is compelling. Indeed, the number of consecutive presidential victories by either party from 1856 to 1980 is indistinguishable from a coin toss.[63] Moreover, many elections are also close, notably including the 2000 contest between George Bush and Al Gore which came down to just 537 votes out of 50 million cast. Finally, Downs' model implies that the two major parties should behave like empty vessels with essentially no fixed beliefs beyond winning. Over the long run, history bears this out.[64]

The short-term picture is more complicated. On the one hand, all organizations are rigid: Even when the public wants change, party members are reluctant to move too far ahead of their colleagues. On the other, withdrawing or amending promises damages credibility. This encourages parties to change their most recent platforms as little as possible.[65] It also makes individual politicians reluctant to change course, although this dynamic is partly offset by the fact that each party includes many voices, with new factions constantly coming onto the scene. The result is that insurgents often advocate platform changes as a lever to oust party leaders and take power themselves.[66] Finally, our "nobody knows anything" principle implies that no politician is ever entirely sure of what the public wants.[67] This is exemplified by the long marathon of presidential primaries, in which the leaders change in rapid and unpredictable ways after each week's elections.

Hotelling's analysis was an enormous improvement compared to earlier accounts. All the same, it could not be the whole story. No matter how

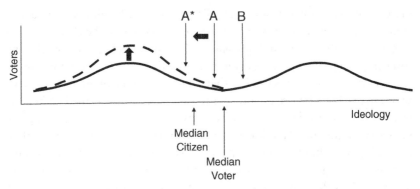

FIGURE 5.1 Downsian abstainers

much voters complained that the two parties "were all the same," their platforms were far from identical and the differences were often bitter. It was left to Professors Duncan Black and Anthony Downs to put the last puzzle piece in place: While Hotelling's argument had referred simply to "voters," he made no distinction between *eligible* voters and those who actually cast ballots on Election Day. But if party platforms are identical, why should any voter show up? It was not enough for both parties to woo the center: They also had to offer enough contrasts to make voting worthwhile.[68] With this final modification, the classical Hotelling–Downs analysis was complete.[69]

Figure 5.1 illustrates this logic in detail. Suppose that the Democratic platform ("A") is initially close to its Republican counterpart ("B"). Then the Democrats' most liberal voters may see so little difference between the parties that they abstain. Doing this deprives them of a choice in the current election. But their absence also cuts into the party's vote totals, and puts pressure on leadership to propose a more progressive agenda next time.[70] Moreover, the liberals may not see abstention as particularly costly: Despising all centrist platforms, forfeiting the chance to support Democrats over Republicans means little to them.

But in that case, the way for Democrats to fix the problem is to move from the original Hotelling result at Point "A" to Point "A*." This lures back the abstainers and increases Democratic Party turnout (dashed line).

Downs' turnout argument shows where Hotelling went wrong: The Democrats, it turns out, do not target the median voter after all; or rather, they target her with a large and deliberate offset. In polarized times when much of their party holds extreme views, this could be very far from what median voters want. On the other hand, the turnout argument comes with an important caveat. When politicians slant platforms to court their base, they have to worry that their words could inadvertently energize their opponents' base even more than their own. This implies that politicians should follow what Bill Clinton called a "triangulation"[71] policy of never taking positions where those who oppose the measure feel more intensely than those who support it. This behavior is socially beneficial since it automatically avoids "tyranny of majority" outcomes and the kind of "repeal and replace" politics that constantly reminds the losers not to forget their anger.

Finally, Democrats' decision to move their platform to the left in our example is not the end of the game: We must also ask how Republicans will respond. Here one might think, in keeping with Hotelling's original argument, that they would move their own platform leftward to capture the centrist votes that the Democrats have just abandoned. But since the Republicans have their own extremists, this strategy would depress their own turnout. So instead, the Republicans' safest move is to make their own, equal-and-opposite break to the right. The result, as Downs pointed out, is that the two parties do not converge after all but instead "remain poles apart in ideology."[72] In this way the abstainers in each party, despite disagreeing about practically everything, find themselves de facto allies in forcing choices that centrist voters dislike.

In the end, the importance of these deliberately polarizing strategies depends on how much each party can raise the dashed line above the solid one. In practice, this is substantial: Modern US presidential turnout seldom exceeds 55 percent of eligible voters,[73] leaving fully 45 additional points potentially up for grabs. Assuming that roughly half of these votes are centrist, this implies that Left and Right can potentially raise their final scores by up to a dozen points apiece – more than enough to swamp most margins of victory.

The result is that modern campaigns nearly always include some combination of extremist views designed to keep "the base" motivated (i.e. angry) and labor-intensive efforts to chide and sometimes physically transport less enthusiastic voters to the polls. In practice, get-out-the-vote drives quickly encounter diminishing returns – trying to persuade someone who has already refused to vote several times is bound to be difficult. Despite this, vigorous door-to-door campaigns in presidential battleground states typically boost total voter turnout on both sides by about ten points – not far short of what ought to be possible.[74] Whether any of this improves democracy is less clear. The fact that so many citizens do not bother to vote suggests that they mostly agree with the status quo. And indeed, survey evidence has found that nonvoters are "virtually a carbon copy of the electorate,"[75] though with the significant caveat that many are poor, and for that reason lean toward candidates who promise more big government and redistribution.[76]

Downs' abstainers insight explained why a polarized society would produce more extreme platforms. Yet the paradox is that the median voter remains as important as ever. The reason is that no party can win a majority unless the median voter remains, if not happy, at least undecided. This forces politicians to balance their own extremism against the other side's. The result is that the Downs–Hotelling mechanism continues to operate, guaranteeing close elections that lead to massive policy reversals every few years. Indeed, the races will be even tighter to the extent that polarization increases turnout, reducing each side's room to squeeze a winning margin from superior get-out-the-vote efforts. The point is nicely illustrated by the very close 2020 election, in which turnout jumped from an average of 56 percent in the previous ten presidential races to 65 percent.[77]

Downs worried that no democratic system could long survive such chaos. Still, his theory offered the saving grace that Hotelling's median voter result would continue to keep centrists in charge unless and until the far-Left or far-Right achieved an absolute majority. This seemed to put disaster safely out of reach – indeed, even Weimar would be considered stable by this criterion. We will argue in Section 5.4 that Downs' reasoning was too optimistic, and that the real American system is significantly less stable than he thought.

The question remains just how much turnout we should hope for. Ideally we might want just enough abstainers to mimic the platforms that parties would offer in an intensity-weighted vote by the entire electorate. The trouble, of course, is that this standard (like voter intensity itself) is nearly impossible to measure. In practice, the best we are likely to do is to make much cruder judgments about whether the country's politics could be improved by boosting current turnout (e.g. by mandatory voting) or else suppressing it (e.g. by reducing the "early voting" period).

Not surprisingly, each option includes both benefits and costs. On the one hand, policies that make voting harder favor extremists, who feel strongly and are therefore the most likely to vote. This could sometimes push the two-party system toward platforms and candidates that are *more* radical than the ones that universal, intensity-weighted voting would generate. This already seems to be happening in local elections, where the turnout for many large cities routinely hovers between 10 and 30 percent.[78] Assuming that only the most extreme voters cast ballots, this means that just 5–15 percent of the population routinely chooses mayors and district attorneys for everyone else.[79] The end result, at least for a time, is a government that is significantly more extreme than the population it serves.[80] But over the longer term this too is unstable: Extremists' power comes from their passion, which in turn reflects the distance between their views and current policy. But once the policy changes, centrists who liked the earlier system suddenly feel just as angry as the extremists did before – and go to the polls to reverse the change. Something like this seems to have happened in 2021–2 when many local officials began refusing to enforce various criminal statutes or else tried to teach Progressive orthodoxies like "critical race theory" to school-children. The result was landslide recall elections against the incumbents,[81] after which many of the previous policies were restored. The irony of course is that the oscillation would never have happened at all if centrists had remembered the importance of voting in every election.

Strangely, policies that make voting radically *easier* often lead to similar pathologies. For now, this is mostly evident in "long ballot" jurisdictions where voters come to the polls for a few high-profile races, but then linger to pass judgment on various down-ballot offices they have never heard of. Given that voters know little or nothing about these candidates, their reasoning is less "rational" or "social" than simply random. In these circumstances, even a tiny amount of positive information about one candidate can propel her to victory. The recent spate of George Soros-backed Progressive district attorneys is an especially successful example of this tactic.[82]

The bottom line here is that optimal turnout should avoid overrepresenting extremist and ignorant voters equally. Operationally, this implies a system where nonvoters disproportionately include citizens "who don't know and/or don't care." At a guess, this might be not too different from the 50–60 percent turnout typically found in recent US presidential elections.[83] If so, there is a strong case for banning practices like paying citizens to vote or filling out ballots for them through "harvesting" schemes.[84] There is also the subsidiary concern that modern turnout campaigns carefully target partisans, diluting the centrist vote.[85] Here the obvious cure, practiced in Australia for nearly a century, is to make voting mandatory by charging nonvoters a modest fine. This has consistently kept turnout above 90 percent.[86] If nothing else, mandatory voting would ensure that the large mass of indifferent and uninformed voters that the major parties already make it their business to mobilize included more centrists. The downside is that it would also aggravate the problem of indifferent and uninformed voters, who are (by definition) among the most easily swayed by politicians hoping to organize tyrannies of the majority.

So far we have considered a Left–Right spectrum that plots polarization as if there was only one issue. This is reasonable to the extent that large numbers of voters really do think that a single issue – traditionally class or income inequality – decides all the others. And indeed, surveys continue to show that voters' opinions are highly correlated from one issue to the next.[87] Despite this, it is also true that many voters agree on some issues and dispute others.

This generalization to multiple issues takes some getting used to. So long as we insist on imagining politics as a one-dimensional spectrum, each party platform reduces to a single, well-defined point. But when there are multiple issues, the party's overall position depends on the sum of each separate issue *weighted by its importance to each individual voter*. Since voters typically assign different weights to different issues, it follows that they can and will disagree about where each party falls on the Left–Right spectrum.[88] Listening to the public discourse, an observer trying to summarize the various opinions will conclude that each party's ideological position is smeared out.

But expanding our one-dimensional spectrum to include the possibility of multiple, independent issues is more than a nod to reality. It also enables new political strategies. Most obviously, we expect voters to arrive at different opinions and intensities for each issue. This opens the possibility of compromises in which each side "wins" on the issues it cares about most. The result is particularly visible in the kind of special interest politics where politicians quietly offer large benefits to some narrow group without telling their other supporters.[89] This tactic is limited only by general voters' disgust with a party that blurs its positions too often, inducing them to switch their support to rivals whose promises, though less appetizing, appear more honest.[90]

Recognizing the existence of multiple, independent issues also opens the door to "single-issue voters," who care about one issue much more than the others. Here Downs made a startling prediction. The major parties, he said, would eject each other from power at approximately regular intervals, which he speculated would last one or two presidential cycles.[91]

To see this, suppose for the sake of argument that most voters oppose abortion but favor gun control. Then the incumbent party has no choice: It must immediately side with the majority on both issues. After all, if it doesn't the challenger will capture the majority and win the next election. But that is not the end of the story. Supposing that the incumbent sides with both majorities, what should the challenger do?

If every voter felt equally strongly about both issues, the challenger's best option would be to agree with the incumbent to produce a tie. But this changes once the electorate includes single-issue voters. Suppose, then, that Tucker opposes both abortion and gun control, but cares much more about the second issue than the first. Meanwhile, Maddow favors both abortion and gun control, but cares more about the first issue than the second. Then the challenger must choose between three possible outcomes. First, it can adopt the incumbent's position on both issues, so that neither Tucker nor Maddow has any real choice on Election Day. Second, it can write a platform that contests just one issue, say gun control. Now Tucker can vote against gun control. But since most voters want gun control, the incumbent will still be reelected and gun control policy will stay the same. Then there is the third choice. Suppose that the challenger contests *both* issues. Since Tucker mostly cares about gun control, he will hold his nose and vote for the challenger despite its abortion stance. Meanwhile, Maddow will similarly vote for the challenger despite its gun control policy. And if there are enough Tuckers and Maddows, the challenger will win the election. The irony is that the new incumbent has now promised *two* minority positions, so that it too will be vulnerable as soon as the former incumbent can convincingly amend its platform. Moreover, new issues are arriving all the time. So the game will continue, with both parties replacing each other at roughly equal intervals.[92]

This kind of alternating government is sometimes interpreted as a sign of voter ignorance, particularly when populist challengers replace centrists.[93] But Downs' argument suggests that high turnover could just as well be the sign of a healthy democracy in which parties seek out trades that reduce net anger across the electorate. There is something redeeming here: A two-party system cannot help reducing voters to a single choice. Yet, barring miscalculation, the choice that politicians do give them will also be the one they care about most.

Does this happen in life? Prof. Downs was careful to emphasize that no one knew "with certainty" how many single-issue voters existed at any given time or how fast they accumulated. Even so, he thought that the chances of a successful challenge would be "high" after a party had held power for several consecutive terms.[94] And certainly, the evidence is suggestive: In presidential races, success in the previous two elections is indeed a negative factor for the incumbent.[95] The surprise is that Downs' prediction works even better today than when he made it. Before World War II, two-term presidents were frequently followed by members of the same party.[96] But since then voters have ejected the incumbent party at the end of the president's second term in seven out of eight contests.[97]

Like most Downsian predictions, the importance of single-issue voters almost certainly varies from one era to the next. In particular, we expect their numbers to diminish in eras of strong social voting when knowing a person's views on one issue reliably predicts his views on all the others. This is bound to weaken Downs' mechanism, so that challengers will have to wait longer to unseat incumbents.

So far we, like the Framers, have imagined majority tyranny in terms of razor-thin majorities. But coalitions become simpler when the minority is small and clearly defined. In America, these lines have usually been drawn around race. For the first century after Emancipation, having the vote did very little to protect 10 percent of the population from legalized inequality. The question remains when majority tyranny is stable, and what procedural protections can do to make it less so.

The first and most obvious observation is the converse of Downs' single voter analysis: If 51 percent of the electorate prefers oppressing the minority to every other issue, all tyranny is stable.[98] Still, if we think that some voters sooner or later change their minds, it might be better to ask what must happen to keep one of the two major parties from championing the issue. Here we expect at least one party to oppose oppression so long as the affected minority includes one-third of the electorate. To see this, imagine counterfactually that America had three major parties. Then we expect debate to be suppressed so long as the two biggest parties can earn more votes by keeping the issue off the ballot than the third party can win by raising it. The punch line, of course, is that American third parties are unstable. This explains why the two parties could remain almost entirely indifferent to slavery before 1840.[99]

All the same, the prospects for minorities smaller than 33 percent are far from hopeless. The catch is that they have to wait for some transient political crisis in which the major parties' struggle for power runs so deep that one of them renounces oppression in order to win. Here the best example is

Irish Home Rule politics in the 1880s and again in 1910. In each case, both of Britain's major parties found themselves short of a parliamentary majority, with smaller Irish parties holding the deciding votes. Liberals were then able to win power by compromising their otherwise strong opposition to Home Rule in exchange for Irish willingness to accept social reforms they had previously opposed.[100] In these cases, any oppressed minority larger than the (typically small) margin between the major parties' vote totals can sooner or later assert itself.[101] John F. Kennedy's political gratitude to the Black Chicagoans who helped eke out an extraordinarily narrow victory over Richard Nixon in the 1960 presidential race was reportedly pivotal in persuading him to launch the legislative initiative that would later culminate in the Civil Rights Act of 1964.[102]

By these standards, at least, contemporary American politics looks reasonably safe for minorities. The reason is that the modern Democrats are an alliance in which each minority pledges to support the others. This lets new groups seeking protection join an already functioning coalition. Given that nonwhite minorities account for 40 percent of the US population,[103] this is well above what is needed to support the country's second party and, provided it can attract a small number of extra voters, achieve a majority. That said, the strategy can only succeed if most minority voters choose the diverse party over the nondiverse one.[104] Moreover, the diverse party must constantly reassure members that its promises of mutual support still hold. This may account for Democrats' extreme sensitivity to anyone who questions transgender groups, whose importance lies much more in the realm of symbolism than in their actual votes on Election Day.

Minorities received still further protections when the United States ratified the Bill of Rights – yet another Madison-authored document – just two years after the Constitution itself.[105] The document fit nicely with Madison's habitual argument that members of today's majority have solidly material reasons to protect minorities since they themselves could just as easily be targeted tomorrow. Still, this argument only works so long as members of today's majority coalition have some substantial chance of becoming victims. The assumption fails badly when the oppression targets groups that are readily distinguishable from other citizens, usually because they belong to some historically or biologically defined "other" whose characteristics are hard to change. Congressional and judge-made law extending similar protections to race,[106] sexual preference,[107] and out-of-wedlock births[108] mark further installments in this pattern. The catch, of course, is that none of these protections is worth much unless judges are willing to assert them. Here, the examples of "separate but equal" segregation in the Jim Crow South[109] and Japanese internment during World War II[110] show how fallible such guarantees can be.

Prof. Downs' great contribution was to see that elections were not identical to product markets after all, and that Hotelling's prediction that both parties would target the median voter would become less and less realistic in a polarized society. Eventually, both parties' platforms would diverge in the direction of their most extreme voters.

Though Downs never says so, his theory of policy-reversals nevertheless implied a hopeful caveat. The oscillations he predicted could only begin once extremists on one side or the other achieved an absolute majority. Yet Jefferson's logic – not to mention practically all modern history since the French Revolution – suggests that a large number of Left extremists implies roughly as many Right extremists, and vice versa. So saying that one group of extremists could command an absolute majority really implied that *both* groups must command numbers close to 50 percent – and therefore that the center barely existed. Yet history offers no examples of this: Even in Weimar the number of centrist voters never dipped much below 50 percent. This seems to imply that Downs' extremist scenario will never occur in life.

Unfortunately, the conclusion is nonsense. Germany's Weimar Republic may have had a near-majority of centrists, but it still collapsed. Instead of reassuring us, what the paradox really tells us is that Downs' bipartisan model is missing something important. The next three sections address this gap.

## 5.3 RELATED MODELS

The strength of Downsian theory, like that of *The Federalist* itself, is that it extracts so much from so few assumptions. Even so, real voters often pick candidates for reasons that have nothing to do with party platforms. Here we consider whether and to what extent Downs' conclusions change when voters decide based on social voting, individual candidate characteristics, and/or their perception of each party's enduring strengths and weaknesses. While it is tempting to ask which of these models offers the closest fit to American life, it is more accurate to admit that all of them have existed side by side throughout US history, with relative strengths shifting from one era to the next.

We begin with social voting. We argued in Chapter 2 that conformist pressures are comparable to, and sometimes stronger than, Downsian ones. Here the good news is that the Downs–Hotelling strategy of targeting the median voter remains good advice so long as "rational" voters constitute a significant fraction of the electorate. The reason is that the social incentives to show solidarity and conformism are beyond the parties' control in any case. Conversely, the ballyhoo and symbolism that social voters crave can be paired with almost any platform that rational voters might potentially care about.

And indeed, history shows that both parties continue to target median voters even when rational voting is weak. We have said that social voting reached an all-time high in the late nineteenth century. Yet despite this, the half-century after 1860 saw the closest presidential races in American history, while control of Congress changed constantly.[111] More recently, social voting has grown enormously since the 1990s. Yet this, too, has been an era of close presidential elections, with control of the House majority changing four times. Evidently, the parties have managed to adopt platforms so evenly balanced that the median voter – though pining for more centrist choices on both sides – continues to see them as tossups.

That said, social voting does modify Downsian theory in other respects. First, our Ising model implies that conformist pressures tend to amplify whichever views are locally in the majority. But in that case we expect each blue or red neighborhood to vote more ideologically as social pressure mounts, exaggerating the number of extremists elected to Congress on both sides. Second, social voting, by its nature, suppresses the number of single-issue voters. After all, there is much less risk in adopting "party line" opinions that are perfectly correlated and therefore predictable. Yet we have also seen that single-issue voters are the key to Downs' argument that incumbents will be regularly ejected from office. The upshot is that challengers in conformist eras need to accumulate more hot button issues to assemble a majority. While power will continue to alternate, the average frequency will decline. Finally, social voting makes the already-substantial barriers to successful third parties even higher. For the two major parties, the best way to maximize votes will always be to side with whichever view is most widely held within their coalition. This forces third parties to pick from whatever long shots remain in hopes that the public will sooner or later come around to what are – for now – less popular choices.

We have also emphasized that Downs' model focused on platforms. But from Colonial times to the early Republic, real voters invariably cared about candidates much more than issues.[112] This helps to explain why the Framers imagined Congress as an atomistic collection of individuals who resembled the voters and could, to that extent, serve as stand-ins for the wider society.[113] This had the nice feature that Congress could never pass laws that betrayed voters without simultaneously hurting itself. Indeed, citizens who accepted this logic could ignore politics altogether, safe in the knowledge that government would do the right thing regardless.

More usually, though, voters have looked to candidates' personal qualities for evidence they will reach wise decisions. Here the oldest logic argues that voters should choose candidates based on such personal characteristics as competence, character, occupation, class, and (these days) race or gender. The persuasiveness of these candidate-specific factors has varied widely across American history. In modern times, however, candidate-specific effects seem to be largest in eras when polarization is weak so that voters have little to choose from on the issues. This is exemplified by the long bipartisan era from the 1950s to the 1980s, when the risk-averse Depression generation produced close elections when no incumbents were running for president, but landslides when they had the chance to reelect candidates who had already shown competence in office.[114]

At bottom, candidate-specific voting follows naturally from Downsian theories where voters' information budgets are so limited that the only affordable judgments involve instantaneous realizations that a candidate belongs to a certain sex or race, or appears capable, or would be fun to drink a beer with. And once a candidate has been picked for her identity, there is nothing left to say. Voters will then go on voting for her until some unusually large fact – say, a scandal or outrageous vote – persuades them to shift their support to some equally unknown challenger with the same demographic descriptors. Conversely, polarization makes voters more partisan and ideological. This necessarily downgrades the importance of politicians' personal characteristics and, with it, their willingness to argue with their supporters when the latter embrace bad ideas.[115]

The question remains which heuristic(s) are most persuasive to voters. Hamilton, alone among *The Federalist*'s essayists, argued that competence and character would trump identity. The reason, he insisted, was that public policy required much more than having one's heart in the right place. Without clever and competent execution, election victories were meaningless. This meant that voters would often choose representatives who looked very different from themselves, though only if they judged them to be both competent and loyal to their supporters.[116] The argument for competence is especially strong when the government's goals are widely agreed, so that the only remaining uncertainty is how best to achieve them. This was usually true in the early Republic, when government seldom strayed beyond a few narrow and well-defined ambitions. Then too, individual competence mattered more in an era of weak institutions when a great debater like Daniel Webster could exercise outsized influence by explaining to less reflective colleagues why some superficially attractive policy was sure to fail or end in political disaster.[117] This advantage is greatly diminished now that every congressman has access to a professional research staff. That said, the fact that candidates like the late John McCain still proudly advertise their "maverick" status suggests that competence remains a significant draw for voters generally and pragmatic centrists in particular.

The traditional "character" argument for voting is similar. The argument is especially strong in eras when voters mostly fear the traditional vices of bipartisan politics, for example that the national party will grant quiet favors to special interests in hopes that its rank-and-file members won't notice.

The analysis is different when the parties' goals are controversial. Here, the simplest heuristics quickly reduce to class, gender, or other "identity" categories. Being inherently one-dimensional, they encourage politicians to act like single-issue voters on whichever descriptor(s) got them elected.

In principle, identity politics can lead to two regimes. In weakly polarized eras we expect identity politics to produce the usual single-issue voter dynamic in which identity politicians trade votes with colleagues who feel strongly about other, nonidentity issues. In the short term, at least, Downsian theory predicts that these trades should reduce intensity on both sides. In the longer run, the political messaging that accompanies this politics will make all voters more receptive to seeing identity-based patterns, reducing the supply of nonidentity politicians in Congress willing to make trades. In the extreme case where most politicians are elected on the basis of socioeconomic categories, we should expect majority tyranny outcomes in which identity-based coalitions run roughshod over everyone else.

The irony is that neither party can do much to enhance its individual candidates' demographic descriptors beyond recruiting more candidates from particularly promising categories like females (for Republicans) or military veterans (for Democrats).[118] This suggests that they will continue to focus on Downsian platforms aimed at rational and social voters. One partial exception is that party platforms that endorse "conscience" or "identity" politics may reassure voters that candidates running on their personal qualities will be allowed to act on them once they reach Congress. Then too, increasing the number of "identity" candidates cannot help changing each party's governance, pushing platforms in directions that pay less attention to the median voter. This will boost candidates in districts where identity politics is popular and handicap them everywhere else.

The fact that the Hotelling–Downs mechanism favors close outcomes also injects a large element of chance into elections. But in that case we should seriously consider the possibility that what we take for "the will of the majority" might only be a statistical fluctuation, or more precisely that every close election reflects some unknowable mix of the two. To see this, consider a thought experiment in which every American voter is equally likely to vote Democrat or Republican. Then the probability of any particular partisan balance in Congress is the same as the number of "heads" in 435 consecutive coin tosses. Yet despite this, the odd number of seats ensures that there cannot be a tie, while the laws of probability predict that chance alone will sometimes produce substantial majorities. For example, it is straightforward to show that one side or the other will gain a twenty-vote majority (or better) 3.4 percent of the time.[119] While such margins are unlikely in any particular election, they are nearly certain to occur every century or so even when the public had no intention of giving either side a mandate. The question is what to do about it. Requiring a modest supermajority in the Senate limits parties' ability to exploit such accidents, but also makes it harder for genuine (if thin) majorities to implement their campaign promises. On recent evidence, we expect each party to randomly enjoy majorities large enough to overcome the filibuster every fifty years or so.[120]

The notion that democratic outcomes can fluctuate from election to election is disturbing. But the damage from random events can linger for much longer periods. Suppose one party spectacularly succeeds or, more usually, fails in office. Should voters understand this as the failing of individual politicians and bad luck, or something more systematic? Voters often attribute enduring personalities to each party, including well-defined competences and failings. And this is not unreasonable: The persistence of prominent leaders and lower-level personnel makes some kind of enduring personality inevitable. For the largest events, the electoral impact can linger for decades.[121] Examples include the Jackson Democrats' domination of the aristocratic Whig party down to 1860,[122] Republican preeminence following widespread disillusion with the Wilson Administration in World War I, and Democrats' string of election victories from the stock market crash through World War II.

The net result in these cases, for a time at least, is to ensure lopsided losses until the public forgets. Even so, targeting median voters remains the disfavored party's best available strategy to beat the odds. Moreover, losing a few elections is hardly fatal so long as the party's chances of eventual victory remain high enough to keep its core supporters from straying. Given the unpredictability of politics, this is usually a reasonable hope. The durability of both the Republican and the Democrat labels after their respective electoral catastrophes in the early twentieth century shows that the parties' names, if not their principles, are nearly indestructible.

## 5.4 COERCIVE POLITICS

The Framers worried that simple majority rule would invite tyrannical majorities, policies that wastefully jittered back and forth, and stand-offs in which "contumacious" minorities blocked needed legislation to blackmail the majority. The surprise, as we have seen, was that political parties alleviated these problems by narrowing their differences through the Hotelling–Downs mechanism. But as Professor Downs warned, the mechanism could only work so long as centrists dominated public opinion. Today the Framers' worries have resurfaced in a polarized environment where extremists on both sides threaten to shut down the *entire* government unless their demands are met. In these cases, at least, the conflict spreads far beyond new legislation, with extremists shutting off benefits that have been agreed for decades for no better reason than to inflict pain and coerce their opponents.

Downs imagined elections producing clear winners who could dictate policy until the next election. Yet real legislatures deadlock, and this happens often enough to matter. This leads to a second, non-Downsian strategy once extremists on the Left and Right approach roughly half of the electorate. To see this, consider a hypothetical America split between the extreme Left (25 percent), Centrists (50 percent), and the extreme Right (25 percent). Neither set of extremists has any hope of winning the Downsian game by persuading the majority. But they do have the numbers to control their respective parties, and therefore the choices the public sees. When this happens, Left and Right each have a 50 percent chance of prevailing in the next election, while the center, despite its near-majority, is left to choose between two platforms it despises. The result is that *one-fourth* of the population can end up dictating their preferred policies to everyone else.[123] The implication, of course, is that the American system is far more vulnerable to polarizing politics than the Framers or Downs – both of whom had imagined extremists achieving something like an absolute majority before they seized control – ever imagined.

The question, of course, is what happens next. Prof. Downs assumed that one or both parties would move to the center for purely competitive reasons, giving centrists at least one acceptable choice. But this depended on two assumptions: (a) that rational politicians would propose whatever platforms seemed likely to get them elected, and (b) that voters' political beliefs were fixed. Yet we have already said that neither is strictly true: Some politicians are inflexible true believers, while voters often change their political judgments from one election to the next. This makes it reasonable to consider alternative political strategies in which each party's extremists stick to their orthodoxies, refusing to offer centrist choices until a frustrated electorate gives in. One might, of course, object that this kind of non-Downsian game is unrealistic. But in fact, history is full of such outcomes.

Europe's political history in the late nineteenth and early twentieth centuries shows an astonishing sameness. In each of the great democracies, large extremist parties on the Left and Right would campaign on promises to overthrow and replace the existing constitution.[124] Meanwhile moderates, in power but under siege, would struggle to govern despite constant attacks from both sides. The end game, all too often, was dictatorship by one set of extremists or the other. As the poet William Butler Yeats despaired, "Things fall apart, the centre cannot hold."[125]

Variations on this story can be found in France,[126] Italy,[127] and Spain.[128] But it was the collapse of Germany's Weimar Republic (1919–33), which brought Hitler to power, that provides the starkest example. Throughout the 1920s, both Left and Right promised to overthrow centrist governments. The silver lining, for more than a decade, was that neither group held anything close to a majority, and for that reason could do nothing. Instead, they used their seats in the legislature to disrupt the government and spread propaganda with hardly any legislative agenda. Even so, the center was able to govern effectively for most of the 1920s.[129]

The real crisis arrived with the Great Depression. With Left and Right preventing the Reichstag from acting, conditions deteriorated rapidly. Moderate voters, seeing the centrist parties' helplessness, soon found themselves choosing between Communists and Nazis. The struggle ended with Hitler's appointment as chancellor in 1933.[130]

For the extremists, timing was everything. Given that each side never held more than roughly 25 percent of the vote,[131] their only path to power lay in persuading voters that the centrist parties were paralyzed. Moderate voters would then find themselves forced to make unpalatable choices between extreme Left and Right. Historians often say that German voters were "radicalized," but this is only true in the limited sense that they stopped voting for centrists. Many if not most supported extremists from the perfectly rational judgment that they were the least-bad choice.[132]

The key, of course, was for both the Left and the Right to keep the political chaos going long enough to outlast the center.[133] More specifically, party leaders knew that they could defect to the center and pass reform legislation any time they wanted to. Still, most ignored the temptation, either because they did not believe that the centrist measures would work, or because they judged their own agendas far more valuable. This made it perfectly rational to continue the blockade for as long as their side had even a modest chance of winning power.[134] And in any case, it would have been psychologically impossible for good communists to support a "social fascist"[135] government, or for good Nazis to join the "November criminals" who had betrayed Germany at the end of World War I.

So long as Weimar's center parties held an absolute majority, they could debate and pass legislation almost as if the extremists did not exist. Formally, this condition was satisfied until the Republic's final year.[136] Thereafter, the crisis deepened as both sides refused to help the center cope with the emergency. But this game also had to end at some point. As soon as one side saw that the other was about to gain power, its only remaining choice should have been to block them by joining the center. The tragedy of Weimar was that the Left did not move fast enough. Like all political parties, the Communists worried that changing course too quickly would discredit them with voters. Then too, a Communist leader who joined the center would have had to renounce a lifetime's faith that history was on his side. Finally, the same propaganda made it hard for rank-and-file constituents to see just how desperate the political situation had become. To them, any leader who called for a tactical alliance with the center was automatically a traitor. The French and Spanish Left,

having seen what happened in Germany, would be more agile in forming "Popular Front" governments. But they too had trouble cooperating
with centrists once in power, leaving the new governments shaky and
vulnerable.

Things are bound to play out differently in the American system.
America's first-past-the-post voting ensures that two – and only two –
major parties can win a majority in Congress. Downsian theory then
expects the centrist plurality to control the biggest party. This is encouraging, since it seems to say that the system has room for just one extremist party at a time. But that is untrue, because the centrists are always
split between Republicans and Democrats. That means that the centrist/
extremist struggle *within* each party will be evenly matched once Left and
Right each number about one-fourth of the electorate.

This sets up two possible outcomes. First, suppose that centrists control
at least one party. Given that roughly half the electorate prefers centrists,
a moderate party will enjoy a nearly insurmountable electoral advantage. But in that case, the extremist party must also move to the center or
become uncompetitive. Alternatively, suppose that extremists simultaneously take over both parties, so that voters have no centrist choice at all.
This is a reasonable description of US politics over the past decade.

Plainly, this is not the old bipartisan politics. Instead of fighting for
a share of federal spoils, extremist voters now hope to change the system entirely. Moreover, they understand that such a large goal requires
patience. So they do not criticize their favored politicians for failing to
pass legislation, but instead praise them for blocking "the other side."
And this is rational. For the foreseeable future, at least, they know that
their chances of winning an outright majority are minuscule. Given the
circumstances, their politicians are already doing the only thing they can
do, condemning each new attempt at compromise and hoping that the
next crisis, when it comes, will be so painful that it forces the rest of the
country to give in.[137]

Of course, such positions would not be sustainable in a perfectly competitive system. But American politics is a duopoly, and like all duopolies
each party knows that any transient advantage from moving to the center
would be immediately erased by a mirror-image response from the other
side. So instead, the radicals in each party enable the other, subject only
to the mirror-image condition that they cannot become so extreme that
alarmed centrists rush to their opponents. The result is a weird codependency. The extremists who regularly denounce each other on television

are no doubt sincere. Even so, neither could exist without the other.[138] The good news, in principle, is that each party's centrists are similarly intertwined, so that talk of nominating moderates by one party immediately strengthens centrists in the other. This was particularly visible during the 2022 midterms, when many Democrats openly criticized their party's support for "wokeness" and "Defund the police," even as moderate Republicans found the courage to criticize ex-President Trump for reducing their predicted "Red Tsunami" to a painfully narrow win in the House.

None of this would be possible without voters' support. The key requirement, of course, is strong polarization. As we argued in Chapter 2, this immediately increases social voters' incentives to conform while encouraging rational voters to trade pragmatism for ideology. The result in both cases is that voters become more willing to back obstructionist politicians. For social voters, the need to show solidarity with friends is satisfied the moment they take a stand. After that, it hardly matters whether the political goal is achieved or not. Strong ideological voters, on the other hand, are (by definition) true believers. Since they know that their policies are right – and everyone else's are useless – they will happily lose a great many political fights so long as they think they can win in the end.

Meanwhile, centrist voters will also develop new behaviors, splitting their votes for president, Senate, and House across both parties. This refuses victory to either side, reducing the possibility of extreme change in either direction. Historically, ticket-splitting first became popular shortly after World War II and has continued down to the present.[139] As usual with Madison's checks and balances, the price that voters pay for divided government is friction and gridlock. Still, this will often be the best available choice for centrists who would have preferred to write "none of the above" on their ballots.

In the long run, centrists can also shift their support back and forth at each successive election. In theory, the resulting policy zig-zags might then approximate a middle course. But tacking back and forth between extremes implies violent course reversals. Prof. Downs insisted that no system could long survive such oscillations.

But in that case, what is the end game? Depending on who gives in first – extremists or the center – we can imagine two outcomes. The first is for extremists on one side or the other to win and then hold power long enough for voters to get used to the new laws and policies. This could take a long time: Republicans' quest to repeal and replace Obamacare dragged on for more than a decade, while voters' antipathy toward Progressive Democrats and Republican Trumpists continued to break evenly down the middle as recently as the 2022 midterms. Even so, it is easy to see how rank-and-file party members could become discouraged and drop out, after which success would become even more remote, driving away still more of the remaining members in the endless spiral. At this point, the new consensus would become permanent until, sooner or later, fresh divisions and conflicts emerged in the usual Jeffersonian way.

The other possibility is for the centrists to prevail. We have described coercive politics as the Weimar end game in American circumstances. All the same, there is an important difference. In Weimar, it did not matter if there were more extremists on one side than the other. American extremism, on the other hand, is only stable so long as it controls both parties. Moreover, the arithmetic is tight. After all, not even Weimar voters ever gave the two extremist parties much more than 50 percent support between them. This implies that both major parties can only be hijacked so long as the Left and Right enjoy exquisitely similar vote totals. Then too, the temptation for one side or the other to defect is enormous. So long as both sides blockade the center, each has a 50 percent chance of winning power. But as soon as one side reverts to a centrist platform, its chances grow enormously. At this point the other party will be practically certain to follow unless its leaders show a very non-Downsian loyalty to ideology over winning elections.

Suppose, then, that the Left-extremists (say) lose control of their party so that it suddenly offers centrist voters a moderate platform. At this point, the Right-extremists' chances of prevailing, so recently at 50 percent, would immediately drop to zero.[140] But in that case the Right-extremists' obvious response is to move to the center themselves. The two-party system would then return to the old Downs–Hotelling pattern of bipartisan choices. On the other hand, we can imagine cases where extremist rule has so completely purged Downsian politicians from one party that only radicals remain. Here, the example of William Jennings Bryan, whose populist platforms captured the Democrat nomination in 1896, 1900, and 1908, shows how such a party could lock itself out of power for a generation. This would also reduce pressure on the now-dominant party to produce platforms aimed at the median voter, while short-circuiting the redundancy that the existence of two parties normally provides against the occasional bad candidate. But either way, centrism would return.

In principle, a centrist rebellion could start either in Congress or in presidential politics. However, a centrist rebellion in Congress seems unlikely. One reason, as we will argue in Chapter 7, is that polarized times tend to tighten leadership's power to control which bills come to the floor. This implies that a centrist rebellion would require members of both parties to form an alliance against their respective leaderships. This is particularly unlikely since congressmen, being comparatively anonymous, would have to defend their breach of party discipline against national donors and extremist challengers in their home districts. Then too, organizing a rebellion poses (as Madison already foresaw) massive coordination problems. This leads to the Catch-22 logic that there is no point in calling for a rebellion until it is likely to succeed, especially since a failed challenge rebellion can only invite retribution.[141]

By comparison, presidential nominations have a large element of unpredictability. But once a centrist was nominated, she could normally count on a landslide victory against her extremist opponent on the Nixon–McGovern (1972) or Johnson–Goldwater (1964) pattern. Flush with success, the newly elected president could then use her influence in Congress to make her party's newfound centrism permanent.

We close this section by counting the costs. The whole point of coercive politics is to short-circuit the Hotelling–Downs tendency for platforms to converge on the median voter. That said, creating a situation where roughly one-fourth of the population can dictate policy to everyone else is bound to generate outsized anger and dissatisfaction.

We can get a rough estimate of this resentment by noting that the prevailing extremists' joy is exactly canceled by unhappy extremists on the other side. The center's disappointment then decides how much unhappiness society feels on net. But in fact, this probably understates the damage. The reason, as we argued in Chapter 1, is that resentment often increases faster than our assumed linear extrapolation. In that case, the best way to minimize unhappiness is to center policy near the largest group of voters. By this standard, coercive politics produces *even more* dissatisfaction than the fully polarized world in which the Left has a 51 percent majority and constantly outvotes the Right's 49 percent.[142]

Beyond this, coercive politics means that power can only be won after an extended period of gridlock. This, however, implies an equally extended political argument which, for reasons already discussed in Chapter 3, will encourage voters to see their opponents as not just misguided but evil.

Finally, a full accounting must consider the wastefulness of a politics in which extremists deliberately block reform for decades. The hope, of course, is that the suffering will be cut short when one side or the other realizes its weakness and returns to the center. But the history of Popular Front initiatives in the 1930s suggests that the momentum of party ideologies makes this about-face difficult even in an obvious emergency. By the time one side finally does win, the disaster may no longer be unrecoverable.

### 5.5 PARTY GOVERNANCE

Downsian theory predicts that rational politicians will methodically search out and offer whichever bundle of policies 51 percent of the country prefers to all the others. Even so, real platforms and candidates routinely fall short of this standard. Donald Trump's 2016 victory over Hillary Clinton shows just how vulnerable the American system can be when both parties pick widely disliked candidates at the same time.

The procedures that the parties use to select candidates have evolved constantly over the years. For the Republic's first three decades, candidates were picked by each party's congressional delegation. But the caucus system lost most of its influence once expanding suffrage conferred power on those who could communicate to mass audiences, notably including incumbent presidents and party organizers. Then too, the new breed of Andrew Jackson-style populists made congressmen reluctant to participate for fear of being demonized as "insiders" and "elites."[143] Then, in 1832, the Anti-Masonic Party – which had no seats in Congress at the time – asked local members to send representatives to a national nominating convention.[144] Seeing this, Democrat Andrew Jackson – who never missed a chance to bypass Congress or establish more links to the public – copied the idea for his own nomination that year.[145]

For the rest of the century, the party system remained mostly unregulated. This was probably a good thing, since competition forced both parties to invent and adopt ostentatiously democratic procedures. But giving the people what they wanted, especially in the rapidly growing cities, also led to machine politics. Starting in the early twentieth century, Progressives angered by insider corruption persuaded government to open the system by holding party primaries.[146] Soon after, Congress passed the Tillman Act (1907),[147] prohibiting banks and corporations from making campaign donations.

The irony is that machine politics was the closest America ever came to Downs' assumption that the parties would place cold-blooded bets on whichever candidate seemed most likely to win. And indeed, nineteenth-century professionals had seen politics "as a trade or task, usually free of moral or ideological considerations."[148] This encouraged them to place what most voters wanted even above their own convictions. More surprisingly, the new system was egalitarian. Despite or perhaps because of its venality, machine politics was far more inclusive than the eighteenth-century practice of leaving government to the wealthy. When Van Buren formalized party patronage in the 1820s, he made political organizing into a middle-class career.[149] At one level, this reliance on graft was a comically *ad hoc* way to fund democracy, especially since voters had so little information that bosses could routinely pocket indefensible sums for shoddy services and still be reelected. And yet, it was not obviously worse than modern parties' reliance on billionaire donors.

The Progressives hoped that primary elections would replace political bosses with something like townhall democracy.[150] Looking back, this ignored the defining problem that most voters would never know enough to make intelligent choices.[151] Moreover, agreeing with a particular candidate's choices is not enough: Voters must also make the additional judgment of how likely she was to win, and discount their choice accordingly. It was hard to see how voters can possibly do this better than professionals who have made a detailed study of the problem.[152]

The primary system also suffers from structural distortions. Without powerful party organizations to back them, candidates are forced to publicize themselves. As Prof. Hofstadter has argued, this gives rich donors even more influence than they had in the Gilded Age.[153] The need for publicity also rewards flamboyant candidates for using shock value to attract attention. Finally, most candidates start as unknowns. This, combined with the press's usual entertainment value focus on asking which candidate will win, ensures that a politician who starts to get noticed can suddenly communicate more of her message to voters. But, as we emphasized in Chapter 3, we expect estimates based on such thin information to swing wildly.[154] Indeed, there may be no enduring winner at all until the bunched elections of "Super Tuesday" give one candidate an insurmountable lead. This is all well and good if the winner has been leading for weeks; if not, though, conferring the nomination on whoever happens to be leading at the moment resembles nothing so much as a hard-fought game of musical chairs.

That said, primaries offer an unrivaled testbed for trying out variations and extensions of the party's platform on scales that cannot otherwise be matched before Election Day. It is one thing for a political strategist to propose some new narrative and quite another to show that a politician can deliver it effectively, still less that large numbers of voters respond to it. The only uncertainty, and it is substantial, is whether the primary system's distortions make such results misleading.

Finally, the remaining wildcard in a process stuffed with wild cards is that candidates who fail in the primary may nevertheless run as independents in the general election.[155] This can be destructive to the extent that it makes voter choice less effective by splitting one party and suppressing its chances in the general election. At the same time, the existence of a third choice lets voters change course when primaries select extremists. One saving grace is that independent candidacies cannot succeed unless voters know enough facts to overcome their usual deference to party-endorsed candidates.

How, then, should we regard the Progressives' legacy? The randomness of primaries means that long-shot bets often pay off, and this encourages a crowded field. Moreover, there is no particular reason to think voters can sort through this field before a winner is declared. So many bad candidates are chosen.

The results are also predictably biased toward extremism. We have already said that modern presidential elections seldom attract more than a 55 percent turnout. But the corresponding figure for primaries is far lower – in 2020, only eleven states saw more than a third of their eligible voters go to the polls.[156] This gives Progressives outsized influence even though they account for just 35–40 percent of all Democrats.[157] Their grip is then further reinforced by the outsized number of Progressive donors,[158] and congressional seniority rules that systematically empower members from safe districts whose strongly partisan voters favor extremists as the furthest thing possible from the other party.

This institutional bias toward weak or extreme candidates also explains why both parties periodically fail to follow Downs–Hotelling strategies. From 1960 to 2012 there were at least three historically weak candidates: Barry Goldwater (1964), George McGovern (1972), and Michael Dukakis (1988). On the numbers, that made it reasonable to think that two bad candidates would run against each other every half-century or so. The Trump–Clinton (2016) matchup was in this sense entirely predictable. Worse, once one party elected a weak candidate, the chances that extremists in the other party would win the next election immediately rose to something like a fifty–fifty coin toss. From that point forward, the codependency would continue indefinitely until one side or the other finally broke the cycle by nominating a centrist.

The primary system also made candidates more dependent on large donors.[159] This made a lottery-like system still more random. Like any investor, donors must balance each candidate's chance of winning against the policies he promises to pursue in office. The problem, of course, is that the donor's preferred policies could be venal or wildly extremist. Moreover, the uncertainty of politics often favors wait-and-see strategies in which donors sit on the sidelines until some suitable candidate starts to pull ahead.[160] This creates the possibility of speculative bubbles in which each sponsor invests simply because the others do.

The question remains how much donors can shift outcomes compared to a world where money was irrelevant. Prof. Downs argued that no amount of money could convince well-informed citizens to vote against their interests. But many voters (the "baffleds") did not know enough to make decisions, and were therefore vulnerable to ad campaigns based on partial or false information. This means that donor influence depends on how the number of baffleds compares to the expected margin of victory.[161] Downs' inference is supported by the outcome of the 2020 election, where Democrats outspent Republicans by 15 percent in House races and an astonishing 65 percent in the Senate.[162] Despite this, the widely touted "blue wave" failed to materialize.[163] Presumably, four years of President Trump had taught voters on both sides more politics than they cared to know. This depressed the supply of baffleds to an all-time low, leaving only a tiny audience for the ads to target.[164]

Finally, the parties' efforts to narrow the issues do not end the day they choose a candidate. If anything, the process accelerates as the winners and losers argue over the party's platform. Here the losers' leverage comes from the near-certainty that they will only turn out for the general election if the nominee adopts some significant part of their agenda.[165] Historically, parties whose factions fail to do this have almost always lost.[166] These tensions are further complicated by a cross-cutting division between the party's presidential and congressional factions.[167] This is only natural given that congressmen are less visible than presidents, face elections twice as often, and represent much narrower slices of the electorate. The resulting intraparty tension ensures that some divided government persists even when one party controls the House, the Senate, and the White House.

## 5.6 FEEDBACKS

We argued in Chapter 4 that a smoothly functioning communications industry constantly develops new narratives and ideologies. Still, none of these matters until the two parties choose the particular issues that voters will see on Election Day.

Professor Downs' theory still provides the definitive guide to party competition in eras when public opinion is broadly centrist. It predicts that both parties will target the median voter, with an admixture of more radical positions designed to mobilize extremists on Election Day. This focus on median voters causes the parties' positions to overlap, suppresses further public debate on many issues, and supplies the indispensable first step toward forgetting and healing old fights. At the same time, the parties' need to motivate their respective supporters gives politics a permanent restlessness: Even if current policies were perfect, the out party would still find fault and offer fixes. This obsessive fault-finding destabilizes the mainstream consensus over and above the various psychological factors described in Chapter 3. Even so, the fact that bipartisanship was stable for most of the twentieth century shows that the effect is fairly modest.

Meanwhile, politicians have a clear incentive to remind voters how much they have accomplished. This narrative further burnishes bipartisanship's reputation for getting things done. To the extent the compromises consummate implicit trades between single-issue voters, they further reinforce bipartisanship by draining intensity on both sides. Conversely, rising polarization promotes ideology and conformism that suppress the supply of single-issue voters. This reduces the number of intensity-reducing trades and allows more anger to accumulate.

Finally, bipartisan eras usually feature widespread normative agreement on what the government's goals should be. This makes it natural for voters to choose politicians on the basis of competence and character. We argue in Chapter 7 that the shifting importance of individual attributes from one era to the next has profound implications for how Congress organizes itself, including the procedural rules that guard against majority tyranny.

Yet despite these successes, Professor Downs' theory is showing its age. First, it overlooks the messy details of how real parties pick candidates and platforms. When one party nominates extremists, the result is an uncompetitive race or "landslide." But when both parties do it, centrist voters will be shortchanged no matter who wins. Worse, there is the ratchet effect that an extremist who reaches the White House makes extremist challengers more viable when he runs for a second term. If the electorate then ejects the incumbent, extremism in both parties can continue indefinitely.

Second, we have argued that turnout rates should ideally give extremists just enough added influence to mimic an intensity-weighted vote across the electorate. But in practice local election turnout often overrepresents extremists so that city leaders are significantly more liberal than the people they serve. This is typically followed by a centrist backlash a few years later. Conversely, national elections that rely on massive get-out-the-vote drives inflate participation by the least informed and least passionate voters. The net result is to make the electorate more confused, volatile, and manipulable by donor-funded ad campaigns.

Third, Downs' model ignored the possibility that legislatures can deadlock, and the coercive politics strategies that this enables. Like George Washington, Downs thought that democracy could not long survive wild swings from one extreme to the other. But his model also implied that the chaos could only start once extremists on the Right or the Left held an absolute majority – something that has seldom if ever happened in human history. This chapter has instead argued that coercive politics lets extremists prevail at less than half that figure. Moreover, Downs' scenario would have angered just under half the country. By comparison, coercive politics lets extremists ignore three-quarters of the population. This builds resentment much faster.

Gridlock also changes the nature of politics. Because debates never end, politicians and media end up teaching voters the same narratives and ideologies for decades. This allows resentments to accumulate and builds polarization to the point that voters value candidates' party loyalty far above their competence and character.

Second, coercive politics strategies are predicated on politicians waiting to seize power in the indefinite future. This encourages a now-or-never willingness to engage in dishonesty and rule-bending when the moment seems to arrive. This can permanently lower honesty standards in both parties, making information impactedness even worse than before.

Third, coercive politics changes the electorate. In bipartisan eras, politicians who refuse to compromise collect fewer benefits for their districts and are voted out of office. The difference in coercive eras is that voters understand that the struggle will continue for years if not decades. This makes it rational to reelect representatives who accomplish nothing at all beyond blocking "the other side."

Finally, the silver lining of coercive politics is instability. Political competition guarantees that if extremists on one side move to the center, the
other side must follow or else lose elections for years. But since American
politics is a duopoly, each side knows that there is no permanent advantage to be gained from moving to the center because the other side will
immediately follow. The result is that Left- and Right-extremists tacitly
cooperate to make each other viable. This metastability is further reinforced by the normal frictions that keep career politicians from abruptly
changing their promises. Even so, if extremists were to suddenly lose
control of either party – for example, by being ejected from their leadership posts in Congress or seeing their party nominate a reliably centrist
presidential candidate – the Downsian politicians on both sides would
quickly migrate to the center until bipartisanship returned.

## Notes

1  *Federalist* No. 10 at p. 39 (Madison).
2  Downs (1957) at pp. 11 and 104 at n. 3. While real elections sometimes end
   in ties, state law typically invokes random methods such as coin tosses or
   poker hands to break the impasse. Levenson (2018).
3  Hofstadter [1959a] at p. 812.
4  *Federalist* No. 10 at pp. 38–9. (Madison).
5  Hofstadter [1959a] at p. 812.
6  *See, e.g.,* Anon (n.d. (j)); Gill (2019); and Churchill [1956] at p. 137.
7  *Federalist* No. 10 at pp. 39–40 (Madison).
8  *Federalist* No. 6 at pp. 20–21 (Hamilton).
9  *Federalist* No. 10 at p. 39 (Madison).
10  Wallace (1968) at p. 454.
11  Wallace (1968) at p. 454.
12  Hofstadter (1969) at pp. 41–2.
13  Churchill [1956] at pp. 133 and 302; Hofstadter (1969) at pp. 41–2. The
    system was made even less democratic by "rotten boroughs." By the early
    nineteenth century nearly 40 percent of the seats in parliament came from
    districts with fewer than 100 electors, a number small enough to bribe or
    intimidate. Wikipedia (50). Such methods were all the more effective in an
    era when electors still cast their vote in open meetings. Anon (n.d. (f)).
14  Hofstadter (1969) at p. 219.
15  Wallace (1968) at p. 455; Hofstadter (1969) at pp. 242–3.
16  Churchill [1957] at pp. 107, 111.
17  Churchill [1957] at pp. 118–25.
18  Churchill [1957] at p. 128.
19  Engerman and Sokoloff (2005) at pp. 812.
20  Brands (2018) at p. 102. As late as 1820, future president John Quincy Adams
    passionately warned against extending the franchise in Massachusetts.
    Engerman and Sokoloff (2005) at p. 14. The requirement that voters pay

taxes lingered in Pennsylvania and Rhode Island into the early twentieth century. Engerman and Sokoloff (2005) at p. 15.

21 England had traditionally limited voting to "freeholders" thought to have a stake in the community. Engerman and Sokoloff (2005) at p. 6.

22 Hofstadter (1969) at p. 210.

23 Anon (n.d. (g)).

24 Engerman and Sokoloff (2005) at p. 16.

25 Ricks (2020) at p. 247.

26 Hofstadter (1969) at p. 121.

27 Hofstadter (1969) at p. 41.

28 Allen (2020).

29 Brands (2018) at p. 265.

30 Amy (n.d.)

31 Gehlbach (2022) at pp. 11–12.

32 Since the whole point of voting is to exercise choice, citizens always derive value by voting for the second most popular party even when its chances of winning are small. Voting for a third party, on the other hand, is wasteful so long as the first two choices are approximately satisfactory. Voters may however support a third party for other reasons, most obviously to show *other* voters that victory two or three elections hence is more plausible than it seems. This lets dissidents lay the groundwork for replacing one of the existing parties if their demands are not met.

33 The most notable example was the collapse of the Whig Party in the 1850s, whose residual support in border states helped split the Democrat vote in 1860. This let Abraham Lincoln win the election. Guelzo (2021b) at p. 234.

34 Prof. Hofstadter argued that America's long series of failed third parties have achieved a great deal: The Liberty and Free-Soil parties led to the abolition of slavery, while the Populists led to railroad regulation, the income tax, an expanded financial system, the direct election of senators, and lavish farm subsidies. Hofstadter (1955) at pp. 94, 101, 109, and 126.

35 Hofstadter (1969) at pp. 31, 345.

36 Hofstadter (1969) at pp. 35–7, p. 115 at n. 43, and p. 123.

37 Hofstadter (1969) at p. 81.

38 Hofstadter (1969) at p. 115.

39 Hopes of eventual vindication played a crucial role in persuading the Federalists to relinquish power after losing to Thomas Jefferson in 1800. Hofstadter (1969) at p. 127. Decades later, Samuel Tilden similarly charged that the 1876 election had been stolen, only to add in the next breath, "Be of good cheer. The Republic will live. The institutions of our fathers are not to expire in shame. The sovereignty of the people shall be rescued from this peril and re-established." Rehnquist (2004) at p. 161. Despite endless talk of "our fragile democracy," the same faith applies today. The US has held elections for so many years that hardly any American politician can imagine a world without them.

40 The Federalist opposition had bitterly opposed the war because conflict with the Royal Navy would hurt business in its New England political stronghold. Despite this, the Federalists appeared vindicated when Madison's Jefferson

Republican Party signed a disappointing peace treaty in 1814. That should have doomed the Jefferson Republicans had it not been for the era's poor communications, which allowed Andrew Jackson to win a spectacular victory at the Battle of New Orleans two weeks *after* the war had ended. Suddenly, Americans decided that the war had been successful after all – and tarred the Federalists with treason for calling on New England to negotiate a separate peace with Britain at the Hartford Convention of 1814. Brands (2018) at pp. 48, 73.

41  Brands (2018) at p. 231.

42  Brands (2018) at pp. 227–8.

43  Meacham (2008) at pp. 281–2.

44  Brands (2018) at pp. 103, 268.

45  Brands (2018) at p. 144.

46  Meacham (2008) at p. 14.

47  Meacham (2008) at p. 73.

48  Meacham (2008) at p. 70.

49  The Whigs, who opposed a strong presidency, took their name from Britain's pro-parliament, anti-monarchist party. Rehnquist (2004) at p. 160.

50  Brands (2018) at p. 262; Meacham (2008) at p. 369.

51  Hofstadter (1969) at pp. 249–50.

52  Wallace (1968) at p. 454.

53  Hofstadter (1969) at pp. 225–6.

54  Hofstadter (1969) at p. 227.

55  Hofstadter (1969) at pp. 229 and 248–9.

56  Hofstadter (1969) at pp. 249–50.

57  Van Buren tied himself in knots trying to explain that, while both parties were necessary, Democrats were still inherently more virtuous so that their opponents should only win often enough to punish corruption. Similarly asymmetric views of the party system continued to dominate American political thought for the rest of the century. Hofstadter (1969) at pp. 257–71.

58  Scholars argue that the American system of two parties running on national platforms was not fully implemented until the 1840s. See, e.g., Quitt (2008) at p. 651.

59  The political discussion in Hotelling's paper is worth quoting in full:

> The competition for votes between the Republican and Democratic parties does not lead to a clear drawing of issues, an adoption of two strongly contrasted positions between which the voter may choose. Instead, each party strives to make its platform as much like the other's as possible. Any radical departure would lose many votes, even though it might lead to stronger commendation of the party by some who would vote for it anyhow. Each candidate "pussyfoots," replies ambiguously to questions, refuses to take a definite stand in any controversy for fear of losing votes. Real differences, if they ever exist, fade gradually with time though the issues may be as important as ever. The Democratic party, once opposed to protective tariffs, moves gradually to a position almost, but not quite, identical with that of the Republicans. It need have no fear of fanatical free-traders, since they will still prefer it to the Republican party, and its advocacy of a continued high tariff will bring it the money and votes of some intermediate groups. (Hotelling 1929 at pp. 54–5)

60 The median voter did not have to be moderate. In a strongly polarized world, the center could be so thoroughly eroded that a hard-right or hard-left voter was just as likely. Nor, for that matter, does the word "moderate" have any particular content: What counts as moderate opinion today could just as easily be vilified tomorrow.

61 Mayhew (2002) at p. 148.

62 Downs (1957) at p. 101.

63 Professor Gans reports that preceding elections are just barely significant at the 0.5 level compared to a simple coin flip. Gans (1985) at p. 231 and Table 2. Furthermore, even this signal disappears when the winning candidate from the first election fails to run in the second. Gans (1985) at p. 232 and Table 3.

64 For example, the Republican Party has been pro-tariff (1850s–1960s), anti-tariff (1970s–2016), and pro-tariff again (2017–present); isolationist (1917–67) and interventionist (1970s–present); and pro-civil rights (1860–1890s) and hands-off (1890s–present). Barone (2020).

65 Downs (1957) at p. 110.

66 Downs (1957) at pp. 110–11.

67 For the large literature modeling how rational politicians adjust their platforms to cope with uncertainty, see Gehlbach (2022) at pp. 27–51.

68 Gehlbach (2022) at p. 98.

69 Also called the "Median Voter Theorem." See, generally, Wikipedia (37). Downs' (1957) result was anticipated by Black (1948), although Downs may not have known this.

70 Downs (1957) at pp. 117–19.

71 Wikipedia (58).

72 Downs (1957) at p. 118.

73 Wikipedia (61).

74 Green and Gerber (2015) at p. 4.

75 Wolfinger and Rosenstone (1980) at p. 109.

76 Leighley and Nagler (2013).

77 Riley (2020).

78 See, e.g., Bailey (2020) (Portland City Council races); Wikipedia (3, 4) (New York City mayoral races).

79 The problem would be much ameliorated if *both* political extremes showed up and canceled each other. However, social voting implies that progressive extremists will normally outnumber extreme conservatives in red states and vice versa in blue ones. The question remains why parties that find themselves in the minority do not close the gap by adjusting their platforms to local beliefs. The answer, almost certainly, is that no substantive policy can persuade social voters who prefer to believe that one national party (and its local affiliates) is inherently more virtuous than the other.

80 See, e.g., Kavanaugh (2021) (detailing deep disagreement between Portland, OR, residents and their city council on funding the police).

81 Fuller (2022).

82 Vincent (2021).

83 Wikipedia (61).

84  In principle, turnout could equally be *suppressed* through race-neutral, income-adjusted voting fees. These however are unlikely, given the 24th Amendment banning poll taxes in federal elections and the ugly historical precedent of such taxes in the Jim Crow South.

85  Polls show that America remains a majority-centrist country – but only if nonvoters are included in the mix. A recent survey by the Hidden Tribes Project found that fully two-thirds (67 percent) of the population has squarely centrist worldviews. Hawkins et al. (2018) at p. 6. The figure comes with the large caveat that it includes a "Politically Disengaged" population (26 percent) who seldom vote. Hawkins et al. (2018).

86  Hawkins et al. (2018).

87  See, e.g., Hawkins et al. (2018). This social fact is reinforced by modern political parties, which constantly hector their coalition members to support each other's priorities.

88  Downs (1957) at p. 133.

89  Downs (1957) at pp. 110 and 135.

90  Downs (1957) at p. 133.

91  Downs (1957) at pp. 56–7.

92  Downs (1957) at pp. 55–60.

93  Guriev and coauthors show that increased voter access to the web has made incumbency more tenuous in Eastern Europe, interpreting the rise of online political news as a dumbing-down that favors populist outsiders. Guriev, Melnikov, and Zhuravskaya (2021). Here, Downsian theory suggests an equally plausible alternative: Giving voters *better* information *always* makes incumbency less stable.

94  Guriev, Melnikov, and Zhuravskaya (2021) at p. 60.

95  Gans (1985) at p. 234 and n. 15.

96  The examples were the presidents following Jefferson, Madison, Jackson, Lincoln, Grant, McKinley, Coolidge, and Franklin Roosevelt. The exceptions were the presidents who succeeded Cleveland and Wilson.

97  The exception was G. H. W. Bush's election in 1988.

98  Downs (1957) at p. 57.

99  Ulysses Grant recalled in his *Memoirs* that "Opposition to slavery was not a creed of either political party before 1848. In some sections more anti-slavery men belonged to the Democratic party, and in others to the Whigs." Grant [1885] at pp. 300–1.

100 Wikipedia (17). Similarly, Israeli Arabs – despite representing 20 percent of the population – never shared power before 2021, when mainstream parties' hatred of Prime Minister Netanyahu overcame their traditional insistence on an all-Jewish government. Wikipedia (62).

101 The main caveat is that the minority must be dispersed unevenly, producing enough local majorities to elect legislators.

102 Risen (2014) at p. 29.

103 US Census Bureau (2020).

104 This asymmetry has existed in one form or another since the early 1800s, with Democrats representing diverse collections of out-groups against

Republicans supported by a much more homogenous constituency that views itself as typically American. Barone (2019) at p. 11; Swaim (2019).

105  Brands (2018) at p. 27.

106  *Shelley v. Kraemer*, 334 U.S. 1 (1948).

107  *Romer v. Evans*, 517 U.S. 620 (1996).

108  *Levy v. Louisiana*, 391 U.S. 68 (1968).

109  *Plessy v. Ferguson*, 163 U.S. 537 (1896).

110  *Korematsu v. United States*, 323 U.S. 214 (1943).

111  Grinspan (2021) at p. 9.

112  Colonial voters typically selected their elected representatives based on social status, reputation, and a willingness to ply constituents with rum punch, without reference to any recognizable issues. Hofstadter (1969) at p. 48. Thereafter, candidates' individual qualities remained dominant through out the 1790s, when many Americans actively disapproved of organized parties trying to influence their representatives in Congress. Hofstadter (1969) at p. 95. And change, when it did come, arrived slowly. As late as the 1820s, astonished foreigners routinely reported that "The Americans ... are infinitely more occupied about bringing in a given candidate" than his platform. Meacham (2008) at p. 90.

113  Given the difficulty of learning about candidates in a crowded field, voters would have chosen winners nearly at random, with a slight preference for those who were already famous or particularly skilled in publicity. See, e.g., Adams (1776) ("The Representative Assembly[] should be an exact Portrait, in Miniature, of the People at large"); Smith and Hamilton [1788] at pp. 759–60 (representatives "should be a true picture of the people" biased toward "those with military, popular, civil or legal talents [who] will be sufficiently well-known to win election in a district of thirty or forty thousand voters"). This would have led to a Congress composed of ordinary men with some slight admixture of talent, wealth, and demagoguery.

114  Barone (2019) at p. 63.

115  Noonan (2021).

116  Smith and Hamilton [1788] at p. 770.

117  See, e.g., Brands (2018) at pp. 49–50 (Daniel Webster) and p. 92 (Henry Clay).

118  Brufke (2019) (Republican women); Weissert (2021) (Democrat veterans).

119  The result can be calculated using the Binomial Theorem. See Maurer and Karapetyan (2021) for details.

120  Showah (2022) reports that Democrats have earned supermajorities twice since the current sixty-vote filibuster rule was implemented in 1975, and held more than fifty-five seats five times. The Republicans have failed to match either feat, hinting that they may face some structural disadvantage.

121  Mayhew (2002) at pp. 91, 147–8, 150. Downsian theory similarly predicts that median voter outcomes will be systematically offset to the extent that the public believes one party is systematically more incompetent, corrupt, or likely to keep promises than the other. Gehlbach (2022) at p. 35.

122  Barone (2019) at p. 43.

123  This is explicit in the Republican Party's "Hastert rule," which holds that no legislation should ever reach the House floor unless a majority of the majority supports it; Fechner (2014). In practice, a minority party's power to propose or amend legislation in the House has almost always been severely limited. Green (2015).

124  Watt (1968) at p. 8 ("Pre-eminent ... was the fact, difficult to grasp for one accustomed to political life in English-speaking nations, that the political opposition ... was not a 'loyal' opposition ... Rather, their aim was to take over the Republic and totally change its form").

125  W. B. Yeats [1919b].

126  Left- and right-wing extremists refused to participate in every French government from the fall of the Second Empire (1870) to the Dreyfus Affair (1894). Watt [1962] at pp. 2–19; Derfler (2002) at p. 7. Thereafter the French left renounced violent revolution and worked with centrists to keep the right from power. Derfler (2002) at p. 29. The strategy was briefly interrupted when rejectionist Communists stopped working with moderates in the 1930s. Brendon (2000) at p. 333. Even then, the Communists soon reverted to cooperation by joining a "Popular Front" government after street riots nearly produced a right-wing coup. Brendon (2000) at 334.

127  Socialists and conservative Catholic parties boycotted Italian governments from 1898 to the start of World War I, although both sides' opposition softened over time. (Anon n.d. (a)). After the war, Communist and Fascist extremists both demanded an end to centrist rule. This ended badly for the left when Fascist thugs used extralegal violence to suppress their enemies. Soon afterward, the government handed power to Mussolini after the latter's "March on Rome." Brendon (2000) at p. 26.

128  Spanish politics in the early 1930s was badly fragmented among nationalist, conservative, clerical, traditionalist, centrist, liberal democrat, separatist, radical, left republican, socialist, and syndicalist parties. All were intransigent and some sought to overthrow the state. Brendon (2000) at pp. 351 and 365. The democratic collapse began with an unsuccessful Communist-backed rising in 1934, followed by a right-wing regional uprising which persuaded the Communists to join the centrists. The resulting Popular Front coalition won power in 1936 but suffered from so many quarrels that it never governed effectively. This led to an attempted coup and the start of the Spanish Civil War. Brendon (2000) at pp. 368 and 372.

129  Mommsen (1996) at p. 355; Ward (1981) at pp. 30, 32.

130  Ward (1981) at pp. 34 and 38.

131  Deutscher Bundestag (2006).

132  Richie (1998) at p. 401 (quoting Josef Goebbels' political speech: "[T]hings cannot go on as they are. We have the choice: from here on into Bolshevist anarchy or from here on into National Socialist order and discipline").

133  The German Communist party's rejectionist politics reinforced the Nazis' attacks on democracy. Moreover, the cooperation was often deliberate, as when some local Communists "invaded Nazi meetings ... to urge collaboration in strikes, protest demonstrations, and defiance of republican

authorities"; Ward (1981) at p. 39. For his part, Nazi leader Josef Goebbels shared the Communists' antidemocratic and antirepublican goals, and even insisted on being called "Comrade Dr. Goebbels." He prioritized toppling the republic over struggling with the Communists for working-class support. Richie (1998) at 386.

134 Prof. Downs describes this logic explicitly:

> The exact probability level at which he switches will partly depend on how important he thinks it is to keep the worst party from winning. For example, let us assume that there are three parties: Right, Center, and Left. Voter X prefers Right to Center and Center to Left, but if he believes that Right has the least chance of winning and is almost indifferent between Center and Left, he is less likely to switch his vote from Right to Center than if he slightly prefers Right to Center but abhors Left. (Downs 1957 at pp. 48–9)

135 Brie (2010).

136 The combined Communist/Nazi tickets polled 51.9 percent in the July 1932 election and 50.0 percent in November 1932. Deutscher Bundestag (2006).

137 The point is neatly summed up by activist Saul Alinsky's aphorism, famously appropriated by Obama acolyte Rahm Emanuel, that radicals must "Never let a crisis go to waste." Morci (2021).

138 The dependency was particularly visible in the 2022 midterm elections, in which Democrats regularly denounced "MAGA Republicans" as "a threat to democracy" while simultaneously spending $53 million to help thirteen of their enemies win primaries against more centrist opponents. Crane (2022). The obvious calculation was that taking centrist choices off the table would increase Democrats' own chances of winning the general election. The fact that it also increased the chances of far-right candidates winning must have seemed an acceptable trade.

139 Barone (2019) at p. 93; Mayhew (2002) at p. 49. In the usual case where voters know the presidential candidates better than the congressional ones, rational vote-splitters will normally name their top pick for president, and then dilute their downside risk by supporting the opposing party in Congress. Ticket splitters further fine-tune their choice by deciding whether to oppose the president's party in just one chamber of Congress or both. The recent trend is for the Senate to remain loyal to the president's party. Seib (2020).

140 Or perhaps just 20 percent. The fact that American elections show substantial randomness suggests that extremists with sufficiently long time horizons could quite rationally decide that it was better to lose several elections in hopes of eventually winning a long-shot victory.

141 One possible exception involves the so-called reconciliation procedures that allow floor amendments in both the House and the Senate. House Budget Committee (2021). In principle, centrists could present a completely new alternative bill at this point. In practice, this will usually be a case of too little too late: Reconciliation is only relevant where the House and Senate have already overcome their deadlock to the point of passing bills in each chamber.

142  See Figure 1.1.
143  Brands (2018) at p. 106.
144  Wikipedia (60).
145  Meacham (2008) at pp. 281–2.
146  Wikipedia (60).
147  52 U.S.C. § 30118.
148  Grinspan (2016) at p. 48.
149  Hofstadter (1969) at pp. 225–6; Grinspan (2021) at pp. 45–8.
150  Hofstadter (1955) at p. 240.
151  The fact that primaries tend to be low-turnout events dominated by extremists makes the problem still worse. This explains why the Democratic Party, in particular, leavens the result by automatically giving elected politicians a "super-delegate" status whose votes can sometimes change outcomes. This notably allowed party professionals to block a Bernie Sanders nomination in 2016. Anon (n.d. (l)). The mechanism is nevertheless awkward, since parties that visibly overrule their own voters will often lose support going into the general election.
152  One could of course argue that financial markets routinely aggregate the "wisdom of crowds" into judgments that outperform the average estimate. This however only works because those who possess better information are allowed to invest more. This is very different from politics, where ignorant voters cast the same number of votes as everyone else.
153  Hofstadter (1955) at p. 242.
154  The fact that voters are most interested in candidates who seem likely to win also adds to frontrunners' popularity at the expense of other candidates.
155  Recent examples include Alaska Sen. Lisa Murkowski in 2010 (Wikipedia (2)) and Buffalo Mayor Byron Brown in 2021 (McKinley 2022).
156  Anon (n.d. (n)).
157  Freeman (2020). Evangelical Christians, who account for roughly one-fifth (22.5 percent) of all Americans, have long played a similar role in the Republican party. Burge (2019).
158  Naively, at least, we expect donors on both the left and right to be extreme. This follows from our usual argument that citizens feel most intensely when there is a large gap between their personal political ideals and current policy.
159  Small donations are mostly valuable as evidence of passion that can boost a candidate's turnout on Election Day or help her to survive a bad news cycle. Palmer (2020). The case is different in congressional politics, where extremist members who mainly rely on small donations can afford to defy party elders. This seems to have driven much of the Republican House Freedom Caucus' resistance to Speaker Kevin McCarthy in 2023. Lange et al. (2023).
160  The reverse can also happen, with big donors pausing support when their preferred candidate suffers a bad news cycle to see if he recovers.
161  Downs (1957) at pp. 93–4.
162  Levine and Funakoshi (2020).
163  Levine and Funakoshi (2020).

164 The result also makes sense for social voters. Normally, massive ad buys shift the "average" message that social voters see on television and therefore their estimates of "mainstream" opinion. The problem in the Trump years was that voters were already saturated with political messaging. This meant that they had more than enough information to estimate the "mainstream," and no feasible amount of advertising could possibly change that.

165 Hofstadter (1964c) at p. 898.

166 Hofstadter (1964c) at p. 898.

167 Hofstadter (1964c) at p. 898.

# 6

## The "Extended Republic"

### Communities, States, and Regions

Madison defined his institutions geographically. At one level, the choice was obvious: English and Colonial governments had always been organized this way. All the same, it was not inevitable. Schemes like medieval guilds, the French Estates, and Fascist Italy's Worker-Management Councils have often downgraded geography in favor of supposedly more fundamental categories like class and occupation. If the Framers rejected such approaches, they must have thought that voters who lived near each were more likely to share a common viewpoint. In the language of Chapter 2, this was a bet that interactions between neighbors – social voting – caused voters' policy choices to converge at least as much as their Downsian self-interest.

At the same time, it was only natural that different problems would be best addressed by different-sized units of government. For the smallest units, this mostly meant making sure that the consensus which social voting produced was faithfully translated into seats in Congress. On the other hand, most states were big enough to host several social networks, each of which was practically certain to disagree with the others. The job of state governments was to resolve those differences so that their citizens would eventually come to support a single shared policy. Finally, the American Revolution had shown how economic and social differences that were barely noticeable at the state level could accumulate into dangerous divisions on regional scales. For some issues, this meant letting each state pursue whatever solutions best fit its voters' beliefs and circumstances. For others, it meant reminding the citizens that a strong federal government could accomplish projects that no single state could possibly aspire to on its own.

But just stating these principles is still not enough to draw boundaries and allocate responsibilities. There are, after all, infinitely many ways to divide the country into 50 states or 435 congressional districts. Worse, every possible map empowers some groups while splitting and disempowering others.[1] This makes it essential that whatever maps do prevail are designed in a principled and transparent way. We argue in Section 6.1 that tradition, law, and social voter theory all imply that political borders should track community. We also explain how this abstract principle can be made to define practical maps. Section 6.2 asks how states can reconcile the various communities within their borders to a single, widely agreed course of action. Finally, Section 6.3 examines Madison's claim that a federal system is the best way to manage material and cultural differences between regions.

## 6.1 CONGRESSIONAL DISTRICTS

The Framers thought that voters would elect candidates that they admired, or trusted, or simply resembled. But that was all. The candidates would say little about the issues before Election Day. Instead, the substantive debate would only start once Congress convened.[2] At this point, Madison's formal rules would step in to moderate democracy's inevitable tendency toward bad decisions.

That's not how it turned out. While Madison's institutions worked much as he imagined, the *internal politics* of Congress, Executive, and courts was only half the story. The surprise was that a second, *external politics* quickly spread the debate to ordinary citizens through newspapers and political parties. This narrowed and sometimes decided issues before the new Congress was even seated. Crucially, this left fewer differences for Congress to argue about and overcome. As Prof. Hofstadter has argued, the Constitution, "for all its ingenuity," might never have succeeded otherwise.[3]

With no Madison to design them, the institutions of journalism and political parties evolved opportunistically in whatever directions seemed most likely to please the public. Even so, the system worked well enough that when Congress and state legislatures finally got around to legislating reform, the changes they implemented (e.g., secret ballots, campaign finance) were narrow enough to leave the Framers' basic architecture unchanged. That said, there was one issue the legislators could not avoid. One way or another, there had to be rules for translating the public's votes into seats in Congress. The accusations of "gerrymandering" began immediately.

The mechanics of gerrymandering are straightforward. Suppose there are three adjoining districts A, B, and C, all of which are so evenly split between Republicans and Democrats that the elections in each are a tossup. Then, if we adjust each district's borders so that a large number of the Republicans who used to live in Districts A and B now find themselves in C, the Democrats will win A and B while the Republicans win C. Suddenly, what used to be a 50–50 gamble sends two Democrats to Congress for every Republican.[4] Now suppose that voters belong to a particular social network or, as we will usually say in this chapter, "community." Then if one community receives its own congressional district, the inhabitants can send a representative to Congress. But if a second community is divided across three districts, its citizens will be in the minority everywhere and receive no representation at all. The upshot is that the first community is much more likely to influence policy than the second, even though both groups are equally deserving.

But if the sin lies in splitting communities, we can also guess at a cure. All legislatures have to do is draw maps that, so far as geometry and arithmetic allow, keep communities together by ensuring that each is contained within a single district.[5] This is traditionally done by letting legislators adjust district boundaries that might otherwise cut communities in half. The counterargument, of course, is that legislators are partisans who cannot be trusted. The question immediately follows whether respect for community can be implemented some other way.

Readers could be excused for thinking that judges and legislators would have found some appropriate criterion by now. In fact, Americans have been trying and failing to find principled rules for over two centuries. Even so, they have made progress. The eighteenth-century Anglo-American world was cursed with "rotten boroughs" where tiny numbers of voters decided who sat in the legislature. The US Supreme Court's landmark decision in *Baker* v. *Carr* (1962) and Congress's passage of the Voting Rights Act three years later ended this pathology by making one-man-one-vote a constitutional principle.[6]

By itself, however, one-man-one-vote is not enough to end gerrymanders. The reason is that there are infinitely many ways to divide states into similarly populous districts. Starting in the early 1800s, state legislators and congressmen began searching for a second principle that would deter partisan mapmakers entirely. In practice, the strategy invariably came down to limiting the particular shapes that legislators were allowed to draw. Then in the 1960s the US Supreme Court,

FIGURE 6.1 Elkanah Tisdale's "The Gerry-mander" (1812)
Source: Bettmann / Getty Images

fresh from its success in *Baker,* joined the hunt. This led to still more geometry-based proposals.

Probably the strangest aspect of this agenda is how much of it was, and still is, inspired by a newspaper cartoon. Even though politicians have manipulated electoral maps since colonial times,[7] modern reform arguments invariably start from newspaper cartoonist Elkanah Tisdale's (1768–1835) sketch lampooning Massachusetts Governor Elbridge Gerry's eponymously self-serving 1815 redistricting map (Figure 6.1).[8] With this one sketch, Tisdale convinced not only his contemporaries, but millions of their unborn descendants, that they could detect electoral dishonesty with a single glance.[9]

Can a sketch really do this? Certainly, there was a grain of truth in Tisdale's satire. The only possible explanation for Governor Gerry's weirdly distorted districts was political advantage. Still, legal rules are supposed to be articulable – and practically all scholars admit that an intuition that some geometries look "strange" fails to meet this standard.[10] Worse, would-be reformers soon leaped to the opposite conclusion that districts which did *not* look "strange" must ipso facto be fair. This led to a long series of state and federal statutes requiring legislatures to draw districts featuring certain favored geometries that could loosely be called "contiguous" and "compact."[11]

Looking back, it's easy to see how flawed the agenda was. Even if Tisdale had been right that *some* gerrymandered maps look suspicious, it hardly followed that they all were. So, while the geometric standard probably did deter the laziest forms of cheating, cleverer ones remained possible.[12] The hard-nosed way to fix this problem would have been to tighten the geometric requirements still further. As the economist William Vickrey pointed out in 1961, it is easy to invent algorithms that generate random maps that no human can predict in advance.[13] This would immediately rule out all possible bias.

The problem, as Vickrey immediately added, was that such algorithms also split real communities at random.[14] Prof. Rossiter and her coauthors have shown that some states split real communities up to one-fifth (17 percent) of the time.[15] Any attempt to make geometric standards more stringent would have necessarily made this worse. At the same time, back-of-the-envelope calculations show that giving legislators the discretion to adjust boundaries on the scale of typical communities would *also* give them the power to change election outcomes in roughly one-fifth of all districts.[16] This is six times larger than the normal statistical fluctuations we would expect if every election was a 50–50 tossup. Not surprisingly, Congress and the states decided to leave things as they were.

Yet even despite these defects, the geometric approach worked reasonably well for over a century. The reason was practical: Creating a visually subtle, honest-looking gerrymander meant collecting small-scale features that systematically favored Democrats in some districts and Republicans in others. This, however, required would-be cheaters to examine thousands of ordinary-looking maps in hopes of finding one violently partisan example, and this exercise was nearly always unaffordable in an era when a single hand-drawn map could take months.[17] The difference since the 1990s is that computers can now draw nearly unlimited numbers of geometrically lawful maps and test them to find the handful that drastically favor one side or the other. The result is that traditional geometric rules now find themselves badly outclassed.[18]

For a time, the US Supreme Court thought it could do better. Recognizing that one-man-one-vote was incomplete, the justices' *Gaffney* v. *Cummings* (1973)[19] decision urged lower courts to find some constitutional principle that would limit partisan mapmakers.[20] Over the next half-century the Court considered several proposals without finding any it approved of. Then in 2019 the justices finally ran out of patience. The 5–4 majority in *Rucho* v. *Common Cause*[21] not only surveyed and rejected all existing approaches, but announced broad objections that any future proposal would have to meet. The basic point was that there had to be an articulable standard for deciding when a particular map was "fair." All existing proposals, the justices explained, did this based on how many votes each party had won in the past.[22] That, however, invariably introduced a "gravitational pull" toward proportional representation.[23] Yet winner-take-all districts *had* to be constitutional: Indeed, nearly every election since the Revolution had embraced precisely this principle.[24] Were they really all invalid? Then too, the policy stakes were astronomical: Winner-take-all races had enforced the country's "strong and stable two-party system" and, through the Hotelling–Downs mechanism, "contributed enormously to sound and effective government."[25] No unelected court could possibly overrule this choice. Having made these comments, the justices admitted defeat: While an acceptable approach might possibly emerge in the future, none of the existing proposals would do.

But if the old geometric approaches are played out, what constitutional principle should replace them? We argued in Chapter 2 that social networks play a central role in most voters' decisions. This immediately implies that democracy should be grounded in community. Moreover, this insight conforms to tradition, going back at least as far as Alexis de Tocqueville, who argued that New England democracy had emerged from preexisting communities of two to three thousand souls each.[26] From the standpoint of legal theory, this made its townships both "sovereign" and "primitive."[27] More practically, de Tocqueville added that the townships were small enough to develop homogenous opinions,[28] and faced problems rooted in human need and the "ordinary relations of life."[29] This, he hoped, would teach voters and politicians alike to value pragmatic solutions above ideology and empty rhetoric.

Still, that leaves the practical problem of how to draw borders that match real communities on the ground. One common suggestion has been to search for geographic areas that vote the same way. But that can't be right. After all, even families disagree. Nor should we follow the politicians' habit of stretching the word "community" to bundle together complete strangers who share some common occupation ("the legal community"), casual interest ("the hobbyist community"), or involuntary attribute ("the Black community"). Properly speaking, these are no more than guesses at what people who share the suggested attribute *should* feel for each other. Worse, the number of possible commonalities is endless.[30] Finally, we have already emphasized that deciding *which* issues voters see on Election Day is properly the job of political parties. Letting judges decide *which* attributes are most likely to unify voters would usurp this function, gerrymandering in favor of some issues and against others.

The only way to avoid these difficulties is to ask how voters themselves understand the communities they belong to. Here, the most probing questions are almost certainly "Do I feel loyal to this collective?" and "Will I defer to them if and when I find myself in the minority?" Moreover, these questions imply a method: Why not *ask* voters which community they belong to? To be sure, we cannot take the suggestion literally, since many voters would probably lie if they knew that political power was on the line. But this is a conventional problem with a conventional solution. On the principle that actions speak louder than words, all we have to do is observe citizens' choices – what economists call "revealed preferences" – to infer which groups they feel the most kinship to.

This was, in fact, the genius of New England townhall democracy. It was not just that people voted with their neighbors. It was *also* that they chose *which* neighbors they would vote with. On the one hand, citizens had to apply to government if they wanted to form a new township, or even join an existing one.[31] On the other, most townships contained more than one village. This made it easy to secede, and many did.[32] And that evidenced community in the strongest imaginable way. Not only did the citizens who attended the townhalls want to be there, but those who didn't were long gone.

The challenge is to match this paradigm today. If we wanted to, we could simply *assume* that the New England model still holds. And indeed, there is some truth to this: Groups of voters sometimes really do secede from existing local governments,[33] while other groups move en masse to form a local majority somewhere else.[34] These, however, are rare events. More usually, only individual Americans vote with their feet. And while migrations from New York and California to Florida and other Southern states[35] probably do express political views at some level, the patterns are too diffuse to say much about individual congressional districts. What we need, then, is some empirical proxy for when people interact, and to draw our districts accordingly.

One possibility is culture. Prof. Rossiter and her coauthors have shown that place names are a powerful tracer of cultural ties and therefore community.[36] All the same, their method has a large drawback: Given that place names and other cultural features are slow to change, whatever districts we draw will almost always be archaic compared to current communities. A second and more up-to-date method is to measure or at least estimate daily contacts between citizens. Mapmakers could then draw whichever district lines separate the smallest number of discussants consistent with the Supreme Court's equal population requirement. The problem, of course, is that finding out how often each pair of citizens talk to each other would be a massive violation of civil liberties. We can, however, do the next best thing by estimating the odds that randomly selected pairs will discuss politics. The question then becomes which variables should be used to construct the estimate. It turns out that the physical distance between voters is by far the most predictive. Work by Huckfeldt and coauthors has shown that the odds that two citizens will regularly talk to each other about politics declines with the square of the distance between their homes, with half of all contacts occurring within a radius of 8.4 kilometers or fifteen minutes by automobile. We show in the Appendix that algorithms based on this principle produce districts that are visually indistinguishable from those drawn by humans.

There is something pleasingly minimalist in constructing districts based on a single, politically neutral variable. All the same, there is no question that adding variables describing, say, citizens' education, or income, or race would improve the estimate still further. The main reason not to do this is that politicians already use these variables to design their platforms. This means that a legislature which groups community by race, for instance, will ipso facto optimize districts in ways that reward race-based appeals. Voters will then be bombarded with more racial narratives, so that elections divide still further along racial lines. Then, ten years later, statisticians updating the algorithm for the next redistricting map will find that race "explains" each party's support even better than it did before. The importance of race in defining "community" will have become a self-fulfilling prophecy.[37]

Finally, we have assumed that external politics takes place exclusively through face-to-face discussions. Yet the Framers often wrote letters to persuade and inform, and the invention of telephones and the web has annihilated distance. This makes it natural to ask whether it would be better to group citizens whose social contacts are mainly electronic in nonphysical congressional districts that only exist in cyberspace. Here the main conceptual problem is avoiding the kinds of factionalism that the Framers feared. Membership in physical districts, after all, is based on people's normally apolitical decision where to live. By comparison, letting voters choose their online congressional district could quickly lead to a runaway feedback in which a glamorous progressive congressman, say, attracted still more liberal voters so that her district became even more extreme. The existence of online districts would then polarize Congress even further, though with the offsetting wrinkle that the migration of extremists online would make centrist candidates in physical districts more competitive. Probably the best way to avoid this outcome, as in the physical world, would be to organize online districts around preexisting communities that have nothing to do with politics.[38]

## 6.2 STATES

Madison's decision to define the new government's architecture in spatial terms immediately reduced the Framers' task to two basic questions: First, how many levels of government should coexist in the same physical space? And second, which levels should address which issues?

That there had to be at least two levels must have seemed obvious. On the one hand, as de Tocqueville would later acknowledge, community was primordial and fundamental. This made local governments inescapable. On the other, the Framers' vision of a single, continent-wide nation meant nothing without a government to speak for it. But the case for an intermediate tier of states was less clear. Probably the best answer is that the states commanded such massive loyalty that the Framers could not have abolished them even if they had wanted to. Instead, the best they could hope for was that the national government would eventually accumulate an even greater loyalty that eclipsed them. But that would be the work of decades if it happened at all.

Yet since the states did exist, it was only natural to take advantage of their strengths. Stripped to its essentials, the goal of the new Constitution, like that of all governments, was to keep the new country's political resentments within bounds. This meant, at a minimum, providing services efficiently. But since Madison's scheme was defined by geography, this mostly came down to the question of how tasks should be allocated across the different levels of government. For a few missions – notably including military power, diplomacy, interstate commerce, and collecting tariffs – only the federal government was big enough to do the job efficiently. But for most tasks, smaller jurisdictions could capture whatever scale economies existed.[39]

Then too, size alone could not guarantee efficient programs. Cleverness also mattered. This often made it sensible to try several approaches before settling on a single, best-practice solution. The existence of parallel state governments created obvious testbeds ("laboratories of democracy")[40] for doing this, while also sharing best practices and potentially shaming underperforming governments in front of their voters. Of course, trying fifty experiments at once might be forty too many, particularly for simple problems where the likely difference between the best and worst outcomes was too slim for second-best jurisdictions to scrap their programs and start over. Still, there was nothing to keep individual states from pooling their resources to design a single set of uniform laws when that seemed most efficient, or even forming several competing coalitions to balance innovation against cost-sharing. The existence of multiple states let them do either of these things.

But physically providing services was only half the problem. The bigger challenge was often the *political* one of deciding which services to provide and who would pay for them. Here, scale did not help: Indeed, including more communities within a given jurisdiction meant more viewpoints to reconcile. The question was how large any state could grow before the resulting political dissatisfactions swamped the physical advantages of size. As in Chapter 3, it helps to analyze this political challenge separately for rational and social voters.

The key fact for rational voters is that we expect many opinions to vary on local scales – a poor neighborhood here, a particular industry there – with no clear trend over longer distances.[41] For the Framers, who considered difference in wealth "the most common and durable source of factions,"[42] this optimistically suggested that opinion in large states might not be significantly more diverse than it was in small ones. If so, states need only be smaller than the regional-scale differences that separated, say, the commercial North from the agrarian South.

The situation for social voters was more complicated. Because it is so overwhelmingly predicated on face-to-face interactions, social conformity is inherently short-ranged.[43] For the Framers, this explained why "factions" hardly ever grew beyond a certain size,[44] and were for that reason more likely to dominate small states like Rhode Island compared to large ones like Massachusetts.[45] This suggested that mid-sized states that spanned several social networks were the best way to reconcile disagreements. The task was greatly facilitated by the fact that (by definition) social voters cared much less about substantive policy than about agreeing with each other. This reduced the problem of compromise and healing to coordinating each network's voters so that they converged on the same opinion at the same time. The task was further facilitated by the early Republic's ferociously strong norm that laws, once enacted, were ipso facto legitimate.[46]

But if states had an optimum size, it was still possible that Congress could sometimes get the answer wrong by admitting ungovernably large states. If so, cutting an existing state into two or more pieces could improve voter satisfaction.[47] This was a popular solution in the early Republic when Congress carved Vermont (1790), Kentucky (1792), Maine (1820), and West Virginia (1863) from existing states. In theory, at least, the case for dismembering states still depends on their internal homogeneity. Where intrastate conflicts routinely deadlock – or one large area consistently outvotes the others – there seems little reason not to accord them the same protections that the populations of small states enjoy.[48]

If the Framers had a blind spot, it was thinking that state and federal politics would proceed independently. The rise of parties changed all that. Since creating and maintaining separate grassroots organizations for state and federal elections was plainly unaffordable, local party branches had to choose whether to design their platforms to win national elections or local ones. From the Civil War to the mid-twentieth century, Democrats often chose the latter. This gave Republicans an outsized edge in presidential elections, where candidates could take advantage of centrists' disgust with Northern Democrats' political machines and Southern Democrats' racism.[49]

The existence of local heterodoxies also blurred national platforms. This was practically unavoidable where the party's national strength depended on politicians like West Virginia's Sen. Joe Manchin who could only be elected as mavericks. In extreme cases, the national party might even embrace these heresies to fend off third-party challenges, as Bryan's Democrats did by adopting various populist positions in the 1890s.[50] Today, though, the influence mostly runs in the other direction, with national platforms forcing local branches to adopt unwinnable views.[51]

The predictable result has been one-party rule in states like New York and California, leading to a politics in which perhaps one-third of the population dictates policy to everyone else.[52] This has turned primaries into de facto general elections in which voters confront large fields of longshot candidates, none of whose platforms is worth learning about ex ante. Meanwhile, the fact that primaries almost always suffer from low turnout forces candidates to woo their party's extremists. When the one-party states are also populous, this same extremism can end up dominating the national platform as well.[53]

This coupling of state and national politics has reacted strangely on the Framers' design. The most tragic consequence came during the Jim Crow era, when Madison's protections against majority tyranny at the national level sheltered state officials practicing their own majority tyranny against local Black people. The problem was especially vivid because Republicans did not need Black votes to win in the North, but had no chance of winning with or without them in the South. Had simple majority rule existed at the national level, Northern majorities in Congress would have made quick work of Jim Crow. Instead, the South's outsized representation in the Senate, coupled with the filibuster, preserved segregation down to the 1960s.

Finally, the erosion of the Framers' original design, with its strictly limited federal government, has massively increased the number of issues that federal voters must fold into their yes/no choice on Election Day. For example, it is perfectly possible that a libertarian would prefer liberal social policies but conservative fiscal principles. This choice was readily available so long as the former were a state responsibility and the latter a national one. Today, however, the extension of federal power into issues like crime and abortion has limited choice to the point where "fiscal conservatives" must be "cultural conservatives" as well. In the meantime, the existence of fifty state governments ensures constant partisan opposition no matter which party rules in Washington, continuing to generate discordant narratives long after most voters have decided to move on.

And if political reconciliation failed, the states would have to preserve themselves by force. This argued for large states with populations that greatly outnumbered any possible faction. The federal government would then act as a kind of insurer, declining to step in unless and until state governments found themselves on the edge of defeat.

There was an obvious economy in this. But there was a deeper principle. State governments, after all, could fall into tyrannies of the majority pathologies just as easily as the national one could. And if that did happen, the example of a functioning tyranny in one state could spread domino-like to the others. These dangers would have seemed especially prominent to the Framers, writing shortly after Shays' Rebellion had nearly toppled the Massachusetts government. So the new Constitution established a federal duty to intervene where a state rejected republican government by, say, becoming a monarchy.[54] The abolitionist argument that the North's obligation to defend slavery through the nasty business of returning runaway slaves would end by coarsening the Free State politics as well was a direct descendent of these concerns.[55] This however meant giving Northern States, and ultimately the federal government, a say in the South's internal arrangements. Once breached, there would be nothing to replace Madison's strict division of state and federal responsibilities except politics.

## 6.3 REGIONS

Some physical, cultural, and historical characteristics change so slowly from place to place as to be nearly invisible on the scale of individual states. Even so, the Framers saw that these strains could accumulate into dangerous differences on larger scales.[56] As Madison later recalled, "The great division in the U. States did not lie between the large & small states; It lay between Northern & Southern."[57] These included deep ethnic, religious, cultural differences[58] which periodically spilled into open contempt.[59] In the short run, the Framers hoped that Americans' broad similarities in religion and customs[60] would hold the country together. But in the longer term the individual states were too small to perceive, much less address, these conflicts. Only the federal government could deliver enough substantive benefits to bring the regions together.

Geography posed particular dangers for voting. We have said that rational voters mostly rely on information gathered in the course of everyday life to form their political opinions. The trouble with regional hatreds was that distance makes such learning almost impossible. Here the classic example came in the years immediately leading up to the Civil War, when Northern and Southern voters quickly convinced themselves that the other side was bluffing and would sooner or later back down.[61] In principle, of course, distance could equally encourage sentimental myths that encouraged each region to celebrate the others. But this was never likely. Part of the reason is physiological: As we argued in Chapter 3, evolution biases our memories to record fear over affection. Then too, political parties must constantly convince voters that real problems exist and are in need of fixing. This encourages them to populate the haze of distant regions with threats instead of reassurance. As Washington observed, local politicians habitually "misrepresent the opinions and aims of other districts."[62]

The implications of social voting were still less favorable. The goal of social voters, after all, is to make friends with the people they actually know and depend on. This means that it is almost always profitable for social voters to express solidarity with their immediate neighbors against distant enemies they will never meet. Worse still, we have argued that prejudice against *local* enemies is self-correcting: When voters encounter dissenters in their social networks they become more tolerant. But this mechanism disappears as soon as the antagonisms are regionally distributed. Finally, physical distance makes it possible for each region to develop its own narratives and ideologies in isolation. Thomas Jefferson, who thought that every human consensus sooner or later dissolves into conflict, argued that geographic segregation could only accelerate the process. On hearing news of the Missouri Compromise in 1820, the aging Jefferson declared himself "terrified" that the new law had confined slavery to some states and not others. Drawing "a geographical line, coinciding with a marked principle, moral and political," he argued, might prove "the knell of the Union." What had started as an arbitrary division would now become permanent. "Once conceived and held up to the angry passions of men," he declared, "the new division would "never be obliterated, and every new irritation will mark it deeper and deeper."[63]

Madison, obsessed as always by majority tyranny, also worried that the most populous states and regions would oppress the others. This led him to endorse the Constitution's principle that low-density states – first in the South and later the West – would receive extra votes to defend their interests in the Electoral College and Senate. Even so, the gamble was breathtaking. In principle, "tyranny of the majority" could just as easily have emerged along nongeographic fissures like class or race. Had that happened, Madison's whole scheme of giving some citizens extra votes would have complicated federal politics for no good reason. Yet today we see that he was right: 230 years later, our biggest political tensions are still geographic, even if the old North/South division has become an argument between "The Coasts" and "Flyover Country."

In the deeper sense, of course, the Framers had no choice. For all its elegance, the Constitution was also a hardheaded political bargain. On the one hand, the populous North knew that a national government would make it enormously richer. But on the other, the South and West would only join if they expected to share the riches, and this was doubtful so long as they were sure to be outvoted each time the federal government parceled out projects and taxes. Territories that expected the country's most populous states to routinely impose unjust or exploitative laws on the smaller ones might easily have decided not to seek statehood at all.[64]

Madison's protections for individual states should have eroded as the Union grew. Instead, Congress's consistent practice of admitting new states of roughly the same geographic size extended his minority protections from the low-density South to the even lower-density West. This preserved the Framers' goal of making sure that no single region could ever dominate the others.

The rise of mass parties complicated this calculus. So long as both parties remained nationally competitive, the Hotelling–Downs mechanism biased the system toward compromise. But it was equally possible for parties to win elections by running on issues that wooed one region and alienated others. As Madison warned in 1819, "Should a state of parties arise, founded on geographical boundaries and other physical and permanent distinctions which happen to coincide with them, what is to control these great repulsive Masses from awful shocks against each other?"[65]

Madison was almost certainly thinking of rational voters contesting narrowly material benefits. But social voting only made his "awful shocks" worse. The real secret of nineteenth-century partisanship lay in how party feeling channeled the myriad loves and hatreds of small-town life. This gave voters an emotional stake in party politics that transcended any merely material interest. Moreover, this emotional commitment, like the small-town cliques it fed on, it was the work of generations. As Martin Van Buren observed, "It would take longer than our lives (even if it were practicable) to create new party feelings."

So long as both parties were nationally competitive, partisan enthusiasm could overcome even the terrifying antipathies of North and South. But that made America's stability hostage to the political health of its parties. And when the Whig Party collapsed over slavery, the system broke down. The disastrous sequel was the four-way election of 1860, which saw the country divided between two parties in the North, one in the Border States, and a fourth party in the South.[66] As Professor Hofstadter observed, "So long as there were two nationally-competitive parties, the Union had held together. When they broke apart, the country had Civil War."[67]

The rub was that the same emotional energy could unify in some eras and divide in others. It all depended on which issues the major parties embraced. Without national parties there were just two possibilities. The first was that national issues would dominate all others so that regional tensions would never emerge at all. But there was no reason to think that such issues were particularly likely, and experience showed that issues like the tariff or slavery could just as easily divide the regions. Moreover, politicians could not avoid regional issues just because they were dangerous. After all, we have said that the supply of narratives and ideologies is always limited, and the whole point of elections was to force politicians to run on the most attractive ones regardless of their private convictions. This suggested that the ratio of unifying to divisive issues was mostly a matter of chance, and that sooner or later the country's politics would become divisive. According to this second possibility, majority tyranny would then emerge along regional lines, creating a significant risk of civil war.

The rise of national parties opened a third option. Now, members of the same party from different regions could trade their support. Like Downs' single-issue voters, each could then swallow what they saw as a flawed platform to achieve the goals they valued most. Here Jackson and Van Buren provided the prototype: an alliance between Western Frontiersmen, Southern planters, and common men in the North. While each shared their party's ideological hostility to big government, their immediate material motives were vividly different: in the North, fear that government would favor wealthy merchants; in the South, that it would meddle with slavery.[68] Later in the century, post-Civil War Republicans would build a similar alliance that spanned manufacturers in the North, farmers in the West, and laborers in the South.[69] And in the twentieth century, Northern Democrats would find themselves supporting pro-union policies at home (which they cared about) but also Midwest farm supports (which they did not) and Southern segregation (which they abhorred).[70]

In practical terms ideology provided a common banner that gave each member of the coalition what it wanted wrapped up in shared, high-minded slogans. But ideologies can change. In the nineteenth century, neither party had any clear consensus on slavery before the 1840s.[71] But when slavery did become an issue, the Whigs found themselves so divided that their party disintegrated. A similar, though less violent shift came in the early 1970s when each party found itself divided over abortion. *Roe* v. *Wade* (1973) forced a choice: Twenty years later, both parties had realigned so that their members held strong, internally homogenous views.[72]

This strategy of building parties around multiple regional issues has served the country well. But it does require that no single national issue predominate. Wars, which almost by definition overshadow all other issues, challenge this model. This may explain why some of the country's bitterest political divisions involved regional disagreements over whether to fight the War of 1812 and, later, the War with Mexico.[73] Then too, there is an element of path dependency. On the one hand, we expect parties that have achieved national competitiveness to downplay strong regional issues that could split their supporters. On the other, new third parties are practically certain to be regional at first. This means that – as in Lincoln's case – appealing to one region is unavoidable. From this standpoint, the enormous obstacles facing American third parties have plainly helped to stabilize the country.

Finally, the Framers tried to preempt regional divisions by delegating most issues to the states. The trouble, of course, was that this strategy only worked on the assumption that citizens in one state would not care what other states thought or did. This made good sense for infrastructure projects whose costs and benefits were both material and local. But social issues rooted in empathy for others were a different matter. While voters' desire to alleviate suffering probably did decline with distance, there was no reason for it to disappear the moment it crossed state lines.

And if federalism failed, the states could become enemies. For Americans to leave the Union, they first had to believe that the federal government had wronged them and, if necessary, that they could organize sufficient forces to resist an invasion. Ordinarily, these obstacles should have been daunting. But the states possessed trusted leaders who could influence their publics toward war. And once war started, their organizational capacity would make the violence that followed much worse. What *The Federalist* did not foresee was that still other states might side with the national government. When the Civil War finally did come, the North's willingness to enforce the Constitution allowed the Union – however narrowly – to prevail.[74] The more general point is that the number, size, and population of the states were themselves policy variables that could be manipulated to make secession less likely.[75] Here the obvious strategy was to break regions into small states that would not be viable on their own. This would have forced them to exit (if at all) as a group, implying negotiations so complex and multisided that they might never have been attempted.[76] Instead, the nineteenth century's various secession crises proceeded with each state debating and acting separately, albeit while paying close attention to what was being done and said elsewhere. The result was a kind of domino effect in which each state that left the Union made it that much easier for others to follow. This gave the handful of states with outsized populations dramatically more influence. The Civil War would have remained manageable had Virginia decided against secession.[77] Indeed, before it left many observers confidently expected the seceded states to come back to the Union after a few months. Instead, Virginia's secession stabilized the Confederacy and turned what had should have been a manageable rebellion into a four-year cataclysm.

## 6.4 FEDERALISM EVOLVING

Most proponents of the Constitution, including George Washington, hoped that Americans would eventually give their primary loyalty to the Union.[78] And this was reasonable: The experience of working together during the Revolution and the Confederation had taught Americans to cooperate on a continental scale. Moreover, citizens had seen this cooperation pay off, and could reasonably hope to see still more benefits under the new Constitution. Even so, the country remained divided over just how strong the new national government should be. In the end Madison's generation bridged the uncertainty with a clever placeholder that made both the states and the federal government independently answerable to the people. The Framers must have understood that this schizophrenic system of two equally fundamental and legitimate governments was asking for trouble. But it was also the best halfway house they could devise on the path to a genuinely nationwide government.

In the meantime, the Framers tried to preempt the skeptics by insisting that the federal government's powers were limited. Even so, they admitted that voters would ultimately decide just where federal powers ended and the states' began. This suggested that, no matter what the Constitution said, the final division of labor would depend on the public's accumulated faith and affection for the national government.[79] But that would depend almost entirely on how well the new government performed. Here the surest way to ensure success was to focus on projects which offered scale economies that no state could match. Rather than simply stating this principle for later generations to argue about, the Framers reduced these responsibilities to enumerated categories, reserving all other tasks to the states.[80]

In the long run, the new government could only succeed if it delivered more material benefits for every state and region than it cost them. For

Jefferson Davis, justifying secession in 1861, this implied that the country had to be sufficiently homogenous so that "the welfare of every portion shall be the aim of the whole. When this does not exist, antagonisms are engendered which must and should end in separation."[81] Yet this was not strictly true so long as the political system was able to allocate the costs and benefits of federal infrastructure projects so that each region benefited. This condition was easily met so long as voters rewarded congressmen who traded favors and then brought the spoils home to their districts.

But not every issue was like that. In the nineteenth century the most notorious examples were the tariff and whether slavery should be extended to the territories. Unlike the typical infrastructure project, each benefited some regions and hurt others. In principle, this might have been resolved by suitable side payments that evened out the benefits and losses.[82] Yet this would have required large transfers in an era of decidedly small governments, while the North's growing population hinted that it could soon impose its will unilaterally. At this point, the win–win politics of congressional favor-trading became a zero-sum struggle between the regions.

Not surprisingly, the politics of both subjects vastly expanded federal powers. For the tariff, this took the form of an argument over the Constitution's enumerated powers. Here most congressmen took the view that powers once granted were not limited to the specific purposes listed in the Constitution.[83] This was already evident by the early 1800s, when Congress used its authority to establish a national postal system to fund a road from the Potomac to Ohio.[84] The fact that the new road would be useful to mail carriers was all that mattered: The fact that Congress would have voted to fund the road even without that purpose was irrelevant. The interpretation made good sense in the usual lawyerly way that it is better to have clear rules than to invite inquiries into Congress's always debatable intentions. All the same, it practically guaranteed that some powers would be used for unforeseen purposes. This became still more evident after the War of 1812, when Kentucky congressman Henry Clay argued that Congress could charter banks to help open the West. Though the power appears nowhere in the Constitution, Clay argued that constructing banks was essential to Congress's responsibility to "regulate" interstate commerce and provide for the collection and disbursement of federal taxes.[85] Yet if that were true, it was hard to think of anything that the Commerce Clause did *not* allow Congress to do, given that nearly every human activity affects interstate commerce in one way or another.

In practice, the idea of using verbal formulae to limit the national government, so seductive in principle, almost always turned out to be impotent. Nor was this the drafters' fault. One could, for example, have imagined the Supreme Court declaring that Congress's Commerce Clause power was limited to projects whose main purpose was advancing commerce across state lines. But if the justices had done that, they would have set themselves against projects that most of the country plainly wanted.[86] This immediately reduced the constitutional limits on Congress to a mere political argument. This came to a head in the 1820s with Sen. John C. Calhoun's argument that the federal tariff on imports, though justified as a measure to raise money for the government, could not be used to shelter Northern factories from foreign competition.[87] While the statute was eventually withdrawn, the decision depended almost entirely on congressional politics and Southern threats to secede.[88] After that, the lesson was clear: So long as the people *wanted* a limited federal government they would have one. But if they ever changed their minds, the Constitution's enumerated powers would do nothing to stop them.

The second wedge in the Framers' scheme of limited powers was slavery. The Constitution had gone out of its way to suppress the issue, most famously by forbidding Congress to regulate the slave trade for twenty years.[89] This must have seemed an attractive political gamble at a time when the institution seemed to be disappearing on its own.[90] No one could foresee that the invention of the cotton gin in the early nineteenth century would revive Southern slavery in a new and still crueler form. By the early 1820s, emotions on both sides began to rise again.[91] Partly this reflected Northern empathy which had been present from the beginning. But the more important influence was purely material, as Northerners realized that their economy could only take advantage of the new lands if they were free.[92]

The Civil War was federalism's greatest failure. Yet the reasons for the conflict remain obscure. After all, the overwhelming majority of Southerners had voted for unionist parties.[93] This should have made the 1860 election a mandate for centrists. That, of course, did not happen. Yet it remained true that Lincoln, though pledging to keep slavery out of the territories, had equally promised not to interfere where the "peculiar institution" already existed,[94] affirming that "whatever concerns only the State, should be left exclusively, to the State."[95] Moreover, Lincoln would never have been elected without the bizarre four-party election of

1860. This made it reasonable to think that the two-party system would soon reassert itself, after which each side would revert to the center in the usual American way.[96]

And in the meantime, Congress had postponed one slavery crisis after another for forty years. Why not again? In fact, the Senate was already mulling a proposal to hold a nationwide referendum that would have banned slavery above 36½° North latitude. This would almost certainly have commanded a substantial majority, in which case it is hard to see how politicians could have persisted in refusing a compromise that voters in both regions had already accepted. In the event, this last, best chance was lost to a dysfunctional Congress in which the collapsing Whig Party[97] held just enough seats to deny both Democrats and Republicans a majority.[98] So in the end, the catastrophe lay less with Madison's institutions than with a two-party system which found both sides' coalitions "realigning" at just the wrong moment.

These political failures were compounded by a still deeper failure of trust, because it did not matter how many assurances Lincoln gave if hardly anyone believed him. Instead, most Southerners interpreted the North's oft-repeated moral condemnation as evidence that it would renounce any and all assurances the moment it took power.[99] Then too, there was a now-or-never aspect to secession. Many Southerners argued that if the South accepted Lincoln as president slavery would sooner or later end without a shot being fired.[100] After all, it was not enough that individual Southerners favored secession: They had to know that others like them were actually willing to fight. Given some sufficiently large provocation, if Southerners did not take action they would begin to see their leaders' fiery calls for secession the same way the North did – as bluffs that need not be taken seriously.[101]

But saying that war could once again have been postponed in 1860 fails to satisfy. The question is whether American politics could have gone on to heal the divide. For the two-party system, this would have required the Republicans to expand out of their Northern stronghold into a genuinely national party that won more districts in the South than it lost in the North.[102] Here the obvious starting point was that most Southerners did not own slaves and were at best ambivalent about the institution.[103] The question was what a Republican platform could offer these voters instead. But that too should have been obvious: Northern politics since the Revolution had wooed the middle class by promising large (for that era) government expenditures on infrastructure and social welfare. It was true that the planter class who dominated the South preferred to keep government small and taxes low.[104] Yet the poor whites who did not own slaves could easily have outvoted them.[105] This class-based politics was already evident before and during the war[106] and continued expanding through Reconstruction[107] into the Jim Crow era.[108] The main obstacle, both then and later, was poor whites' desperate fear that racial equality would invite lawlessness and drag down white wages.[109] This kind of populist ideology – light on civil rights, but heavy on government-funded infrastructure – would have appalled modern-day Americans. But it would have provided a launching pad – aided in the usual way by the president's control over federal patronage[110] – for the Republicans to compete in the South. Madison's checks and balances would then have worked exactly as intended, giving Southern states the pro-Union choice that they had been denied in the 1860 election.[111]

But all of this is speculation. War did come, and permanently changed Americans' understanding of the federal government. Here the most obvious change was that the national government gained a new, if still imperfect, ascendancy over the states. By declaring state and federal governments equally legitimate, the Constitution had left open the possibility that the states could defy or even leave a government that exceeded its powers. Indeed, Jefferson himself had led the way by quietly discussing the possibility of secession with other politicians in the 1790s.[112] By 1800 the talk was sufficiently open to help convince Congress that it was better to reject the Federalists and make Jefferson president.[113] Thereafter, New England and later the South threatened to leave the Union every decade or so.[114]

To modern ears, the secession debate puts much too much weight on legal niceties. Like any business contract, the thinking ran, The People had agreed to the Constitution and thereafter could not unilaterally renege. That was "revolution," and could only be excused if others had broken the rules already. Of course, The People could still tire of the Constitution and get rid of it. But they would still have to follow its rules by amending it out of existence.[115]

Granted that all this seems terribly formal now, elevating fidelity to procedure above any particular political outcome made eminent sense. With memories of the Revolutionary War still fresh, the idea of replacing violence with agreed rules would have seemed an excellent trade. But in that case, it also followed that people who breached the norm had to be stopped – by force if necessary. The trouble with secession was that it blurred the legalities: If the federal government was subservient to the states, then the latter could leave whenever they wanted to. As Lincoln pointed out, arguing that secession was lawful meant that "good men" could support it after all.[116]

There was also a softer option. Instead of seceding, states could simply refuse to obey, or "nullify," federal law. Nullification had first been asserted in the 1790s when Kentucky and Virginia announced their resistance to the Alien & Sedition Acts. And indeed, this made good sense: At a time when the US Supreme Court had not yet claimed the right to declare federal acts unconstitutional, there was no other arbiter available.[117] Moreover, nullification – unlike secession – stopped short of a final split. Instead of immediately dissolving the Union, it only diluted its benefits and burdens. In the nineteenth century, nullification was primarily used by state legislatures against national laws designed to compel the return of escaped slaves,[118] and became one of the slavery debate's most visible flashpoints. Centrists repeatedly argued that Lincoln could end the crisis by forcing Northern courts to honor the South's slave laws.[119]

The civil war rewrote, even if it did not entirely erase, such theories. Southerners like Robert E. Lee, Thomas "Stonewall" Jackson, and Jefferson Davis all vehemently opposed secession. Yet when the time came, they saw their own states as the more sovereign entity.[120] Lee, to his credit, would eventually reconsider when faced with an even worse choice between rejoining the Union and launching a guerilla war that would have destroyed Southern society – and his own class interests – forever.[121] "The War," he would later write, had "originated from a doubtful question of Construction of the Constitution, about which our forefathers differed at the time of framing it," and had now been settled "by the arbitrament of arms."[122] Since then, there has been no reasonable prospect of states leaving the Union.[123] This effectively means that the federal government's size, power, and responsibilities can be whatever Congress decides and the Supreme Court allows.[124] Strikingly, this includes involving itself in what the Framers would have considered purely local fights like abortion and education.

Other constitutional changes were more explicit. This was particularly true for the federal government's power to set national civil rights standards. Lincoln had justified the Emancipation Proclamation (1863) in the old pretextual way, as a war measure needed to achieve military victory.[125] But this was quickly followed by extending the written Constitution to civil rights through the Thirteenth Amendment (1865) ending slavery, the Fourteenth Amendment (1868) granting former slaves citizenship, and the Fifteenth Amendment (1870) guaranteeing all male citizens the right to vote.[126] For the moment the government's expanded responsibilities were mostly confined to race, even if the Fourteenth Amendment's Equal Protection guarantees were potentially more general.

The final expansion came in the twentieth century. The Framers had imagined that – with or without formal constitutional limitations – politics would ensure that the national government remained small[127] and distant from voters.[128] For a long time they were right. What they could not see was the rise of modern issues like regulating railroads and coping with the Great Depression that no single state could possibly address on its own. In some ways, these new federal responsibilities followed from the Framers' old scale economy argument that some responsibilities were inherently federal. But they also contained a distinct element of circularity: Once the federal government implemented big government programs – and especially the taxes to pay for them – trying to erect parallel state solutions seldom made much sense.

Meanwhile, the Supreme Court's willingness to find federal power had undergone a parallel expansion. More often than not, the Supreme Court found the required powers in a wildly expanded Commerce Clause. Though the Framers had limited the provision to "Interstate Commerce," the justices soon stretched its meaning to include every conceivable product including grain that farmers never intended to sell, but only grew for their own consumption.[129] Meanwhile the Court found its own authority to discover new civil rights in successively looser "penumbras" that could be inferred from the Constitution's enumerated rights. The question remains whether there are any limits on these rights beyond the Court's unavoidable political caution as an unelected branch. As Prof. John Hart Ely observed in the case of *Roe* v. *Wade*, rights should at the very least hinge on "the sorts of evils the framers had sought to combat." By comparison, *Roe* stretched "invasion of privacy" to include a right where there was no invasion at all. In this instance, at least, the Court had given "almost no sense of an obligation" to explain why its ruling implicated what the Framers had written or even intended.[130]

## 6.5 FEEDBACKS

As soon as the Framers decided to define their new government geographically, their choices quickly narrowed to (a) drawing the boundary lines for the various jurisdictions, and (b) allocating the tasks that each level of government would perform. Since then, judges have invested enormous effort into developing clear constitutional principles to answer these questions. In practice, however, the limits to gerrymandering are mostly political while the overlap of state and federal responsibilities continues to generate needless duplication and conflict.

Despite two centuries of effort, American law has yet to develop a sensible theory for translating votes cast into seats in Congress. But as Justice Byron White once observed, there are fundamentally two possibilities. At one extreme, legislators can create safe seats, in which case congressional delegations will change little from one election to the next. This maximizes deadlock. At the other, legislators can create competitive districts so that control of Congress rockets back and forth and each year's winner enjoys such large majorities that it can ride roughshod over the loser.[131]

No doubt there is a balance. But if so, American constitutional law has yet to articulate it. This leaves judges to strike down maps that depart "too much" from proportional representation, where "too much" is defined by what still other courts have allowed in the past. Probably the most that can be said of this system is that it limits how fast maps can drift between Justice White's extremes. All the same, it is safe to assume that partisan legislators will always press for more gerrymandering, and this will be doubly true in polarized times when judges, legislators, and voters become more partisan. The difference today is that the computational challenges of drawing normal-looking maps have largely disappeared. Barring reform, we should therefore expect more gerrymandering, more safe seats, and more extremists in office.[132] And that will lead to still more aggressive gerrymanders at the next redistricting. We have argued that the only practical way to break this feedback is to exclude human discretion by drawing districts algorithmically. The Appendix describes one very basic way to do this, though there are others.

Meanwhile, the Framers' decision to make state and national governments coequal has ensured endless fights over the federal government's proper responsibilities. Looking back, attempts to create formal constitutional guardrails were always doomed. Once it was admitted that the Constitution had not settled the matter, there was nothing to stop the federal government's proper sphere from being renegotiated and expanded with each new piece of legislation. Post-Civil War amendments that authorized the federal government to guarantee civil rights formerly left to the states have added to the overlap. This poses a deep embarrassment to Madison's system by expanding the number of issues that voters' single yes/no choice must resolve and inviting massive duplication and conflict when, inevitably, federal and state offices are controlled by different political parties. Then too, contemporary public opinion nearly always varies by region. This has revived Madison's nightmare of two regional parties struggling for control of the national government and, with it, the power to dictate policy everywhere. Small wonder, then, that the US has drifted to some of the most geographically polarized politics in its history.[133]

## Notes

1 See *In re Legislative Districting*, 475 A.2d 428, 445 (Md. 1984); *Hastert v. State Bd. of Elections*, 777 F. Supp. 634, 660 (N.D. Ill. 1991).

2 Individual candidates did, of course, tell voters where they stood on the issues. But without party platforms, voters had no way of knowing whether other congressmen would agree, and hence whether the ideas they heard had any chance of becoming law. This gap disabled elections from performing anything like the narrowing function they do today.

3 Hofstadter (1959a) at p. 812.

4 It is true that the Republican margin of victory in District C will be a landslide compared to the Democrat wins in Districts A and B, but in a winner-take-all system this changes nothing.

5 Casual references to "social networks" and "communities" can be confusing. Depending on which definitions we choose, it is possible to describe the same underlying reality in terms of many small, tightly linked groups or a few large, loose ones. Fortunately, the ambiguity is mostly linguistic. In practice, the only thing that matters is the number and strength of bilateral ties between voters. So long as we draw district boundaries that cut as few of these links as possible, our maps will respect "social networks" and "communities" no matter how we define them.

6 See Voting Rights Act of 1965, Pub. L. No. 89-110, 79 Stat. 437; *Baker v. Carr*, 369 U.S. 186, 208 (1962). In practice, courts usually limit themselves to insisting that the population of each congressional district should fall within 10 percent of all the others. See *Brown v. Thomson*, 462 U.S. 835, 842-43 (1983).

7 Pennsylvania governors often drew legislative districts that split cities so that suburban votes could decide outcomes, or else centered districts in places where the governor's friends were especially thick on the ground. See, e.g., *Vieth v. Jubelirer*, 541 U.S. 267, 274-75 (2004).

8 Tisdale [1815].

9 The conceit was even more tempting because conventional legal methods required challengers to comb through mountains of legislative history to find evidence of dishonesty. Since corrupt legislators could reliably be counted on to dissemble, the task was almost always backbreaking. That said, it is surprising how often such evidence exists. This was nicely illustrated in the

*Rucho* case, where one Republican argued that he favored a biased map because "I think electing Republicans is better than electing Democrats." For his part, Democrat Steny Hoyer cheerfully confessed that he was a "serial gerrymanderer." See *Rucho* v. *Common Cause*, 588 U.S. ___, 139 S. Ct. 2484 (2019) at pp. 2 and 5.

10  Legal scholars have been remarkably confessional on this point. See, e.g., McDonald (2019) at p. 20 (the "'interocular test'" is "a scientific-sounding restatement of Justice Stewart's celebrated obscenity definition, 'I know it when I see it'"); Grofman (1991) at p. 165 ("[T]he most powerful statistical test for partisan gerrymandering is … 'Does the evidence for gerrymandering leap up and hit you between the eyeballs?'"); and Polsby and Popper (1991) at p. 302 ("The diagnostic mark of the gerrymander is the noncompact district. Anyone who eyeballs a few legislative maps quickly will learn to recognize gerrymanders, although admittedly with imperfect accuracy").

11  For a definitive history, see Altman (1998) at pp. 168–70.

12  Even strange-looking maps could be innocent. No one would have thought twice if Tisdale's long, thin district had coincided with the thickly settled Massachusetts coast. But why? Clearly, we have no quarrel with "strange" geometries when they follow actual settlement patterns. See also Maurer and Karepetyan (2021).

13  Vickrey's scheme required redistricting authorities to pick a location within their state at random. After that, a previously agreed algorithm would generate maps without further human intervention, showing that the scheme was both transparent and impossible to predict.

14  Vickrey (1961) at p. 107. Vickrey was probably less concerned with community per se than with the administrative efficiency of making congressional districts match existing "political sub-divisions such as towns, counties, wards, and the like." In the end, the Supreme Court's decision to enforce one-man-one-vote caused split counties to proliferate anyhow. Crocker (2012) at p. 11. See also *Prosser* v. *Elections Bd.*, 793 F. Supp. 859, 863 (W.D. Wisc. 1992) ("[T]he achievement of perfect contiguity and compactness would imply ruthless disregard for other elements of homogeneity; would require breaking up counties, towns, villages, wards, even neighborhoods").

15  Rossiter, Wong, and Delamater (2018). The figure would presumably be higher except that most districts are much larger than most communities. Rossiter, Wong, and Delamater (2018) at p. 610. This places most communities deep inside districts where splitting is impossible.

16  Karapetyan and Maurer (2020) present a simple model for three perfectly square districts. They show that even much stronger versions of today's one-man-one-vote, compactness and contiguity requirements would still permit 17.6 percent of all congressional seats to be gerrymandered on average. Alexeev and Mixon (2018) similarly consider the efficacy of compactness rules in a hypothetical state where each voter's location and partisanship are decided at random. They find that even very strict compactness rules cannot stop partisans from drawing districts that shift 70 percent of legislative seats to their own party.

17  Grofman (1985) at p. 91; Newkirk (2017).

18  Newkirk (2017).

19  *Gaffney* v. *Cummings*, 412 U.S. 735 (1973).

20  Readers may ask why the Court only sought to limit unfairness instead of ending it entirely. The reason is the Court's own long-standing position that legislators should have broad discretion to draw whatever maps seem reasonable.

21  *Rucho* v. *Common Cause*, 588 U.S. __, 139 S. Ct. 2484, (2019).

22  State-of-the-art analyses before *Rucho* almost always relied on so-called wasted votes methods to make traditional geometric intuitions more articulable and precise. In the first step, researchers created thousands of computer-generated maps, each of which followed the state's districting statutes. Then they added precinct-level data from past elections to see how each map favored one party or the other. Finally, they compared these results to the state's actual map to conclude (in North Carolina's case) that the legislature's districts were more biased than any of the computer's 3,000 offerings. *Rucho* rejected this approach, arguing that if 3,000 was an acceptable threshold, there was no principled way to decide whether 500 or just 50 might also suffice. This arbitrary numbers game was very different from the usual legal argument that reading a statute leads to a well-defined class of outcomes that the legislature could not possibly have intended. Worse, judges could choose whatever cutoffs they wanted, and this choice would sometimes decide whether a particular election was reversed. Finally, "wasted votes" methods penalized maps that departed from whatever voter coalitions had dominated recent elections. This created a built-in incentive for politicians to replicate their existing coalitions over and over instead of trying out new platforms that might attract more supporters or make their existing ones happier.

23  *Davis* v. *Bandemer*, 478 US 109.

24  Eighteenth-century political thinkers saw single-member districts as a hedge against a few big cities dominating elections. The problem was urgent in a world without parties where personal fame was the only way to reach voters – and fame was easiest to acquire in cities. Anon [1787] at p. 261.

25  *Davis* v. *Bandemer*, 478 US 109 at pp. 144–5 (O'Connor concurring) (1986).

26  De Tocqueville [1835] at pp. 60–1 and 65–6.

27  De Tocqueville [1835] at pp. 64 and 67.

28  De Tocqueville [1835] at p. 61.

29  De Tocqueville [1835] at p. 61.

30  Judges trying to implement "communities of interest" approaches in the 1980s routinely found "interests" in everything from regional aviation industries to freeways; Malone (1997) at pp. 469 and 477. Over time, most concluded that the concept was "too nebulous for principled application in apportionment plans." Malone (1997) at p. 475.

31  See Labaree (1962) at pp. 165–6.

32  Syrett 1964 at pp. 353 and 354; Labaree (1962) at pp. 166–7.

33  Residents of the Atlanta suburb of Buckhead recently voted to secede rather than continue under the city's current soft-on-crime policing methods. McWhirter (2021).

34    See, e.g., van Frank (2015) (nineteenth-century Mormons); Wollaston (2018) (Rajeneshee cult in Oregon); Pauly (2016) (libertarians in New Hampshire); Etahad (2020) (white nationalists in Oregon). Recent survey evidence suggests that these are exceptions, and that politics plays little or no role in most Americans' decision to move. Motyl, Prims, and Iyer (2020).

35    Kerns and Locklear (2019).

36    Rossiter, Wong, and Delamater (2018) at p. 612.

37    No matter how the community principle is implemented, courts will also need to reconcile it with *Baker* v. *Carr*'s equal population requirement. Here, the simplest answer is to embrace the Supreme Court's *ipse dixit* that equal population need only be enforced to within 10 percent. However, a more principled answer starts by recognizing that voters face a tradeoff. On the one hand, citizens do not want their vote diluted, which leads to the one-man-one-vote ideal. But on the other, splitting the community's debate across two sets of candidates necessarily means that voters will know less about each, making voting more random and therefore less valuable. In principle, the tradeoffs can be measured by asking how much turnout is depressed when (a) districts have larger than average populations, or (b) citizens mostly talk politics with interlocutors outside their districts.

38    In some ways, defining web-based districts would be easier than drawing physical ones. We have already said that it makes sense to assign voters to physical communities based on distance. The difference on the web is that actual communications between pairs of voters can be measured directly. Redistricting could then draw districts that prioritize groups in which voters communicate directly over those who only communicate indirectly through mutual friends.

39    They would also eliminate externalities including the kind of beggar-thy-neighbor politics in which each community tries to offer better tax breaks than the next one.

40    Politics having a large element of randomness, it was practically certain that each state would pick different solutions to problems, and that some would work better than others. As Justice Brandeis famously observed, this made states the "laboratories of democracy." See *New State Ice Co.* v. *Liebmann*, 285 US 262 (1932) (Brandeis, dissenting) at p. 311.

41    This is most obvious in Madison's comment that "Taking each State by itself, ... its interests [are] but little diversified." *Federalist* No. 56 (Madison) at p. 259. He admitted that this was likely to change as the nation developed "those branches of industry which give a variety and complexity to the affairs of a nation." *Federalist* No. 56 (Madison) at p. 260.

42    *Federalist* No. 10 at p. 40 (Madison).

43    This is reflected, among other things, in modern studies showing that public opinion can and often does change from one neighborhood to the next. See, e.g., Johnston et al. (2004) at pp. 369 and 377–9; Huckfeldt (2014) at pp. 45, 50, and 63.

44    *Federalist* No. 10 at p. 43 (Madison).

45    Stevens [1787] at p. 460 ("[S]mall states ever have been, and from the nature of man ever must be, the nurseries of parties, factions, discord, discontent,

wild uproar, and seditious tumults"); Pinckney (1788) at p. 586 (arguing that "factious men" were able to "infect" the whole people of Rhode Island, while in Massachusetts "the more temperate and prudent part of society [was able] to correct the licentiousness and injustice of the rest"). While both men treat the proposition as an empirical fact, Pinckney also implies a mechanism when he suggests that size is limited to "factious" men's ability to assemble a crowd "at one time, and one place." Pinckney (1788). Probably the best-known nineteenth-century examples are the interminable conflicts between the coastal and interior hill country communities in South Carolina and West Virginia. Tullos (2004) and Catton [1961] at pp. 414–15. Today, the division is more apt to center on conservative strongholds within otherwise liberal states. Familiar examples include upstate New York, downstate Illinois, and James Carville's cartoonish summary of Pennsylvania politics as "Philadelphia in the east, Pittsburgh in the west, and Alabama in the middle." Wikipedia (43).

46 De Tocqueville [1835] at p. 807 ("[A]s long as the majority is still unde- cided, discussion is carried on; but as soon as its decision is irrevocably pro- nounced, a submissive silence is observed, and the friends, as well as the opponents, of the measure unite in assenting its propriety").

47 Wikipedia (40); Erwin (2016).

48 Splitting existing states would also give regional minorities outsized weight in choosing US senators and Electoral College delegates. This need not change the balance of partisan political power, since reliably Democrat and Republican states would almost certainly be admitted pairwise on the nineteenth-century pattern. The deeper problem is that an expanding Senate would simultaneously increase *both* protections against majority tyranny *and* the chances for deadlock and coercive politics.

49 Barone (2020) at pp. 70–1.

50 Hofstadter (1955) at pp. 94–5.

51 For Democrats this may reflect the shift from the twentieth-century coalitions that relied on in-kind support from unions in the Midwest and conservatives in the South to new strategies fueled by cash donations from billionaires who lived on the coasts. Showah (2022).

52 The archetypal example is California, where 47 percent of the state is Democrat and another 12 percent leans Democrat. Public Policy Institute of California (2021).

53 Alexandria Ocasio-Cortez's unexpected victory over powerful incumbent Joe Crowley in 2018 is widely credited with shocking centrist Democrats into adopting radically more "woke" positions than they had previously. Anon (2022i).

54 US Constitution, Art. IV, Sec. 4.

55 The strong version of this complaint held that Southern elites had formed a "Slave Power" conspiracy to depress white wages and even enslave working- class whites. The argument is widely credited with helping the North's anti- slavery feeling spread beyond its abolitionist roots. Nye (1946) at pp. 263 and 270–2.

56 *Federalist* No. 60 at pp. 275 and 281 (Hamilton).

57 Ricks (2020) at 218.

58  Pinckney [1788] at pp. 582–3.
59  See, e.g. Winthrop [1788] at pp. 762–3.
60  *Federalist* No. 2 at p. 6 (Hamilton).
61  See, e.g., Grant [1885] at pp. 307 and 314; Ayers (2003) at pp. 65–7, 69, 90, 103, 104, and 114; Bates [1860] at p. 48; Adams [1860] at p. 144; Lowell [1861] at p. 415; Douglass [1860] at p. 60.
62  Washington [1796] at p. 11.
63  Quoted in Brands (2018) at p. 86.
64  The US granted statehood to Missouri and Texas at least partly to prevent them from becoming independent. Brands (2018) at pp. 93, 298–9. This would have permanently derailed the Framers' ambition to make the US a continental power.
65  Madison's immediate fear was the Missouri agitation, which he saw as an attempt to launch a regionally based second party. Hofstadter (1969) at p. 202. The point would become painfully obvious by 1860, when Stephen A. Douglas, running for president against the Northern-dominated Republicans, declared sectional parties "the great evil and curse of this country." Catton [1961] at p. 101. South Carolina fire-eater William Lowndes Yancey made the same point in a backhanded way by complaining about "the foul spell of party which binds and divides and the South." Catton [1961] at pp. 1–2, 9.
66  Beschloss (2018) at p. 170. Lincoln did not receive a single Electoral College vote outside the North. Beschloss (2018).
67  Hofstadter (1964c) at p. 897.
68  Hofstadter (1969) at p. 237; Grinspan (2016) at p. 28.
69  Rehnquist (2004) at p. 74.
70  Showah (2022).
71  Grant [1885] at pp. 300–1.
72  Barone (2020) and Bravin (2022).
73  Madison's decision to declare war against Britain in 1812 immediately alienated New England, which saw ruin in a British Navy campaign against its shipping. By comparison, the South and West welcomed the land war as an easily winnable way to expand their economies. Brands (2018) at pp. 29 and 40–1. The result was that not a single House Federalist voted for the war, which remained the almost exclusive project of Madison's party. Beschloss (2018) at pp. 68–9. The War with Mexico was similarly regional, promising new lands to the South but opposed by large numbers of Northern Whigs. Guelzo (2021b) at pp. 121 and 137.
74  Catton [1961] at p. 333.
75  It also mattered, in the usual gerrymandering way, just where state boundaries fell. Western Virginia's generally pro-Union population made the whole state more centrist, and to that extent made secession more difficult. That said, it would have been almost impossible to gerrymander against secession by predicting which communities would and would not oppose secession seventy years hence.
76  But see New England's "Hartford Convention" during the War of 1812. Brands (2018) at pp. 48, 72–3, and 161.

77 Guelzo (2021b) at p. 305. Virginia included nearly 20 percent of the Confederacy's white population, produced one-third of its industrial goods, and grew 40 percent of its wheat.

78 Washington [1796] at p. 7.

79 *Federalist* No. 17 at p. 73 and No. 27 at p. 118 (Hamilton); *Federalist* No. 46 at p. 216 (Madison).

80 US Constitution, Tenth Amendment.

81 Davis [1861] at p. 204. South Carolina's John C. Calhoun had similarly emphasized that the only way to preserve the Union was by "[d]istributing equally the benefit and burden of the Union." Brands (2018) at p. 180.

82 President Lincoln endorsed national legislation to compensate slaveowners for emancipation, passing a statute that prohibited slavery in the District of Columbia while paying owners an average of $300 ($8,000 today) for each slave freed. Similar legislation was considered but failed in Delaware, Maryland, and Missouri. Wikipedia (18).

83 Judges found the view particularly attractive, since any inquiry into whether Congress had acted for merely pretextual reasons would have forced courts to conduct difficult and politically fraught inquiries into legislators' motives.

84 Brands (2018) at p. 68.

85 Brands (2018) at pp. 66–7 and 78–9.

86 The justices did try to limit Congress's power to manufactured goods; *Federal Baseball Club v. National League*, 259 U.S. 200 (1922). This distinction was later abandoned.

87 Brands (2018) at pp. 68, 105, and 148–9. "Protective" tariffs were readily distinguishable because they deterred imports so effectively that they raised hardly any revenue at all. Brands (2018) at p. 166. New protective tariffs were enacted after the Civil War [Brands (2018) at p. 204] and remained an intense source of controversy between pro-Southern Democrats and pro-Northern Republicans for the rest of the century. Rehnquist (2004) at p. 164.

88 Rehnquist (2004) at p. 186.

89 US Constitution Art. 1, sec. 9, cl. 1. The Framers carefully avoided any explicit mention of slavery or race in the Constitution because, as Madison prissily insisted, they "thought it wrong to admit ... the idea that there could be property in men." Madison [1787b].

90 When the Constitution was adopted the great majority of Americans believed that slavery was doomed. And the view was justified: Slavery really did disappear in the North, and came within a single vote of being abolished in Kentucky and Virginia. But that was before the cotton gin restored its profitability. Du Bois [1915] at pp. 965–6; Grant [1885] at p. 317. Even then, many prominent Americans down to the Civil War continued to believe that the institution would wither away. See e.g. Brands (2018) at p. 2 (Henry Clay); Guelzo (2021) at p. 235 (Robert E. Lee); Catton (1961) at p. 244 (Edward M. Stanton).

91 The new, factory style of slavery arose in the second decade of the nineteenth century. At this point, the South stopped making excuses for slavery and began to defend it both rhetorically and practically through the imposition of harsh new slave codes. The crackdown was predictably met with resistance in the form of Gabriel Prosser's attempted insurrection in Virginia

(1800), Denmark Vesey's in South Carolina (1822), and Nat Turner's in Virginia (1831). DuBois [1915] at pp. 965–6.

92  Strong [1860] at p. 46.

93  Brownlow [1860] at p. 52.

94  Catton [1961] at p. 116 et passim.

95  Lincoln [1861b] at p. 438.

96  President Buchanan told Southerners that Lincoln's election had been a fluke, based "on a transient and temporary cause which may probably never again occur." Buchanan [1860] at p. 69.

97  The Whig Party was also unlucky in nominating John Tyler, a Southern slaveowner, for vice president in 1840 to allay suspicions that William H. Harrison might secretly sympathize with abolition. When Harrison died after just one month in office, Tyler promptly started to veto key pieces of Whig legislation. It took just six months for the Whigs to eject the sitting president from their party. Heartily disliked by both parties, Tyler achieved little in Congress. He ran for reelection as a third-party candidate in 1844, but lost to Democrat James K. Polk. See Brand (2018) at p. 275; Wikipedia (32).

98  Catton [1961] at p. 199.

99  Stephen A. Douglas told Lincoln after the election that the South's fears did not turn on any immediate threat, but rather on the North's condemnation of slavery as an institution. Catton [1961] at p. 114. This had been underscored by the North's enthusiastic response to John Brown's raid on Harper's Ferry, which many Southerners saw as endorsing mass murder. Catton [1961] at pp. 18–20; Gwynne (2014) at pp. 42–4. Apart from Lincoln's assurances, this meant that there was nothing to stop the North from banning slavery within the South itself as soon as the admission of new states eclipsed the South's outsized power within the national government. Guelzo (2021b) at p. 159.

100  Catton [1961] at p. 99.

101  Catton [1961] at pp. 107–8.

102  The Republicans would have had to soften their already soft stance of slavery, but in a two-party system this would have cost nothing. There was never any realistic chance that an abolitionist third party would eject the Republicans from their Northern majority.

103  Robert E. Lee held to the traditional if maddening belief that Black people were being steadily Christianized and would be freed at some indefinite point in the future. Guelzo (2021a). Shortly after Fort Sumter, Lee told General Winfield Scott that he did not believe in secession, that if he owned every slave in the South he would free them all to bring peace, but that it was not in him to fight against Virginia. Catton [1961] at p. 338. Thomas J. "Stonewall" Jackson was a slaveowner but also a unionist. His widow later insisted "that he would never have fought for the sole objective of perpetuating slavery." Gwynne (2014) at p. 32.

104  The planter or gentry class had dominated American politics from colonial times, and this was especially true in the South. Schlesinger (1962). The contrast deepened in the first decades of the nineteenth century as the party system opened government to middle-class Northerners. Hofstadter

(1969) at pp. 225–6. Ulysses S. Grant similarly recalled that the slaveowners dominated both parties in the South as "a sort of divine right" while looking down on other voters "as poor white trash who were allowed the ballot so long as they cast it according to direction." Grant [1885].

105  Catton [1961] at p. 116.
106  Ulysses S. Grant argued that "The great bulk of the legal voters of the South were men who owned no slaves; their homes were generally in the hills and poor country; their facilities for educating their children, even up to the point of reading and writing, were very limited; their interest in the [Civil War] very meager – what there was, if they had been capable of seeing it, was with the North, they too needed emancipation." Grant [1885] at pp 314–15. Loewen (2011) and Catton [1961] at p. 99 make similar points.
107  Before the war Andrew Johnson had believed that slavery was legitimate and only opposed the slaveowning aristocracy on class grounds. Levine (2021) at p. 25. After Lincoln's death, now-President Johnson sought to restore the Confederate states to the Union without demanding any significant concessions beyond abolishing slavery. Levine (2021) at p. 65. Southern voters could then have rejected Black suffrage just as their counterparts in Connecticut, Wisconsin, and Minnesota had done in 1865. Levine (2021) at p. 67. Congress finally ended the argument by passing the Fourteenth Amendment (granting Black people citizenship) and the Fifteenth Amendment (granting voting rights). Levine (2021) at pp. 117 and 213. It then impeached Johnson for opposing Reconstruction and firing Cabinet members protected by the constitutionally dubious Tenure of Office Act. Levine (2021) at pp. 127 and 156. But most white Northerners had little interest in helping Black people and the Radical Republicans lost seats in the 1868 elections. Levine (2021) at pp. 173, 207, and 211.
108  Demagogic politicians like Louisiana's Huey Long would repeatedly enlist poor white people in populist crusades to expand public works and welfare while raising taxes on the upper classes. Anon (n.d. (i)). Poor white people's schizophrenic attitudes to race and class continued to drive Southern politics well into the 1960s. McWhorter (2001).
109  Catton [1961] at p. 203.
110  Many Southerners thought that the Lincoln Administration would use federal patronage to "build up an abolitionist party in every Southern state." Catton [1961] at p. 99. And indeed, many white Southerners wanted federal jobs much more than they wanted slaves. Guelzo (2022b) at p. 235.
111  Abolitionists feared that Lincoln would bring the South back into the Union without addressing slavery at all. Douglass (1860) at p. 59. Moreover, this hope persisted well into the war. Ulysses S. Grant spoke for many when he wrote that "My inclination is to whip the rebellion into submission, preserving all constitutional rights. If it cannot be whipped in any other way than through a war against slavery, let it come to that legitimately."
112  Ricks (2020) at p. 273.
113  Ferling (2004).
114  The earliest threats came from the North when a young Daniel Webster declared that New England would never have joined a Union whose foreign

policy made it impossible to earn a living at sea, and that the War of 1812 gave the region every right to secede. Brands (2018) at pp. 21 and 41. Since New England had already agreed that the new government would set foreign policy, this necessarily implied that the national bargain could be renegotiated whenever one party or another felt shortchanged. The threat was sufficiently real that Madison worried that some antiwar states would secede, igniting a civil war. Beschloss (2018) at p. 76. Starting with the Missouri Compromise of 1820, Southerners saw each attempt to add new states as a Northern gambit to gain permanent control of the Union – and threatened secession if that happened. Brands (2018) at p. 83. Soon South Carolina Sen. John C. Calhoun had persuaded his state to ignore US Supreme Court rulings on slavery (1822) and federal tariff legislation (1824). By 1832 the state's local politicians were organizing armed resistance, stopping only when President Jackson ordered federal troops south to conduct what he promised would be a "civil war of extermination." Meacham (2008) at pp. 10, 82–3. Despite this, Southerners resumed their threats in the Crisis of 1850 over admitting California. On that occasion, too, they refused to back down until President Taylor threatened to hang those advocating secession. Guelzo (2021) at p. 157.

115  Of course, if one side refused to follow the Constitution that would excuse the other. Indeed, Lincoln himself said that "revolution" – a word not yet lumbered with the Marxist implication of class warfare – would be justified "If, by mere force of number, a majority should deprive a minority of any clearly written constitutional right … [and] certainly would if such right were a vital one." Lincoln [1861a] at p. 215.

116  Lincoln [1861b].

117  Brands (2018) at p. 27. The *Federalist* repeatedly imagines the states resisting federal overreach. See, e.g., *Federalist* No. 17 at p. 73 (Hamilton).

118  Strong [1860] at p. 46 (describing Vermont's refusal to repeal its nullification statute). In Southern eyes the refusal was all the more alarming since the then-existing US Constitution required (Article IV, Sec. 2) that all escaped slaves be "delivered up" to their owners.

119  See, e.g., Greeley [1860] at p. 9; Hill [1860] at pp. 15–16 and 27; Houston [1860] at p. 38; and Catton [1961] at p. 103.

120  It is easy to forget that Jefferson Davis became the Confederacy's president because secessionist fire-eaters needed to mend fences with the recently defeated moderates. This made Davis, who had opposed secession, the ideal unity candidate. Catton [1961] at p. 213.

121  See Guelzo (2021) at pp. 463–7.

122  Quoted in Guelzo (2021) at p. 481.

123  Southern threats to renew the war did play a role in the 1876 election and the end of Reconstruction. Rehnquist (2004) at pp. 20, 89, 92, and 155.

124  Nullification would have a strange afterlife. Where nineteenth-century nullifiers had refused to support the distant evil of slavery, their successors used nullification to protect local practices they saw as virtuous from federal law. For Southern opponents of school desegregation in the 1950s, this meant daring federal authorities to implement integration forcibly. If the

authorities hesitated, integration would be exposed as a dead letter; but if they used force, they might alienate their own supporters. Similar defiance since the 1950s has been a mixed bag. Then San Francisco mayor Gavin Newsom's support for gay marriage was eventually overturned by the California Supreme Court under state law. Tolan (2018). On the other hand, federal authorities have so far hesitated to enforce immigration law on "sanctuary cities" or drug laws on states where marijuana use is legal.

125 Dueholm (2010) at p. 25.
126 The Eighteenth Amendment later expanded the list of federal responsibilities to include alcohol prohibition, though this was soon repealed.
127 *Federalist* No. 66 (Madison) at p. 215.
128 *Federalist* No. 66 at p. 215 (Madison) and No. 17 at p. 73 (Hamilton).
129 *Wickard* v. *Filburn*, 317 U.S. 111 (1942).
130 Ely (1973) at p. 929.
131 *Davis* v. *Bandemer*, 478 U.S. 109 at p. 130 (1986).
132 Kilgore (2019); Seib (2021).
133 Strassel (2021).

# 7

## Making Law

### *The Congress*

We turn now to Madison's core focus on institutions. The Framers feared that Congress would dissolve into self-interested cabals writing laws that favored the politically organized few at the expense of everyone else. The good news, Madison insisted, was that each new crop of congressmen and senators would arrive in Washington as strangers and only afterward start to build up their contacts and power. Since cabals were hard to organize, there would be no great danger so long as the country's legislators were both numerous and frequently replaced.[1] Today we know better. The rise of mass parties guaranteed that elected officials would come to Washington with their cabals and alliances (now renamed "party caucuses") already organized. More than that, the president, House, and Senate would often belong to the same party. When that happened, the Framers' celebrated checks and balances would be short-circuited.

None of these developments is necessarily fatal. Indeed, we argued in Chapter 5 that the two-party system has often *improved* Madison's design. Still, the impact of parties is far from obvious, and Prof. Downs' usually insightful theory says nothing about Congress. Instead, Downs simply ignored legislatures and assumed that the winners of each election could pass whatever laws they wanted. In fairness, this was not a bad model in the bipartisan 1950s, when both party platforms were so close to each other that Congress spent most of its time debating legislation targeted at or near the median voter. The difference today is that a polarized electorate has changed congressional politics from the old bipartisan model to something much more confrontational.

This chapter asks how the existence of legislatures changes Professor Downs' theory. We begin with some context, describing in Section 7.1

how and why Congress evolved the complex and seemingly arcane rules (e.g. the filibuster) that define its structure. Section 7.2 then turns to the particular case that Downs concentrated on, in which centrists dominate public opinion and extremists are rare. Here, the Hotelling–Downs mechanism reliably leads both parties to converge on similar positions, paving the way for compromise when their members reach Congress. We explore the dynamics of this bipartisan politics regime in Section 7.2. Section 7.3 describes how a second, non-Downsian set of strategies becomes possible once roughly half the electorate becomes polarized. This coercive politics is marked by a deadlock in which radicals on both sides repeatedly take centrist solutions off the table. Finally, Section 7.4 argues that some gridlock is unavoidable if we hope to protect members from Madison's tyranny of the majority, although today's tradeoff might possibly be improved. Section 7.5 concludes with a short review of how politics in Congress is influenced by and reacts back on the wider political system.

## 7.1 CONGRESS EVOLVING

The Framers focused obsessively on how the Constitution's rules, coupled with elected politicians' self-interest, would keep any one branch of government from dominating the others. Yet they say nothing about how such bodies function *internally*. And this is doubly true when it comes to Congress. When Madison imagines congressmen, he sees them debating, joining factions and cabals, telling lies, and sometimes panicking. What he does not do is imagine them following any particular rules and procedures, nor does he imagine how those rules could shape and limit the kinds of statutes they produced. For aught that appears in *The Federalist*, the Framers saw little difference between Congress's internal dynamics and any other turbulent mob.

To some extent, this silence was deliberate and tactical. After all, *The Federalist* had been written as an extended polemic for the Constitution, and there would have been no point in arguing about "details" that the document did not address. All the same, the Framers must have known from the long history of colonial and state legislatures and, more recently, fifteen years' experience with a national Congress how much rules and committee structures mattered. Moreover, the ground was shifting under their feet. In the eighteenth century it was still possible – just barely – to see the New York legislature, for example, as a tangle of personal relations punctuated by occasional formal votes. By comparison, the rise of party caucuses, platforms, and voting discipline in the early nineteenth century would show that rules and organized institutions were at least as important as individual politicians.

More than two centuries later, the Framers' self-restraint has paid off: Left to constantly invent and revise their own rules, legislatures have produced new mechanisms beyond anything *The Federalist* could imagine. We argue in what follows that these include solutions to majority tyranny as important as anything in the formal text of the Constitution itself.

We start by asking how anything as ephemeral as Congress's procedural rules can protect against majority tyranny.[2] After all, Congress adopts and revises its own rules in every session, and if a majority suddenly voted to discard them there is nothing the minority could do to stop them. Then too, members know that preserving the existing rules will almost always come at the cost of fewer legislative achievements. This suggests that rules are most likely to fail in polarized times, when legislators on both sides feel most intensely.

Our answer is an extension of Madison's argument that factions would resist the tyranny of the majority even when it favored them.[3] Yes, frustrated members of the majority can see that jettisoning protections for the minority would immediately win today's argument. But they also know that some new majority could target their own interests tomorrow. On the usual insurance logic, this makes it wiser to pay a "premium" by honoring procedures that limit their power today than to suffer abuse if they should find themselves in the minority tomorrow. All the same, Madison must have known that the argument proves too much: If self-restraint was so obviously in legislators' interest, majority tyranny could never happen at all. Instead, real legislators had oppressed minorities constantly throughout history. Looking back, it is easy to see that while Madison's basic logic was sound, he had swept some important difficulties under the rug.

Probably the biggest problem was his assumption that a legislator's decision to refrain from abuse when she was part of the majority would encourage others to protect her when she later found herself in the minority. To a cynic, this kind of unenforceable promise seems worthless and even delusional. The surprise, as twentieth-century economists showed, is that favor-trading has a bootstrap quality: Each side knows that the other has repeatedly honored the rule despite its immediate interests in the past, and also that the rule, once broken, cannot be restored. So, it honors the rule because this is the only way to protect itself the next time it joins the minority. And since both sides know the same facts and make the same calculation, the rule becomes self-fulfilling. At the same time, the argument is not nearly so general as Madison implied. More specifically, the calculation only makes sense so long as each side faces risk for the foreseeable future: As soon as one side decides that the risk will definitely end at some point, it will betray the other.[4] Moreover, this understanding can change. Betrayal is especially likely under what we have called coercive politics, where one party persuades itself that it stands on the brink of a "permanent majority." Something like this seems to have happened in 2020, when many Senate Democrats called for abolishing the filibuster.

Minority protections can also erode gradually. Advocates of new and controversial legislation often claim that existing rules can be relaxed in some harmless way that permits action today while still protecting members going forward. Historically, such arguments have been most tempting when, as we argued in Chapter 5, the minority is limited to some plainly defined biological or cultural "Other." Still, thinner distinctions can sometimes satisfy the majority.[5] The question is how far down this path legislators are willing to go. In bipartisan eras when trust is strong, a suitably bright line distinction may sometimes suffice. This seems to be what happened in 1974, when senators diluted the filibuster by exempting so-called reconciliation bills so long as they did not contain "extraneous" items unrelated to revenues and expenditures.[6] This change required both substantial trust and a bright line to confine the exception. By comparison, neither was present in 2021 when Democrats proposed a similar carveout for voting rights because, President Biden said, "it is the single biggest issue."[7] The fact that only one party supported the issue – over the other's vehement objections – made it almost certain that more exceptions would follow. In the event, at least two Democratic senators refused to open the loophole, so that the filibuster survived.

The principle of rules and procedures is, of course, much broader than "tyranny of the majority." It also sets the balance of power between members and their leadership. For example, recent Congresses have routinely suspended the "regular order" by which bills proceed through a specified process of hearings, committees, and floor votes to become law. Instead, they have let their respective leaders draft important or controversial bills in secret and then disclose them just hours before the vote is taken. The result is to make amendments impossible so that members face a take-it-or-leave it choice. This greatly increases the leadership's own power compared to ordinary members, who would otherwise have been able to examine the bill and offer amendments.

One might ask why members would ever agree to this. But as we argued in Chapter 5, one of the few disadvantages of incumbency is that voting makes it hard to hide one's real views, which in turn breeds single-issue voters that challengers can mobilize at the next election. Reducing the number of votes held each year drastically slows this process. Then too, some members are happy to surrender power to like-thinking party leaders. In coercive eras when extremists capture one or both leaderships, preventing centrist members from offering amendments ensures that *only* extremist solutions have any chance of passage. This drastically restricts the possibility of bipartisan legislation, and therefore what the media finds newsworthy. In this instance, at least, congressional rules systematically suppress the centrist messages that voters would otherwise hear, reinforcing polarized opinion throughout the society.

In the meantime, the existence of procedures also defines a crucial constitutional variable. The Framers designed their system of overlapping congressional, senatorial, and presidential terms on the theory that voters would be able to change course before too much damage was done. But their Constitution defines the interval between elections in calendar time. By contrast, the amount of legislation that Congress can produce in a single session depends on procedure. At one extreme, Downs assumed that the government could pass any laws it wanted to before the next election. This would indeed be possible if members were willing to pass every new law instantly on the same party-line vote. But real members want to monitor and participate in drafting new laws, and this takes time. The reason, contrary to Downs' assumptions, is that voters sometimes expect their representatives to oppose their own parties. At a deeper level, the number and size of these departures depend on how much the average voter values local issues and the candidate's personal judgments compared to the national platform.

Beyond even majority tyranny, Congress's ability to set rules also decides whether democracy can persist at all. On the one hand, Congress can refuse to seat new members. On the other, this necessarily means, at least in theory, that extremists on one side could potentially eject some or all of their duly elected opponents. Moreover, the situation is unstable: While a first wave of expulsions would require help from a large number of centrists, a second wave would have fewer opposing votes to overcome, a third wave still fewer, and so on. The accelerating spiral would then continue until a tiny extremist majority controlled whatever rump legislature remained.

Unfortunately, the scenario is anything but fanciful: Many if not most historical revolutions have proceeded in precisely this fashion.[8] The Constitution sets guardrails by insisting that ejections require a two-thirds supermajority.[9] This was a high bar when members voted as individuals, and is still higher in party systems where the Downs–Hotelling mechanism encourages close elections. The downside is that the supermajority could keep Congress from acting in a legitimate case. In practice, Congress has seldom used the power.[10] Instead, most cases have been limited to treason, notably including secession during the Civil War, while the rest involved well-defined crimes like election fraud and corruption.[11] This narrowness confirms our argument that members will almost always insist on bright lines (here, criminal conduct) so that enforcement is not endlessly repeated until average members find themselves at risk.[12]

## 7.2 THE BIPARTISAN REGIME

For most of the twentieth century, the hallmark of American politics was "reaching across the aisle" to pass compromise legislation that benefited both sides. This followed from the Hotelling–Downs mechanism's reliable tendency toward similar, and sometimes overlapping, platforms that usually sent both parties to the nation's capital already convinced that certain pieces of legislation were desirable, subject only to their differences on how to divide the spoils. This section examines this "bipartisan" regime.

We said in Chapter 5 that Downsian theory specifically assumes that voters choose candidates based on party platforms, and that it is easy to construct variant theories in which voters rely on other cues. Here we emphasize that each of these variant(s) has profound consequences for how Congress is structured and behaves as an institution. For example, Downsian theory assumes that each politician is perfectly loyal to their party's platform. But if that were true, Congress would pass or reject every piece of legislation by the same party-line vote. Since this does not happen, it must also be true that large numbers of congressmen – and the rational voters who elect them – find other rationales more persuasive. A well-designed Constitution should be able to function no matter which rationales predominate at any given moment.

Broadly speaking, a rational voter who ignores parties and platforms has three choices. The first and oldest is to choose politicians who look like her. When voters do this, the result is the specific type Congress that John Adams called "an exact Portrait, in Miniature, of the People at large."[13] Here, the key advantage was, as one eighteenth-century pamphleteer explained, that the legislature would possess "the same interests, feelings, opinions, and views as the people themselves would were they all assembled," with the single exception that they would also be the "best informed."[14] After that, democratic institutions were child's play: All the Constitution had to do was ensure that the legislature was subject to the same laws as ordinary citizens. Indeed, voters did not even need to learn the issues because their representatives would, by definition, suffer from bad laws just as much any voter.[15] Congressmen might, of course, still disagree about the best way to achieve the country's goals. But since there was no fundamental disagreement among them, they would simply reason with each other until they found the right policy.

The second possibility was for voters to choose candidates who, in Madison's phrase, "show both fidelity and competence."[16] Here the main problem was defining some ideal against which "fidelity" could be compared. Most commonly, the Framers followed the Roman example by assuming that there existed some single best policy that would make the country better off than all the others. This view was exemplified, *inter alia*, by John Jay's prediction that voters would choose representatives who had proven their "patriotism" regardless of birth,[17] and George Washington's even plainer hope that "virtuous men" would serve in Congress.[18] The more practical answer is that government in the eighteenth century was small and unambitious. This ensured that any normative disagreements among voters could be safely ignored. Finally, if differences over "civic virtue" did happen, they might still be the kinds that reasoned discussion could resolve. As Madison noted, Congress would be able to "refine and enlarge the public views, by passing them through the medium of a chosen body of citizens, whose wisdom may best discern the true interest of their country, and whose patriotism and love of justice will be least likely to sacrifice it to temporary or partial considerations."[19] Modern scholars often adopt a similar approach by arguing that the public seldom knows its own mind – and that it is Congress's job to "invent solutions that it anticipates the public will approve of."[20]

The other half of Madison's heuristic – "competence" – was more straightforward: Once the country's various goals were defined, policies that achieved more of them were unambiguously superior to those

that achieved fewer. Even so, it led to the strange prediction that voters would often choose representatives who did *not* resemble them.
Indeed, Hamilton stressed that the less literate classes had no choice if
they wanted effective representation.[21] The case was even easier for a
man like Washington, who thought that the right policies would follow
automatically if only Congress evolved into a natural aristocracy limited to "the most disinterested" and "able" men.[22] This view had largely
disappeared since the 1840s,[23] although it is not hard to see a survival
of the instinct in modern voters' nostalgia for aristocrats on the John F.
Kennedy pattern.

The third and last possibility was for rational voters to choose candidates who supplemented the national party's platform with their own
individual promises. Given individual candidates' limited access to publicity, these were nearly all small in number.[24] Probably the easiest tactic was to make promises that selectively supplemented or else opposed
particular planks of the national platform. Among other things, this let
politicians show their independence in states where public opinion differed markedly from the party's national positions. Alternatively, politicians could embrace labels that factions within the party had already
established. For Democrats, these have notably included the moderate
"Blue Dog" label of the 1990s and its "Progressive" successor in the
2020s. In either case, the effect was to blur the national party's positions.
Depending on the faction, these shifts could either facilitate bipartisan
compromise or stiffen the polarization of coercive politics.

The importance of these various non-Downsian voting models is
always changing. Partly this is a function of the radically different
value that voters place on ideology and political platforms from one
era to the next. But it also depends on Congress's constantly changing
procedures. On the one hand, it makes no sense for voters to worry
about their representative's fidelity and competence if the rules make it
impossible to ever influence her party's leadership. On the other, it is
not enough for voters to value character and competence. They must
also be able to estimate it. Here, House and Senate leadership's current
power to "protect" members from going on the record in floor votes
preserves ambiguity, making character and competence less measur-
able, and therefore less important.[25]

The question remains how these non-Downsian voter strategies trans-
late into policy.[26] To understand the connection, imagine that you are
a party leader and that your caucus's loyalty to the national platform

is limited. More specifically, you know that no congressman will vote for a bill unless it benefits his constituents on net. If the initial bill does not do this for a particular member, you have three choices. First, you can rewrite it to get his vote. Second, you can enlarge the transaction through "logrolling"; that is, trading votes for some other piece of legislation against this one. Finally, you can promise to return the favor at a future date, and hope the member trusts you enough to accept the offer. No matter what choice you make, though, you have certain advantages. Your deputies are constantly counting heads, so at every given moment you know whether you have the votes to win more accurately than any ordinary member does. It follows that members never know how much their vote is worth to you. This gives you a substantial advantage when you approach uncommitted members one by one to haggle over which promises and side deals you are prepared to make.

Now put yourself in an ordinary member's shoes. There's a new spending bill being considered and the leadership wants your vote. If you say yes right away, they will reward you. But just how many bridges and highways will your district receive? You are bound to get some, but that won't stop challengers at the next election from saying you could have gotten more. Then too, House politics is opaque: the leadership is always promising side deals to individual members, negotiations are secret, and you probably won't find out what other members have received until the bill becomes law. So, you worry that you could be short-changed. And of course, every other member thinks the same thing and tries to sell her vote as dearly as she can.

Meanwhile the bill is being constantly being renegotiated – more highways in some districts, fewer in others – and uncommitted votes are getting scarce. If the leadership needs these holdouts, it will have to pay a high price. This encourages ordinary members to wait until the last possible moment to say yes. But if they wait too long the leadership may find a way to assemble its package without them, or else time will run out and the bill will fail so that no one gets anything. As the leadership's offers get sweeter and sweeter, the holdouts wonder whether it's finally time to say yes. And those who have already signed wonder if they should renege and renegotiate. Regardless, members know that they can't be seen as pushovers. If leadership starts to take their vote for granted, they'll be treated like suckers forever after. Sometimes, they may even vote against the leadership just so they can command a higher price the next time.

In all of these dilemmas, the basic timing problem of when and on what terms to join the majority is a special case of what economists call a "game of chicken." While details matter, the formal models generically show that members will almost always earn higher returns by adopting a "mixed strategy" in which they randomly support most, but not all, legislation that benefits them. More concretely, members should hold out long enough on average so that the bill occasionally fails without them. However painful in the short term, such losses are an investment in the future: Once the leadership sees that it cannot take members' votes for granted, it will offer them more.

Finally, we have said that leadership can sometimes win votes by promising to "repay the favor" at a later date. Naively, this kind of unenforceable promise might seem worthless. The surprise is that a long string of successful favor-trading has a kind of bootstrap quality. On the one hand, both sides know that breaking the string will automatically forfeit all of the favors that they would otherwise receive in the future.[27] On the other, each side knows that the other understands this logic. So, in the end, the leadership grants the favor so that the expected trades become self-fulfilling. Granted that members are bound to discount the promise, it still has value. And each granted favor makes promises on both sides more credible. From this standpoint a history of successful trades becomes a shared asset – call it "trust" – that makes both parties better off.

The trades also have consequences for Congress as a whole. A long history of kept promises reduces the mistrust that keeps large deals from happening. This increases the chances that the next bill will pass as well. Then too, the logic of favor-trading means that it is valuable to *do* favors as well as receive them. This encourages leadership to share benefits even when they are not strictly necessary to obtain a majority. This spreads the benefits of new legislation more widely across members, softening the otherwise strong majority tyranny incentive to concentrate benefits in just enough districts to win.

Trust incentives can also change from one era to the next. Everything depends on history: When everyone has kept their promises for a long time, new promises are valuable and people see their reputations for honesty as assets worth preserving. But when promises have been routinely violated, there is no point in keeping them. The deeper lesson is that trust has no "natural" level: It can be high in some eras and low in others. Economists typically formalize this logic by analyzing "trust games" where players trade favors that are neither simultaneous nor enforceable by contract.[28] According to the "Folk Theorem," such systems are indeed stable so long as the exchanges are expected to continue indefinitely.[29] That said, trust is dynamic: As soon as one player breaks a promise, every other player immediately revises their trust estimate downward. This can lead to still more violations and a downward spiral.[30]

Of course, the trust dynamic is about much more than vote trading. It also includes the expectation that norms will be observed, and rules applied predictably and fairly. As with vote-trading, this is most likely to happen when a long history of adherence encourages people to continue to respect norms despite their short-run incentives to renege.

We also expect congressmen to accumulate more and more trust over their careers. This lets them negotiate still bigger deals so that voters may decide to reelect them even over challengers who seem to offer better personalities and ideas.[31] At one level this seems antidemocratic, and there is no question that it dilutes the competition that keeps Downsian politicians focused on giving the median voter what she wants. All the same, the advantage of being able to pass large packages is entirely real, so that if voters feel better off voting for the incumbent we should accept this.

So far, we have stressed simple transactions between party leadership and ordinary members. But in fact, Congress's complex hierarchy gives many intermediate players power as well. Here the most prominent examples are committee chairs.[32] In practice their power comes through various channels. First, ordinary members rely on chairs to keep them informed about legislation that they lack the time and resources to track on their own. This gives chairs the usual "trusted intermediary" power to slant information and shape opinions. Second, chairs have various formal powers, including the ability to hire and fire staff. This further tightens their grip over what information is developed and transmitted to ordinary members. Third, chairs have broad discretion to schedule or delay the hearings that bills need to move forward.[33] This lets them advance their own preferred bills and also trade favors with other chairs. Finally, chairs decide which bills reach the floor for take-it-or-leave-it votes. This lets them choose which version of the legislation passes so long as the median congressman sees the chosen bill as at least a small improvement over the status quo.[34]

The average congressman surely resents these advantages. Even so, some version of the committee system seems unavoidable. Indeed, the practical necessity for dividing Congress's work among various standing committees was already evident to the very first Continental Congress.[35] In the end, the system reflects what members themselves want. After all, their power ultimately depends *both* on their right to intervene and comment *and* on the total number of bills that Congress can pass each year. This paradoxically suggests that letting a few powerful individuals control which bills do and do not receive a floor vote enhances the average members' influence as well. Then too, the existence of parties adds a second layer of discipline. Ever since Martin Van Buren, American party leaders have tried hard (though not always successfully) to subordinate rank-and-file members to the will of the group,[36] sometimes to the point of forcing them to embrace and defend embarrassing inconsistencies in the party's policies.[37] So there can be no real surprise if leaders try to impose a similar discipline on their congressional delegations.[38] This discipline is almost always strongest for House members who – being comparatively obscure – have the least ability to explain themselves to voters if and when they rebel against the party's platform. Conversely, congressmen correctly fear that every vote will make them a better target for critics at the next election. From this standpoint, giving the House Speaker nearly unlimited control over which bills reach the floor saves them from going on the record with embarrassing votes.[39] The trouble is that this same discipline gives leaders outsized influence, even as incumbency makes them safe from electoral challenges in their own districts. This means that when extremists become leaders, they can often force their views onto more moderate colleagues with little danger of losing their seats in the next election.[40]

Member self-interest has also changed Congress's personality over time. In practice, this usually happens when an outsized class of new members sets out to challenge the existing order. For example, seniority hardly mattered before the early twentieth century when Congressmen seldom ran for reelection.[41] Then, as terms grew longer, the growing bulge of senior Republicans and (somewhat later) Democrats banded together to pass seniority rules.[42] This led to a Rules Committee dominated by Republicans and conservative Democrats, making it comparatively easy for centrist proposals to reach the floor. Looking back, mid-century seniority rules slowed change by tying power to politicians who had first been elected in a particular era, and to that extent prolonging whatever ideological fashions had prevailed in the past. At the same time, seniority also disproportionately elevated members who represented safe districts, giving extremists more power than they might have had otherwise. The fact that the first effect worked against the second tended to keep both manageable for most of the twentieth century.

The seniority system lasted into the 1970s, and was only definitively overturned by the bulge in young Democrats who were elected after Watergate. They forced the secret ballot election of chairs, which prevented incumbents from using the threat of reprisals to keep their posts. That, in turn, forced the chairs to greenlight more liberal legislation to please their members. The insurgents also changed the Rules Committee so that two-thirds of its members were appointed by the Democratic leadership, giving liberals still more sway. The changes were mirrored in the Republican caucus, which soon gave their leaders more power to overrule seniority. This included forcing out incumbent chairs after six years to make room for young members who had raised money for their colleagues' campaigns.[43]

Finally, individual congressmen also form *ad hoc* alliances to gain power. This is most obvious in the roughly 440 caucuses that press for mostly narrow interests like "American-Belgian Friendship" or "Zoos and Aquariums." Beyond their obvious educational function in pooling and disseminating information that favors particular viewpoints, they also provide a nucleus of agreement which makes the leadership's job that much easier when and if it takes up the cause. At the same time, membership is self-limiting. This is most obviously true for groups dedicated to inherently local issues like, for example, the "Interstate-11" and "I-14 Caucuses." More generally, lobbyists always try to enlist a few interested members to put their issue on Congress's radar. After that, however, the value of signing up still more members falls off steeply. This gives congressmen little incentive to join caucuses that are already oversubscribed.[44]

The main exceptions to this rule are the various ideological caucuses on the Left and Right, which sometimes threaten to withhold support from their own parties in order to force results that could never pass otherwise. Probably the best-known example is the House Freedom Caucus, which routinely threatened to vote against the Republican leadership in the early 2010s unless it tacked to the right,[45] and later provoked a prolonged standoff over Kevin McCarthy's fight to become Speaker in 2023.[46] However, it is worth noting that Progressives practiced similar tactics when Democrats recaptured the House in 2018.[47] This included repeatedly refusing to vote for President Biden's bipartisan $550 billion infrastructure bill in 2021 unless and until Congress agreed to a parallel $3.5 trillion package as well.[48] Such tactics were all the more costly because threats to kill legislation must occasionally be carried out to remain credible.[49]

## 7.3 THE COERCIVE REGIME

We argued in Chapter 5 that American politics sometimes crosses over into a coercive politics regime in which extremists promote gridlock in hopes that centrists will become frustrated enough to accept more radical policies. Naively, we would expect this to happen when the total number of Left- and Right-extremists crosses 50 percent, although the existence of party discipline means that that actual transition could come somewhat sooner if extremists manage to capture key leadership posts and attract more donors than centrists.[50]

The available evidence suggests that the country has already entered this era. Most obviously, empirical studies of Congress show a sharp rise in gridlock around 2010 or so.[51] Then too, it has become common for politicians,[52] journalists,[53] and ordinary citizens[54] to not just understand but openly advocate a politics of blocking compromise to get what they want. Indeed, many Progressives no longer even pay lip service to compromise, insisting that the very idea of bipartisanship is outdated.[55] Finally, coercive politics provides by far the most parsimonious explanation for the recent history of healthcare, gun control, abortion, and immigration legislation. In each case, the pattern is the same: Some new bill is introduced on the basis of strong centrist support. The backers then open negotiations with whatever conservative or progressive votes are needed to push the bill across the finish line. Then, after a months-long drama, the talks collapse and the bill dies.[56]

Blockading centrist solutions makes excellent sense for extremist congressmen who could never hope to assemble a majority for their own proposals otherwise. All the same, the strategy can only succeed if members are willing to enforce, or at the very least tolerate, gridlock for long periods. We now ask when and under what circumstances rational politicians are willing to do this.

We start by revisiting some basic assumptions. Recall that Downsian politicians prioritized winning the next election over every other concern. But this is not the only possibility, and we can equally imagine a second type of politician (call them "Idealists") who prioritize substantive policy changes over their own reelections. While they must win at least some elections to reach this end,[57] they might equally decide to forfeit reelection once the goal seems within reach. More specifically, we expect such politicians to embrace the risk, and sometimes the certainty, of losing the next election to achieve their policy goals.[58] Certainly there is not much doubt that Idealists exist: Indeed, voters who follow the "character" heuristic demand it and would be disappointed if their candidate jettisoned some core belief to save her party.

But if all politicians are either Downsians or Idealists, we can immediately say something about how gridlock is possible and also how it ends. As in Weimar, Idealist politicians have a definite strategy. On the one hand, they cannot win unless they outlast the center. On the other, seeing their ideological opposites win is literally the last thing they want. It follows that we expect them to defect to the center as soon as their odds of losing get high enough.[59] The problem, as in Weimar, is that this turnaround might easily come too late, either because Idealist politicians misjudge how much the political tide is running against them, or because they are secret Downsians who know that a turn to the center could anger their followers and cost them reelection.

The end game for Downsian members is similar. As centrists, they always face a choice between obeying their leadership or joining Downsians in the other party to pass compromise solutions. In principle, the defections should start the minute centrists in each party see that they are closer to each other than to their own party's extremists. Still, there is a problem. Because individual defections change nothing, they only make sense as part of a coordinated centrist rebellion in both parties. This is hard to organize and sure to invite reprisals from leadership if it fails. Even so, the situation is unstable. If for some reason there are actual or rumored cross-aisle defections, the chances for centrist legislation will suddenly improve. At this point, the incentives for still further defections would likely become self-sustaining in a kind of avalanche.

In the meantime, coercive politics could do permanent damage. Because extremists know that they are a minority, they expect power to be fleeting. This encourages them to push their advantage as hard and as fast as they can. This explains why Democrat Idealists pursued President Obama's Affordable Care Act (2010) and President Biden's "Build Back Better" (2021) spending package *knowing* that the backlash would probably cost them the next election.[60] But in that case, why not jettison protections for the minority? If departing from "regular order" or ending the Senate's sixty-vote supermajority lets them pass more legislation faster, so much the better. Meanwhile, those centrist politicians who resist this destructive politics are more likely to pay the price in polarized eras when voters value representatives' commitment to ideological goals more than integrity or conscience.[61]

The only constraint is that the violations cannot be so large that they shock centrist voters into joining their ideological enemies. This, however, is a moving target, since Idealist politicians can almost always point to previous acts by the other side to justify their actions.[62]

The damage from breaking norms is sure to be long-lasting. After all, the existence of rules like the filibuster and supermajority depends on an expectation of mutual forbearance. Once one side repeals a rule, there is no real doubt that it would do the same thing a second time. Knowing this, the other side would be crazy to restore the rule when it takes power.[63] At this point, restoring the necessary level of trust will almost always require a long period of renewed favor-trading, if not an entirely new generation of politicians too young to have been involved in overturning the old rule.

Finally, coercive politics generates messaging that tends to make the wider society more radical. We have said that new narratives and ideologies are constantly being developed, and some could bring Americans closer together. But that cannot happen unless politicians and media personalities are first willing to embrace them. This is markedly less likely in coercive eras, when most of these actors are strong partisans looking for narratives to justify gridlock and pillory the opposing party.

### 7.4 INSTITUTIONAL RULES: FRICTIONS, STABILITY, AND HEALING

Madison worried that majority rule would set policy even when most voters did not feel intensely or might still change their minds. In the former case, the country would get majority tyranny and more resentment. In the latter case, policies would endlessly jitter back and forth.

The Framers addressed these fears in their usual way, by adding deliberate frictions including a divided legislature, staggered terms for elected representatives, and the presidential veto. Yet in the end, their most consequential decision was to let Congress set its own rules. This eventually led to genuinely effective guardrails against majority tyranny and jitter, most notably the Senate's filibuster and (more recently) sixty-vote supermajority. The downside was that these procedures were and remain lowly procedural rules. This has invited endless tinkering, not always for the better. Despite this, they remain "constitutional" in the only sense that matters – their undoubted impact in shaping both politics and outcomes.

The Constitution established three safeguards against tyrannical majorities and jitter. The first of these was a divided or "bicameral" legislature that required the House and Senate to agree before passing legislation. This would slow the passage of pernicious legislation until the public came to its senses, assuming it ever did.[64] That must have seemed a substantial safeguard to the Framers, since we naively expect two evenly divided bodies to disagree half the time by chance alone.[65] In the event, of course, the rise of mass parties, coupled with direct elections to the Senate, undercut the safeguard by ensuring that election outcomes in the two bodies are strongly correlated.

The Constitution's second innovation was staggered elections. Even if some demagogic faction were to sweep elections in any given year, two-thirds of the Senate – and sometimes also the president – would still be holdovers from earlier cycles. This meant that American policy could not change completely in one and sometimes two aberrant elections. That said, the mechanism was fragile, since the barrier would evaporate unless the public fever broke in less than four to six years. That was a tight but unavoidable schedule if, as the Framers believed, elected officials had to be continually replaced to stop cliques and cabals from forming.[66]

The Framers' third and final safeguard was the president's veto.[67] Unlike the first two mechanisms, this was much more than a simple friction, though it is not entirely clear how well the Framers understood this. Strangely, *The Federalist* says that its primary purpose had nothing to do with majority tyranny, but was designed to help the president defend himself if Congress tried to abridge his powers. Even so, the Framers quickly added a second justification that vetoes could also be used to block bad legislation. The wrinkle, of course, was that Congress could overcome the president's judgment by a two-thirds vote. Whether or not the Framers realized it, the result was to create a supermajority that the president could switch "on" for bad legislation and "off" the rest of the time. This was of course only a half-measure: When the president shared the majority's bad judgment, the veto might just as well not exist. All the same, a mechanism that improved legislation in even a few cases was better than nothing.

But in that case, there was still the question of just when the president would act. Hamilton predicted that vetoes would be rare, so that "there would oftener be a charge of timidity" in the president's use of the veto "than of rashness in the exercise of it."[68] This made sense if the president wanted to be reelected: At the very least, the fact that the bill had passed the democratic House was good evidence that the most voters wanted it, while Senate passage implied that the country's wisest and most reputable men agreed. All the same, the president could still question this logic if the House and Senate majorities were narrow. For Hamilton, the two-thirds override was thus a guarantee that the president would only use the veto when a "very respectable portion of the legislative body" was willing to support him, thereby endorsing "the propriety of his conduct in the public opinion."[69] Here was a hint, at least, that this particular friction would *only* come into play following the kinds of passionate, knife-edged majorities most likely to produce majority tyranny and jitter. We will return to this point later.

Still, the most striking aspect of these strategies was their timidity. The first two were nothing more than simple frictions, coming down in the end to Madison's hope that given time, Congress or the voters would change their minds. The third, despite its intricate incentives, would only matter on those rare occasions when the president sided against the majority. This was decidedly small beer for men who feared majority tyranny as a mortal threat to the Republic.

The Framers could have gone further. Some colonial legislatures had already adopted supermajorities that let minorities block all new business by simply refusing to show up for a quorum. Indeed, Congress itself had adopted the practice during the Articles of Confederation.[70] Despite this, the Framers refused to continue the rule in their new Constitution.[71] The reason was experience: Past supermajorities, they insisted, had encouraged minorities to blackmail the majority into "contemptible compromises of the public good," or else left important measures "injuriously suspended or fatally defeated"[72] when the majority refused. Conversely, a majority that gave in would suffer its own version of tyranny, this time at the hands of a "pertinacious minority."[73] Finally, they added – and here they anticipated Weimar – that the tactic almost always worked best in times of crisis.[74] This would encourage minorities to practice their brinksmanship at just those moments when the Republic could least afford it.

Even so, the example of the president's veto hinted that more sophisticated solutions were possible. Unlike a simple supermajority, the veto only happened when the president's own passion was so great that it outweighed his fear of alienating the public. Though no one could know it at the time, the US Senate would try out variations of this same basic design for the next two centuries.

Before introducing this history, it is useful to set a baseline by examining the old supermajority idea and its failings more carefully. Figure 7.1 graphs the number of votes (horizontal axis) against the intensity (vertical axis) that

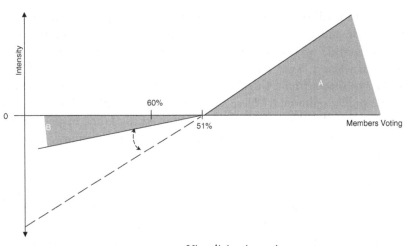

FIGURE 7.1 Visualizing intensity

each senator feels. For convenience, we show the simple majority rule case where a new law passes by a single vote. Then the total intensity across all senators (and implicitly the voters they represent) is represented by positive area "A" and negative area "B." Readers should note that even though the legislation depicted in the figure passes by fifty-one votes to forty-nine, majority rule *does not* guarantee that passage will make the population happier on net. Instead, what matters is the relative size of triangles "A" and "B," which determines the net intensity across all of the winners and losers.

As before, we have assumed a simple Euclidean estimate in which each legislator's passion for or against the proposed legislation increases linearly with her preferred legislation's distance from the median.[75] This, however, immediately tells us that that the new law will only improve legislators' net happiness if the "knee" that divides winners and losers is either flat or points upward, compared to a simple downward extension of the winners' estimated intensity (dashed line).

Now consider how adding a supermajority changes the analysis. By moving the deciding "pivot" or swing vote to, say, 60 percent in Figure 7.1, the rule ensures that A's area will exceed B's unless the "knee" points downward and is very, very sharp. Provided that this is rare, members as a whole will find themselves better off. All the same, moving the pivot from 51 percent to some higher threshold is a "one-size-fits-all" solution. After all, it is bound to be too small or too large in any particular case. When it is too small, majorities can still pass laws that cause net resentment, even if there are fewer such instances than there would be under simple majority rule. And when the supermajority is too large, minorities will be able to block legislation that generates good feelings on net, ushering in all the pathologies that the Framers feared. We argue in what follows that Senate filibusters and shutdowns are best understood as attempts to address these gaps.[76]

The supermajority also has a second function. We have argued that narrow majorities invite each new Congress to reverse its predecessor's handiwork, so that laws and policy become unstable. Supermajority requirements suppress this jitter by ensuring that the losers – who would have to overcome the same margin to repeal the law – are too discouraged to seek a rematch.[77] Provided that the margin is big enough, this automatically rules out reversals from all but the rarest statistical fluctuations from one election to the next. The trouble, of course, is that it is not enough for the supermajority "friction" to stop good laws from being revisited. It should also be low enough to fix bad ones if and when their defects become obvious. Unfortunately, there is no reason why both goals should be simultaneously achievable. In 2010, the Senate's 60 percent threshold nearly stopped an historically large Democrat majority from passing the Affordable Care Act. Yet the same supermajority *failed* to deter angry Republicans from spending the next decade pursuing "repeal-and-replace." Evidently, the current sixty vote figure is, at best, no more than a least-bad compromise.

   Despite these advantages, the supermajority would be much improved if there were some veto-like mechanism that turned it "off" and "on" depending on intensity. Here the starting point is that measurements of intensity necessarily require some reference standard. The veto did this by making the president choose between personal political risk and legislation he disagreed with. It follows that measuring intensity in Congress must similarly force members to choose between dropping their demands and suffering some definite penalty. The problem with the supermajority was that it cost nothing to frustrate the majority. The filibuster filled this gap for over a century.

Like many institutions, it began as an accident. In 1789, the first US Senate adopted rules that let senators end debate by a simple majority vote. Over time, however, many senators decided that the rule was unnecessary and, giving in to the usual lawyer's weakness for rewriting functional language that seems inartful, repealed it in 1806. At this point, debates could theoretically drag on indefinitely.[78] All the same, no one actually attempted a filibuster until 1826, when Virginia Sen. John Randolph unsuccessfully tried to derail the Adams Administration's plans for a diplomatic conference in Panama.[79] Even then, the tactic only became popular when Democrat Sen. William R. King used it to stop a new bank charter in 1841. After that, senators regularly filibustered to block controversial bills for the rest of the century.[80] This lasted until twelve antiwar senators successfully stopped a bill designed to arm US merchant ships against German submarines on the eve of World War I. At this point, an angry majority added a "cloture" rule that let members end debate by a two-thirds vote of those then present on the Senate floor. This meant that even though the Senate, like the House, could pass legislation by a simple majority, the vote itself had to be agreed to by a two-thirds (now three-fifths) margin.[81] That let substantial minorities – forty senators in the rule's definitive mid-twentieth-century version – halt all new legislation unless and until the majority withdrew its bill.[82] This is the same rule that older Americans remember from Frank Capra's *Mr. Smith Goes to Washington*. In real life, the filibuster's most spectacular and consequential example came with the Civil Rights Act of 1964. Having filibustered for sixty days, Southern Senators saw that they could not win – and that they much preferred passing programs that benefited their districts to what had become a pointless defense of Jim Crow laws.[83]

Most readers will know that this classic filibuster no longer exists. All the same, the fact that it survived for half a century tells us something important. Evidently, a majority of senators believed that whatever legislation might be lost was worth the price of stopping legislation that they and at least thirty-nine other members felt strongly about. At the same time, they were *not* willing to let smaller and presumably more extreme groups stop senate business, since that would have invited the crankiest members to bring constant challenges. In this sense, the supermajority margin reflected members' best judgment of the particular tradeoff that promised the biggest net benefit for themselves and their constituents.[84]

On the face of things, the filibuster seems wasteful. And certainly, the costs of gridlock were real enough. But once senators decided that it was both possible and desirable to account for members' intensity, the need for some benchmark test of passion and, more precisely, pain became inescapable. The prospect of lost Senate business – benefits to constituents that representatives can brag about when seeking reelection – provided this.

It helps to think about the process in detail. For every day that went by, senators knew that they would have fewer chances to pass legislation.

Moreover, the losses would continue to mount until the deadlock ended. At this point those who cared the least about the issue at hand – moderates near the deciding sixtieth vote – would ask themselves whether it was better to end the contest by defecting to whichever side seemed closest to winning. That, however, required them to estimate who would give up first. Here the simplest and most natural guess was that whichever side felt most passionately was on the steeper side of the knee and would be the last to defect.

If this were all, we could safely assume that Figure 7.1's "knee" pointed upward in every case where the ayes successfully defeated the nays.[85] In practice, however, swing senators seldom have complete information, which makes them vulnerable to mistakes and gamesmanship. Most obviously, a burst of early defections could persuade other swing voters that a trend was emerging. But of course, the early defections could just as well be random and mean nothing at all. In that scenario, at least, the less passionate side could still bluff its way to victory.[86]

Finally, the filibuster's test of intensity was also transparent to onlookers. This proved particularly valuable in the great Civil Rights Act filibuster of 1964, which showed segregationists throughout the South that their leaders, for all their fire-breathing rhetoric, were hypocrites who much preferred the usual pork barrel of Senate business to a Pyrrhic defense of segregation.[87] From this point, Jim Crow ceased to be a viable issue, allowing politicians in both parties to finally change the subject.

Beyond this core function of measuring intensity, the classic filibuster also offered economy. When we say that a political tactic is "wasteful," we usually think of how it damages society as a whole. But the filibuster's pain was disproportionately focused on senators themselves. Some of this they felt personally in everything from the strain of giving marathon speeches[88] to Majority Leader Joe Robinson's fatal heart attack in 1937.[89] Still other pain was political, preventing senators from passing laws that might help them win votes at the next election. Finally, even this pain was limited. Because swing voters cared less about the issue than anyone else, they could almost always be counted on to end the contest as soon as the eventual winner became obvious. More than that, senators could see when bills were likely to spark a filibuster, and whether the minority was likely to block it. This suggests that many politicians knew better than to propose controversial legislation (or threaten filibusters) in the first place.

Against these strengths, the filibuster did nothing to protect views held by fewer than forty senators. Based on the geometric arguments sketched in Figure 7.1, this did not matter so long as the minority's intensity was only slightly greater than the majority's. That said, this was a dangerous gap in a world where small minorities often suffer harsh treatment.

The filibuster's decline began in 1970 when the Senate, trying to limit the tactic's pain and inconvenience, adopted a "two-track system" so that the majority and minority leaders could agree to consider two bills at once. Filibuster or not, senate business could now continue so long as both major political parties agreed. The reform also excused filibustering senators from being physically present on the floor.[90] This was quickly followed by post-Watergate reforms that reduced cloture (except for rule changes) to sixty Senators,[91] and ended it entirely for budget items which could now be passed on a simple majority through "reconciliation."[92]

The net effect of these changes was that forty senators could now block legislation painlessly. For several decades, things did not change much. Apparently, senators who had lived under the old rules still held reciprocal expectations that the step would not be taken lightly. By the early 2000s, however, so many items were being obstructed that Senate and House leaders felt obliged to respond.[93] Their answer was to bundle appropriations into massive, last-minute "omnibus packages." This would end the supermajority problem since, they reasoned, no politician would ever court the voters' wrath by shutting down the federal government.[94] At the time, the House's disastrous 1995 shutdown seemed to support this judgment.[95] Despite this, the supposed deterrent has not stopped Ted Cruz (2013),[96] Chuck Schumer (2018), and Donald Trump (2018) from blocking "must-pass" legislation for what they claimed were more important goals.

Still, the question remains whether these crises resolve disputes better than the filibuster did. Here the filibuster's clearest advantage was that it focused the pain of gridlock on the personal and political comfort of the senators themselves. By comparison, shutdowns inflict pain indiscriminately on millions of citizens.[97] Then too, filibusters – which occurred throughout the session and considered one issue at a time – were reasonably transparent. By comparison, shutdowns bundle multiple issues together and then use deliberately tight deadlines to intimidate members.[98] As Madison would have been the first to point out, this engineered chaos is bound to make outcomes less predictable. Given these advantages, it is hard to escape the conclusion that government shutdowns are a poor trade for the classical filibuster.

## 7.5 FEEDBACKS

Madison designed his system to keep political resentments from accumulating. During bipartisan eras Congress furthers these goals by (a) deciding political arguments quickly and decisively, (b) avoiding majority tyranny outcomes that generate new resentments, and (c) stressing common ground and compromise. The paradox is that the mere existence of a Congress also introduces the possibility of gridlock. This facilitates a second, coercive politics regime when public opinion is polarized.

Congress has developed various rules to contain majority tyranny. This balance is constantly changing depending on how much the public values individual representatives' character and competence compared to party loyalty. It follows that rules in highly polarized eras will almost always expand congressional leaders' power to limit amendments and jam through legislation. Conversely, bipartisan era holdovers like filibusters and supermajorities will be particularly vulnerable. Yet these procedures remain as necessary as ever. Jettisoning them would massively increase jitter by making it easier for each new Congress to reverse the work of its predecessors. Worse, once discarded it would probably take years to reinstate the rules when bipartisanship returned. In the interim, the barriers would remain low, encouraging still more tyranny-of-the-majority outcomes along with the anger and resentment that follow in their wake.

The politics of deadlock depends on blockading centrist legislation even when there are enough moderates in both parties to pass it. But in that case, Congress can debate issues for years without resolving them. This necessarily puts pressure on both the executive and the courts to step in. Unlike statutes, however, court decisions and executive orders have no inherent finality. That makes it easy for future administrations and Supreme Court justices to revise or undo their predecessors' policies. The resulting executive and judicial activism then invites further cycles of controversy and policy reversals. Voters are never allowed to forget, and instead become still more angry with each passing year.

The silver lining is that coercive politics cannot begin until extremists in both parties capture their respective congressional delegations. This naively suggests a sharp transition when the total number of extremists on both sides crosses 50 percent. In practice this is almost certainly blurred by subsidiary factors like the number of gerrymandered safe districts, the existence of extremist donors, and Congress's seniority rules.[99] Empirically, control seems to become feasible when extremists number as low as 40 percent of each party.

The good news, of course, is that the extremists' control is unstable: If one party were to announce a centrist agenda, the other would be compelled to follow or else lose the next election. In principle, the rebellion could start with centrists in Congress reaching across the aisle to pass compromise legislation that their leaderships opposed.[100] This, however, would require unprecedented coordination and trust, and would subject members to retaliation if they failed. In practice, rebellion is more likely to begin outside Congress, with a convincingly centrist politician winning her party's primaries followed by a landslide victory on Election Day. At this point, Downsian politicians on both sides of the aisle would insist that their parties move to the center to remain competitive.

Finally, senators and congressmen are second only to the president in their ability to influence which of the media's many narratives and ideologies become mainstream. This, in turn, shapes voters' political imaginations and, eventually, their choices on Election Day. In bipartisan eras when Congress resolves most disputes quickly, issues come and go before voters can build significant anger and resentment, after which they are quickly forgotten. The difference in coercive politics eras is that deadlock lets many if not most debates drag on for years. The result is that voters are constantly reminded of their opinions, so that polarization and anger can build indefinitely.

### Notes

1   *Federalist* No. 37 at p. 161 (Madison).
2   One could equally ask why the Constitution is binding. But here at least we have a recursive answer. So long as citizens respect it and can detect violations, Congress has no choice in the matter.
3   *Federalist* No. 51 at p. 240 (Madison).
4   The result corresponds to what economists call the "Folk Theorem," which holds that if players value the future highly enough there exist equilibria where each acts based on her trust that the other will reciprocate. See generally Fudenberg and Maskin (1986). The Folk Theorem derives its ironic name from the fact that it circulated within economics departments for years before anyone thought to publish it. Its discoverers are unknown and therefore anonymous.
5   The *reductio* of such arguments would be to claim something plainly false about the Constitution, for example that Trump's 74 million votes in the 2020 election were "actually" larger than Biden's 81 million. Since we expect

partisans to embrace any convenient argument, the only real guardrail is centrist voters' willingness to punish politicians who fail to play by the rules. Even then, voters will usually need intermediaries to see through whatever lies partisans invent to obfuscate the issue. The US Supreme Court has traditionally supplied this linchpin.

6  Wikipedia (49).

7  Gittleson (2021).

8  See Brinton (1938) at pp. 176–81.

9  U.S. Constitution, Art. I, § 5, cl. 2.

10  But see Democrat Congressman Bill Pascrell's (D-NJ) call to exclude 126 Republicans from Congress for seeking to overturn the 2020 election. Solender (2020).

11  Over the years, Congress has expelled or else forced seven House members and twenty senators to resign; apart from advocating secession during the Civil War, the reason has almost always been bribery. US House Dept. of History, Art & Archives (n.d.) (a, b); US Senate (n.d.). The House's most "political" expulsion was a Wisconsin congressman who had received a twenty-year sentence for opposing America's entry into World War I. It then refused to seat him a second time after voters reelected him. Barry (2005) at p. 207.

12  Congress refused to seat minority members fifty-nine times in the hyperpartisan era from 1875 to 1903. Even then, however, it limited itself to cases where the winning margin was razor thin or else involved fraud within the Jim Crow South. Congress has refused to seat just two members since. Rove (2021a).

13  Adams (1776).

14  Anon [1787] at p. 254.

15  The Framers did not anticipate the hypocrisy of modern Congresses, which regularly exempt members and staff from labor, civil rights, insider trading, and other statutes. Restoring the traditional argument that representatives should face the same laws as their constituents seems like an obvious reform. Skoning (2015).

16  *Federalist* No. 62 at p. 285 (Madison).

17  *Federalist* No. 2 at p. 8 (Jay).

18  Ricks (2020) at p. 234.

19  *Federalist* No. 10 at p. 42 (Madison).

20  For example, Prof. Letwin writes:

> Congress does not merely enact its private dogmas, nor does it simply supply whatever the people order. Public opinion is not so precise. Far from demanding a particular law, the public desires at most a certain kind of law, and more often only wants to be rid of a general evil. Sometimes, indeed, public opinion is practically silent and yet effective, for Congress often refuses to pass laws because it expects that the public would object, or adopts them anticipating that the public will approve. (Letwin 1956 at p. 221)

21  *Federalist* No. 33 at p. 151 (Hamilton).

22  Ricks (2020) at p. 234.

23  Quitt (2008) at pp. 631 and 635.

24  Promises that have not been endorsed by the party's leaders are also inherently less likely to pass, further reducing rational voters' incentive to learn about them, much less find them persuasive.

25  This provides some of the best evidence that many members are Downsian politicians at heart; that is, that they care much more about being reelected than about influencing legislation.

26  I am indebted to Sebastian von Engelhardt for clarifying my thinking on this issue.

27  In more sophisticated variants the parties might choose to ignore one or two violations, or refuse cooperation for a limited period followed by new cooperation in hopes that the other side has learned its lesson and will reciprocate.

28  Economists usually model the situation in one of two ways. First, they consider trust games in which Alice helps Bob because she thinks he will return the favor. If Bob makes a reciprocal calculation, the assumptions become self-reinforcing even though neither favor is enforceable. The second approach assumes that each actor is born with a fixed amount of trustworthiness which, however, cannot be directly observed by others. Parties then update their estimates each time a request is honored or refused. For a mathematically rigorous account of the literature, see Cabral (2005).

29  See, e.g., Tadelis (2013) at pp. 190–6.

30  See, e.g., Tadelis (2013) at p. 198.

31  Incumbents may also possess tactical advantages in influencing legislation from their accumulated understanding of how to manipulate Congress's procedural rules and/or the substantive issues facing the country.

32  Berry and Fowler (2018) at p. 10.

33  Berry and Fowler add that committee chairs also have the power to expedite or block hearings and markup; run committee meetings; withhold staff support from members; invite opponents of the bill to testify; refer the bill to friendly subcommittees; represent it favorably to the media; name members to the conference committee; and schedule hearings to influence the way bureaucrats implement the law. The net result is that "the proposer can often achieve favorable policy outcomes or extract a significant portion of resources for herself because voting against her proposal is costly, either because extra rounds of voting are costly or because the policy will revert to an undesirable outcome." Berry and Fowler (2018) at p. 2.

34  Gehlbach (2022) at p. 125. Some scholars argue that House rules against floor amendments give committees more power over the final outcome, and for that reason encourage them to examine legislation more carefully. Gehlbach (2022).

35  The Continental Congress organized various bodies to manage the war, including a Committee of Secret Correspondence, Treasury Board, Board of War and Ordnance, and Navy Board. Still more work was done in small *ad hoc* committees. One of these drafted the Articles of Confederation (1777) that became the country's first constitution. See Wikipedia (19).

36  Hofstadter (1969) at p. 244.

37  Hofstadter (1969) at pp. 246–7.

38  Hofstadter (1969) at p. 245.

39  Members elected for their character, independence, and/or ideological purity sometimes see recorded votes as a policy lever. Many of the Freedom

Caucus members who initially refused to support Kevin McCarthy for Speaker in 2023 did so to force rule changes that would ensure *more* votes. Centrists, they argued, would be less likely to authorize spending under a return to "regular order" rules that meant going on the record multiple times. Rove (2023).

40 Strassel (2021).

41 Congressional Research Service (2019) at p. 1.

42 Barone (2019) at 21.

43 Barone (2019) at pp. 84 and 89.

44 Ballotpedia (n.d.) (b).

45 See, e.g., DeSilver (2015).

46 See, e.g., Rove (2023) for a detailed account of the various factions opposing McCarthy along with their motives.

47 See Chamberlain (2019), Bolton (2021), and Collins (2021).

48 See, e.g., McCaskill (2021) and Rove (2021b).

49 In principle, extremists could even threaten to leave the party if it refuses their demands. That was precisely what happened in 1860, when Southern Democrats demanded that their Northern colleagues endorse slavery in the territories. This forced Northerners to choose between making themselves unelectable at home or seeing their party lose the next presidential election. When Northern delegates predictably chose their own political survival, Southerners walked out of the party's nominating convention, paving the way for Lincoln's victory that Fall. Catton [1961] at p. 28.

50 In principle the transition could also be delayed until extremists on both sides total *more* than 50 percent of all representatives. Probably the most obvious way for this to happen would be if centrists retained outsized influence under Congress's remaining seniority rules.

51 Binder (2014).

52 O'Neil (2018) (quoting Senator Lindsey Graham: "What you want to do is destroy this guy's life, hold this seat open, and hope you win in 2020"); Anon. (2019) (quoting former presidential candidate Hillary Clinton: "Some Republicans, mainly in the House Freedom Caucus, think Mr. Trump can win an extended game of chicken with Democrats"); see also Reilly (2016).

53 Henninger (2018) ("This looks like the future of American politics: Play to a base jacked up by social media, hold it with scheduled feedings of red meat and simply force the rest of the bewildered electorate to sort it out and choose between two poles"); Goodwin (2018) ("Still, there is danger when two sides both think they can outlast the other"); Rall (2019) ("[M]any Progressives would rather see a second Trump term than a President Biden, who would govern through Clintonian triangulation. Winning the next election isn't necessarily more important than the long-term objective of winning over the Democratic Party. Progressives' broader aim is moving the 50 yardline of American politics to the left").

54 Goodwin (2018) (describing conversations with readers: "Responding to my concern that America might be sleepwalking into a second civil war, a number of readers agreed. Some said they welcomed it. Curt Doolittle wrote this:

'We aren't sleepwalking into it, we know exactly what we're doing and why. The hard right and hard left are planning on it, ready for it, and looking for an opportunity'").

55 Anon (2021d). The most celebrated House Progressive, Alexandria Ocasio-Cortez, has never authored a single bill. Congress.gov (2022).

56 On healthcare, see, e.g., Starr (2001); Pear (2017); Kreiter (2017); Goldstein (2016); Anon (2019) (arguing that polarization on immigration has led to "two decades of legislative frustration"). On immigration, see, e.g. Kane (2019) (polls show that Democrats and Republicans would agree to compromise immigration bill if Speaker Pelosi allowed a vote); Galston (2019) (reviewing survey evidence that major party orthodoxies ignore the "nuanced center on this long-contested issue"); Salam (2022) ("Both coalitions have their nonnegotiable demands, and both have made it clear that they'd rather see the border crisis continue than give ground to their political opponents")

57 It is tempting and probably accurate to assume that most Downsian politicians hold centrist views, while most idealists side with the extremists. That said, it would be perfectly rational for Downsian politicians representing highly polarized, "safe" districts to take extreme positions. They can, after all, count on voters reelecting them whether or not their policies cause their party to lose seats overall. Conversely, an Idealist politician could rationally adopt the Downsian strategy of offering centrist solutions to her moderate district, waiting for the day when more extreme measures stand some chance of passing.

58 The distinction between Downsian and rational Idealist politicians is an abstraction. Real politicians almost always mix these strategies in proportions that change over time. For example, a rational politician who harbors strong ideological views would still place her own reelection above all else when there is no chance of fulfilling them. But the same politician could behave quite differently when her private goals suddenly seemed within reach. In practice, many extremists never face the choice because they come from safe districts whose voters expect Progressive agendas no matter what happens.

59 More specifically, we expect rational extremists to defect to the center when the risk-adjusted benefit of achieving their own goals is less than the risk-adjusted downside of seeing their ideological enemies prevail. There is also the additional caveat that they must see the center's proposals as at least a slight improvement over extremist agendas on the other side. Politicians who see no difference will presumably fight to the end.

60 Strassel (2021).

61 Richard Nixon, for all his faults, used his personal authority to stop Republicans from pursuing voter fraud theories after the 1960 election. Gellman (2021); Noonan (2022). This would have been impossible in a world where loyalty to ideology exceeded loyalty to the man.

62 This is particularly evident when the stakes are high, most obviously when scandal threatens to unseat whichever party won the preceding election. In 1973 norms against personal misconduct were still strong enough that President Nixon could see that the Republican Party would not stand by him and resigned. A half-century later President Clinton (1998), Virginia

Governor Ralph Northam (2020), and New York Governor Andrew Cuomo (2021) all tried to brazen it out, although Cuomo failed in the end.

63 The fact that Democrats failed to overturn the filibuster by just two votes in Congress's 2021–2 session is similarly disquieting.

64 *Federalist* No. 63 at p. 290 (Madison).

65 Suppose the House outcome favors the legislation. Then the chances that the Senate or President will disagree are ½ × ½ = ¼. And of course, the same argument applies equally if the House opposes the legislation.

66 On the need for frequent congressional elections, see, e.g., *Federalist* No. 37 (Madison) at p. 161. The Framers never said whether they favored presidential term limits, although Hamilton plainly worried that a second term would give the president time to form dangerous alliances with the federal bureaucracy and other elected officials across the country. *Federalist* No. 69 (Hamilton) at p. 315. In practice a two-term limit was set by custom and example at the end of George Washington's presidency, even if Grant and Wilson, neither particularly successful in their second terms, still dreamed of reelection. Beschloss (2018) at p. 367 (Wilson); Rehnquist (2004) at p. 165 (Grant). Theodore Roosevelt, who had served nearly two full terms after President McKinley was assassinated, actually took the plunge by running for a third term as an independent in 1912. Wikipedia (46). The custom was then suspended by Franklin Roosevelt in the emergency of World War II before being permanently formalized by the Twenty-Second Amendment (1951). This was yet another instance where practical experience with the Constitution eventually persuaded Americans to accept rules that the Framers had been too hesitant to set in advance.

67 U.S. Constitution Art. I, § 7, cl. 2.

68 *Federalist* No. 73 at p. 338 (Hamilton).

69 *Federalist* No. 73 at p. 339 (Hamilton).

70 See e.g., Guelzo (2021b) at p. 37; *Federalist* No. 58 at p. 270 (Hamilton). Hamilton adds that minimum quorum requirements would "foster the baneful practice of secessions … a practice which leads more directly to public convulsions, and the ruin of popular governments, than any other which has yet been displayed among us." The point is well taken: Once dissenters permanently refuse to attend, the majority must choose between continuing without them and having no government at all. For a brief history of quorums and minority obstruction in the Anglo-American world, see Wallner (2020).

71 The single exception is that constitutional amendments require a two-thirds vote in both houses of Congress followed by three-fourths ratification by the states; U.S. Constitution, Art. V.

72 *Federalist* No. 22 at pp. 96–7 (Hamilton).

73 *Federalist* No. 22 at p. 96 (Hamilton).

74 *Federalist* No. 22 at p. 97 (Hamilton).

75 While the real distribution is surely more complicated, this linear model is probably the best we can do given the current state of research.

76 We usually justify our insistence that new legislation should reduce legislators' net anger on the normative ground that it prevents tyranny. That said, it is instructive to mention the variant argument in which the supermajority

is less about guaranteeing fairness than the state's physical security. Given that population is the sine qua non of military power, a large supermajority guarantees that dissenting minorities cannot topple the national government no matter how strongly they feel. The fact that the South failed to secede at the very moment when the Northern population was about to cancel its constitutional advantage in the Senate and Electoral College is striking. Coincidence or not, the constitutional balance must have been nearly identical to the military one.

77  Jitter can be considered a version of majority tyranny in the limiting case where the winning side is both minuscule and changing.

78  Wikipedia (26).

79  Brands (2018) at p. 127.

80  The House also experimented with filibusters in the nineteenth century, but quickly abandoned them. Wikipedia (26). Though not technically a filibuster, House Democrats also used procedural delays to block presidential vote counts in the disputed election of 1876, only lifting their blockade when the new president agreed to end Reconstruction. Rehnquist (2004) at pp. 137–8.

81  Whitener (2021).

82  S. Res. 285, 113th Cong. Rule XXII.2 (2013).

83  Hoppe (2021).

84  The Senate practice of "blue slips," which gives members a courtesy veto over judicial appointments in their home states, is consistent. Tobias (2018). Even more than the filibuster, this insurance is tightly limited to the two members likely to be most affected by the nominee.

85  To be sure, all of this was rough and ready given that the measurement was limited to the dozen or so least passionate swing voters in the middle. While this seems a reasonable sample for the full Senate, it is easy to imagine cases where a 20 percent minority might feel more intensely than the rest of the body combined.

86  For a blow-by-blow account of defections in the 2019 Trump shutdown struggle, see Restuccia et al. (2019).

87  Hoppe (2021). The Civil Rights Act underscored the connection by making any state or local program that practiced discrimination ineligible for federal funds. Southern whites quickly made their choice by abandoning Jim Crow. Risen (2014) at p. 6. Crucially, the filibuster was instrumental in advertising this choice. Far from trying to evade the showdown, Senate Majority Leader Mike Mansfield embraced it as a necessary test of strength, promising members that there would be no trickery, "not in the seeking of short-cuts, not in the cracking of nonexistent whips, not in wheeling and dealing, but in an honest facing of the situation and a resolution of it by the Senate itself." Hoppe (2021).

88  Senator Ted Cruz read bedtime stories as part of his twenty-one-hour speech during the 2013 shutdown. Fitzpatrick (2013).

89  Mayhew (2003).

90  Wikipedia (26).

91  Fallows (2012).

92  Wikipedia (26).

93 Hughes and Wise (2020).
94 Hanson (2015) at p. 1.
95 Gonyea (2019).
96 Fahrenthold and Zezima (2016).
97 It also matters how the pain is applied. An ideal mechanism would start sanctions high enough to immediately attract swing senators' attention and then quickly escalate their severity until there were enough defections to end the struggle. By this standard both mechanisms seem to be reasonably efficient. Thus, the filibuster blocks the Senate from considering other business so that the pain of unpassed legislation continues to climb until one side gives in. Similarly, past shutdowns have almost always been carefully calibrated to inflict just enough pain to persuade opponents, while stopping short of levels that might make their own side capitulate. For example, the 2019 Trump shutdown was tailored to affect less than one-fourth of the Federal budget. Paletta (2019). The fact that past shutdowns have (so far) ended quickly suggests that politicians are reasonably good at making this estimate.
98 It might be argued that disposing of several issues simultaneously takes less time than considering the same number of filibusters seriatim. This however is illusory so long as senators' votes are correlated across issues. In these cases, at least, whichever side demonstrates that it can outwait the other on the first issue is unlikely to be challenged again for months if not years. Where senators' votes are uncorrelated, the Senate may indeed save time, though at the cost of transparency in considering multiple bundled issues together.
99 For example, it seems obvious that recent politics would have looked very different had Nancy Pelosi not become Speaker. On the history and financing of San Francisco's Progressive political machine, see, e.g., Wilentz (2020).
100 This is essentially what happened in 1910, when Progressives from both parties joined forces to restrict Speaker Cannon's power to control legislation. The reforms endured for nearly a century. Meyer (2023). In principle, centrists could also reach across the aisle to elect a "compromise speaker" who was less extreme than the majority party's leadership preferred. Axelrod (2022).

# 8

# Implementing Law

## *The Executive*

The Framers imagined a simple division of labor in which the Congress would announce national policy, and the president would carry it out. The surprise in the Jackson era was that voters had come to know the president better than their own congressman. And often liked him more. Suddenly, the chief executive could ask the electorate to choose between him and his congressional opponents at the next election. If he had to, he could even fight his own party.

This political change took more than a century to play out. The revolution came in three acts. The first made presidents into legislators, albeit voteless ones. The Framers had thought – correctly at first – that presidents would be timid in using the veto. But Jackson, having demonstrated his influence with voters, injected the president into Congress's deliberations by announcing which bills he favored – or would veto – in advance. If voters did not like this meddling, they could always punish him at the next election. Otherwise, voters would punish the congressmen who defied him, constantly resetting the balance of power between the branches. In emergencies, presidents could even claim powers that neither Congress nor the Constitution had given them, ruling by fiat and only later asking the voters to ratify what they had done.

Jackson was equally prominent in the drama's second act, tightening the president's grip on the bureaucracy and asserting the executive branch's right not just to carry out the legislature's policies, but to originate its own.[1] Where presidential influence had previously consisted almost entirely of the power to hire and fire, Jackson now extended his control by imposing a complex system of paperwork and signoffs on the country's government. Finally, Jackson aggressively expanded

government patronage jobs, trading efficiency for (he claimed) democratic responsiveness. This form of presidential control reached its apo-
gee shortly after the Civil War, only to be cut back by civil service laws
from the 1880s onward. The result by the early twentieth century was
to insulate the federal bureaucracy from presidential interference, so that
government agencies became a source of policy in their own right.

The final act came with Big Government. However effective in the
short run, Jackson's web of signoffs also encouraged bureaucrats to trade
favors, establishing personal fiefdoms and sclerotic "agency cultures." By
the 1930s the bureaucracy was so large as to be nearly impervious to outside monitoring and control. Instead, most decisions now emerged from
a complex web of internal interactions with little or no outside input. On
the one hand, it was clear that Americans wanted this bureaucratic state,
and that no democratic system could deny them their wish. On the other,
it was almost impossible to say whether agency policies were democratically responsive, or could be made so in the future.

We proceed as follows. Section 8.1 details the president's relations
with Congress, concentrating on the executive branch's rise as a nearly
coequal player in setting policy. Section 8.2 reviews the accidents of history that shaped the federal agencies we know today. Section 8.3 analyzes how the various strategies developed to constrain and democratize
bureaucratic action over the years now combine to set policy. Section
8.4 examines the limits of Madison's rule of law model, focusing on the
president's war powers as an example. Section 8.5 examines how the
presidency, uniquely in Madison's system, lets a single person push back
against and sometimes correct the other branches of government when
they stray into error.

## 8.1 THE PRESIDENT AND CONGRESS

The Framers had assumed that each state would back its own favorite
son for president, so that no candidate could obtain a national majority. According to the Constitution, that reduced the Electoral College to
picking five semi-finalists, leaving the final choice to Congress. And in
fact, this scenario played out repeatedly between 1800 and 1824.[2] But
if Congress could choose presidents, it was only natural for it to choose
pliable ones. Nor would the meddling end on Inauguration Day, since an
angry Congress could block the president's reelection, withhold honors
and rewards, and even impeach him. By modern standards at least, most
of the early Republic's presidents were weak.

But that was not the Framers' plan. Their idea had been that the president would slow Congress when the public's worst impulses took hold. This could only work if the president's reputation was strong enough for the public to respect him even when he overruled their wishes. Some of this influence would accrue naturally: The president was bound to be a prominent and respected man within his home state, and would usually have burnished these credentials by serving in Congress or the military.[3] Potentially, at least, the president could also increase his reputation still further once in office. The rub was that this required large projects that a jealous Congress might deny him by issuing detailed instructions and prohibitions.

The deeper handicap at first was that state legislators elected the Electoral College. This limited candidates' chance to build their popularity and influence directly with voters. But change was coming. In 1800 state legislators chose presidential electors in fourteen of the country's sixteen states; by 1830 citizens were electing them directly in all but one of the country's twenty-four states.[4] Meanwhile, the rise of the two-party system meant that presidential candidates were no longer just local favorite sons, but could campaign throughout the country, demonstrating their strength for all to see on Election Day.

It was only a matter of time before presidents would convert this popularity into influence in Congress. The turning point came with Jackson's fight to abolish the Bank of the United States. Presidents before Jackson had made only limited appeals to the public. But where the Framers had imagined the president standing up to a deluded House, Jackson flipped the script by helping the more democratic House stand up to an elitist Senate. Indeed, Jackson insisted that *he* was more visible and hence more democratic than the House itself, whose permanent cliques cared only about themselves. He then called on newspapers to punish congressmen who obstructed his policies, even as lawmakers who backed him received patronage and favorable writeups in party-controlled newspapers.[5]

Jackson had given the president the stature to make policy. But it was the Constitution that, somewhat unexpectedly, gave him the tool he needed to shape legislation. The Framers had given presidents the power to veto Congress's worst ideas. But in that case, why wait silently for mistakes to happen? So long as Congress was the only elected branch, the president had been loath to challenge it. Once Jackson established his own link to the people, though, Congress had to take his veto threats seriously. Instead of wielding an essentially reactive veto, the president now became a legislator, albeit a voteless one,[6] demanding that Congress consult him *before* it passed legislation. Where the first six presidents had vetoed a total of just nine bills, Jackson vetoed a dozen.[7] Furthermore, Jackson's formal power was paired with his unofficial status as leader of one of the country's two major parties. This usually gave him the dominant voice in deciding platforms and issues for roughly half the Congress.

In one sense, the new arrangement spoiled the symmetry of Madison's design in which an impulsively democratic House was counterbalanced by the cooler, unelected president and senate. Still, it added something important. Jackson – unlike any congressman or senator – was the only politician who could claim to speak for the nation.[8] This made him the natural choice to resist parochial interests in Congress, smoothing over the benefits and burdens of national projects so that they did not expropriate some regions to benefit others.

But of course, passing laws was just the curtain-raiser: In the long run, the broader struggle over just how the federal government would implement Congress's statutes was just as important. Yet the Constitution, normally so rich in detail, failed to say who government officials would answer to. This left the president and Congress scrambling for whatever carrots and sticks they could muster. Superficially, the requirement that the laws be faithfully executed seemed to give Congress, as the author of those laws, the final say in deciding when its intent had been honored. But Jackson's direct appeal to voters implied a very different theory. More than 100 years later, the Supreme Court would write this directly into the Constitution, holding that

…the President is the active agent not of Congress, but of the Nation. As such, he performs the duties which the Constitution lays upon him immediately, and as such, also, he executes the laws and regulations adopted by Congress. He is the agent of the people of the United States, deriving all his powers from them and responsible directly to them. In no sense is he the agent of Congress. He obeys and executes the laws of Congress not because Congress is enthroned in authority over him, but because the Constitution directs him to do so.[9]

This made it clear that at least some of the president's powers were rights derived from the people and existed independently of Congress.[10] At one level, this was the only possible answer if the government was to save itself from sudden, unforeseen emergencies. But that did not make the authority any less dangerous, and the dangers were multiplied when, as often happened, Congress stayed silent for political reasons.[11] In either case, it was hard to see how presidential rule by decree could end unless courts stepped in or voters elected a challenger at the next election. This made the prospects for reestablishing the normal rule of law seem strangely indefinite.

The question of emergency powers is especially poignant when Congress deadlocks. While the old choices no longer command a majority, neither has Congress formed some new consensus to replace them. The National Emergencies Act[12] tries to address this by letting the president repurpose existing spending by declaring an emergency when Congress is silent. This makes good sense in bipartisan eras when new issues are typically addressed by compromise legislation within one or two legislative sessions. Here, the duration implied by the word "emergencies" is unlikely to exceed Congress's usual cycle for passing new legislation. Then too, Congress can correct the president if he goes too far.[13] The only real difficulty is the president's constitutional power to veto legislation when Congress votes to reverse his allocations.[14] While this makes sense on the purely formal ground that it takes a new law to negate an old one, the perverse result is that Congress must sometimes muster a two-thirds majority to negate its own intent.

The trouble, as usual, is worse in eras dominated by coercive politics. Now an extremist president can use the National Emergencies Act to fund projects that his allies in Congress have tried and failed to pass for decades.[15] At this point, the US starts to imitate the Weimar pattern of government by endlessly renewed "emergencies," with the president's power limited only by the need to face reelection in a country where a slim majority of the electorate may be all too happy to oppress everyone else. Given that most of the system's safeguards against jitter and majority tyranny are found in Congress's internal procedures, presidential rule immediately lets narrow, fluctuating majorities run roughshod over everyone else. The results are certain to inflame political resentment on both sides, further reinforcing polarization and coercive politics.

Finally, the Constitution gives Congress the power to remove presidents, government officials, and judges who disregard the law through impeachment. The challenge is to protect the president from casual removal long enough for him to show that his programs can work. This implies, if nothing else, that a new majority in Congress should not be able to remove him the first time his party loses an election. The Framers' solution combines a procedural rule (a two-thirds supermajority in the Senate) with a legal inquiry (whether the president has committed "high crimes and misdemeanors")[16] to achieve this balance.

This is yet another instance where Madison's machinery works differently depending on whether the country's politics is predominantly "bipartisan" or "coercive." In the former case, the requirement provides ample protection against impeachment for unpopularity alone. Most obviously, the two-thirds requirement ensures that voters must swing the Senate's partisan balance by at least 16 percent to remove a president whose party originally commanded a majority.[17] In practice, this is comfortably larger than the electoral swings against such historically unpopular incumbents as Jimmy Carter (–9.7 percent) and George H. W. Bush (–5.6 percent).[18] The second, "high crimes" component then reinforces the protection by requiring senators to find objective wrongdoing. While this adds nothing unless senators are sufficiently honest to put law and evidence above party, this is a reasonably low bar so long as voters reward politicians who show respect for the rule of law.[19] The fact that senators are elected for six-year terms and are almost by definition widely respected then further insulates them against the kind of bare-knuckle partisanship that pretends to see "high crimes" where none exists.[20]

The surprise is that impeachment's "high crimes and misdemeanors" requirement *also* suppresses partisanship in the coercive regime. This is because the two-thirds conviction rule amplifies the importance of those centrist senators who are most likely to apply the "high crimes" standard honestly. To see this, consider a simple benchmark example where the Senate is evenly split between the two parties and is populated by Left-extremists (25 percent), Centrists (50 percent), and Right-extremists (25 percent). Now suppose that a centrist is president. Because presidential succession is rigidly defined by law,[21] extremists on both sides already know who would replace the current president if he was removed from office. If that person is herself a centrist, extremist senators on both sides might conceivably join forces to vote out the incumbent, but this would not change much. If, on the other hand, the successor is an extremist, it is hard to see why the other party's extremists would ever vote to put their enemies in the White House. In that case the most either can muster is fifty votes. So, while we have argued that Left- and Right-extremists may often join forces to blockade a centrist agenda, they will *not* cooperate to remove a centrist president outright.[22] This implies that the president can only be removed by the other party's centrists' sincere judgment that the president really has committed "high crimes and misdemeanors."

Now consider the coercive politics case when an extremist is president. He starts with 25 percent support from his extremist allies and 25 percent opposition from his equally extremist enemies. This however means that he needs just nine centrist votes to survive impeachment. Knowing this arithmetic, an extremist president who wants to maximize his agenda will moderate his excesses to stay in power. Whether or not this nine-vote margin is good policy, it is reassuringly close to traditional notions of fairness. Indeed, the fact that the president needs nine of the fifty centrists to vote against impeachment is only slightly less lenient than insisting on unanimity in a twelve-member jury, or "Blackstone's Rule" that it is better for ten guilty men to go free than to punish one innocent man by accident.[23] Of course, the argument will become steadily weaker if polarization increases or the rule of law declines. That said, the failure will at least be graceful, with instability growing gradually instead of all at once.

## 8.2  BUREAUCRACY EVOLVING

Patronage had been rife in the British system, and nowhere more so than in the American colonies. Independence and the rise of modern political parties did nothing to change this, but only shifted the recipients from royal cronies to political hacks. Yet even that change was momentous. The eighteenth century's gentry politics had been a game for wealthy amateurs. By Jackson's day the new political campaigns required manpower, and the "volunteers" had to be paid. Suddenly, politics was a middle-class profession like any other, and just as businesslike, with professional politicians careful to insert as many hacks into undemanding government jobs as they possibly could.

Congress began the Revolutionary War by acting as its own government, forming *ad hoc* committees to micromanage every tiny detail down to, in one instance, "intercepting two [enemy] vessels *en route* to America." But as the war dragged on, it began delegating this kind of day-to-day supervision to permanent "departments." Initially, these bodies were staffed by congressmen; however, they soon expanded to include outside officials, followed by a free-standing government when Congress created independent Foreign Affairs, War, Marine, and Finance (later The Treasury) Departments in 1781. Both then and forever afterward, each department was headed by a single executive nominated by the president and acceptable to Congress.[24]

The question remained who would supervise this government. Today's Americans mostly remember *The Federalist* for arguing that government administrators "ought to be considered as the assistants or deputies" of the president, and "subject to his superintendence."[25] But the

Constitution itself is silent, and in other moods the Framers imagined, for example, that Senate consent would be needed to fire as well as hire the president's deputies.[26] So the first Congress made an enormous concession when it authorized the president to remove administrative officials unilaterally. At least in the short run, this made Washington and Adams the undisputed masters of their governments.[27]

Still, Congress soon found other ways to bend the departments to its will. The fact that congressional caucuses nominated presidential candidates was particularly corrosive: Since many department heads hoped to be president themselves, they often heeded Congress as much as their nominal boss. Starting with the War of 1812, Congress also increased its own supervisory capacity by dividing itself into committees that mirrored (and tried to direct) each of the main departments.[28]

The first government departments were headed by patrician elites who believed that gentlemen were born to command. The result was that agencies were organized much like the era's cavalry units, as fiefdoms built in the image of whichever prominent personality led them.[29] Whatever its advantages, this improvisational style demanded well-educated followers. That reinforced the leaders' already strong tendency to staff agencies with people from their own class, including relatives and friends, no matter which party held the White House. Many posts were effectively inherited from one generation to the next.[30]

The system could not last. Geography and the sheer growth of government hiring soon pushed operations to scales that no single person, however gifted, could control. But that did not stop elite agency heads from asserting their independence from the White House, and the resistance took on a class tinge when the country's rapidly expanding suffrage made that quintessential outsider, Andrew Jackson, president. He pointedly insisted that no elite training was necessary: "The duties of all public officers," he said, "are, or at least admit of being made, so plain and simple that men of intelligence may readily qualify themselves for their performance."[31] In any case, he added, his Administration had no choice: Any government that sought to serve the people needed to appoint its own staff.[32] If the people were displeased, they could always turn him out of office.[33]

The underside of this high-toned rhetoric was patronage. Jackson removed and replaced twenty times as many government employees in his first term as any previous president.[34] Government was also dumbed down. In place of gentlemanly improvisation, bureaucrats now followed detailed instructions that subdivided tasks into such tiny pieces that even indifferently educated men could do the job. The need for more checks and balances was also becoming clear, never more so than when one enterprising bureaucrat absconded with 5 percent of the US annual budget. Jackson found a cure for this in red tape: Henceforth, no moneys could be paid out, or actions taken, without signoffs from multiple offices backed by periodic audits to make sure the procedures were actually being followed.[35] This would have important long-run consequences: Bureaucrats who were supposed to act as checks on each other would eventually figure out that it was better to trade approvals back and forth, creating a landscape of small bureaucratic empires that resisted outside direction. For now, though, the system not only worked, but also gave Jackson and his successors a handy way to pay the armies of "volunteers" who got them elected.[36]

Nathaniel Hawthorne, of all people, has left us a detailed memoir of what it felt like to be a cog in this federal machine. Soon after John Tyler became president in 1845, politician friends wangled Hawthorne a job at the Customs House in Salem, Massachusetts. The job came with an annual salary of $1,200 ($37,500 today) in exchange for a half a day's undemanding work, which left plenty of time to write and raise a family.[37] For the most part, Hawthorne's memoir is an indictment of how patronage bleeds initiative and creativity from government employees.[38] Nor did he lack for evidence: Most of the workers he supervised held what we would now call "no-show" jobs, staying at home for most of the winter and barely working the rest of the year. There was also rampant corruption: On one occasion Hawthorne even watched as smugglers trundled wagon-loads of untaxed goods past the office at high noon.[39]

But Hawthorne's most illuminating passages involve his squeamish reaction to patronage close up. Certainly, he knew that elected officials care about paying off political connections at least as much as doing the government's work.[40] Yet despite having arrived "with the President's commission in my pocket," he kept most of his inherited subordinates apart from the handful of miscreants who appeared guilty of "evil and corrupt practices" or had shown some egregious "lack of efficiency." Then too, he knew that holding the legal power to fire was not everything. Like every previous administration for the past twenty years, he did not dare remove the head of the Customs House – formerly "New England's most successful soldier" – or the underlings whom that elderly gentleman had made it his business to protect. Evidently, there was a practical limit to how far partisans could go without calling down the wrath of the local power structure.[41]

Yet Hawthorne himself was already an anachronism. Despite boasting of his own softheartedness, he knew perfectly well that a "professional politician" would have fired and replaced the entire office before the first month was out. And things were only getting more mercenary. However eager for patronage, Jackson's Democrats had still known "how to spare." By comparison, the new Whig Party showed only "a bitter spirit of malice and revenge." The predictable result was that Hawthorne was himself removed when the White House changed hands three years later. He consoled himself with the knowledge that his misfortune would now persuade "brother Democrats" to forgive him for not firing others when he had had the chance, let alone for his stubborn habit of socializing with friends outside the "narrow paths" of partisanship.[42]

Most of the pre-Civil War government's growth had been concentrated in the Post Office. Starting with the Department of Agriculture (1862), however, interest groups discovered the value of having a government agency dedicated to looking after their needs. This soon led to bureaus for Education (1869), Labor (1884), Commerce (1913), and a greatly expanded version of what is now the Veterans Administration. The bureaucracy also began to regulate private industry, though this was at first limited to the railroads, food, and drugs.[43] The rapidly growing federal workforce, in turn, expanded patronage jobs to the point where young professionals could begin to choose politics as a career like any other.[44] But it equally sparked growing complaints of incompetence, featherbedding, and a corrupt trade in government jobs. Talk of test-based civil service reform began soon after the war and was intensively studied by the Grant Administration.[45] But it took President James Garfield's assassination by a former campaign worker (and disappointed office seeker) to change the system.[46]

The Pendleton Act (1883) established a Civil Service system that hired and promoted bureaucrats based on performance.[47] The rub, as Jackson had stressed, was that making bureaucrats harder to fire also made it easier for them to ignore or defy elected leaders. Regardless, the change proved irreversible, with each new administration expanding the Civil Service to protect its appointees from being removed by its successors.[48] This steadily grew the Civil Service from 10 percent of federal employees in the 1880s to more than 99 percent today.

Finally, the decline of patronage and, especially, the president's power to fire employees created new opportunities for Congress. Now more than ever, presidents found it hard to overrule the goals of whichever legislative coalition had created the agency. Though this sort of special interest politics was only doubtfully democratic, it at least reduced jitter by making sure that policies did not change after every election.[49]

The third revolution began with Franklin Roosevelt. Wars apart, state and local governments spent twice as much money as the national government down to World War I. Boosted by the New Deal, federal spending finally reached parity in 1939. But World War II changed everything. Ten years later, the federal budget was twice as large as the states', with a similar increase in regulation.[50]

The worry, of course, was that this new government was too big for the Constitution's short list of elected officials to oversee. One response was to beef up the rule of law by installing a kind of miniature legislature and court system within the executive branch itself. Beginning with the Interstate Commerce Commission (1887), Congress started to create self-governing bodies that were at least formally beyond presidential control. These almost always featured a collegial leadership of five to seven members, nominated on staggered terms so that no single president could dominate the agency.[51] In 1935, the Supreme Court confirmed the arrangement by deciding that while the president could fire officials from agencies that were "an arm or an eye of the executive," this did not include administrative bodies that were limited to "quasi-legislative" or "quasi-judicial" functions.[52] In theory, at least, the former were required to make a record showing that they had listened to citizens and tried to achieve the kind of least-unpopular outcomes that Congress would. Conversely, quasi-judicial bodies were supposed to apply existing statutes and rule as judges would. In both cases, any remaining discretion would be technocratic; that is, well below the large choices that the Constitution gave to the president and Congress.

The Administrative Procedure Act (1946)[53] or "APA" built on this start by requiring *all* agencies to solicit comments and hold hearings before issuing new regulations. Agencies now had to keep elaborate records of their decisions and, in theory at least, make efforts to discern and implement what citizens wanted. The APA also created semi-independent "Administrative Law Judges" to decide when agency rules had been violated. This deliberate imitation of courts and Congress injected still more friction into the executive branch. But like most frictions, this at least had the useful side effect of reducing jitter. First, the new procedures required massive time and effort, limiting the number of new regulations that any single administration could pass. And second, they placed limits on agencies' ability to reverse policies from previous administrations.[54]

In principle the APA inserted democracy directly into the bureaucracy, at least to the extent that citizens bothered to participate.[55] But while the statute laid down formal channels for democratic input, it could not force bureaucrats to listen, or if they did listen to simulate how a democratically elected Congress or president would share out the benefits and burdens of regulation to keep the country's various interest groups happy. Instead, determined bureaucrats could almost always feign deference to public comment while pursuing their own agendas. This forced interest groups to choose between accepting new regulations despite their flaws, or else bringing court challenges to force a new round of hearings with possibly better outcomes. Conversely, agencies had to decide what their draft regulations should concede to avoid drawing challenges, with their inevitable cost in time, energy, litigation expense, and delay in having any rule at all.

## 8.3 DEMOCRATIZING THE BUREAUCRACY

The preceding section has traced elected officials' long, losing fight to control the federal bureaucracy, and the rise of Big Government institutions that nervously claim to govern themselves. All of these governance strategies still survive to one extent or another. Here, we analyze each in detail.

The oldest strategy for controlling the bureaucracy, and the only one explicitly anchored in the Constitution, is the president's power to hire and fire subordinates. Analytically, the arrangement corresponds to what economists call a "principal–agent game"[56] where the president (the principal) hopes to achieve certain goals, but relies on subordinates (the agents) who may have different agendas. The question then becomes how efficiently the president can detect and punish cheating when they ignore his instructions. As Max Weber emphasized, bureaucrats can do what they like so long as monitoring is weak and there is little chance of getting caught. Thus, "Every bureaucracy hides its knowledge and conduct from criticism as well as it can." Moreover, the bureaucracy will usually slant whatever information it does reveal to make its own preferred options seem more attractive. Knowing this, the president's problem is to take advantage of the bureaucracy's superior knowledge while still making the final normative and political choices himself.[57]

But implementing policy requires loyalty and initiative at many levels further down the bureaucratic chain of command. Since the president cannot possibly know all of the best candidates for these jobs, he often lets his subordinates pick their assistants, and so on.[58] Then too, the impossibility of day-to-day contact limits the president's ability to monitor the people he does hire. The further one descends into the bureaucracy, the more the president and his agenda fade into a distant rumor.

Finally, the president sometimes finds it useful *not* to assert control either tacitly or by visibly disabling himself. Here the best known examples are the Department of Justice regulations that divorce decisions to prosecute from presidential direction, and in exceptional circumstances can even require that special counsels be are immune from "day-to-day supervision."[59] But the absence of presidential control does not guarantee that such efforts are apolitical, and indeed examples from Ken Starr to Robert Mueller have not been.

These limits to presidential power are unavoidable. But Madison's system dilutes the president's hiring-based influence still further by requiring the Senate's "advice and consent" for appointments to the highest 1,200 or so "offices of the United States."[60]

The Framers optimistically hoped that voters would hold bad appointments against *both* the president *and* the Congress. This, they argued, would force the president to make quality choices to defend his own reputation and reelection prospects, and also force the Senate to agree, absent "specific and strong reasons" to challenge the nominee's competence and qualifications.[61] Self-interested politics would then lend content to the Constitution's otherwise vague "advice and consent" language by giving the Senate strong political reasons to confirm the president's candidates so long as they held "mainstream" views and could be trusted to apply the law honestly. The problem, in practice, is that it is almost impossible for voters to know when a partisan senator blocks someone whom she privately believes is qualified. As the Framers already knew, this opens the door to a second game in which Congress demands slanted candidates to push policy in some preferred direction,[62] or else cripples an administration it dislikes by blockading cabinet members indiscriminately.

Even so, these are aberrant cases. The system has worked surprisingly well in most eras, with Democrats routinely approving Republican

nominees and vice versa down to 2010 or so.[63] Some of the change since
then is due to the court system: The rise of open-ended doctrines that
establish rights not expressly mentioned in the Constitution has created so many close cases that judges' personal views are bound to affect
outcomes. This makes judges' personal and political biases much more
relevant than they were before. But this still cannot explain the vast
majority of nonjudicial fights where the nominee will never face a single
hot-button issue. Here, the obvious interpretation is that extremists are
using Advice and Consent to blockade the executive, hoping to cripple
the administration so that it accomplishes as little as possible. Evidence
from the highly polarized Trump era suggests that senators do both. On
the one hand, the *average* Democrat voted "no" 57 percent of the time
compared to just 1 percent for Republicans. On the other, some senators
within this group remained far more partisan than others.[64] This shows
that the Framers' argument for Senate deference still exercises a significant restraining influence on centrists.

Patronage attacks the problem from a second angle. Instead of forcing
recalcitrant bureaucrats to follow orders, why not install people who are
already invested in the administration's success? Naively, these partisans
should want policy achievements nearly as much as their government
pay. Unfortunately, there is a catch: Patronage jobs are only a reward if
they offer better terms than the jobs recipients could get in the private
sector. This means some combination of higher wages (seldom true in
government), lighter duties ("featherbedding"), and a greater tolerance
for incompetence.

Partisan voters might still accept this trade if the resulting waste was
justified by greater thoroughness in implementing the president's policies. But where the drawbacks of graft outweighed the benefits, such
systems could only survive by hiding their waste. Given that voters
were very unlikely to break through their limited information to decide
which party was more culpable, the most natural result was some permanent level of corruption and inefficiency no matter who held the
White House.

Even so, the question remains whether patronage is any more wasteful
than the alternatives. The constitutional power to fire and replace would
deliver total control if monitoring were perfect and firing costless. But, in
practice, neither assumption is true, and Civil Service has made the problem worse.[65] In the end, the basic problem with both the president's power
to fire and political patronage was that whatever control they offer falls off

quickly beyond the president's immediate circle. Moreover, this limitation became steadily more painful as the American government expanded. Yet if presidents could not control the bureaucracy, then neither could voters hold them accountable: After all, the other party would do just as badly. Plainly, other control strategies were needed. In the nineteenth century, the rule of law was the only alternative.

As Madison already knew, deference to the rule of law is more than just virtuous. It can also be cold-bloodedly rational. While individual bureaucrats might prefer to do whatever they want, they equally fear arbitrariness by others. This gives them a powerful motive to reward and promote colleagues who follow the law – understood to include both formal statutes and the agency's consensus "mission" – over those who do not. Crucially, the fact that this logic extends to *every* employee means that we expect its strength to remain roughly constant at every level of government. At some point far from the White House, it may even become more powerful than direct control.

In principle, the rule of law eliminates discretion altogether. In practice, there are limits to how well real bureaucrats can interpret statutes even if they want to.[66] More fundamentally, discretion is inevitable where laws are unclear – and insisting on perfect clarity would mean that Congress passed no laws at all. The question then becomes how to distinguish what might be called "legitimate vagueness" from deliberate abdications in which politicians avoid responsibility by letting bureaucrats decide.

There are, of course, many reasons why vagueness might be legitimate. First, language is imprecise.[67] Much as "strict constructionists" might regret it, there will always be sincere differences in how humans understand even the plainest text. As Judge Richard Posner remarks,

> Statutes and constitutions are written in haste by busy people not always of great ability or diligence, and we are not privileged to ignore the hasty and hackneyed provisions and reserve our attention for the greatest. Moreover, they are products of a committee (the legislature) rather than of a single mind, and of a committee whose numerous members may have divergent objectives .... To suppose that its every word probably has significance, that every statute is a seamless whole, misconceives the legislative process.[68]

In principle, the cure for this is for Congress to spend more time drafting. But that quickly runs into diminishing returns, and in any case it often makes sense for Congress to spread its attentions over several issues even if each individual statute is less precise. Then too, legislators cannot foresee the detailed facts under which the statute will be applied.

This means that judges will sometimes find themselves confronting what Professor Lessig calls "latent ambiguities"[69] that no one anticipated. The Mann Act,[70] RICO,[71] and federal wire fraud[72] are all examples of statutes that have evolved to cover offenses that Congress never imagined. Then too, even deliberate vagueness can be efficient where the best strategies for addressing a problem are poorly known, yet waiting for further study is unacceptable. In such cases, at least, Congress could reasonably decide that the best policy was to give government broad discretion, trusting the president and cabinet heads to keep individual bureaucrats from acting unfairly.

If these were the only reasons for vagueness we would have no reason to limit it. The problem for separation of powers is that Congress *also* uses vagueness as a *political* excuse to abdicate choice and responsibility to the bureaucracy. The Supreme Court's "Non-Delegation Doctrine" tries to prevent this by limiting the president's ability to perform "legislative" functions even when Congress has authorized him to do so. But just what is "legislative" and what "executive"? Justice Marshall made a start at answering the question in 1825, when he announced that while it is constitutional for bureaucrats to issue "minor regulations," they may only do so "within the great outlines marked out by the legislature in directing the execution."[73] Though Marshall conceded that the line between "great outlines" and "minor" details had "not been exactly drawn," some modern scholars argue that the basic approach is viable.[74] The line between what is and is not acceptable would then emerge in the usual common law way, with the lower courts asking whether challenged statutes were closer to those that the Supreme Court had struck down or else upheld in the past.

Still, this approach can only work if the justices are at least occasionally willing to strike down statutes. In practice, the court has found just two unconstitutional delegations in its entire history – both in 1935[75] – and has discredited both by refusing to reach the same result in similar cases since. The result is that modern judges find verbal formulas to avoid the doctrine. And technically, at least, this seems reasonable. Legal reasoning, after all, is less about uniform rules than uniform outcomes.[76] So, while several justices have hinted that they would like to reinvigorate the doctrine,[77] simply calling on lower courts to get tougher cannot change much unless and until the Supreme Court actually strikes down statutes. This is decidedly unlikely, if only because any significant tightening would immediately call thousands of existing statutes into question.

If Congress's tendency toward improper delegations is a sin, the corresponding offense for judges is to refuse to correct the executive branch when it ignores the law. The leading modern case, *Chevron v. National Resources Defense Council*, involved a statute that authorized the Environmental Protection Agency to regulate "major" sources of pollution. Strikingly, the Supreme Court refused to second-guess the agency's interpretation of the word "major," announcing that in the future it would uphold any "reasonable" interpretation of "silent or ambiguous" statutes even when the justices themselves would have reached a different conclusion.[78] This made some sense: Since courts move more slowly than agencies, waiting for judges to speak would either stop agencies from acting or repeatedly reverse policies that had been in place for years. In these circumstances, adopting the agency's interpretation was not terribly different from the *stare decisis* tradeoff (Chapter 9) that courts face when they are forced to choose between correcting some poorly reasoned precedent and protecting citizens who relied on it. The trouble, of course, is that the analogy only holds when the agency's interpretation was made in good faith. But what happens when the "errors" are part of a strategic campaign to seize power that Congress never intended? While the court has so far shown itself willing to stop the most outlandish interpretations,[79] its announced deference privileges any interpretation that large numbers of lawyers claim to believe. That said, the Court's recently introduced "major questions" doctrine significantly reduces the loophole by holding that agencies cannot discover large new powers that Congress surely would have debated, but did not, when it passed the legislation at issue.[80]

So far we have assumed rule of law in the traditional sense of statutes, rules, and judge-made common law. But if the underlying imperative is predictability, almost any coherent belief system will do. The classic description of the bureaucracy's actual norms is due to Max Weber, who elaborated Jackson's groping instinct of using hierarchy, paperwork, and signoffs to constrain power into a formal theory. Noting that predictability is of "primary importance,"[81] Weber emphasized that bureaucracy necessarily elevated learnable rules[82] over idiosyncratic influences like sympathy, favor, mercy, or anger.[83] But even then, the fact that laws and executive orders are always slightly indeterminate meant that at least some "creative" decisions were unavoidable. These, he said, would be guided by "an objective notion of the national interest" defined by agreed norms that balanced recognized goals[84] through design principles learned in universities and professional schools.[85] The 1960s fashion for "technocratic" management made these professional habits still more explicit.

Beyond this, Weber also recognized a parallel loyalty to one's agency which was ultimately rooted in the bureaucrat's personal sense of worth from performing her duties.[86] This encouraged bureaucrats to side with their agency's internal sense of mission against outsiders.[87] While this tribal behavior might sometimes be pathological, it was fundamentally inescapable. After all, missions exist for the same reason that militaries adopt doctrines: first to suppress endless unproductive debate over matters which cannot be constantly revisited without paralyzing action;[88] second to yield quasi-automatic answers so that different employees can act consistently without constant communication; and finally to provide a focal point around which social and professional conformists can bond and trade favors. Like politics more generally, missions often take the form of official agency narratives and ideologies.

Even so, mission comes at a price. One problem is the bureaucracy's classic vulnerability to "groupthink"; that is, the bureaucratic habit of elevating the agency's working hypotheses into unquestionable truths.[89] The other problem is that bureaucracies recruit from well-defined class and educational demographics that have evolved their own characteristic beliefs and allegiances. When new hires join the agency, it is only natural for them to bond around these commonalities. The trouble comes when these same shared beliefs *also* align with a particular political party or ideological agenda, so that bureaucrats go on supporting a particular policy long after the politicians who sponsored it have been voted out of power.

The acid test of Weber's system comes when bureaucrats receive an illegal order. Predictability requires that they refuse. But if they obey, what Congress and the courts say no longer matters, so that Madison's system falls to the ground.

In recent history the most prominent test was the so-called Saturday Night Massacre, when President Nixon ordered Attorney General Elliot Richardson and his deputy William Ruckelshaus to fire Special Prosecutor Archibald Cox. Both men refused and immediately resigned. Rather than continue a stalemate that would have depopulated the Justice Department to no purpose, Solicitor General Robert Bork then obeyed the order.[90] Though Nixon seemed to have prevailed, this proved a Pyrrhic victory as public anger soon forced him to resign. Since then, presidents have had a healthy appreciation for just how dangerous resignations can be. The reason, presumably, is their unique transparency: While few voters can judge the legalities for themselves, resignations immediately evidence an intense and unambiguous judgment that the president is in the wrong. The fact that this judgment comes from subordinates who would normally be expected to side with him only underscores the condemnation.[91]

Despite its happy ending, the story has an important caveat: The fight took place within the uniquely favorable confines of the Justice Department, among trained lawyers who had no difficulty judging the law for themselves. Elsewhere, however, government employees would have less confidence that all but the most flagrant orders were illegal, and might more easily give them the benefit of the doubt. The result would then depend on whether the Supreme Court and Justice Department spoke out, and if they did were trusted to rule impartially. The fact that Washington's politicians and journalists periodically indulge in coup d'état rumors suggests that the idea of a rogue executive is not entirely outlandish.[92]

Presidential oversight, rule of law, and patronage are with us still. At the same time, none of these control methods worked particularly well even in Victorian times. Their limitations have become exponentially more painful now that the federal workforce has grown to four million federal employees,[93] far too many for Congress or the president to oversee in detail.[94]

The question is what to do about the problem. For the most part, the twentieth-century response was not to try. Instead, most scholars presented what amounted to apologies for the system. Individual bureaucrats, they insisted, had less personal power than met the eye. This was true, first because their freedom of action was constrained by the internal politics of their agencies, which Congress had deliberately engineered to favor some policy choices compared to others; and second the fact that agencies had their own ambitions required them to woo partners in Congress and the public. In this sense, at least, the bureaucracy was itself enmeshed in – and might respond to – the wider society after all.

In order to judge these claims, we first need some theory of agency politics. By analogy with Prof. Downs' theory of politicians, we begin by assuming that high-level bureaucrats are profit-maximizers who seek salary, reputation, postretirement opportunities, and tradeable favors from other bureaucrats.[95] Because each of these scales with their agency's budget and regulatory responsibilities, we expect bureaucrats to constantly seek out new policy missions.[96] At the same time, the fact that every action requires multiple signoffs means that these would-be policy entrepreneurs still need their colleagues to cooperate – and their colleagues cannot be compelled to do so. This fosters a web of favor-trading relationships or, as we said in Chapter 7, "trust and reputation games." Here the simplest games are based on bilateral favor-trading. But bureaucrats can also cultivate a general reputation for making decisions that are invariably faithful to the agency's mission and institutional interests. This is particularly helpful when they have to trade with colleagues they have never met before. Not only are both sides predictable partners, but each is more likely to follow through on her promises since this burnishes her reputation still further.

What makes these games interesting is that the content of the bargains is always evolving. On the one hand, the fact that bureaucrats continually trade favors means that their fidelity to the agency's existing mission and ways of doing things is steadily reinforced. This explains why many agencies become sclerotic on the twenty-year timescale of a typical employee's career. On the other hand, presidential policy initiatives consist almost entirely of trying to break and reform existing bargains (in the jargon, "agency culture") around new missions. In theory, agencies must live with and, however grudgingly, immediately incorporate presidential orders into their missions. But in practice, many employees will resist and cling to the old ways until they are bought off with countervailing rewards ("carrots") or else punished ("sticks") using "for cause" disciplinary procedures that require enormous time and effort from supervisors. In either case, we expect the president's cost of intervening to increase with the size of the agency. For their part, presidents often decide that it is better to build on agendas that already command widespread support within particular agencies than to impose whatever goals they might prefer in the abstract.

Agency inertia also creates important dilemmas for Congress. On the one hand, it encourages legislators to create new agencies instead of trying to reform and repurpose old ones. This however puts pressure on drafters to write statutes that balance the flexibility bureaucrats need to do their jobs against the definiteness needed to block actions that Congress would never have voted for. And even then, enforcing these statutory restrictions requires Congress to perform continual oversight or else give interested groups the power to sue agencies that violate the law.[97]

On the other hand, legislators can decide that it is better to assign new tasks to whichever agency has shown itself most sympathetic to similar goals in the past.[98] Moreover, entrepreneurial bureaucrats understand this, and therefore advocate new legislation that lines up with their agency's existing track record.[99] This adds to agencies' inertia.[100] Beyond this, the logic of bureaucratic entrepreneurship favors the growth of government more generally. This is obvious for bureaucratic entrepreneurs, who almost by definition seek bigger missions for their agencies. But it is also true for outside groups, who only find lobbying profitable when they stand to benefit from new programs. By comparison, taxpayers are nearly always too numerous and diffuse to organize and fund offsetting lobbying campaigns. This means that supporters of "Doing less" seldom have anyone to speak for them except, sometimes, the White House.

So far, we have mostly discussed government agencies in isolation. But in fact, they are embedded in wider ecosystems. These "iron triangles" or "subgovernments" typically include agency bureaucrats, the clients they serve, and a handful of congressmen who specialize in the topic.[101] In practice, triangles have nearly complete discretion to set policy, provided only that they avoid actions that are so large or controversial as to attract the attention of outside actors who possess enough political influence to overrule or even permanently break the triangle's power. Where this intervention is expensive, iron triangles can do almost anything they like. Where it is cheap, they degenerate into permanent "issue networks" that include a broad range of viewpoints.[102]

For their part, voters seldom know what the triangles are doing, or else do not care enough to switch their vote to another candidate. By comparison, the agency's clients invariably expect enough benefits to make lobbying worthwhile. The result, as Prof. Downs remarks, is that government will almost always "risk imparting a slight injury to one voter if, by doing so, it gives a great boon to another one."[103] It follows that large diffuse groups like taxpayers and consumers have comparatively little influence in government, although intermediaries like "public interest" lobbyists partly make up for this.[104]

Finally, some issues cut across multiple agencies. When this happens, policy emerges either from bilateral negotiations between agencies or multisided "interagency" committees. Superficially, this might seem like a prescription for deadlock, with each agency pulling against the others. But in practice the standoff is broken by selection of a lead agency which, being more visible, is also more likely to be blamed by its constituents if it fails. This makes it visibly more willing to invest whatever political resources it needs to get its way. The result is that other members end up deferring on close questions, so that the lead agency becomes a first among equals.

One might argue that a system in which Congress establishes different agencies, each with its own fixed mission, would produce a microcosm of the wider society and its ambitions.[105] Indeed, one could even hope that jointly negotiated "interagency" agreements between the various bureaucracies would arrive at policies that the country agrees with. While this is probably true at some level, it is also highly approximate. After all, Congress's decision on which groups "deserve" their own agencies will always be deeply political, and to that extent is largely a matter of chance. Then too, the fact that Congress only creates agencies at long intervals suggests that the balance of political forces will usually be out of date. Finally, agency hearings can never implement the public will as well as Congress, whose members spend the better part of each day trying to figure out what voters want. Even if bureaucrats were inclined to do this, nearly all of their interactions involve special interests with atypical views. Conversely, the vast majority of the electorate will never care enough to participate in agency hearings. This practically guarantees that voters will constantly come across outcomes they would have bitterly opposed "had they only known."

These gloomy conclusions were recently reaffirmed by the COVID-19 pandemic, which cast a particularly harsh light on the notion that interagency negotiations can usefully approximate democracy. While many federal agencies advocated for public health, no obvious institutional champion ever emerged to speak for the economy. Moreover, Presidents Trump and Biden were mostly content to adopt whatever policies the bureaucracy proposed. The result was to give previously obscure public health officials control over government-mandated lockdowns and masking policy.[106] This abdication nevertheless made excellent political sense by minimizing politicians' association with the kind of directly felt restrictions that voters most resent.[107] Strikingly, the federal bureaucracy might never have restored the balance at all if it had not been for the example of red state governors who rebelled against the public health orthodoxy based on their own political values and mounting pressure from constituents. The experience of looser restrictions in states like Florida also provided a powerful, if far from conclusive, counternarrative,[108] generating essential evidence to help voters decide how well incumbents had managed the crisis.

Finally, the Framers – who feared both standing armies and an ignorant public – would have understood the dangers posed by excessive secrecy and the national security state. In keeping with our arguments in Chapter 2, we expect secrecy to aggravate all of the American system's "imperfect information" problems. These results will normally include less predictable elections, a shift from rational to conformist voting, and increased apathy among voters. Just as importantly, overclassification increases the number of embarrassing facts that the government keeps secret. This gives bureaucrats the power to hit back against their elected bosses with anonymous "leaks" in an obvious inversion of the democratic order. One can, of course, argue that leaks inform voters and to that extent are worth the cost. But that seems superficial in the usual case where the disclosed information is only secret because it would embarrass those in power. Indeed, the situation is almost certainly worse than that: In keeping with Weber's analysis, it is enough that the secrets protect the *agency* even when those responsible are long since dead.[109]

The question is what to do about overclassification. Ideally, secrecy should serve some purpose beyond the usual Big Government instinct to "protect one's agency." The current system, where agencies decide what to classify and then defy citizens to sue them, fails badly in this regard. The reason, of course, is that Freedom of Information Act (FOIA) litigation is costly, especially since courts hardly ever award fees large enough to cover private litigants' costs.[110] A better solution would be to create a new government body to promote openness by impartially resolving government refusals to produce requested records. Funding this would be expensive, but probably no more so than what private parties currently spend challenging bad faith refusals. More importantly, agencies that saw their operating budgets eroded by repeated fines would sooner or later discover that overclassification was no longer in their interest.[111]

In the meantime, leaking remains a felony even if the post-Watergate folklore invariably romanticizes leakers.[112] The fact that Trump-era FBI Director James Comey bragged openly about his leaks[113] shows just how weak this deterrent has become. The basic problem seems to be safety in numbers: There are now so many leakers that prosecuting them all is not just unaffordable, but would significantly disrupt the government if everyone responsible was actually punished. This paradoxically suggests that *reduced* punishments might be more credible and effective. These could include publicly naming offenders or freezing Civil Service advancement for a fixed term.

## 8.4 WAR AND FOREIGN POLICY

From the moment hostilities start, the politics of war – being both directly felt and filled with imagery that triggers the brain's emotions – nearly always dominates every other issue. Despite this, *The Federalist* pays almost no attention to the president's war powers, and then mostly on the secondary question of whether foreign governments might try to bribe US officials.[114] Most likely, the Framers considered more discussion redundant. After all, the basic scheme was the same as for domestic policy: Congress would pass laws and the president would execute them, exercising whatever discretion the legislature gave him.

Sometimes, the system works that way. Over the years, Congress has occasionally passed laws to fund or defund wars and prohibit government from taking particular steps.[115] It has also defined US war aims. In some cases, these statements have been earnest and valuable.[116] More usually, though, declaring goals has shaded into empty symbolism like sanctioning foreign leaders or moving the US embassy to Jerusalem.[117] The fact that Congress's resolutions nearly always allow presidential waivers suggests that their real purpose is to blame the executive for disregarding "instructions" that were never serious to begin with.

And for the biggest issue of all – armed conflicts – Congress often keeps silent altogether. Moreover, this has an undeniable logic. If the war goes well the president will get most of the credit anyway, whether members endorse his actions or not. And if the war goes badly, staying off the record will make it easier to distance themselves later.[118] Given that the downside is so much larger than the upside, it is almost always better to say nothing.

The Constitution tries to compensate for this *political* reluctance by adding the *legal* stipulation that only Congress can "declare war."[119] This is different from the usual constitutional practice that Congress can choose to speak or not, and just why the Framers wanted this affirmative obligation is unclear. Long afterward, Madison argued that the president was more prone to war than the Congress, and this has become the mainstream view among scholars.[120] This is a particularly strong version of the Framers' usual argument that procedural frictions stop more bad laws than good ones. All the same, a clause that deliberately favors pacifist outcomes plainly violates our principle that the Constitution should be policy neutral. Then too, history since the War with Mexico provides little evidence for presidential adventurism.[121] This probably reflects Americans' quite rational response to reaching the Pacific. At that point, the security case for expansion that had obsessed the Framers no longer existed,[122] while the economic rationale for acquiring still more territory had very little constituency outside the South.[123]

But the Declaration clause has worked badly. In principle, this could be fixed by authorizing lawsuits to force a vote when Congress is silent.[124]

But that only exposes the second, deeper question of just when small-scale hostilities shade into "wars." This is harder than it sounds: Americans usually assume that the US has fought eleven wars in its history, but this is just over 10 percent of the eighty-eight armed conflicts the country has actually engaged in.[125] Requiring declarations for each of these would defeat the requirement's purpose as a solemn occasion for the country to pause and think through the wisdom of fighting. Forcing Congress to debate conflicts that most citizens considered beneath their notice would turn it into just another formality. But in that case the question arises of how any constitutional requirement can identify which wars matter *politically*. Probably the best solution, on the pattern of the filibuster, would be to give some specified minority of congressmen the right to demand a vote.[126]

Finally, Congress, being only loosely hierarchical, lacks the institutional capacity to manage day-to-day diplomacy and military operations.[127] This leaves presidents plenty of leeway to engineer clashes. After that, as President Ulysses S. Grant said of the Mexican war, it is "Better" for a politician "to advocate 'war, pestilence, and famine' than to act as obstructionist to a war already begun."[128] And this is especially true once a foreign power – whether justified or not – has taken American lives.[129] Once hostilities do start there is seldom any unilateral way to disengage and stop the conflict. In these circumstances, voters will almost always support the war on the theory that it is better to win than to lose. To be sure, these initial attitudes can change if the war goes badly, or just appears unwinnable.[130] But so long as the president appears to have more facts at his disposal – something which is almost always true at the start of any conflict – we should expect the public to take his word for it.

One might have hoped that two-party competition would cause decisions to fight to be debated even without the Declaration clause. Sometimes, it has. Democratic debate worked reasonably well for many of the country's biggest foreign policy choices, including whether to become a continental power in the first half of the nineteenth century, or a Pacific power ("Manifest Destiny") in the second half.[131] More recently, however, the major parties have typically offered voters little to choose from. In the first half of the twentieth century this included taking generally middle of the road positions from the Spanish-American War to World War I, before becoming mostly isolationist in the 1920s and 1930s. Since Pearl Harbor they have both been at least mildly interventionist, though only weakly so after Vietnam.[132]

On shorter scales, however, the record is even more disappointing. Some of this can be excused as bad timing. None of the issues that led to the Spanish-American War (1898), Korea (1950), and the two Gulf Wars (1991, 2003) was sufficiently ripe to have been aired at the preceding presidential election. That said, the record is not much better when the timing is favorable. The two major political parties did give voters a clear choice in the War of 1812[133] and, to a lesser extent, the War with Mexico.[134] But the pattern has not been repeated since, with the ambiguous exception of the two Gulf Wars.[135] Certainly, the risk of war was obvious for the elections that preceded the Civil War, World War I, World War II, and Vietnam. Yet none of them gave voters a clear choice on whether to fight. The reason was that elections are unavoidably limited to binary choices. This fits awkwardly with wars, which almost always present three logical alternatives – yield, compromise, or fight.[136]

This tendency to avoid hard choices is all the greater because the idea of finding a middle path between hostility and capitulation is so seductive. The pattern of avoiding a clean decision to fight was repeated in the 1898,[137] 1916,[138] and 1940[139] elections, where both sides promised that they could resolve matters peacefully. Barry Goldwater, uniquely, ran on promises to *escalate* the Vietnam War beyond what he saw as the Johnson Administration's feckless temporizing.[140] At the same time, politicians' reflexive instinct to promise voters some painless compromise also makes public opinion profoundly unstable: As soon as one side declares war, middle-ground positions on both sides abruptly become untenable. Suddenly, temporizing voters must choose between war and peace. At least in the short run, this tends to boost pro-war sentiment.[141] But in the longer term public opinion can and often does change dramatically depending how the war progresses.

For the president, war enlarges the political stakes, simultaneously expanding upside reward and downside risk. On the one hand, Lincoln suffered massive unpopularity in the Civil War, as did Johnson in Vietnam.[142] On the other, unexpectedly successful wars with Mexico and Spain let Presidents Polk and McKinley deliver far more than voters expected.[143] Militaries understandably criticize presidents who go beyond their originally stated goals as giving in to "mission creep." But it is hard to see what the alternative might be: When new opportunities arise it would be irresponsible to ignore them, and a politician who failed to take advantage of changing circumstances would be justifiably criticized as a bad leader.

So long as the war's outcomes remain unclear, the president's own party finds it nearly impossible to refuse him. And this makes sense: Even if they broke with the president, voters would still find the other party more credible as a source of change. Conversely, the opposition party must do more than simply endorse the president's war. This forces it to choose between claiming it would be more competent and offering the clear alternative of promising peace. In practice, challengers in the early stages of wars usually choose competence. This encourages them to nominate military heroes for president.[144] What happens next depends on how well the incumbent handles, or seems to handle, the war. Voters in 1944 and 1972 rewarded Roosevelt and Nixon for their perceived competence.[145] Conversely, peace candidates tend to emerge once the war seems to have failed, as happened in Vietnam, nearly happened in the Civil War, and happened belatedly in the messy aftermath of World War I.

Not surprisingly, the president's party in Congress usually tracks its leader's fortunes. The Democrats lost ground in World War II's House and Senate midterms in the grim year of 1942 and again in Vietnam's 1966 midterms.[146] However, voters seldom hold their congressmen as accountable as the president himself, whether on the up- or the down-side. Thus, Democrats suffered relatively small losses after the Chinese intervened in Korea in 1950 despite Republican claims that Truman had "lost" China and invited aggression through diplomatic incompetence.[147] Members also try to distance themselves from unpopular wars. This let Democrats limit their losses compared to their presidential candidates in 1952, 1968, and 1972.[148]

Conversely, presidents receive a larger share of both credit and blame. This is even more true when they ostentatiously seize control of the war, a tactic that hurt Johnson but buoyed Nixon in their respective reelection bids.[149] This same blame can also extend to their hand-picked successors, as the examples of both Adlai Stevenson (1952) and Hubert Humphrey (1968) attest.[150] As with members of Congress, the natural instinct for such candidates is to distance themselves. This however forfeits their main advantage of being able to continue familiar policies that may appear less risky to voters. In the end, Vice President Humphrey found he was unable to distance himself from the Johnson Administration so that he, too, ran as a competence candidate. This meant that voters had to wait until 1972 for a peace candidate. But when George McGovern finally did run he was solidly rejected by voters still seeking a middle ground.[151]

Finally, we have said that the comparative handful of government policies that voters feel directly in their daily lives are far more influential than those they only read about. Wars quintessentially present such issues, even though economic impacts and conscription typically bulk larger than casualties. Moreover, the imbalance becomes even stronger as victory approaches. Thus, gasoline rationing and labor controls ate into FDR's victory margin in 1944.[152]

The crisis of war also expands presidential power. *The Federalist* continually reminds us that politics exist wherever humans live in groups, and that the changes introduced by constitutions and formal institutions pale in comparison. When Congress has not foreseen or just not addressed a problem, the president is thrown back on this unstructured politics, and can do whatever the public will accept. Sometimes, this executive discretion is unavoidable and even desirable. "The Constitution," as Justice Jackson reminds us, "is not a suicide pact."[153] But the case is different where Congress could speak but chooses not to, as has happened in most wars and, more recently, the executive branch's various COVID-19 policies.

Most of what we know about the executive's emergency powers dates from the Civil War, when secessionist mobs in Maryland threatened to cut off Washington, DC, and win the war for the Confederacy. Lincoln responded by executive fiat, softening the implied constitutional challenge by simultaneously announcing that Congress would meet a month later on July 4.[154] But while his suspension of habeas corpus and use of martial law were at least arguably lawful,[155] the Constitution clearly said that only Congress could call for volunteers, expand the Army and Navy, and blockade Confederate ports. Lincoln went ahead anyhow, declaring that the measures, "[w]hether strictly legal or not, were ventured upon, under what appeared to be a popular demand and a public necessity; trusting, then as now, that Congress would readily ratify them."[156] As Civil War historian Bruce Catton explained, "What was done ... was effective because in the long run it somehow corresponded to what most of the people dimly wanted. Ruthlessness, then, is acceptable as long as it is ultimately acceptable to the majority ... the shakiest of moral principles, but the one on which a great war began."[157] And if Congress thought the president had overstepped his authority, Lincoln added, it could always impeach him.[158]

Here, the prospect of a reconvened Congress set an endpoint to what would otherwise have been open-ended emergency rule. At the same time, the party system also made impeachment an empty threat. The chances that Republicans would oust even a failed president were tiny.[159]

Nor did the pattern end there. Later in the war Lincoln would say that he would not stop conscription unless and until the Supreme Court ruled it unconstitutional.[160] And he would take an even bigger step by justifying the Emancipation Proclamation "as a fit and necessary war measure for suppressing [the] rebellion,"[161] adding that his oath to preserve the Constitution imposed a duty to preserve the Union "by every indispensable means," and that "measures, otherwise unconstitutional, might become lawful, by becoming indispensable to the preservation of the Constitution."[162]

These actions were at least taken in full view of the courts and Congress. The situation is even more dangerous when presidents ignore the constitutional framework in secret so that the executive branch becomes the judge in its own case.[163] While the same raw politics of emergency powers applies here too, the cycle of secrecy, threats to expose, and eventual shaming has historically taken decades to play out. In this sphere, at least, the American system has probably spent more time outside the law than within it.

So far, we have stressed the president's power to limit individual rights. But in many ways his ability to regulate society and the economy in national emergencies presents an even deeper challenge to the constitutional order. This is especially true since, as COVID-19 reminds us, the "emergencies" are not limited to wartime, but can include any event that large numbers of Americans see as a crisis.

Despite this, Supreme Court Justice Robert Jackson's verdict that there is "[a] poverty of really useful and unambiguous authority applicable to concrete problems of executive power as they actually present themselves"[164] is as true today as it was when Harry Truman was president. For now, the elderly decision in *Youngstown Sheet & Tube Co.* v. *Sawyer* (1952)[165] remains our clearest guide to what presidents can and cannot do in an emergency. Asked to define the limits of presidential authority, the justices gave three overlapping answers. The first is largely semantic, and is based on the Constitution's *ipse dixit* that the president possesses "executive powers." Since these are nowhere defined, the only real limit comes from separation of powers, which by negative inference implies that the president cannot "legislate." This ban clearly includes rules that would allow the president to define new crimes or seize assets,[166] though the permissibility of other orders is less clear. Additionally, the use of executive power cannot be disproportionate to the crisis at hand.[167] With these exceptions, the Court's view is not noticeably narrower than Harry Truman's mystical claim that the Constitution contains unwritten "intentions and powers" which are "there to be used by a President in emergencies."[168]

The Court's second answer is more comforting. Whatever unwritten powers the president might have, Congress can enlarge, or constrict, or negate them by passing a statute.[169] The trouble in practice is that such statements are seldom clear. It is one thing for Congress to address a particular situation or class of situations. But the crises facing the country change constantly, while Congress's last word on the subject often dates back decades. At the very least, this leads to the usual judicial inquiry into whether the new problem is sufficiently like the old one that Congress would have felt the same way. The danger, of course, is that judges will invent strained interpretations to validate acts that they are afraid to overrule. This is nicely illustrated by some of the *Youngstown* justices' assertions that Congress's approval of various Cold War treaties gave presidents a blank check to resist "global aggression" more generally.[170] Given this elasticity, the most one can say is that the Court would side with Congress if it later revoked the supposed authorization. Even then, however, the president could still veto the measure, in which case legislators would have to muster a two-thirds override vote under *Chauda*. This is unlikely in the best of times, and nearly impossible in polarized eras when partisanship punishes congressmen who defy their party's leader in the White House.

Finally, the justices noted that presidents can act from "urgency," and the claimed impossibility of consulting Congress, to take steps that the Constitution would not normally allow.[171] This codifies Lincoln's logic that the US can pass from rule of law to raw politics for temporary, if somewhat elastic intervals, with impeachment as the only deterrent. In such cases, at least, the normal rule of law is effectively suspended with no clear time limit beyond the Constitution's requirement that "the Congress shall assemble at least once in every year."[172]

The danger, of course, is that a presidential emergency could be extended so many times that it becomes habitual. Here the paradigmatic example is the Weimar Constitution's infamous Article 48, which let German chancellors rule by emergency decree. While the first uses were limited to discrete problems like suppressing right-wing militias or addressing the Depression, they soon degenerated into a handy way to implement policy without a parliamentary majority. When Hitler became chancellor, he predictably used the same practice to crush civil liberties and seize unlimited power.[173] This was of course grossly illegal. Even so, that would not have been clear to much of the German public, who had seen chancellors repeatedly declare emergencies from expediency. For the US, the corresponding weakness would come if presidents in a coercive politics era were to seize power because of the purely *political* emergency of a deadlocked Congress. There is some evidence that this is starting to happen.[174]

## 8.5 FEEDBACKS

Jackson's great innovation was using the veto to make the president a legislator in his own right. Making the president a player brought a national constituency to what had been an unrelievedly parochial Congress, especially since the president's influence depended on his popularity and was to that extent whatever voters wanted it to be.

The veto's impact in bipartisan eras, when Congress can be counted on to pass compromise legislation with some regularity, has been all to the good. But its implications for coercive politics are problematic. The good news is that the veto still suppresses jitter when Congress changes hands, damping down the kind of violent oscillations that Prof. Downs warned against. But it also provides a handy tool to practice the kinds of blockading tactics that coercive politics depends on. In the most benign scenario where a moderate president finds herself confronting an extremist Congress, we expect the veto to serve its original Madisonian purpose by slowing radical legislation until the public has time to repent. But the case is different where an extremist president faces a Congress controlled by moderates or else extremists on the other side. In both cases, we expect the president to blockade Congress unless and until it accedes to her agenda. Moreover, these destructive standoffs lead to the usual endgame. If neither side gives in, the public will eventually give one side undivided control of the presidency and Congress. Alternatively, one or both sides, seeing that they are about to lose, will break the fever by reverting to the center so that voters receive at least one centrist choice at the next election.

Finally, the dangerously obscure "high crimes and misdemeanors" requirement protects the president from being replaced when his party holds fewer than thirty-four seats in the Senate. The question remains how far politicians' (and voters') respect for rule of law can erode before the power to impeach becomes merely political. This would immediately convert Madison's design into a parliamentary system where presidents could be removed by what amounted to a no-confidence vote, albeit subject to a two-thirds supermajority. This very broad change would almost certainly exert large and frequently unforeseen consequences on the rules that Americans have lived under since 1790.

Deadlock in Congress also lets problems fester, tempting the president to intervene by issuing executive orders to impose his own solutions. But executive orders are comparatively easy to reverse from one administration to the next. This brings back the legal uncertainty and constant waste of jitter. Then too, each new review invites politicians on both sides to reargue the underlying issue. This continually reminds the public of old resentments, creating still more anger and polarization. If anything, the rise of Big Government has made the problem worse by devolving more and more authority from the president to federal bureaucrats. Particularly in polarized eras, these unelected actors will often pursue goals and defend values that look very different from the general public's. We expect the effect to be especially large in coercive politics eras when gridlock prevents Congress from overruling agencies and Senate extremists leave the administration's cabinet appointments unfilled.

The deeper danger is that the president sometimes finds it convenient to rule without Congress – and that Congress and the Supreme Court often have good political reasons not to protest. When that happens, rule of law is suspended and Madison's elaborate safeguards for the minority – most of which are rooted in congressional procedures like the filibuster – are abruptly disabled. The judge-made "Non-Delegation Doctrine" has been ineffective against weak versions of the problem where the president fills in policy details that Congress has deliberately failed to address. For more extreme cases, the president sometimes invokes national emergencies to rule by fiat. At this point, democracy stops entirely, subject only to vague assurances that normal processes will eventually restart. This is manageable in bipartisan eras where there is broad public support for restoring constitutional rule as soon as possible. What happens in coercive eras, when half the public may favor "their" president wielding indefinite emergency powers, remains, for now, uncharted territory.

## Notes

1  Meacham (2008) at p. 367.
2  McIntee (2018). In a nod to federalism, the vote followed the old continental Congress pattern that gave each state delegation a single vote. McIntee (2018).
3  Early presidents who had risen to prominence in the Revolution uniformly followed this pattern. Since then, the heuristic's strength has fluctuated depending on recent history. Dwight Eisenhower was elected in 1952 based on defeating Hitler's armies in World War II. In 2012, Mitt Romney's credentials rested on having organized a successful Winter Olympics.

4   Hofstadter (1969) at p. 209.

5   Meacham (2008) at pp. 120, 194, and 359.

6   Meacham at pp. 191–2. The power to veto is partly offset by Congress's ability to attach "riders" to appropriations that force the president to choose between unpalatable new laws and continued government funding; Rehnquist (2004) at p. 159. While the tactic plainly implies a threat to shut down the government, the more usual outcome if the president vetoes the bill is for both sides to compromise.

7   Meacham (2008) at pp. 191–2.

8   Meacham (2008) at p. 367.

9   *Youngstown Sheet & Tube Co.* v. *Sawyer*, 343 U.S. 579, 690–691 (1952) (Vinson, Reed, and Minton dissenting).

10  This was a reasonable extension of the British pattern, in which Parliament grew up as a check on the king's government rather than a policymaker in its own right. The hapless John Tyler had similarly insisted that the president, not Congress, should set policy. Wikipedia (32).

11  The situation was even less democratic in cases where the president also holds his tongue and let unelected bureaucrats decide.

12  National Emergencies Act, 50 U.S.C.A. §§ 1601–51.

13  More precisely, we expect a savvy president to repurpose spending just short of the point where it would be worth Congress's time to correct him.

14  *I.N.S.* v. *Chadha*, 462 U.S. 919, 954 n.18 (1983).

15  Recent examples include President Trump's successful declaration of an emergency to obtain funds for his hotly contested border wall, and President Biden's rumored mulling of a similar declaration to declare a "climate emergency." Anon (2022h).

16  The Framers probably inserted the mysterious "high crimes and misdemeanors" phrase into the impeachment clause hoping, in the usual common law way, that it would become clearer with use. As things turned out, impeachments have (thankfully) been too rare to supply much meaning. That said, Profs. Tribe and Matz argue persuasively that the word "high" denotes *political* violations that injure the state whether or not they would have provided grounds for prosecuting a private citizen. The offending acts must also reflect something more than ordinary partisan politics and policy differences, and be "so awful we must seriously consider removing [the president] without waiting for the next election." Tribe and Matz (2018) at pp. 53–5. This suggests a reasonably concrete test: senators should find "high crimes and misdemeanors" if, and only if, they honestly believe that the country would never have elected the president knowing how he would behave in office.

17  The argument assumes that the president's winning margin is a reasonable predictor of how many seats his party holds in the Senate.

18  See Nag (2017).

19  The faux sophistication of politicians who insist that "high crimes" are whatever two-thirds of the Senate say they are has visibly corroded this safeguard ever since future president Gerald Ford invented the trope in a futile bid to remove then Supreme Court Justice William O. Douglas; Black (2019).

20  *Federalist* No. 65 at p. 300 (Hamilton).

21  3 US Code §19.

22  The case might be different in a parliamentary system where the crisis of removing the chief executive could force a snap election, but that is not the American system.

23  Wikipedia (14).

24  Nelson (1982) at pp. 750–3.

25  *Federalist* No. 72 at p. 331 (Hamilton).

26  *Federalist* No. 77 at p. 350 (Hamilton).

27  Nelson (1982) at pp. 750–3.

28  Nelson (1982) at pp. 753–4.

29  Nelson (1982) at p. 756.

30  Nelson (1982) at p. 758.

31  Nelson (1982) at pp. 757–9.

32  Baracskay (n.d.)

33  Meacham (2008) at p. 117.

34  In all, Jackson removed just under 10 percent of the government. Meacham (2008) at p. 117. It is hard to appreciate just how new his argument that the president needed patronage to fulfill his campaign promises actually was. True, Thomas Jefferson had come close, arguing that civil servants should be partisan in rough proportion to the parties' overall voting strength. But Jefferson had shrunk from firing all but the most virulent partisans, hoping that normal attrition would balance the federal workforce. Hofstadter (1969) at p. 235.

35  Nelson (1982) at pp. 760–2.

36  Grinspan (2021) at p. 58.

37  Bauerlein (2011).

38  Hawthorne constantly laments how each man's "proper strength departs from him" the longer he works for the government. Hawthorne [1850] at p. 40. Like modern Department of Motor Vehicles employees, his workers displayed "lack of energy" and had no "power of thought "or "depth of feeling" beyond "a few commonplace instincts." Hawthorne [1850] at pp. 12 and 21. Hawthorne did recall one worker who was "honest and regular in the administration of affairs," but gives the system no credit for this, remarking that "integrity … was a law of nature with him." Hawthorne [1850] at p. 28.

39  Hawthorne [1850] at pp. 17 and 19.

40  Salem had long since yielded most of its trade to New York and Boston. Hawthorne [1850] at p. 11.

41  Hawthorne [1850] at pp. 16–18.

42  Hawthorne [1850] at pp. 13, 18 and 42–3.

43  Nelson (1982) at pp. 764–72.

44  Grinspan (2016) at p. 24.

45  Rehnquist (2004) at p. 23.

46  James Garfield came to the presidency in 1881 hating patronage, albeit for the selfish reason that it forced him to "consider[] all day whether A or B should be appointed to this or that office." Grinspan (2021) at p. 162.

47  Wikipedia (42).

48  The practice continues in "burrowing in," by which political appointees sometimes morph into Civil Service employees shortly before their party leaves the White House. Mazmanian (2018).

49  Baracskay (n.d.)

50  Hofstadter [1959b] at p. 820.

51  Wikipedia (28). Many of the bodies also require a balance of Republicans and Democrats, thereby grafting the unexpected advent of mass political parties into Madison's design. The Supreme Court has since held that structures based on a single director who is only removable for cause are unconstitutional. See *Seila Law LLC* v. *Consumer Fin. Protection Bureau*, ___ S. Ct. ___, 2020 WL 3492641, No. 19–7, slip op. (June 29, 2020).

52  *Humphrey's Executor* v. *United States*, 295 U.S. 602 (1935).

53  5 USC § 500 et seq.

54  Perhaps the most spectacular application of the principle came in 2020, when the Supreme Court ruled that the Trump Administration's attempt to suspend the Obama-era amnesty for so-called Dreamer immigrants without a reasoned explanation was invalid. See *Department of Homeland Security* v. *Regents of the University of California* (June 18, 2020) slip op. 18–587, ___ US ___. www.supremecourt.gov/opinions/19pdf/18-587_5ifl.pdf. The following year a district judge struck down the original DACA order on the same ground. Kendall and Hackman (2021).

55  Our "ignorant bliss" principle argues that citizens who lack the time and energy to intervene will normally be content whatever policies are adopted. This is reasonable so long as agencies are careful to avoid controversies that would bring more groups into the struggle.

56  The difficulty of enforcing even the simplest orders was famously summarized by Harry Truman, who predicted that his successor would "sit right here and he'll say do this, do that! And nothing will happen. Poor Ike – it won't be a bit like the Army." Truman [1973]. Just why Truman said this is unclear. Eisenhower, who had held high positions in the Army, knew more about bureaucratic resistance than any man alive. Truman, himself a former Army captain, should have known this.

57  Weber [2015] at pp. 60 and 64–5.

58  Then too, agency appointees are usually politicians in their own right, with their own need to hand out patronage to friends and followers. From this standpoint, the president's decision to let them choose their assistants provides a further reward for having been loyal in the past and, hopefully, the future.

59  Anon (2020g, h).

60  Carey (2012).

61  *Federalist* No. 76 at p. 349 (Hamilton).

62  Hamilton expresses both views in *Federalist* No. 66 at pp. 305–6.

63  Uhrmacher and Schaul (2017) ("Opposing senators were mostly deferential to the president's picks until about four decades ago, and more voted 'no' on President Obama's picks than those of any previous president. Trump's nominees broke that record"). Anon (2020e). Senate deference began unraveling in George Bush's first term, when Democrat members

blocked multiple appellate court appointees. The practice stopped after the Republication Party regained the majority and threatened to change Senate Rules. Anon (2020e).

64  Andrews (2017). The top half of Democratic senators voted "nay" 70 percent of the time compared to just forty-four "nays" for the bottom half. Not surprisingly, partisanship was most pronounced (86 percent "nays") for declared presidential candidates. Andrews (2017).

65  The anecdotal evidence is mixed. One Nixon official recalls how "a longtime department employee came into my office and told me that he didn't like Nixon, didn't support his agenda and wouldn't support me. He told me that I couldn't fire him nor take away his supergrade." But another veteran disagrees, arguing that the bureaucrats he knew were "highly responsive" since they could "easily be transferred to a less important position or a different location." Drake and Gordon (2022). J. Edgar Hoover's legendary influence over the FBI depended on a statutory "quirk" that let the FBI hire and fire without regard to the Civil Service. Gage (2022) at pp. 133–4.

66  Hawthorne's memoir suggests just how limited rule of law could be. While his office possessed a small legal library (Hawthorne [1850] at p. 12), Hawthorne gives no indication that the books were consulted, or if they were that the employees understood them. Instead, officials' deference to law consisted mostly of an ostentatious enthusiasm for applying "sealing wax" and other "formalities of office," and then only when some recent scandal had drawn criticism. Meanwhile the office's old and now obsolete records were stuffed into barrels or lay as "rubbish ... lumbering the floor." Hawthorne [1850] at p. 31.

67  Hamilton notes that "[a]ll new laws, though penned with the greatest technical skill, and passed on the fullest and most mature deliberation, are considered as more or less obscure and equivocal, until their meaning be liquidated and ascertained by a series of particular discussions and adjudications." And again:

> But no language is so copious as to supply words and phrases for every complex idea, or so correct as not to include many equivocally denoting different ideas ... And this unavoidable inaccuracy must be greater or less, according to the novelty of the objects defined. Whoen the Almighty himself condescends to address mankind in their own language, his meaning, luminous as it must be, is rendered dim and doubtful by the cloudy medium through which it is communicated. (*Federalist* No. 37 at p. 162)

68  Posner (1989) at p. 248. The problem is compounded when laws are amended by different congressmen years if not decades after they were originally enacted. The federal Constitution provides a particularly good example of this phenomenon. In Madison's mind, the document imposed a rigid separation on the missions of state and federal governments. But later drafters added amendments authorizing the national government to intervene in a variety of topics ranging from civil rights to (for a time) alcohol consumption. While it is plain that Madison's strict demarcation has been overruled, the new overlap between state and federal responsibilities has remained highly uncertain – and contentious – for more than 150 years.

69  Lessig (2006) at p. 189.
70  Weiner (2008).
71  Racketeer Influenced and Corrupt Organizations Act; Selan (1987).
72  Raleigh (2017).
73  *Wayman v. Southard*, 23 US 1, 445 (1825) (Marshall, J.)
74  Wallison (2018) at p. 126. The court further confused matters by declaring in 1920 that statutes that contained an "intelligible principle" were acceptable. The problem with this standard compared to Marshall's rule is that a principle can be "intelligible" and still authorize discretion that cannot be dismissed as a "detail." Wallison (2018) at p. 130. Given this difficulty, it would probably be better to accept imprecision except where Congress seeks to avoid hard political choices. Cf. *Industrial Union Department v. American Petroleum Institute*, 448 U.S. 607 at 687 (1980).
75  *A.L.A. Schechter Poultry Corp. v. United States*, 295 U.S. 495 (1935) and *Panama Refining Co. v. Ryan*, 293 U.S. 388 (1935).
76  Lamond (2006).
77  Among those who currently sit on the Supreme Court, Justices Thomas, Roberts, Alito, and Kavanaugh have all expressed interest in demanding more specific standards from Congress. Wallison (2018) at pp. 142–3.
78  *Chevron USA Inc. v. Natural Resources Defense Council, Inc.* 467 US 837 at pp. 843–4 (1984).
79  This was evident, for example, in the Supreme Court's recent decisions striking down Biden Administration orders that claimed to impose vaccine mandates as a workplace safety measure and stop foreclosures in the interests of public health. See *National Fed. of Ind. Business v. Department of Labor* 595 U. S. __ (2022); *Alabama Assn. of Realtors v. Department of Health and Human Servs.*, 594 U. S. __ (2021).
80  Congressional Research Service (2022).
81  Weber (2015) at p. 98.
82  Weber (2015) at pp. 78–9, 123–5.
83  Weber (2015) at p. 98.
84  Weber (2015) at p. 102.
85  Weber (2015) at pp. 78–9, 123–5.
86  Weber (2015) at p. 79.
87  Weber (2015) at p. 98.
88  Jervis (2010) at p. 11.
89  As Prof. Jervis says of the intelligence failures that led to the Second Gulf War, "once the belief that Iraq was developing WMD was established, there were few incentives to challenge it, and each person who held this view drew greater confidence from the fact that it was universally shared." Jervis (2010) at p. 130.
90  Wikipedia (52). Bork had also planned to resign until Richardson and Ruckelshaus persuaded him to stay on for the good of the Department; Wikipedia (52). Threats of resignation similarly forced George W. Bush to cut short his government's "Stellar Wind" electronic surveillance plans in 2003. Goldsmith (2019) at pp. 147–9.
91  The threat is effective even against presidents who strongly favor a particular strategy. For example, President Kennedy felt unable to remove Jupiter

missiles from Turkey against the unanimous advice of senior officials on his "ExCom Committee." Instead, he proposed the idea to Khruschev in secret after revealing it to a rump membership that excluded Vice President Johnson and the Chairman of the Joint Chiefs of Staff. Plokhy (2021) at p. 255. The time and effort required to obtain Senate confirmation for replacement officials gives presidents still more reason not to provoke resignations.

92 Otherwise serious journalists and political figures traded concerns that Nixon wanted to suspend the Constitution in 1970; that Ronald Reagan planned to cancel the 1984 election; and that George W. Bush would suspend the Bill of Rights following 9/11. Terzian (2019). The best-known recent chatter is almost certainly Joint Chiefs Chairman Mark Milley's warning that his subordinates should be on guard against a postelection coup. Gangel et al. (2021).

The question of what might happen following a *successful* coup is beyond the Constitution, and hence outside the scope of this book. However, former President Clinton's comment that "I actually think there is a fair chance we could completely lose our constitutional democracy for a couple of decades if we make bad decisions" contains a backhanded admission that even dictatorship would be temporary. Severi (2022). If so, the habit of democracy would presumably persist in public opinion through some version of the hysteresis discussed in Chapter 2. The gloomier view is due to Jefferson, who believed that people could get used to living under despotism if it continued long enough. This is the basis of his famous comment that "God forbid we should ever be 20 years without ... a rebellion." Jefferson [1787a] at p. 310. In modern language, Jefferson believed that the capacity for organized rebellion requires habits of trust and cooperation that atrophy if left unexercised.

It is hard to say anything very definitive as to whether Clinton or Jefferson is right. However, history seems to be at least weakly on Clinton's side. England's flirtation with Oliver Cromwell's dictatorship (1653–8) lasted just five years, while even Stalinist repression reverted to something milder once its organizers were safely dead. Taubman (2003) at pp. 13, 367, 369, et passim.

93 Baracskay (n.d.)

94 The numbers also make agencies insular in another way, ensuring that the average mid-level bureaucrat interacts dozens of times with colleagues for every outside encounter. This encourages her to follow the trajectory of her department's internal discussions while decoupling from the broader society.

95 See, e.g., Niskanen (1968) and Wilson (1989) at p. 166. Like Downs, Niskanen and Wilson ignore bureaucrats' personal political views, arguing that even bright-eyed idealists end up adopting whichever policies yield the most material benefits. As with politicians, this is reinforced by self-selection: Environmentalists go to the EPA, union activists go to the NLRB, and, as the country learned in the second Trump impeachment, expatriate Ukrainians go to the White House's Ukraine desk.

96 Breton and Wintrobe (1982); Mixon (2019).

97	Gehlbach (2022) at p. 118; McCubbins, Noll, and Weingast (1987). Political scientists analogize direct oversight to "police patrols" which actively search for lawbreakers, while lawsuits (or simply complaining to one's congressman) are more like "fire alarms" that rely on the general public to report violations. The latter have the obvious advantage that they only occur when voters are upset, and to that extent measure what politicians care about most. While Congress plainly uses both methods, "fire alarm" methods seem to have the biggest impact. By comparison, the executive branch often possesses significant active monitoring resources. This makes the White House especially influential over topics like national security whose constituencies are geographically dispersed and find it hard to organize. McCubbins et al. (1987).

98	See Gehlbach (2022) at pp. 108–9 for a detailed model and analysis.

99	Gehlbach (2022) at pp. 112–14.

100	Moe (1998); see also Berry (1989), McCubbins et al. (1987), and Ripley and Franklin (1976).

101	See, e.g., Berry (1989); Cater (1964); Pulitzer and Grasty (1919); and Wikipedia (29).

102	Berry (1989).

103	Downs (1957) at p. 92.

104	Downs (1957) at p. 255.

105	The notion that Big Government should be left to itself became suddenly fashionable during the Trump Administration, when some scholars argued that presidents were limited to supervising agency deliberations but could not compel particular outcomes. Strauss (2019) at p. 443. This interpretation made some sense in the traditional paradigm where rule of law was the country's main lever for controlling bureaucracy. However, the more likely outcome in the Big Government era is to free agencies to pursue their own internally agreed policy preferences. This only makes sense on the somewhat astonishing theory that letting presidents intervene will make outcomes *less* democratic than leaving unelected technocrats in charge.

106	National Conference of State Legislatures (n.d.) (describing public health powers in all fifty states).

107	Politicians had other reasons to err on the side of stringency. Even the best epidemiology models seldom ruled out the possibility of large, sudden outbreaks in the near future. While these outcomes were unlikely, incumbent politicians also understood that they were potentially career-ending. This reinforced their instinct to take strong precautions even when the estimated risk was modest.

108	For a short review of the decidedly messy evidence on both sides, see, e.g., Smith (2021b).

109	Agencies' motives for classification are almost always conjectural. That said, it is hard to imagine a legitimate reason for keeping the twenty-year-old September 11 files, let alone the sixty-year-old Kennedy assassination files, secret; US National Archives (2016) (9/11 files); Pruitt (2018) (JFK assassination files).

110	FOIA Project Staff (2019b).

111 The rise of ubiquitous police bodycam footage has made the declassification problem still more difficult. Prosecutors' usual instinct to delay public release until a jury has been selected probably makes sense in most cases. But it also gives the handful of people who have actually seen the footage – almost always prosecutors, but sometimes including the victim's lawyers and family – the opportunity to "spin" facts in the interim. This invites the public to imagine events in whatever ways their political preconceptions suggest, leading to still more polarization and, sometimes, riots. In these cases, at least, authorities would be better off empaneling and sequestering a jury for months so that everyone else could see the footage immediately.

112 The fact that Watergate started with one of J. Edgar Hoover's senior aides trying to retaliate against an elected president suggests that the "lesson" should be taken with a large grain of salt. Wikipedia (20).

113 Department of Justice (2019). On the prevalence of leaks generally, see Tau and Viswanatha (2018) and Department of Justice (2018) at Attachments G and H.

114 See, e.g., *Federalist* No. 64 at p. 298 (Jay). The openness of the American system has repeatedly tempted foreign governments to intervene in the country's politics. The practice dates back at least as far as the War of 1812, when the British ambassador cruised up and down the Eastern Seaboard criticizing President Madison's warlike stance and endorsing various Federalist politicians' peace platforms. Beschloss (2018) at p. 51. More recent attempts include Iraqi officials' various interviews with American media in the runup to both Gulf Wars. Being public, these at least let voters make their own judgments about how persuasive their messages are. The problem is worse when foreign governments seek to influence the president in secret. For example, Soviet leader Nikita Khrushchev repeatedly told John Kennedy's emissaries that he wanted to help JFK win the 1960 election, and later that he would avoid raising difficult issues before the 1962 midterms. Khrushchev loudly declared himself outraged when Kennedy failed to make foreign policy concessions in return. See Plokhy (2021) at pp. 36, 37, 45, 80, 114, 161, and 180.

115 Andrew Jackson dropped plans to use military force against France after the Senate refused a modest budget for hostilities. Anon (n.d. (i)). Similarly, President Madison withdrew US forces from Eastern Florida after Congress refused to ratify his actions and President Cleveland deferred to House and Senate instructions not to use force in Hawaii. Bobbitt (1994) at pp. 1390–1. In the twentieth century Congress defunded President Nixon's air and ground wars in Cambodia and blocked President Ford's efforts to save South Vietnam from ground invasion and to intervene in Angola. Beschloss (2018) at p. 283.

116 Most obviously, the House considered the "Wilmot Proviso" that would have barred the US from acquiring territory following the war with Mexico, but ultimately rejected it. Brands (2018) at p. 313. Fifty years later, Congress voted to declare war on Spain while stipulating that any military action in Cuba must end by returning the island to its people. Beschloss (2018) at p. 283.

117  Wikipedia (30).

118  Alone among presidents, Madison reversed this political logic by ostentatiously stating the case for war, but made no recommendation beyond asking Congress to choose. This was at least consistent with the separation of
powers principle that Congress's role was to make policy and the president's
to execute it. Politically, however, it did nothing to absolve Madison when
the war went badly, especially since critics focused on the president's supposed incompetence as much as the war itself. Later presidents have avoided
Madison's gambit, either by *requesting* declarations or by making war without any declaration at all. Brands (2018) at p. 32.

119  The meaning of the Declaration of War clause remains controversial. The
majority view is that it gives Congress the sole power to start hostilities. But
the evidence for this consists almost entirely of a letter that Madison wrote to
Jefferson ten years after the fact when both men were looking for arguments
to stop then President Adams from starting a war with France. Madison's
description is short enough to quote: "The constitution supposes, what
the History of all Govts. demonstrates, that the Ex. is the branch of power
most interested in war, & most prone to it. It has accordingly with studied
care, vested the question of war in the Legis." Madison then declares a few
lines later that Congress is "the Body which alone can declare it." Madison
(1798). However, Prof. Yoo points out that most eighteenth-century English
wars were undeclared and that nations sometimes sent forces into combat
when they were not technically at war. Yoo (2002) at p. 1643. He argues
that declarations are less about combat than about triggering the executive's
*domestic* powers to seize foreign property, conduct warrantless surveillance,
arrest enemy aliens, and commandeer the country's transportation systems.
Yoo (2002) at pp. 1672–3. Whatever its limitations, the reading neatly fits
the modern argument that wars are chiefly dangerous as a threat to civil
liberties. Finally, declarations of war only apply to nation-states. Lincoln and
Truman both refused to declare war against opponents that they insisted
were not legitimate states. Beschloss (2018) at pp. 197 and 471.

120  Yoo (2004) at p. 795.

121  The trope of presidential adventurism was a reasonable assumption for the
Framers looking back to Europe's absolute monarchs and the Greek republics' many demagogues. Whether American history since 1789 teaches the
same lesson is more doubtful. Federalists and Jefferson Democrats debated
a war with Britain for nearly twenty years without doing anything, with
Jefferson bragging that he had resisted the push to war. Beschloss (2018) at
p. 42. Indeed, Madison himself hoped to avoid war as late as 1811. It was
only when the British refused to compromise that he began hoping that
Napoleon would distract them long enough for the US to seize Canada.
Beschloss (2018) at pp. 62 and 68. The case for presidential adventurism
is clearest for the War with Mexico (1847). Hoping to make the US a continental power, President Polk engineered a series of tit-for-tat diplomatic
insults with Mexico and then ordered the Army to the Rio Grande despite
Mexico's insistence that Texas stopped at the Nueces River. Beschloss (2018)
at pp. 111–12 and 117.

Later wars have shown much less evidence of adventurism. Lincoln was anxious *not* to start hostilities before the South did, only acting after South Carolina militia attacked Fort Sumter. William McKinley similarly resisted popular pressure to declare war against Spain, to the point where many observers worried that Congress would declare war without him. Hofstadter [1952] at p. 632.

In the twentieth century both Woodrow Wilson and Franklin Roosevelt ran for reelection promising to keep the country out of war. While Roosevelt was plainly insincere, he was also careful not to exceed the public's very limited appetite for intervention. Instead, the most he promised the British was that the US would become "more and more provocative" and "if the Germans did not like it, they could attack the American forces." Meanwhile, on the other side of the world, the admiral charged with defending Pearl Harbor would later complain that "It's obvious [FDR] wanted the Japanese to attack." Beschloss (2018) at pp. 394, 403. Presidents Kennedy and Johnson similarly resisted the slide to war in Vietnam, hoping that "signaling" American resolve would convince the enemy to back down. The strategy led Johnson to authorize aggressive naval operations culminating in what turned out to be mistaken claims that US forces had been attacked. McMaster (2011). This led to the so-called Gulf of Tonkin Resolution formally authorizing intervention. Beschloss (2018) at pp. 532–40. While the two Gulf Wars were plainly wars of choice, both were brought on by Saddam Hussein, the first through his invasion of Kuwait and the second through his persistent refusal to honor the surrender terms that he himself had agreed to in ending the first war. George W. Bush also persuaded the United Nations that Iraq was developing weapons of mass destruction – Beschloss (2018) at pp. 601–2 – though whether Bush actually knew that the claim was false remains unclear.

122 We said in Chapter 1 that the Framers were haunted by fears that North America would evolve into an analog of Europe, with other Great Powers sharing the continent with the US. Most of these fears evaporated when President Monroe announced his eponymous Doctrine with Britain's support in 1823. Thereafter, there was little danger of a third power establishing bases in North America. The War with Mexico (1846–8) consolidated the achievement by taking American power to the Pacific. In theory, extending the country to the north or south would have improved the situation still further. However, neither British Canada nor Mexico posed a substantial threat, while expansion would have embedded large French- and Spanish-speaking populations within the US, diluting the stabilizing effects of a shared culture. Indeed, President Tyler's generals worried that a prolonged occupation of Mexico would spark an unwinnable guerilla war. Guelzo (2021b) at pp. 129 and 135.

The US would later extend "Manifest Destiny" beyond its original West Coast terminus all the way to the Philippines. But as Prof. Hofstadter has argued, this break with the country's earlier defensive focus on the American continent was thrust on it by unexpected developments in what was supposed to have been a limited war to free Cuba. Hofstadter [1952] at pp. 624–5 and 628. This was a fateful choice, since US interventions in the Philippines and its "Open Door" policy toward China put it on a collision course with Imperial Japan. This led to some of the bloodiest fighting in US history. Rose (2007) at pp. 14–20.

123  Some scholars argue that democracies inherently resist aggressive wars, though this is disputed. Wikipedia (21). A better answer is that the New England states, whose economies were anchored in manufacturing and trade, saw little need to expand, and for that reason resisted wars with Britain in 1812 and Mexico in 1846. This left Southerners, whose economy depended on agriculture, as the main proponents for acquiring new lands. Guelzo (2021b) at p. 136. US naval ambitions also occasioned various expansionist urges to secure distant bases after the Civil War, most spectacularly in the Grant Administration's attempt to make the Dominican Republic a US state. Rehnquist (2004) at p. 22.

124  President Truman decided against seeking Congressional authorization to intervene in Korea simply because the fighting seemed to be going well. Beschloss (2018) at p. 482. "If Congress wanted to do it on its own initiative, that would have been all right with me," he said. "I just did what was in in my power, and there was no need for any Congressional resolution." Beschloss (2018) at p. 479.

125  Wikipedia (35). The conventional list includes the War of 1812, the War with Mexico, the Civil War, the Spanish-American War, World War I, World War II, Korea, Vietnam, the First Gulf War, Afghanistan, and the Second Gulf War.

126  The number cannot be so small that ideological pacificists, say, could demand perpetual votes when no real political question was at stake. Nor should it be so large that party leaders could block a legitimately controversial vote. Unfortunately, there are no guarantees that these conditions can be simultaneously satisfied. The "correct" number may be nothing more than a least-bad alternative.

127  The high-water mark for congressional meddling came in Radical Republicans' attempts to micromanage the Civil War. Their Committee on the Conduct of the War routinely denounced any compromise of Republican Party principles as illegitimate and blamed military setbacks on disloyal Democrat generals. Tap (2002) at p. 5. The rhetoric was second nature to politicians from safely Republican districts who had relied on harsh anti-Southern rhetoric to get elected in the first place. Lincoln, on the other hand, had a national constituency that included border states and Democratic areas. If he wanted to maintain wartime unity or win reelection, he had to respect their feelings. Tap (2002) at p. 6.

128  Grant [1885] at p. 106. Grant thought it "very doubtful" that Congress would have declared war if President Tyler had not successfully maneuvered Mexico into attacking first.

129  Senator Thomas Hart Benton declared that absent American casualties it would have been "difficult – perhaps impossible" for President Polk to persuade Congress to declare war against Mexico, but that once Mexico had spilled American blood the vote was nearly unanimous. Beschloss (2018)

at p. 128. More than a century later, President Johnson warned his coldly rational defense secretary that casualties would change everything: "Do you know how far we're going to go? ... I would imagine if they wiped out a thousand boys tomorrow, we might go a hell of a lot further than we'd do if they just wiped out four." Beschloss (2018) at p. 552.

130 George C. Marshall argued that no democracy can match the staying power of a dictatorship. Recalling World War II, he wrote that "We had to go brutally fast in Europe. We could not indulge in a Seven Year's War. A king perhaps can do that, but you cannot have such a protracted struggle in a democracy in the face of mounting casualties." Quoted in Bolger (2021) at p. 341 and n. 24.

131 It helped that Manifest Destiny was achieved on a shoestring when America's tiny Asiatic fleet gunboats sank Spain's Philippines squadron at anchor. Costello (1982) at p. 21. Thereafter, the US repeatedly made moral and diplomatic claims in China and the Western Pacific that far exceeded the Navy's power to enforce them. Congress did not authorize a truly adequate fleet until 1934. Costello (1982) at pp. 16, 20, 49, 58, 68, et passim.

132 Having led America into the Spanish-American War (1897), Republicans remained slightly more hawkish than Democrats through the 1916 election. Wikipedia (1); Anon (2016d). Thereafter Germany's unrestricted submarine warfare drove the Democratic Wilson Administration into a moralistic "War to End All Wars." Massive casualties and the rise of Bolshevism led to a Republican landslide in 1920. Cotton (1986) at p. 627. This gave both parties a decidedly isolationist tinge down to 1935, when FDR could still insist that he had "come around entirely" to Bryanist neutrality. Like Wilson, he then began patiently moving his party toward intervention. Beschloss (2018) at p. 381; AmericanForeignRelations.com (n.d.) Any remaining isolationist sentiment collapsed after Pearl Harbor so that both parties remained strongly interventionist into the 1960s. This forced President Johnson to intervene in Vietnam despite private fears that he could neither win nor negotiate an acceptable compromise. The prophecy proved correct, but by then Republican Richard Nixon was running the war, while the Democrats selected peace candidate George McGovern to run against him in 1972. Since then, neither party has been clearly identified with either position, though the Democrats are arguably less interventionist.

133 Nearly half of Congress and most Americans opposed the war, with the Federalist Party voting against war loans and conscription even after the conflict began. Beschloss (2018) at pp. 80–1 and 99–100.

134 While President Polk successfully maneuvered Congress into declaring war, many Whigs argued that he should have consulted them earlier. The results of this rhetoric were mixed: Polk's Democrats gained four seats in the Senate but lost control of the House. Beschloss (2018) at p. 138. The House then voted 85–81 for a resolution saying that Polk had launched the Mexican war "unnecessarily and unconstitutionally." Beschloss (2018) at p. 154.

135 Among Democrats, just 18 percent of Senators and 32 percent of House members voted to authorize the First Gulf War. Wikipedia (9). Similarly, 39 percent of House Democrats voted to authorize the Second Gulf War,

breaking ranks with the 58 percent of their Senate colleagues who voted against the measure. Wikipedia (10). But in both cases, Democrats' opposition was largely pro forma. Once the conflicts started, Democrats did little to criticize or stop hostilities until the Second Gulf War began to go badly.

136  The system's greatest failure was the Civil War. Republican frontrunners William Seward and Abraham Lincoln spent the summer of 1860 denying that war would happen, assuring Northern voters that Southern threats to secede were just talk. Catton [1961] at p. 97. Moreover, none of the campaign's four major party nominees called for secession, and only Douglas said he was willing to fight. Catton [1961] at pp. 102 and 109. The remaining candidates ignored the issue. This meant that voters never got to say whether they preferred fighting to dissolving the Union. If Southern voters had voted to stay, or Northern voters had foresworn fighting, the war could never have started.

137  McKinley, who wanted peace, continued to seek diplomatic solutions even after becoming president. Beschloss (2018) at pp. 263–4.

138  Most voters wanted neutrality in the 1916 election, but changed their minds once Germany launched unrestricted submarine warfare and encouraged Mexico to attack the US. Wikipedia (2). At this point President Wilson admitted that he, too, had been wrong. Beschloss (2018) at pp. 325–7. Congress declared war by a vote of 373–50 in the House and 82–6 in the Senate. Beschloss (2018) at p. 334.

139  Following the widespread public approval of FDR's destroyers-for-bases deal with England, Republican presidential candidate Wendall Willkie repositioned himself as the man who could keep America out of the war. Beschloss (2018) at p. 390. FDR brazenly promised the same thing, despite knowing that war was inevitable. Beschloss (2018) at p. 391.

140  Anon (1964).

141  Presidents Jackson and Lincoln were obsessed with the middle ground's fragility, emphasizing that the Union should not strike first because it would drive middle-grounders in still more Southern states to leave the Union. See e.g., Meacham (2008) at pp. 290 and 301–2; Simpson, Sears, and Sheehan-Dean (2011) at pp. 12 and 113; Guelzo (2021b) at p. 242. They were right: Fort Sumter produced a steep increase in public support for the war on both sides. Simpson, Sears, and Sheehan-Dean (2011) at pp. 243, 245, 271, 301, 503, and 531; Harris (2011) at p. 36; Catton [1961] at pp. 107–8; Beschloss (2018) at p. 334. Despite this, many Americans continued to hope for a middle ground. Even after secession, most Virginians expected their state to mediate a new Union that would make fighting unnecessary. Guelzo (2021) at pp. 252 and 258–60.

Middle-grounders also posed challenges for FDR. While six in ten Americans wanted to take "firm action" against Japan in 1940, only four in ten were prepared to "risk war" to do it. Costello (1982) at p. 76. This limited FDR's ability to help the Allies until his Republican presidential opponent helped him pass the Lend-Lease Act. Costello (1982) at p. 72. Isolationist opposition did not finally disappear until Pearl Harbor made war unavoidable.

142  Robert E. Lee launched his 1862 campaign hoping that a Confederate army rampaging across the North just before the midterms would overthrow Lincoln's congressional majority and force a negotiated peace. Guelzo (2021) at p. 329. In the event, the Union Army stopped Lee at Antietam, although Lee still sent J. E. B. Stewart's cavalry to raid Pennsylvania hoping "to depose the party now in power." Guelzo (2021) at p. 341. Meanwhile, Lincoln used Antietam to publish his Emancipation Proclamation, reasoning that it would bring "greater gain than loss" in the election. In fact, the Republicans gained one seat in the Senate but lost one-fifth of their House contingent. Beschloss (2018) at p. 224; Tap (2002) at pp. 5–6. Lee's desire to overturn Northern politics also drove his Gettysburg campaign in 1863, and survived into his last full season of campaigning in 1864. Guelzo (2021b) at pp. 369–70 and 418. As late as August 1864, Lincoln predicted that he would be "badly beaten" in the fall election, though he was still hoping that fresh military victories would overcome public unhappiness with his policies. Beschloss (2018) at pp. 224 and 230.

143  Beschloss (2018) at p. 370.

144  Voters often take military experience as a marker for competence. In the nineteenth century presidents Jackson, Harrison, Tyler, and Grant had all been successful generals, while Mexican war veteran Winfield Scott and Civil War general George McClellan received major party nominations but failed to win. In the twentieth century, Douglas MacArthur publicly hinted at running in 1944, 1948, and 1952 despite being a serving general at the time. Beschloss (2018) at pp. 438, 475, and 494.

145  Cotton (1986) at p. 629.

146  Cotton (1986) at p. 631.

147  Beschloss (2018) at pp. 420 and 489. Two easy naval victories and a reasonably successful land campaign followed by peace negotiations limited losses in the 1898 midterms and were taken as an endorsement of America's expansionist policies. The conclusion was further strengthened by the 1900 presidential campaign which returned McKinley to power. Cotton (1986) at pp. 625–6.

148  Cotton (1986) at pp. 629–30 and 631–2.

149  Cotton (1986) at p. 632. Franklin Roosevelt took the opposite course by appointing Republicans to head the Army and Navy in 1940. Costello (1982) at p. 70. Bringing interventionist Republicans into the Cabinet helped outflank the large isolationist factions that had previously blocked either party from embracing intervention. The price was that Republicans received their full share of responsibility and, eventually, credit for the war.

150  Cotton (1986) at pp. 629–30.

151  Cotton (1986) at p. 632. Democrats probably would have nominated Robert Kennedy as a peace candidate in 1968 had he not been assassinated. Cotton (1986) at p. 631.

152  Cotton (1986) at p. 628; Beschloss (2018) at pp. 436 and 439. FDR himself believed that he would have lost if the war's end had been closer. This was confirmed by Democrats' disastrous loss of their congressional majorities in the inflation-driven "beefsteak election" of 1946, when voters turned to the

Republicans as the party more willing to take on unions whose recurring strikes seemed to be aggravating the era's high inflation. Cotton (1986) at p. 628; Rude (2016). Winston Churchill was less fortunate. With Germany defeated, voters chose Labour because they correctly saw that Conservatives were less committed to building the welfare state they had been promised during the war.

153 *Terminiello* v. *City of Chicago*, 337 U.S. 1 (1949) at p. 37 (Jackson dissenting).

154 Beschloss (2018) at p. 197. The Supreme Court later affirmed the blockade, saying that there had been no time for the president to convene Congress. Beschloss (2018) at p. 254. By comparison, Jefferson had *delayed* calling a "Convention of Congress" after the *Chesapeake* affair, hoping to cool public opinion against England. Beschloss (2018) at p. 26. Truman maintained there was no time to consult Congress about Korea, nor did he promise to seek consent going forward. Beschloss (2018) at p. 477. The reason, according to Truman, was that "we have to be able to respond quickly in the circumstances that are typical of this era." Beschloss (2018) at p. 482.

155 The Constitution lets the government suspend habeas corpus in "Cases of Rebellion or Invasion when the public Safety may require it"; Art. 1 §9(2). It does not say whether the suspension must be authorized by Congress and does not mention martial law at all. Beschloss (2018) at p. 200.

156 Simpson, Sears, and Sheehan-Dean (2011) at p. 433.

157 Catton (1961) at p. 361. Lincoln also ordered soldiers to block a writ issued by Chief Justice John Taney (sitting as a federal appeals judge) that would have restored habeas corpus. Lincoln then expanded his earlier order to cover the entire country. Catton (1961) at p. 360; Beschloss (2018) at pp. 201 and 223. In the end, the Army used its new authority for such doubtful purposes as arresting civilians for showing Confederate colors in shop windows or on children's clothes, arresting clergy for leading unauthorized prayers or refusing official ones, and putting soldiers in polling places to decide who was loyal enough to vote. Catton [1961] at p. 358. Eighty years later, Franklin Roosevelt similarly ordered that nine Nazi saboteurs be tried in military tribunals instead of civilian courts, and then had them executed after refusing habeas corpus writs over the objections of his own attorney general. Beschloss (2018) at pp. 424–5; *Ex Parte Quirin*, 317 US 1 (1942).

158 Beschloss (2018) at p. 203.

159 However small, the threat of impeachment is seldom zero. Most obviously, Nixon left office when a delegation of Republican senators – no doubt fearful for their own seats – told him it was time to go; Von Hippel (2020). Similarly, Kennedy believed he would have been impeached if he had not responded strongly when the Soviet Union installed nuclear missiles in Cuba. Plokhy (2021) at p. 186. Just how much the threat of impeachment deters presidents is unclear. The fact that impeachment was seldom invoked before the Trump years is consistent with *either* a very weak deterrent or an extremely strong one.

160 Beschloss (2018) at p. 231.

161 Dueholm (2010) at p. 25.

162 Dueholm (2010) at pp. 25–6. Just what Lincoln meant by the word "indispensable" is unclear. Certainly, the North could have physically prevailed with or without the Proclamation. At worst, the effort would have been costlier in lives and treasure, implying that disproportionate costs are a sufficient stand-in for "indispensability." Then again, Lincoln may have worried that the added costs would have made victory *politically* impossible, implying that violations required to save the entire Constitution outweigh any single provision. During World War II, Franklin D. Roosevelt would similarly threaten to act unilaterally if Congress did not vote to authorize new taxes and wage and price controls. Congress gave in. Beschloss (2018) at p. 416. A few years later, Truman would invoke the same logic to mobilize American industry during the "police action" in Korea: "[W]henever the President knows what he's doing, and knows it's right, he can always convince the Congress [and] tell them what the situation is and why certain things have to be done. You never have any trouble with them after that." Beschloss (2018) at p. 461.

163 FDR gave FBI boss J. Edgar Hoover blanket authority to wiretap despite a Supreme Court case requiring warrants, arguing in a secret memo that the Court could not have wanted the rule in national security cases. A decade later, Eisenhower's attorney general used the same reasoning to authorize breaking and entering to install surveillance equipment, even after the Court held that such acts "flagrantly" violate the Fourth Amendment. By the 1960s the government had expanded its national security rationale to wiretap hundreds of targets including organized crime figures, civil rights leaders, congressional staff, federal officials, reporters, and lawyers. The practice finally became public in 1966 when Solicitor General Thurgood Marshall, arguing before the US Supreme Court, admitted that the FBI had bugged a lobbyist and various mafiosi without any court authority. The Court responded by imposing new Fourth Amendment restrictions on wiretaps, followed a year later by Congress's decision to pass new legislation requiring warrants. But even then, the Court still did not say whether it would have ruled the same way in a foreign espionage case. This last point was only resolved in the early 2000s, when the Justice Department refused to approve the Bush Administration's plans for monitoring suspected terrorists. President Bush briefly decided to go ahead anyway, but changed his mind on learning that several senior officials were about to resign in protest. Goldsmith (2019) at pp. 122, 124, 125, 141–2, and 146.

164 *Youngstown Sheet & Tube Co.* v. *Sawyer*, 343 U.S. 579 (1952) at p. 634.

165 *Youngstown Sheet & Tube Co.* v. *Sawyer*, 343 U.S. 579 (1952).

166 Justice Douglas argued that seizure was inherently a "legislative power"; *Youngstown Sheet & Tube Co.* v. *Sawyer*, 343 U.S. 579 (1952) at p. 630. Justice Black partly agreed, with the caveat that Truman's actions could have been implied from the Constitution if Congress had not previously passed a statute regulating the president's power to seize assets. *Youngstown Sheet & Tube Co.* v. *Sawyer*, 343 U.S. 579 (1952) at p. 597. Justice Jackson argued that "executive power" was inherently limited and could not, for example, give the president totalitarian powers or "supersede representative

government of internal affairs." *Youngstown Sheet & Tube Co.* v. *Sawyer*, 343 U.S. 579 (1952) at pp. 641 and 644. Clark argued that the president could "in ways short of making laws or disobeying them ... be under a grave constitutional duty to act for the national protection in situations not covered by the acts of Congress," or specifically mentioned in the Constitution. *Youngstown Sheet & Tube Co.* v. *Sawyer*, 343 U.S. 579 (1952) at pp. 690–1. Finally, dissenting Justices Vinson, Reed, and Minton argued that the president could act in situations "which have not, though they might have, been actually regulated by Congress." *Youngstown Sheet & Tube Co.* v. *Sawyer*, 343 U.S. 579 (1952) at pp. 690–1.

167  *Youngstown Sheet & Tube Co.* v. *Sawyer*, 343 U.S. 579 (1952) at p. 662 (Clark, concurring).

168  Beschloss (2018) at p. 461.

169  Justices Black, Frankfurter, and Clark argued that the president's power could only come from the Constitution or statute, and that since Congress had laid down procedures covering the emergency, Truman was obliged to use them. *Youngstown Sheet & Tube Co.* v. *Sawyer*, 343 U.S. 579 (1952) at pp. 585 and 609.

170  *Youngstown Sheet & Tube Co.* v. *Sawyer*, 343 U.S. 579 (1952) at p. 669.

171  Justice Black left open the possibility that he might have approved the seizure "had [it] been only for a short, explicitly temporary period." *Youngstown Sheet & Tube Co.* v. *Sawyer*, 343 U.S. 579 (1952) at p. 597. Douglas disagreed, arguing that no amount of urgency could overrule separation of powers. *Youngstown Sheet & Tube Co.* v. *Sawyer*, 343 U.S. 579 (1952) at p. 630.

172  US Constitution at Amend. XX, § 2. The House and Senate frequently adjourn on condition that the Speaker and Senate Majority Leader can reconvene their respective bodies if needed. See, e.g., 114th Congress (2015). As with the Declaration of War clause, it is not clear how or whether courts would enforce these terms if the majority party found it politically expedient to let the president rule without Congress.

173  Wikipedia (6).

174  President Obama famously declared in 2014 that "I am going to be working with Congress where I can ... but I am also going to act on my own if Congress is deadlocked. I've got a pen to take executive actions where Congress won't." Keith (2014).

# 9

# Interpreting Law

## *The Courts*

Rule of law provides finality. Without it, votes in Congress settle nothing, but only transfer fights to the executive branch, where they go on forever. At the same time, finality depends on the average voter's willingness to vote out officials who defy the law.[1] The trouble, as often happens in politics, is information impactedness: Voters hardly ever know enough to make their own judgments about just what the law requires. This makes some trusted intermediary – an umpire to call the balls and strikes – essential. In the end Madison's entire system depends on the public's faith that this intermediary's answers are both selfless and objective.

But that raises a contradiction. Archimedes boasted that with a long enough lever he could move the earth – only to add more soberly that he would first need a place to stand. Likewise, the Framers placed a similar requirement on judges. Unlike every other actor in Madison's system, judges are supposed to ignore their personal beliefs and partisan loyalties. This is asking a lot, and some claim that the very idea is impossible. Section 9.1 begins by explaining why the rule of law is feasible after all. We then ask how the court system furthers the Framers' scheme by limiting government arbitrariness (Section 9.2) and regulating private power (Section 9.3), while still preserving room for private groups to act in the public interest. Section 9.4 concludes with a brief discussion of how the court system's failures can infect the rest of government.

## 9.1 LAW AND PRECEDENT

*The Federalist* seems modern not least because it relentlessly diagnoses politicians' self-interest and uses it to predict how they and ultimately the whole political system will behave. Still, there is one glaring exception.

For Madison, the ideal judge would have no private political goals at all. Unlike every other actor in the scheme, the judge must display "neither FORCE nor WILL, but merely judgment."[2] The question, of course, is whether such a thing is possible, or more precisely whether properly designed incentives can persuade judges to disregard their own material interests and beliefs. If the Framers had been pressed on this point, they would almost certainly have pointed to judges' lifetime appointments: Unlike, say, congressmen, judges never face reelection and have no further promotions in prospect, and to that extent have nothing to gain. Suffice to say, modern social science is skeptical. There is almost always more to be gained, and practically all economic models make "nonsatiety" a standard assumption.

There are not one but two questions here. The first is whether the common law system, in which judges consider themselves bound by previous legal decisions or "precedents," offers determinate answers even in theory. The second question is why, assuming it does, we should trust judges to honor it.

The question of whether law has a determinate meaning is usually presented as an issue in legal philosophy. Suffice to say, the debate quickly degenerates. On the one hand, "traditionalists" insist that close textual reading invariably yields clear and unique answers. On the other, "legal realists" and more recently "postmodernists" claim that judges can always find some verbal formula to do what they like. The net result, almost always, is that the argument founders on the apparent conflict between the observed "reality of disagreement among equally competent speakers of the native language" and those who dream of "the possibility of a science of criticism."[3]

This all-or-nothing debate is inescapable so long as we assume – as both sides invariably do – that law consists entirely of an exercise in logic, and for that reason has just three possible answers: "Yes," "No," or "Insufficient information." Yet in everyday life we see *both* that equally competent lawyers frequently disagree, *and* that large majorities find one interpretation more convincing than the other.[4] This is, of course, just what we would expect from our Chapter 3 argument that humans approach most problems through pattern recognition, or, as practicing lawyers say, "judgment." In what follows, therefore, we *define* the "better" reading as whatever view a majority of judges would independently arrive at. Doing this allows us to replace the fiction of a single Yes/No answer with a probability that can take any value from 0 to 100 percent.

This probabilistic interpretation gives content to federal Judge Richard Posner's suggestion that the existence of "better" and "worse" readings can usefully "box in" judges' discretion even when some ambiguity remains.[5] None of this would have surprised the Framers, who saw no contradiction in arguing that "strict rules and precedents" can limit judges' discretion, while simultaneously admitting that men can have reasonable disagreements about how to interpret them.[6] The difference today, as we saw in Chapter 3, is that psychologists have shown that people who study subjects intensely tend to arrive at similar judgments, even when they have different educations or were born into vastly different cultures.

We do not say that all legal questions are clear in this way; indeed, calling judgment "probabilistic" implies that the choice between competing interpretations is sometimes fifty-fifty, or as Judge Posner says a "hard case." The average newspaper reader could be pardoned for thinking that just about every dispute fits this description. This, however, is an illusion, at least if we assume that litigants never bring – and judges never see – cases they are bound to lose. This makes it reasonable to think that, despite appearances, the law is usually clear enough that no government official ever thinks to defy it.

So far, we have imagined judges following something we have imprecisely called "The Law." But as we saw in Chapter 8, executive branch officials now often make decisions based on their shared sense of professional standards and agency mission at least as much as formal statutes. In much the same way, many federal judges admit that their rulings reflect common sense and good public policy as much as parsing the actual words enacted by Congress. By itself, this need not change the analysis: If, as we have argued, interpreting "The Law" is an exercise in pattern recognition, the raw materials of that pattern hardly matter so long as judges use them impersonally and predictably. The problem only comes when they start legislating their own personal preferences from the bench. As Prof. John Hart Ely once noted, judges usually try to avoid this by limiting their policy judgments to "their best estimate of what over time the American people will make it – that is, they should seek 'durable' decisions."[7] This implies, among other things, enforcing normative principles that they believe are so widely accepted that they fall outside politics entirely. As Prof. Ronald Dworkin pointed out, where statutes admit multiple interpretations, judges must decide "as a question of political theory" which one Congress intended. In such cases, the only way to avoid charges of legislating from the bench is to choose the political theories based on their perceived "fit" without regard to the judge's own personal politics.[8]

But no matter what elements go into the analysis, Madison's system can only work so long as American lawyers consistently find some interpretations better than others. Just why this should be true is subtle: Probably the most popular hypothesis is that it is a product of training and socialization; that is, that lawyers are taught to favor some patterns over others. But this is not the only possibility. As Prof. Child pointed out sixty years ago, we know that artists who contemplate aesthetic problems for long periods often make the same judgments no matter what culture they were born into or where they were educated.[9] This makes it reasonable to think that some and even most of the judgments that lawyers make about "better" and "worse" legal interpretations would be common to any thoughtful person who practiced law long enough. This, however, would also mean that professionals' legal judgments stand outside any particular culture or educational system. So, the traditionalist claim that textual interpretation can be divorced from one's individual political and personal prejudices might be correct after all, with the large caveat that the convergence is only probabilistic, so that there will often be substantial disagreements in the "hard cases" that real judges usually face.

Still, showing that judges tend to reach similar opinions is only the beginning. Because even if the laws do have better and worse interpretations, why should judges honor them over their own private policy preferences? The answer is that judges, like the media companies we described in Chapter 4, do what their audiences want them to. More specifically, their reputations and prospects for promotion require Bar Association endorsements, which in turn depend heavily on the good opinion of the lawyers who appear before them.[10] Yet these same lawyers earn their living by negotiating and sometimes litigating business transactions.[11] Since risk makes deals less attractive, they much prefer predictable outcomes. This implies that judges are rewarded for reaching the same interpretations as the average lawyer. Whether judges who consistently meet these expectations revere the law instinctively or cold-bloodedly simulate the correct outcome hardly matters.

The trouble with this system is that the legal community's ability to detect judges who deliberately ignore the law is highly imperfect. The reason, as we have said, is that equally competent lawyers can and often do disagree. This makes it difficult to know when judges who reach unorthodox outcomes are dishonest or simply mistaken. Of course, large and repeated departures would clarify the issue soon enough. But this still leaves significant room for judges to indulge their cronyism, or partisanship, or personal beliefs at little risk of detection. Despite this, there is good anecdotal[12] and statistical[13] evidence that real judges – on average at least – respect precedent without regard to their personal political views.

The deeper danger lies less with judges than with their legal audiences. If lawyers – and especially the bar associations charged with reducing members' diffuse opinions to clear recommendations for or against particular candidates for judicial promotion[14] – start to prefer partisanship and "legislating from the bench," judges will give them that too. This is especially true in polarized eras, when many judges' personal feelings may already be strong enough to outweigh normal career incentives to apply the law as written.

The question remains whether formal institutions can make individual judges' rulings still more predictable. Because legal judgment is ultimately probabilistic – and since courts invariably face close cases – it is often hard to know when the first ruling on some new legal question represents the mainstream. If it doesn't, the legislators who wrote the law will be disappointed. Worse, private citizens who paid for expensive legal advice that later turned out to be wrong may find their investments in jeopardy. This argues that the courts should have some capacity to second-guess bad decisions. At the same time, having a stable meaning can be just as valuable as having the right one. This suggests that the judicial system should reach some definitive interpretation quickly. The challenge for real court systems is to balance these goals.

In practice, the federal courts do this through two distinct channels. The first is precedent. Because of the Anglo-Saxon respect for earlier rulings, judges who might have initially considered a particular legal issue close will defer to what other judges have said. On the other hand, judges who do feel strongly can disagree for years. This process by which judges at the same level defer or disagree is formally identical to "social influence" models in economics. Here the central idea is that each member of the group starts with her own idiosyncratic belief, but sometimes changes her mind when she learns what others think.[15] For example, Alice might influence Bob, who influences Carl, who then closes the circle by influencing Alice. But there could also be a second path by which Alice talks to Carl, who gives his opinion directly back to Alice. The existence of messages simultaneously traveling across multiple paths, some longer than others, injects a measure of] randomness into which opinions eventually prevail. Even so, most models turn out to be well-behaved in the sense that members' opinions eventually converge on a stable long-run consensus. This strongly suggests that the court system naturally evolves toward definite rules.[16]

There is also an important feedback effect. If litigation were costless, litigants would always challenge every legal interpretation no matter how many courts had previously endorsed it. But of course, real litigation is costly. This means that if the litigant has a one-in-four chance of overturning the case, she will normally pay her attorneys up to 25 percent of the amount at stake to escape liability. But in that case both parties can achieve an even better outcome by settling the case and pocketing the cash that they would otherwise pay to their attorneys. This explains how marginal legal theories can linger for years without finding a plaintiff rich or desperate enough to test them in court.[17] Still, the argument only applies to litigants who see cases as a for-profit investment. Governments and well-heeled advocacy groups have bigger litigation budgets and can bring cases over and over, hoping to nudge the law in their preferred direction.[18]

The second way in which courts correct outlier opinions is through appeals. Since these typically come late in the process, appellate judges can often see how several lower courts have ruled before deciding themselves. This helps identify which opinions are outliers and which mainstream, though at the cost of significant uncertainty in the interim. Then too, we have already said that appellate judges have above-average skills in recognizing outcomes that other lawyers will accept as correct. Finally, appellate courts often convene three-judge panels and occasionally their full membership to hear cases. If we assume that lawyers, like Prof. Child's artists, agree on the correct rule 60 percent of the time, a three-judge panel should arrive at the right answer 65 percent of the time, a five-judge panel 73 percent, and so on.[19]

The doctrine of *stare decisis* discourages this by putting a judicial thumb on the scale to "reduce[] incentives for challenging settled precedents" so that citizens and investors know what to expect.[20] While the doctrine operates differently in different courts, the general point is that judges should only overturn existing law based on something more than a desire to second-guess earlier decisions.[21] Nevertheless, they may still decide to change the law when the challenged rule generates perverse results, or is inconsistent with the rationales adopted in more recent cases. Perhaps most importantly, *stare decisis* is itself a legal doctrine, implying that courts' willingness to change the law can evolve from one era to the next.

As usual, there is a balance: Given that precedent is almost always laid down piecemeal by different judges at many different times, rigorously logical efforts to follow all previous decisions can sometimes lead to unanticipated and unjust results. British courts typically rely on the House of Lords to correct the law when this happens.[22] This makes sense since the Lords, being hereditary, can at least claim to put the good of the country above politics. Unfortunately, that was never an option for the Framers. Not only is the American Senate explicitly political, but giving senators the power to correct court decisions would have immediately collapsed separation of powers' guardrails against legislative tyranny. So the Framers left discretion in the Supreme Court, presumably hoping that the justices would only overrule results on grounds so widely accepted as to be outside politics.

## 9.2 LIMITING GOVERNMENT POWER

The Constitution does not say which branch has the final word on the constitutionality of statutes. But the Framers assumed that the Supreme Court would decide,[23] and the Court itself soon staked out this claim in *Marbury v. Madison*.[24] Two centuries later, it is easy to forget that many contemporary lawyers looking back on English practice declared themselves flabbergasted by the Court's *ipse dixit*.[25] The idea that the states and even the president could similarly declare laws unconstitutional would continue to haunt American politics down to the Civil War.[26]

At bottom, *Marbury* was less important as a statement of law than as a political marker. Even if the Constitution had been more explicit, the Court's orders were only as good as the executive's willingness to enforce them.[27] If the president refused, the Court would be forced into the desperate expedient of asking government employees to defy him. This, however, could only succeed if they or the wider public were willing to accept its legal opinions. Since no one could say that the Court was incompetent, this would usually mean overcoming accusations that it had been deliberately dishonest in delivering a partisan result. And even then, the public might still hesitate to overrule the executive in the midst of some national emergency. All of these considerations make the "rule of law" more elastic than we like to think.

Historically, the limits have most often been tested in wartime. In theory, the Bill of Rights requires courts to step in immediately when individual rights are restricted. In practice, however, courts have usually been silent in the panicky early phases of large wars, famously including Lincoln's suspension of habeas corpus during the Civil War[28] and Franklin Roosevelt's internment of Japanese citizens in World War II.[29] In both cases courts eventually declared the president's acts unconstitutional – but only after the public could see that the crisis had passed. Whether or not we admire this deference, it is at least understandable. In times of crisis, the country wants and needs a functioning commander in chief. So, judges let the president use the challenged measures long enough for the crisis to pass, after which any decision to overrule him is certain to be submerged in the public's broader estimate of how competently he has managed the emergency.[30]

It is hard to escape the conclusion that, on such occasions at least, the American system skids into lawlessness, with only the vaguest limits on how long the emergency can last or when courts will agree to hear a challenge. Presumably the length of this interlude depends on the justices' political judgment of when the crisis is sufficiently past that the president will not defy them, or rather that voter outrage would force him to give in if he tried. Yet it is not clear that the justices can make these estimates better than anyone else, and in any case their personal desire to avoid confrontation will almost always cut the other way. If the president appears competent and claims that some particular measure is needed to save the country, it will take a brave judge to argue.

It would be comforting to say that the courts' wartime pliability is unique. But the country's recent encounter with COVID-19, where court challenges to mandates waited until after the case numbers had started declining, shows the same pattern: Apparently, any emergency will do if the public mood supports presidential action. Moreover, the executive has occasionally defied the Court without any emergency at all. When the Supreme Court declared in 1830 that the State of Georgia had no right to control Cherokee land, President Jackson ignored it and removed the tribe anyhow. More recently, South Carolina governor (and former Supreme Court justice) James Byrnes urged President Eisenhower to ignore the Supreme Court's *Brown* v. *Board of Education* decision in the 1950s. Eisenhower, of course, refused the advice and sent troops to see that school integration was carried out.[31] But the example is sufficiently recent to remind us that the taboo against executive defiance is nine-tenths political, and could easily be discarded the next time passions run high.

There was also the opposite problem of when the Court should take hold of public controversies that, in theory at least, it could safely avoid. In the most prominent cases – abortion and gay rights come to mind – intervention is often rationalized on the ground that the political struggle has become irreversible, so that the Court can safely perform a public service by declaring that the subject has now passed outside of politics. This is plausible where public opinion for the challenged position is both conformist and weakly held, so that those who hold it will take the Court's ruling as a signal to simultaneously switch to the new consensus. The collapse of opposition to gay marriage after the Supreme Court declared it a constitutional right fits this scenario.[32] Yet if the justices miscalculate, enough social voters may hold to the old view to form a hard core of resisters, which then makes overturning the outcome plausible enough to attract rational voters as well. In that case, the Court may instead find that it has created interminable legal challenges, protests, and legislative fights on the pattern of *Roe* v. *Wade*.[33] And if the opposition goes on to capture a major party, the constant messaging on both sides could make voters even more polarized than they were to begin with.

Extremists have also threatened the court, though so far only in times of exceptional political change. Evidently, the idea of demanding specific substantive outcomes from the justices is so foreign to Madison's system that only highly polarized voters can tolerate it. Apart from some modest nineteenth-century precedents,[34] serious threats date from President Theodore Roosevelt's presidency when the Administration's allies hinted that court resistance to expanding the Interstate Commerce Commission would lead to legislation stripping it of jurisdiction and even amending the Constitution itself. Later, in 1912, Roosevelt himself campaigned on a platform of recalling uncooperative justices.

The most dramatic threat was, of course, Franklin Roosevelt's 1937 scheme to "pack" the Supreme Court with justices faithful to New Deal causes. This was promptly withdrawn in the face of a horrified public.[35] Yet despite the setback, most court watchers claimed to see new deference from the justices after the incident.[36] At the same time, the fact that a politician as well loved as FDR could fail so spectacularly seems to have stopped lesser politicians from attacking the court for the rest of the century. That changed in 2012 when the liberal media loudly warned of damage to the court – and to Chief Justice Roberts' reputation – if the court struck down the Affordable Care Act.[37] Moreover the tactic seemed to work, with Roberts writing what many saw as a deliberately distorted decision to save the statute. Since then, senators and congressmen have reliably mouthed new threats each time a hot-button issue comes before the court.[38]

The question remains what judges should do when politicians threaten them. One could argue that the best institutional strategy is for judges to ignore the threats and rule honestly. Instead, the received wisdom is that courts give way when the pressure is high enough. The justification, presumably, is that courts should aim for the greatest *sustainable* rule of law, and that graceful failures are better than standoffs that end with the president or Congress defying or cutting back the court's authority. But of course, outcomes and strategies are related: If the justices could be counted on to follow their best legal judgments, politicians would see no point in making threats to begin with. Conversely, if politicians know that the Court sometimes gives way, the two sides will immediately find themselves in a game of bluff and counter-bluff. At this point, the size of the Court's departures from the rule of law will depend on the justices' estimate of what the politicians will do, or rather what the public will stand for. The trouble, according to our "nobody knows anything" postulate, is that the justices have, at best, only a very rough idea of what this is. Then too, the justices will almost always know less than the politicians who make it their business to track the public mood. This suggests both that politicians will try to bluff the justices, and that the bluff will often succeed. Worse still, once voters see that the Court gives in to threats, the Court's claim to be an impartial referee is bound to ring hollow.[39] At this point, extremists on both sides will make threats endlessly in a downward spiral. And when one side succeeds, the losers will start agitating for legislation to pack the Court or disable it from hearing various types of cases.

Finally, courts have erected formal procedural obstacles to hearing cases. This often prevents Americans – even including elected officials – from bringing constitutional challenges to government actions and statutes in open court. Probably the most spectacular recent example is the 2020 election, where more than sixty courts refused to hear a sitting president's claim that his opponent had won by fraud. This was done on several grounds including "standing"; a finding that the president's complaint, even if true, failed to state a legally cognizable claim; a "summary judgment" that the president's attorneys had produced so little evidence that a full trial could not possibly find in his favor; or else denying preliminary injunctive relief based on a finding that the president was unlikely to prevail at trial. Additionally, the US Supreme Court exercised its own broad discretion by refusing to hear President Trump's attempts to overrule the various state and federal court decisions against him.[40]

The theory behind most of these rulings was that no court could possibly have reached a different result, so that a full trial would have been so much wasted energy. But the trusted intermediary function of courts is about more than reaching the correct result. It equally means reaching judgments in ways that will be believed, which often requires live testimony backed by generous discovery to uncover whatever evidence might exist. Here judicial economy is penny wise and pound foolish: Leaving no stone unturned was precisely what the broader society needed to see, and the benefits of doing this would have outweighed any conceivable cost to the court system.[41]

The cases which addressed the president's "standing" to bring suit were still more provocative. Formally, the doctrine requires plaintiffs to prove (a) a concrete and particularized injury that is (b) caused by the challenged conduct and (c) redressable by the courts.[42] Here the first and third terms are the most important. The first implies that litigants cannot simply be affected in the same way as millions of their fellow citizens: For example, just being a taxpayer is not enough to challenge the constitutionality of US government actions.[43] The instinct here seems obvious: Giving millions of people the right to challenge government policy would ensure that every action was litigated. Moreover, the imperfect nature of all legal systems would then strike down some statutes that ought to be upheld. Even so, President Trump's inability to challenge elections that concerned millions of Americans was deeply disturbing.[44] As with our discussion of the filibuster (Chapter 7), a well-designed system should trigger judicial review so long as a dispute remains relevant within the country's normal two-party politics. Looking forward, it might be better for Congress to give some threshold number of state governors, US senators, and/or congressmen the right to sue.

The deeper issue with standing is buried in the third requirement. "Redressability" implies that courts can only intervene when there is some "constitutional directive or legal standard[]" to constrain how they exercise their power.[45] This implies, among other things, that judges cannot settle purely "political" issues,[46] create "comprehensive schemes" to address social goals,[47] or assume functions that the Constitution has reserved to state and local authorities.[48] This seems sensible on the separation of powers ground that departures from rule of law are best left to the elected president. Despite the doctrine's obvious vagueness, the central point – that courts should respect the separation of powers by sticking to strictly "judicial" functions – is hard to argue with.

### 9.3 MANAGING PRIVATE POWER

American thought has always linked political freedoms to competitive markets backed by the Myth of the Frontier, which held that settlers who did not like existing economic and social arrangements could simply move on. In Thomas Jefferson's words, "I think our governments will remain virtuous ... as long as there shall be vacant lands in any part of America."[49] The political argument for competition also resonated with the deeply felt, if sometimes vague, hatred of monopolies that the colonists brought from England. In medieval times the word "monopoly" had extended to all exclusive privileges, including even the right to incorporate a business.[50] Americans would spend most of the nineteenth century deciding which privileges were abuses, and which benign.

President Andrew Jackson opened the battle with his long fight to abolish the Bank of the United States. Where advocates had promoted the Bank as a way to strengthen the American financial system, Jackson called it favoritism to the country's elites and argued that the country should not renew the Bank's charter. The Bank, predictably, fought back by paying to place hostile ghost-written articles in newspapers and offering favorable loans to congressmen.[51] But this was not all: The Bank also called in loans and restricted credit to businesses because, said its president, "Nothing but the evidence of suffering abroad will produce any effect on Congress."[52] Jackson was outraged. His polemics paired the traditional English complaint against "privileges" with a new argument that no private entity should ever grow big enough to threaten democracy itself.[53]

Voters embraced this framing. In time, the old "privileges" objection faded as Americans grew blasé about big corporations. But their fear of plutocracy only deepened, climaxing with the Sherman Antitrust Act in 1890. By then sponsor John Sherman had sharpened Jackson's argument, insisting that "If we will not endure a king as a political power, we should not endure a king over the production, transportation, and sale of any of the necessities of life."[54] Though couched in economic terms, this made the Sherman Act a *political* response to the *political* problem of limiting private power.[55]

Stripped to its essentials, the new creed held that democracy could not tolerate private monopolies big enough to buy whole legislatures or vandalize the economy.[56] Still, the question remained just how far government should go to enforce the principle. The Bank had been an easy case: Refuse to renew its charter and it simply disappeared. The situation was different, though, where private power rose up without government's help. This did not matter so long as the "invisible hand" of markets ensured plenty of competition. But after the Civil War, voters suddenly saw giant corporations springing up everywhere.

And just what did the Sherman Act require? Because Congress had made it a criminal statute, courts soon limited it to deliberate wrongdoing. This gave companies that became dominant through, say, clever products or scale economies had a complete defense. By the Theodore Roosevelt Administration antitrust's original hostility to monopoly per se had narrowed to a focus on whether defendants had achieved or maintained their advantage by unfair methods; the last efforts to modify the statute to include size alone petered out in the Wilson Administration.[57] The trouble, of course, was that even innocently acquired power can be abused. Still, the inconsistency was tolerable in the old physical economy where companies almost always ran into diminishing returns before they were big enough to monopolize their respective markets. This meant that, absent illegal behavior, there was usually plenty of room for other firms to compete even without government intervention. This comfortable situation lasted until the 1980s. As Profs. Varian and Shapiro stress, what made the new Silicon Valley economy different is that its businesses could not operate without access to shared "interoperability" standards. And unlike older technologies, the benefits of these standards continued to grow until every last customer joined.[58] The result was that a statute that had successfully contained monopoly for nearly a century found itself outclassed by digital monopolists like Facebook, Apple, Netflix, and Google. This led to a massive resurgence of private power not just economically but also in politics.

So far, we have said that courts must guard against public and private power. But the danger is still greater when the two conspire. Chapter 4 described how the Wilson Administration worked with self-styled Progressives to slant and suppress media coverage during World War I. But the Administration went much further than that, using its Justice

Department to recruit more than a quarter million volunteers who harassed antiwar speakers, spied on coworkers, and searched neighbors' homes and mail for evidence of disloyalty.[59] Caught up in the enthusiasm, many publications went still further by monitoring their rivals for seditious content and also asking readers to report infractions.[60] Now, a century later, history seems bent on repeating itself. Private activists have successfully "canceled" a wide variety of targets including former President Trump,[61] TV shows,[62] journalists,[63] books,[64] websites,[65] speakers,[66] and opinions.[67] And when they have not canceled voices outright, they have reduced their audience by manipulating search results[68] and cutting off access to credit card services[69] and servers.[70] Nor are the attacks limited to public targets: Indeed, activists have pressured employers into firing, among others, a short-order cook, a tile installer, and a real-estate agent.[71] Most alarmingly of all, media gatekeepers and social media companies systematically suppressed coverage of an influence-peddling scandal that threatened to derail Joe Biden's election.[72]

No surprise, then, that the Biden White House has both privately and publicly pressed social media to suppress "disinformation."[73] The problem, as President Wilson discovered, is that controlled speech is not believable. As in 1918, democracy needs an independent press not so much to say when the government is lying as when it is telling the truth. It follows that discrediting the press increases the costs of information to the point where some rational voters decide not to vote at all while others turn to marginal news outlets where "fake news" is common. Similarly, driving opposition speech from the biggest platforms drives social voters who oppose the president to whatever niche channels remain. This makes opposition viewpoints less predictable and sometimes more extreme.

If this were all, stronger antitrust laws would be a reasonable solution. But that would make *private* collective actions harder, even though these often address problems more efficiently than official solutions. The challenge for the courts is to find some way to make private initiatives acceptably democratic without telling them what to do.

Americans have experimented with private governments since the 1890s. Most of the early examples took place in the so-called shadow of hierarchy when government agencies ordered industries to self-regulate, or private groups "spontaneously" adopted codes to preempt government intervention. In both cases, the private entity's rules usually ended as watered-down (if sometimes more efficient) versions of what government would have imposed. Soon, however, private bodies found themselves regulating issues that formal government had ignored. In the nineteenth century this typically meant defining acceptable business behavior. Here the archetypal example was Underwriters Laboratories, which created and enforced a private safety code so that insurers could take on fire risks for clients and premises they had never seen. But since every business needs insurance, the private code soon acquired the force of law. And when legislatures did finally regulate safety, they took the private code for a model.[74]

The rub is that private collaboration can also mask antitrust violations. For example, companies could agree to standards that systematically disadvantaged their competitors' technologies, or else required members to pay license fees that helped maintain high prices for consumers.[75] The tension became acute during the Great Depression, when women's clothing suppliers tried to ban "unethical" competition and haul offenders into their own private court. The Supreme Court struck down the arrangement in an opinion that claimed to outlaw "private tribunals" entirely.[76] But this created its own confusion: Today there are hundreds of thousands of private standards bodies, and federal officials say they want more.[77] Which standards, then, should be targeted for antitrust scrutiny? Eighty years later, we still don't know.

In the meantime, private governance is undergoing a renaissance. Unlike earlier examples, the new standards are almost always organized and enforced by the purchasing power of large, consumer-facing retailers. Most are neurotically sensitive to consumer opinion and see self-regulation as a way to protect their brands. Moreover, the regulation is substantial: The compliance costs for private coffee, lumber, fishing, and apparel standards are often comparable to government regulation.[78]

The question remains how reliably corporations track public opinion. For now, the answer seems to be "not very." Even though consumers closely resemble the overall electorate,[79] data from the "2d Vote" Project[80] suggests that 80 percent of US corporations donate to at least one liberal cause compared to just 3 percent for conservative ones.[81] Some of this may reflect that Left's longer experience of organizing boycotts, although the recent experience of conservative backlash against transgender initiatives by Bud Light and Target shows that conservatives are rapidly closing this gap.[82] However, the fact that the disconnect is strongest for creative industries like entertainment, high tech, and finance suggests deeper reasons.[83] First, these industries almost always feature strong intellectual property and/or network effects that help insulate them from competition. This makes it easier to take stands their customers resent.[84] Second, creative employees need autonomy to work effectively. Unlike traditional corporate hierarchies, this often includes having a say in their company's politics; indeed, many employees would rather quit than sign a "no politics at work" pledge.[85] Finally, creative industries often recruit their employees from comparatively narrow class and educational backgrounds. The median views within these groups are then then further amplified inside the company as workers try to bond with one another in the usual conformist way.

At the same time, customers have become more militant.[86] As with cable television markets (Chapter 4), this suggests that other industries may soon cross the threshold where it becomes profitable to segment consumers by politics. If so, employees will likely amplify the trend by self-selecting into politically congenial employers in the same way that conservative television journalists currently gravitate to Fox.

But if private – and politicized – governance is the wave of the future, what should courts do about it? It is no answer to say that private entities can do what they like. Indeed, the US Supreme Court has said that core government functions must respect civil rights no matter who performs them.[87] It follows that private collective action that includes unwilling members must similarly meet certain minimal standards. In practice, American courts typically insist that organizations follow written rules, though they need not be as elaborate as government ones. Enforcement must also be sufficiently transparent for outsiders, including judges, to confirm that the asserted reasons for private action are more than just pretextual.[88] At the same time, courts almost always defer to private rulings except where bodies violate their own rules,[89] or some announced public policy.[90] The question is whether Congress should force some larger intervention. Probably the most common proposal would be for legislators to pass a statute requiring platforms to permit all speech that the government itself must tolerate.[91] Judges would then be required to to rule on particular acts of private censorship and speech, just as they currently do for government.

Finally, politics also extends to illegal actions like civil disobedience and rioting. Indeed, these tactics can be disproportionately effective politically. One reason is informational. So long as violence is rare, rioting lets activists *create* newsworthiness for media companies that would never cover their causes otherwise. Then too, violence evidences intensity and, since viewers' brains preferentially respond to emotion, is inherently eye-catching. Granted that rioters represent perhaps one in ten thousand citizens,[92] Downsian politicians often see their anger as a clue that more typical voters also feel strongly. Finally, the ability of small groups to create permanent trouble in the streets changes the government's political calculus.[93] Granted that politicians can always put down the violence by force, doing so tests their sincerity much more than the "parchment act" of passing a bill.[94]

At the same time, violence is an inherently unreliable guide to public opinion: Instead of sincerity, it may often show nothing more than good organization. Worse, the feasibility of violence changes with time. Since people cannot riot alone, it follows that they will not even attempt violence unless they expect others to join them. This can deter violence even when anger is high. But after the first riot, this barrier is abruptly diminished. This makes violence easier to organize even when the anger is no greater than before. Then too, rioters' motives may only be secondarily political. There is good evidence that bored young men enjoy brawling, even for such apolitical causes as European soccer rivalries.[95] The forced inactivity of COVID-19 lockdowns greatly inflated this demographic and was almost certainly causal in the George Floyd riots of 2020.

## 9.4 FEEDBACKS

Rule of law provides the foundation for everything else in Madison's system. But the concept itself is far from obvious. For judges there is the puzzle of how to maintain a body that possesses "neither Force nor Will." For everyone else, there is the related problem of why Americans should believe that judges have truly achieved this status, and therefore defer to them. Both problems become especially acute in eras of polarized opinion and coercive politics, when the incentive for judges to "legislate from the bench" is at its highest.[96]

We have argued that neutral judging is rooted in judges' desire for promotion, which in practice means giving their audience – nearly always practicing lawyers – predictability. But predictability can be achieved in many different ways, ranging from "originalist" legal reasoning, to "common sense" policy arguments, to nakedly partisan outcomes, and this mix is constantly changing. The silver lining is that the changeovers tend to occur slowly, moderated by judges' lifetime appointments.

Yet when judicial activism does become more common the consequences can quickly ripple across Madison's system. Now, new legislation settles nothing, but only initiates a long series of court actions and still more jitter. This, in turn, stokes further polarization and anger. Finally, judicial activism makes statutes less predictable so that legislators become more reluctant to pass new laws in the first. At this point judicial activism and legislative gridlock can start to reinforce each other in an endless cycle.

Meanwhile, the fragility of courts also makes them vulnerable. In bipartisan times most politicians refrain from making threats for fear of outraging voters. However, this deterrent fades in polarized eras when partisans praise almost any tactic that furthers their party's policies. And since threats *do* influence some courts, we expect the most extreme politicians to make them, followed by still more politicians if the threats succeed. In the end, the practice could become so common that voters do not even try to punish offenders at the next election. Political restraint will then disappear entirely, leaving the law still more fluid and unpredictable than it was before.

But this is not the only danger. Instead, events can also evolve in the other direction, with courts seizing control of issues originally committed to lawmakers. This is especially tempting in eras of gridlock, when judge-made law can sometimes step in to reify consensus around issues like desegregation and gay marriage and remove them from politics. Even so, the cost is high. Once the Supreme Court starts intervening, senators have every right to question prospective justices about their politics. Then too, each decision to recognize some new right depends on a *political* estimate that the public will accept it. Yet the Court has no special instinct for politics, and when public opposition does not collapse a controversial ruling can actually *exacerbate* public anger.

Widespread polarization also encourages more coercion by private organizations. Yet the injuries and anger from private coercion are no less real than the public kind. Worse, private power typically confers outsized influence on such comparatively narrow slices of the population as billionaires, tech workers, and customers who buy athletic shoes. While these effects were traditionally limited by competition (and antitrust law), the rise of Silicon Valley since the 1980s has made monopoly power vastly more common than it was at mid-century. The situation becomes even worse when elected officials urge private firms to take on tasks like censorship that the Constitution prevents them from doing directly. In either case, private efforts to slant news and "cancel" political enemies cannot help stoking new anger and resentments.

Finally, the executive branch can seize dangerous if sometimes necessary power in emergencies where Congress has no chance (or sometimes, desire) to speak. Here the president must fill this gap as she sees fit, limited only by the raw politics of her own popularity and the possibility of being blamed later. The fear, especially in coercive politics eras, is that the "emergency" will never end. This makes the Supreme Court the last line of defense against a Weimar-style politics of endlessly renewed "emergency" powers.

## Notes

1 *Federalist* No. 44 at p. 208 (Madison).
2 *Federalist* No. 78 at p. 354 (Hamilton) (emphasis original).
3 Levenson (1982) at pp. 379 and 380.
4 Levenson (1982) at p. 384 (In law, not even "radical critics defend the position that any interpretation is as good as any other"); Armstrong makes a similar point for literary criticism; Armstrong (2013) at p. 9.
5 Posner (2008) at p. 13.
6 *Federalist* No. 22 at p. 98 (Hamilton) and No. 50 at p. 235 (Madison).
7 Ely (1973) at p. 946.
8 See Dworkin (1996) at pp. 160–1.
9 See Chapter 3, Part B.
10 Profs. Epstein, Landes, and Posner show that judges respond to various incentives including private satisfaction from having "done a good job," "reputation, prestige, power, influence, and celebrity," and the possibility of promotion to a higher court or lucrative private-sector job. Epstein, Landes, and Posner (2013) at p. 48.
11 The argument assumes that the same lawyers simultaneously write contracts and appear before judges. While this is not always true for individual lawyers, most law firms do both.
12 See Posner (2008) at pp. 42–4 and 49–50 (reporting that many judges decide cases according to formalist ideals).
13 See, e.g., Chen, Frankenreiter, and Yeh (2016) (finding that US federal lower court cases filed after higher court decisions are 29–37 percent more likely to rule the same way as the appellate court).
14 Severino (2019).
15 Jackson (2008) at pp. 228–35.
16 Economists have also found solutions where members' opinions oscillate indefinitely. However, this only happens in the relatively special case where every path leading from Alice back to herself has the same length. See Jackson (2008) at pp. 230–3. This is unlikely for real court systems, where the order in which different judges decide legal questions is almost entirely random.
17 One of the most spectacular examples derives from antitrust law, where litigants stopped writing contracts authorized by the Supreme Court's decision in *United States* v. *General Electric Co.*, 272 U.S. 476 (1926), even though the Court has twice declined to overrule it since. Weinschel (2000).
18 Law students sometimes wonder why the middle third of their antitrust textbooks consists entirely of cases decided in the 1940s. The reason is the Roosevelt Administration, which saw the "little Depression" of 1937 as evidence that monopolies were strangling the economy. FDR responded by expanding the Justice Department's Anti-Trust Division from a few dozen lawyers to nearly three hundred. The statute's reach expanded dramatically over the next decade. Kennedy (1999) at p. 359.
19 The estimate assumes that each judge decides independently. In practice judges influence each other, so that panels probably reach consensus somewhat faster than our estimates suggest.

20 *Kimble* v. *Marvel Entertainment LLC*, 576 US 446 (2015) at p. 455.

21 As Judge Posner points out, courts are loath to abandon "even patently erroneous interpretations." See Posner (1989) at p. 251. By comparison, the US Supreme Court is willing to revisit existing rules based on their "workability ... the antiquity of the precedent, the reliance interests at stake, and ... whether the decision was well reasoned." This is particularly true for bad constitutional precedents, which only the Court can correct. See generally Mead (2012) at pp. 789–91.

22 Carty (1981) at p. 68.

23 See, e.g., *Federalist* No. 78 at p. 356 (Hamilton).

24 *Marbury* v. *Madison*, 5 U.S. 137 (1803).

25 Brands (2018) at p. 74.

26 The idea that states would decide, and if necessary enforce, the constitutionality of federal actions is most prominently associated with US Senator John C. Calhoun. Brands (2018) at p. 150. The reliably combative Andrew Jackson similarly denied that he was bound by the Supreme Court's rulings, arguing that "Each public officer who takes an oath to support the Constitution swears that he will support it as he understands it, and not as it is understood by others ... The opinion of the judges has no more authority over Congress than the opinion of Congress has over the judges, and on that point the President is independent of both." Meacham (2008) at p. 271. A shadow of Jackson's doctrine persists in "presidential signing statements," which sometimes declare that new legislation is partly unconstitutional, and that the president plans to ignore or interpret the defective parts in ways that avoid the infirmity. Woolley and Peters (n.d.).

27 *Federalist* No. 78 at p. 355 (Hamilton).

28 *Ex Parte Merryman*, 17 F. Cas. 144 (C.C.D. Md. 1861); Guelzo (2021b) at p. 479.

29 *Korematsu* v. *United States*, 323 U.S. 214 (1944).

30 Historian Bruce Catton argued that Lincoln's behavior, though unconstitutional, was nevertheless the only way to save the Union so that his actions "somehow corresponded with what most of the people dimly wanted." Catton [1961] at p. 361.

31 Breyer (2013).

32 *Obergefell* v. *Hodges*, 576 US 644.

33 This was exemplified by the court's futile plea urging both sides "to end their national division." *Planned Parenthood* v. *Casey*, 505 U.S. 833 (1992). A plea that asked one side to accept defeat was probably doomed from the outset.

34 Jefferson expanded the lower courts to put in his supporters, but refused to pack the Supreme Court itself. Grant increased the Court from seven members to nine, and was later accused of court packing when the new members reversed a politically controversial case decided the previous year. Hofstadter (1969) at pp. 163–4; Rehnquist (2004) at pp. 102–3.

35 Hofstadter (1969) at pp. 163–4.

36 Hamburger (2021).

37 Roy (2012).

38  See, e.g., Walsh (2020) (Senator Schumer on abortion rights); Anon (2021c) (Senator Whitehouse on gun control).

39  The 2016 Clinton–Trump debates, in which neither candidate even pretended that they would nominate justices without regard to ideology, marked an important sea change in this regard. Bobelian (2016).

40  For a comprehensive list of the various cases and their outcomes, see Danforth et al. (2020).

41  Courts normally argue that judicial economy outweighs any possible errors from forgoing a trial, and for private suits they may be right. The difference in a disputed presidential election is that the issues are so much greater. Holding a trial would have put the president's team to their proof, and (assuming Trump lost) allowed centrists and most conservatives to move on. We have a hint of this missed opportunity in the Michigan State Senate Republicans' report on the election, which methodically examines the evidence for each charge before finding "no evidence of widespread or systemic fraud." Michigan Senate Oversight Committee (2021).

42  Wikipedia (43).

43  Wikipedia (54).

44  Some courts also refused to hear challenges on the ground that President Trump should have brought them earlier. Even assuming that these refusals were justified, future presidents are unlikely to make the same mistake.

45  *Rucho v. Common Cause*, 139 S. Ct. 2484, 2508 (2019).

46  *Gilligan v. Morgan*, 413 U.S. 1, 10 (1973) (Constitution's text "commits" certain issues to "the political branches of government").

47  *Juliana v. United States*, 947 F.3d 1159 (9th Cir. 2020).

48  See, e.g., *Spallone v. United States*, 493 U.S. 265, 277–80 (1990) and cases cited therein.

49  Jefferson (1787b) at p. 213. Lincoln, who knew the hardships of small-scale farming at first hand, loathed such sentimentality. Guelzo (2015).

50  Letwin (1956) at p. 226. Several state constitutions (and very nearly the US Bill of Rights) banned all of these privileges outright. Letwin (1956).

51  See, e.g., Brands (2018) at p. 189 and Meacham (2008) at p. 268.

52  Meacham (2008) at pp. 347 and 358.

53  Meacham (2008) at p. 228, 349, and 352. See also Letwin (1956) at p. 228 (quoting Missouri Senator Thomas Hart Benton).

54  Hofstadter (1964a) at p. 667.

55  Hofstadter (1964a) at p. 665.

56  *United States v. Columbia Steel Co.*, 334 US 495, 535–6 (1948) (Douglas dissenting).

57  Hofstadter (1955) at pp. 227, 229, and 284.

58  Varian and Shapiro (1999) at p. 179.

59  Barry (2005) at p. 206; Trickey (2018); and Vaughn (1980) at p. 342.

60  Vaughn (1980) at p. 342.

61  Kessler (2021). Meta later reversed the ban in February 2023, though only after Republicans had retaken the House and begun holding hearings to investigate private censorship. Bond (2023).

62  Flint (2020).

63  Malenga (2021).
64  Pollack (2021).
65  Palmer (2021); Gray (2020).
66  Bokhari (2020a); Bokhari (2020b).
67  Wikipedia (38) (Wikipedia bans user descriptions voicing opposition to gay marriage).
68  Wells and Lovett (2018).
69  Andriottis, Rudigeair, and Glazer (2021).
70  Palmer (2021).
71  Rall (2021). The attacks are, for the moment at least, more common on the Left than the Right. Nearly one-third (31 percent) of all Americans would support firing a business executive who voted for Donald Trump, and this number rises to 50 percent for strong liberals. Meanwhile, only 22 percent would feel the same way about a Joe Biden donor, rising to just over one-third (36 percent) for strong conservatives. Ekins (2020).
72  Jenkins (2022b).
73  The Biden White House privately "flagged" what it saw as COVID-19 disinformation for Facebook to consider. Nelson (2021). This was followed up by what company employees called "tough questions" about why journalist Alex Berenson "hasn't been kicked off from the platform." Ramaswamy and Rubenfeld (2022). CEO Marc Zuckerberg has similarly admitted that he limited Facebook's coverage of a corruption scandal involving then-candidate Biden's son based on an FBI warning that it might be "foreign interference." Romero and Goggin (2022).
74  Maurer (2017b) at pp. 11–19.
75  For full technical details, see Maurer and Scotchmer (2015).
76  *Fashion Originators' Guild of America* v. FTC, 312 U.S. 457 (1941).
77  Maurer (2017b) at p. 165.
78  Maurer (2017b) at pp. 23–47 and 69.
79  The numbers of consumers actively boycotting companies in 2020 were evenly divided between Democrats and Republicans, pro- and anti-maskers, and pro- and anti-Black Lives Matter (BLM) supporters. Holmes (2020). Like voting, willingness to boycott also increases with income, possibly because rich consumers spend proportionally less on necessities: 53 percent of households earning more than $100,000 are currently boycotting at least one company compared to just 28 percent earning below $25,000. Holmes (2020).
80  2d Vote (n.d.). All quoted statistics refer to a random sample of 144 name-brand companies performed by the author in September 2020.
81  The percentage doubles if we include the special case of sporting goods firms that support gun rights.
82  Consumers only join boycotts when there is a reasonable chance that other consumers will participate. This is a comparatively low bar for liberals, who have organized a long string of successful boycotts going back to the 1950s. Maatman (1981) at p. 219.
83  On a scale where 5.0 is strongly conservative and 1.0 strongly liberal, the most reliably liberal corporate donors are found in Communications (1.61),

Entertainment (1.46), Automobiles (1.56), Internet Travel Sites (1.72), and Finance (1.5). Traditional businesses like Restaurants (2.76), Retailers (2.17), Retail Clothing (2.53), Airlines (2.79), Cheap Motels (2.7), Convenience Stores (3.0), Oil Companies (2.43), Retail Clothing (2.54), Grocery Stores (2.70), and Food Producers (2.63) are markedly more centrist. See 2d Vote (2021).

84 Palmer (2021) (describing how employees pressured Amazon to stop hosting Parler's minimally moderated discussion site).

85 See, e.g., Murphy (2020); Newton (2021).

86 About half of Generation Z (51 percent) and Millennials (52 percent) are currently boycotting at least one company compared to one-fifth of Baby Boomers (22 percent) and Silent Generation members (16 percent); Holmes (2020).

87 *Marsh v. Alabama* 326 U.S. 501 (1946).

88 Maurer (2017b) at p. 177.

89 In practice, this requires organizations to draft articulable and nondiscriminatory rules, adopt them by majority rule, avoid arbitrary enforcement, and include such basic procedural protections as giving participants fair notice and an opportunity to comment. The requirements are generally stiffer where the accused has important interests at stake. Maurer (2017b) at pp. 166–77.

90 Maurer (2017b) at p. 167.

91 Montgomery (2020).

92 Even France, with its rich tradition of romantic revolution, probably hosts fewer than 3,000 hard right extremists in all. Décugis, Guéna, and Leplongeon (2021) at p. 5. It is reasonable to think that the American appetite for political violence is even thinner. For example, nonpolitical murders occur at a rate of roughly one one-hundredth of 1 percent per person per year. By comparison, the rate for presidential assassinations is perhaps one every fifty years, which is only two hundred times higher. This suggests that partisans who feel as strongly about politics as everyday life are extraordinarily rare.

93 Prominent American examples include race riots in 1967 and nearly continuous Antifa and BLM rioting for much of 2020.

94 Andrew Bonar-Law, later British prime minister, warned Parliament in 1912 that it could pass any laws it liked for Ireland, but that if Northern Ireland rejected them "there are stronger influences than parliamentary majorities." No government, he added, "would dare to use their troops to drive them out." A government that tried "would run a greater risk of being lynched in London than the loyalists of Ulster would run of being shot in Belfast." Coogan [1993] at p. 45.

95 British soccer hooligans in the 1980s and 1990s routinely traveled long distances – sometimes overseas – just to fight with each other and the police. Like Antifa, they would routinely show up by the hundreds, execute elaborate preplanned street tactics, inflict life-threatening injuries, and get arrested. Whatever their political views, their principal motivations were boredom, lack of regular jobs to absorb their energies, and a love of

street-fighting. Bufford (1993). Small wonder, then, that European soccer hooligans and Neo-Nazi brawlers often turn out to be the same people. See, e.g., Anon (n.d. (d)); Anon (2020i). Etahad (2020) similarly describes how Antifa grew out of a Seattle punk rock scene where politics was originally quite secondary.

96  The number of high-profile, nationwide injunctions rose sharply following President Obama's "phone and pen" governance in 2014. They increased still further with the wave of challenges that met President Trump's policies in 2017. Anon (2021e).

# 10

# Democracy Evolving

## *The Future of American Politics*

We like to imagine the Framers as infallible, or nearly so. But Madison knew that the Ancient republics had repeatedly fallen for bad ideas, and only hoped that the Constitution's various frictions would give Americans time to repent. Still, this was largely a matter of chance and there was no guarantee that The People would regain their sobriety fast enough. Though the Framers never say so, their system was living on borrowed time.

Perfection is still out of reach today. That said, the Framers would want us to take stock and do better where we can. Moreover, they left many important details about conducting elections, structuring the courts, and debating legislation for Congress and the states to fill in afterward.[1] More than two centuries later, Americans know much more about what works and ought to be made permanent. We begin this chapter by reviewing the most important examples and argue that it is past time that we wrote them into the Constitution. Indeed, the greater danger comes from opportunists who might seek to change them to win this or that policy fight. We should put the temptation out of reach. The rest of the chapter turns to deeper issues. This book has paid special attention to the interactions and feedbacks that made the country's slide from bipartisanship into coercive politics possible. Our goal should be to fix enough problems so that the slide toward coercive politics can begin to reverse itself. We suggest modest changes to do this. We end by addressing the Constitution's biggest design defect – the Framers' failure to invent institutional checks and balances for debates that drag on for decades. For concreteness, we focus on the polarizing topics of race, climate change, and COVID-19. If Madison's system can meet these challenges, the rest will be easy.

## 10.1 THE STORY SO FAR

Earlier chapters have divided the US political system into sectors and explored how each interacts with and amplifies the others. This lets us summarize the country's recent political history as a sort of fable:

At some point in the early twenty-first century, many Americans became receptive to political rhetoric promising large changes over the existing order. Just why this happened is unclear. However, the causes probably included a long period of peace and prosperity, the financial crisis of 2007, and the rise of monopolies which made it easier to blame individual villains than anonymous market forces. Soon, the country's conservative and liberal narratives began to diverge so that each side knew less and less about the other. This encouraged voters to believe that "the other side" was not just mistaken, but stupid or dishonest. In principle, some new unifying ideology could have rescued the situation. But none emerged.

America's private institutions accelerated the confrontation. On the one hand, the big media companies discovered that they could segment the market – and increase their revenue – by targeting narrow audiences. This segmentation quickly reached the point where some outlets suppressed important stories entirely. Meanwhile, the major political parties lost their old instinct for moderation. By the early 2000s politicians in many parts of the country saw that there were enough extremist voters on the left and right to get elected on a purely negative promise to block one's opponents. This led to a new politics in which gridlock dragged on indefinitely. Worse, the polarization was geographic. This reawakened the old nineteenth-century nightmare of regional parties, though this time between "The Coasts" and "Flyover Country."

The new politics hit Madison's institutions hard. Deadlock in Congress ensured that both parties now repeated the same complaints year after year, endlessly stoking voters' resentments. Polarization was aggravated still further when a congresswoman from one of the country's most reliably Progressive districts became House Speaker in 2007. Though in some sense accidental, the event was made enormously more likely by a combination of House seniority rules, a reliably safe district, and rich donors. Thereafter, Speaker Pelosi used her power to control which bills reached the floor to promote legislation that pleased her San Francisco constituents far more than the average Democrat. This further polarized elections, convincing Progressives that they could finally effect permanent changes to American life. But it also deprived centrist voters of congenial choices, so that their support veered from Obama's Progressivism to Trump's "Make America Great Again" to Biden's still more extreme Progressivism.

And when legislation did pass, other extremists vowed to "repeal and replace" it. Ten years after its passage, President Obama's Affordable Care Act should have been old news. Instead, it was constantly rehashed, so that resentments never faded. The irony, never far from the surface, was that a centrist candidate would have handily won the White House. But voters never got that choice. Instead, Democrat and Republican extremists found themselves locked in a weird codependency that allowed each side to nominate weak candidates simply because the other did.

The good news was that the situation was palpably unstable. Sooner or later one party would break the impasse by offering a centrist candidate. The only question was how much damage overheated partisanship could do in the meantime. Madison's system had always depended on Americans' willingness to settle disputes according to the Constitution's rules. But now the rules were being stretched and ignored. This was mainly visible in presidents' increasing use of executive orders which were later reversed in court or rewritten after the next election. The result was that the old issues were constantly rehearsed so that polarization grew year after year…

Like Madison, this book has emphasized institutional design, less for its power – though there is good evidence for that – than because it is the only policy lever we have. The question now is how effectively Madison's institutions have delayed the slide toward coercive politics, and what reform can do to promote a return to bipartisanship. We should approach the project with optimism: America's long periods of centrist politics show that bipartisan regimes, once established, tend to stay that way. Yet we also know that politics since the 1990s has become increasingly unstable, suggesting that coercive politics, once established, is also self-sustaining. The question is how much sensible reforms can do to destabilize coercive regimes, and promote bipartisan ones.

## 10.2 FIXES (1): ROUTINE MAINTENANCE AND MODEST REFORMS

We begin with the good news. The Framers' machinery still works for the short-term fevers it was designed to manage. Here, the Constitution's main weakness is that it left so many items for Congress and the states to fill in. This tentativeness was surely wise at the time. The difference today is that we have enormously more experience in what works and what doesn't. What would have been adventurous or reckless for Madison should be routine maintenance for us. All the same, the maintenance is not just necessary but overdue. It is dangerous to leave the de facto Constitution's ground rules – most notably, the filibuster, the nine-member Supreme Court, and the principle of winner-take-all elections – to statute or custom. Too many extremists see Madison's safeguards as the last barrier to recasting society in their preferred dream image. Rules that are constitutionally important in shaping outcomes should likewise be constitutional in law.

*External politics.* Democracy requires that at least some voters think for themselves. But imperfect information dominates Downsian theory, and most voters will never make more than tiny investments in information.

There is, however, one towering exception: For the first few years of our lives, the state dictates how much we learn. It follows that K-12 education provides the greatest opportunity to improve voting. Before World War II, children were usually taught the kinds of facts that rational voters would want to know. Since then, however, the emphasis has shifted toward teaching the mainstream viewpoints that social voters care about. That was not all bad: We have said that pattern recognition requires practice, and a suitably socialized child should be able to anticipate (and tolerate) most narratives and ideologies. At the same time, we have argued that the public's short window for learning and remembering facts leads to shallow opinions and wild reversals. It follows that a return to teaching more facts would help to stabilize our politics. And to the extent that schools do continue to teach narratives and ideologies, teachers should approach the most common views impartially, without elevating any one of them above the others.

*Elections.* From the start, American democracy depended on *both* the internal politics of Madison's institutions *and* the external politics of citizen debate and mass political parties. But while the first sector was carefully planned, the second grew up without much guidance beyond a competitive pressure to please the public. Still, there was one place where explicit design was unavoidable. Somehow, citizens' opinions – votes – had to be converted into seats in Congress. And here evolution took a wrong turn. Starting in the early nineteenth century, legislators and judges lost themselves in a legal kudzu of geometric criteria like "compactness" and "contiguity." Whatever its faults, the Supreme Court's *Rucho* decision was right to call off the quest. The question now is whether Congress and the courts can replace the old geometric rules with something better. Here, the principle of one-man-one-vote has worked well since the 1960s, but remains incomplete. We have argued that a coherent approach to districting will require a second principle of community and, ideally, a third principle codifying the traditional American system of "winner-take-all" elections.

The devil will be in the details. We show in the Appendix how the principle of community can generate unambiguous congressional maps. But this is just one possible implementation, and the US Supreme Court's traditional deference would almost certainly let state legislatures choose from a range of variants. The simplest possibility would be an algorithm that generates maps based on voters' physical locations alone. But states could equally add factors that the Court has recognized in the past like limiting the rate at which existing districts change, enhancing minority representation, or even giving future legislatures the power to make limited adjustments to algorithmically drawn maps as they see fit. Finally, our social voter theory suggests that the dominant voices in each electoral district should belong to the community itself. This implies that limits on how much outside donors can donate to state and local races should be constitutional.[2]

The third, "winner-take-all" principle is potentially the most controversial. As the Supreme Court pointed out in *Rucho*, calls for electoral "fairness" nearly always display a "gravitational" attraction toward proportional representation.[3] This was not particularly dangerous at mid-century, when Americans still remembered how proportional representation had wrecked Germany's Weimar Republic. But today only specialists know the story. Enshrining winner-take-all in the Constitution would not necessarily imply that proportional representation is a bad principle – indeed, most Europeans prefer it – but only that casual or unthinking change would alter the American system in large and unpredictable ways.[4]

Still other reforms could fine-tune the system. We have argued that well-designed institutions should pay attention to voter intensity. This implies that people who come out to vote should be better informed and/or feel more passionately than those who do not. From this standpoint, modern "get out the vote" campaigns that systematically mobilize partisans who would never vote otherwise offer the worst of all worlds: inflating the number of extreme viewpoints relative to centrists, depressing average voter knowledge, and diluting the votes of people who feel strongly compared to the mostly indifferent. Given that we cannot uninvent the tactic, the best we can hope for is make it nondistortionary. Mandatory voting is by far the simplest and most straightforward way to do this.

The idea is not new: Australia has fined nonvoters for almost a century. During this time turnout has never fallen below 90 percent,[5] far above the American rate. Meanwhile, academics confirm that the provision has indeed suppressed Downsian incentives to inflame the electorate through fiery "appeals to the base."[6] In the short term, at least, mandatory voting is probably the most important step the US could take to push Madison's political system back into its usual, bipartisan state. Surveys show that fully two-thirds (67 percent) of the American population remains squarely centrist.[7] These numbers would almost certainly ensure a centrist national politics if they did not include a very large, low-intensity "politically disengaged" population (26 percent) that seldom votes.[8] Mandatory voting would immediately shift the balance against extremists on both sides, although there are no guarantees that American politics would not eventually recross the threshold if polarization continues to grow.

Finally, American federalism still makes sense. Our divisions have always contained a large regional component and still do. Meanwhile the Electoral College continues to fulfill its historic function by ensuring that presidential races are decided in centrist "battleground" states. This makes it hard to elect presidents who enrage large parts of the country.

*The media.* America has traditionally relied on the invisible hand of markets to rein in publishers, politicians, and advertisers. Yet private suppression and slanted coverage have reached alarming levels. There is probably little to be done about slanting, which is practically inevitable once Hotelling strategies become profitable. Suppression, on the other hand, requires cartel members to possess sufficient monopoly power to ignore market signals. Here the simplest prescription is to reinvigorate the antitrust laws throughout the economy. Among other things, the problem of billionaires buying up newspapers will be less noticeable when there are fewer billionaires. Conversely, recent proposals to prop up newspapers by *exempting* them from the Sherman Act seem spectacularly short-sighted.[9]

Government subsidies, though controversial, are also worth considering. Here the main question is whether voters would consume appreciably more political news if the price fell to zero. Econometric studies should have no difficulty determining this. Additionally, subsidies should not depend on content or viewpoint. This could most easily be done by scaling support based on each outlet's total circulation.

The most difficult questions concern search engines and social media platforms. Politicians often say that the dominant platforms should be broken up, and this reliably pleases constituents. But social media companies are monopolists for a reason: Consumers derive more benefit from joining one large platform than several small ones. The problem is to introduce competition while still preserving the benefits of one-stop shopping. In the spirit of "first, do no harm," Congress would be wise to try less intrusive interventions, leaving divestiture is a last resort. One obvious possibility is to require more transparency from platforms that restrict speech. While almost all platforms claim to censor based on published guidelines, these are frequently vague and companies often refuse to explain their application in specific cases. This makes it hard to tell how much speech is suppressed, or why.[10] Requiring platforms to generate an automated record each time they suppress speech and specify the in-house rule(s) they purportedly relied on would go a long way toward fixing this. Making the full archive of censored posts available to regulators, congressmen, and scholars would then encourage rival platforms to compete over which company offered the best moderation. Whether this would reduce censorship is unclear, but Silicon Valley monopolies have often changed behaviors to preempt seemingly minor competitive threats in the past.

A second possibility is to impose open standards on large platforms so that users can seamlessly access content from rival sites. Many digital products like games and word processing already operate under shared standards that let providers "interoperate." Here the main danger is that forced openness could impair the intellectual property incentives needed to fund other inventions going forward. This can be a strong objection where judges decide with twenty–twenty hindsight that a particular invention was obvious and for that reason deserves only a small reward. But Google and Facebook are not close cases: Indeed, it seems obvious that their founders never dreamed how rich they would be. Then too, forced openness is unlikely to deter future investments so long as markets view it as a one-time event that is unlikely to be repeated.[11]

Finally, we have seen that libel law provides a powerful lever against abusive publishers. Congress could readily reinstate this sanction by making platforms that censor content subject to defamation actions.[12] Alternatively, Congress could simply extend First Amendment protections to all speech posted on social media sites, or else require companies to deanonymize users so that they could identify and sue each other directly.[13]

*Political parties.* American elections give voters just two choices on any issue, and we have seen that this is not always enough. When one party nominates a weak candidate, the resulting landslide eliminates choice entirely. It is easy to complain that the modern emphasis on primaries is too random, and that professional politicians who know more and only care about winning elections should have more influence. Yet our "nobody knows anything" principle suggests that these human experts can make mistakes too. Then too, the natural tendency of politicians to trade favors makes it hard for newcomers to win no matter how strong they are as candidates.[14] For now, we should be reluctant to legislate and hope instead that competition will encourage one or both parties to try incremental reforms.

*The Congress.* Madison's "checks and balances" act mostly as frictions that slow all new legislation indiscriminately. The filibuster filled this gap by blocking majority tyranny for the most intensely felt issues. However, its status as a simple legislative rule made it a perpetual target for tinkering. A run of good luck in the rule's first century led to the supremely functional "talking filibuster" from 1917 to 1975. Since then, changes designed to save senators political pain and personal inconvenience have steadily degraded the rule. This was and is quixotic: the idea of substituting politicians' personal discomfort for the public's offers large savings. Possible sanctions could include suspending members' salary,[15] pension contributions, medical benefits, and nonessential travel[16] until the filibuster ends. More draconian measures would increase the pressure still further by fining members or extending sanctions to include their staff. The deeper reform would be to change Senate rules to restore some version of the talking filibuster. Yet this, too, would only be a half-measure: Leaving the filibuster as a lowly procedural rule will merely invite more attacks the next time extremists use some transient majority to try to remake the country. A constitutional amendment would put this temptation firmly out of reach.

Congress would also work better if members had more opportunities to vote on centrist choices. The trouble for now is that representatives have given leadership the power to block votes to "protect" them against having to go on record for controversial legislation. The situation would be much improved if party discipline could be turned off whenever centrists in both parties had the votes to pass bipartisan legislation. This will not stop the politics of blockade if extremists ever command a majority of the whole House. But it will at least delay its onset, and accelerate the return to bipartisanship. The House "Problem Solvers Caucus" has long proposed rule changes to do this.[17] The practical political obstacle is that the change would weaken the dominant factions within each party, who can be counted on to resist unless and until the public demands reform.

A second reform concerns debate. Under the Constitution neither chamber can adjourn for more than three days without the other's consent. Since this is hard to change, leadership often uses the fixed date to rush through bills at the last moment, giving members no time to assert their rights or even read what they have been asked to vote for.[18] The result is a forced choice in which members must either take the bill as is, or vote it down. This could easily be remedied by guaranteeing a fixed period for debate, possibly increasing in proportion to the proposed legislation's word count, before any final vote.

*The executive.* The Republic's most dangerous moments have almost always come when Congress has not spoken and the president must act. The question remains how to restart the rule of law once it is interrupted. The Declaration of War clause was an early and ultimately incoherent attempt to force the president to consult Congress before starting hostilities. But hostilities have a way of starting on their own, and the political impossibility of undeclaring wars afterward has made the clause a dead letter. Even so, the instinct was sound: Hostilities are very much a special case, and many crises (e.g. COVID-19) do not involve armed conflict. This makes it sensible to insist that Congress vote to affirm any emergency power that the president chooses to assert within some reasonable time. Lest Congress simply ignore the requirement, practical legislation should also require a vote whenever some substantial number of members – say one-third of the body – demand it.

A second set of reforms should address Big Government's dangerous romance with secrets. Probably the simplest reform would be to create a separate agency to hear Freedom of Information Act (FOIA) claims with an institutional mission to declassify as much as possible. Agencies found to have indulged in bad faith might also be required to pay citizens' litigation costs out of their operating budgets, so that stonewalling became less attractive in the first place.

Finally, we should ask what can be done to reinvigorate the rule of law. Washington's recent culture of leaks suggests that it is not enough to have strong punishments on the books: Leaking was and is a felony.[19] The problem instead is that enforcement is no longer credible. If there are laws there need to be prosecutions; if there are "unwritten exceptions" Congress should make them explicit. This suggests that smaller but more certain punishments could actually improve enforcement. Against this, one might object that such reforms would only be superficial, relying on fear without doing anything to change what bureaucrats feel in their hearts. Here, the silver lining is that no government worker really knows how much their colleagues' respect for norms reflects sincerity as opposed to fear. This means that, even if the sanctions were later lifted, bureaucrats would have no way of knowing how many of their colleagues preferred the new regime, and were ready to punish anyone who reverted to the old ways by withholding favors. In this way, a long period of increased enforcement could improve the underlying culture as well.

*The judiciary.* Madison's system requires judges to interpret the law as written. We have argued that judges can, in fact, do this. But this is only one possible outcome, and there are others. If the rule of law does fail, there will be nothing to keep policies from jittering back and forth after each election. And the accompanying political debate will become perpetual so that polarization never ends.

The supposedly realist course of nominating right-leaning judges to counter a left-leaning bench and vice versa cannot fix this. Indeed, it can only end in two outcomes: dictatorship by one side or violent alternations in policy. The principled solution is to make it clear when judges deviate from what most lawyers see as the correct legal answer, and encourage the legal community to vote for or against judges on that basis. In the American system correct legal judgments typically reflect a mélange of precedent, principles so widely agreed as to be "outside politics," and partisanship. We have argued that these criteria can nevertheless produce reasonably predictable results. The trouble is that the lay public is ill-equipped to decide when a particular judge has jettisoned these principles in favor of personal preferences. More transparent records that let the public know, for example, how often judges are overruled on appeal would go some distance to fixing this.

The law of standing is also troubled. When a sitting president like Donald Trump wants to challenge an election, he should be heard. At the same time, eliminating the requirement so that any citizen could sue would swamp the courts and – since legal interpretation is to some extent always probabilistic – invalidate so many statutes that Congress would become even less efficient than it is today. The better solution is to tie challenges to an estimate of when some large fraction of the country objects. This could be done by specifying that any challenge endorsed by one-third of the House or Senate would receive a full trial on the merits. The fraction is of course arbitrary, though using the old filibuster threshold would provide some assurance that it was high enough to deter Congress's more incorrigible complainers.

An even more obvious reform would be to fast-track challenges to federal authority ahead of other court business. In the American system this would probably mean granting the US Supreme Court original jurisdiction to hear and decide some cases from the outset. The downside of this kind of fast-tracking is that the Court is more likely to be intimidated if the case is heard while whatever emergency raised the issue is still ongoing. But this would still be better than the current system where challenges take years during which time government policy remains in limbo.[20]

Finally, much of the Supreme Court's authority – how many justices sit on it, what cases they hear, and how long they can sit on the court – is set by statute. This invites Congress to threaten the court in an attempt to influence rulings. But if we believe that law has meaning, at least probabilistically, we should let judges do their job, impeaching them only when there is evidence that they have violated this trust. The nine-member court has been with us since 1869: There is no great risk in amending the Constitution to put it beyond the threat of politically motivated revisions.

Our commitment to democracy should depend on substance rather than labels. This means that collective action should respect basic democratic procedures even in the private sector. It follows that the usual formalist argument that the First Amendment only applies to government action, and that private entities like Google can therefore censor as much as they wish, is fundamentally dishonest. As the Supreme Court held more than seventy years ago, even a company town must meet minimum standards for democratic rule.[21] Despite this, the principle remains elusive. First, it has never been clear when private bodies' attempts to regulate members cross over into illegal price-fixing. This disables communities from trying to solve problems that formal governments lack the time, resources, or will to address. One obvious bright line would be to shield any private agreement that leaves profit margins unchanged. There is also the second problem of deciding when speech becomes coercion. Here, our argument that voting always involves social pressure provides a clear dividing line: Purely verbal statements of approval and disapproval must always be legal so long as they stop short of concerted action. By this standard, physical blockades on the pattern of "Occupy Wall Street" are illicit and can be cleared by force. But appeals to conscience aimed at persuading individual consumers to boycott would still be lawful.

Similarly, Congress should resist attempts to regulate or discourage speech. We have argued that ideology is dynamic, and that new ideas will be needed to end the current standoff. One might argue that exceptions should be made to ban particularly reprehensible ideologies. The problem is that there is no obvious way to keep such bans from expanding to suppress every challenge to orthodoxy. Following the Framers, we can take comfort in the hope that legislators will resist banning views knowing that their own opinions might be next. Moreover, exposing voters to minority views provides a form of inoculation. The real danger, in the Hegelian way, would be to suppress new arguments and fact patterns for so long that they seemed new and exciting when, inevitably, voters finally encountered them. Additionally, we have argued that developing counter-ideologies takes time, so that new ideologies can sometimes push against a vacuum for months if not years. The current practice of establishing "safe spaces" to exclude particular viewpoints is dangerous precisely because students who are "protected" from dangerous arguments have less chance of thinking them through, and therefore rejecting them when they threaten to become mainstream. This suggests that First Amendment-type limits should apply to private censorship as well.

## 10.3 PERENNIAL DISPUTES AND ABSTRACT PERILS

Madison believed that most public arguments would last a year or two, after which the public would clear up any confusions and know its mind. He then designed a government to match. At the time, it was hard to fault him: Short, sharp debates really were the best reading of history when newspapers first began serializing *The Federalist* in 1788. What he could not foresee was that the French Revolution would break out the following year, unleashing ideological struggles over class and equality that echo down to the present.

The silver lining for the American system was that, in Yeats' happy phrase, the center held: The total number of extremists on the American Right and Left has always been modest. This diluted what could have been a European-style death struggle to an incrementalist argument over just how much generosity the country could afford. The current version of the fight dates back to World War II. Knowing how much they were asking their populations to sacrifice, the Allied nations had all promised to establish a welfare state when the war ended. But where Britain and the European continent followed through, the US hesitated when a Republican Congress rejected President Truman's proposed medical reforms. After that not much happened until Medicare (1965).[22] And far from resolving the issue, this only set the stage for another half-century of stalemate between Democrats and Republicans until Obamacare very modestly increased insurance coverage from 85 percent to 92 percent.[23] Since then the fight has become perennial, with Democrats pressing for this or that component of FDR's blueprint (healthcare, transfer payments, education …) and Republicans resisting. This did not stop extremist ideologies from evolving on both the Left and the Right, and sometimes breaking out in angry protests. But for all that, the country's actual policies remained overwhelmingly centrist, incremental, and pragmatic.[24]

The issues that dominated 2020 – global warming, COVID-19, and BLM – were different. On the one hand, incrementalism was largely impossible: Solutions, assuming that they existed at all, would have to be implemented on scales guaranteed to cause significant, direct pain to voters. And on the other hand, even serious experts could and did disagree bitterly over which policies made sense or even, in the first two cases, how significant the underlying problems were. But in that case, it was impossible for even diligent voters to learn enough to arrive at a rational opinion. This left the "debate" almost entirely to social voters, leading to predicably emotional responses on both sides. As a result, partisanship and polarization rose to levels not seen since the "Great Quieting" more than a century before.

Chronologically, global warming was the first issue to become mainstream. The idea that humankind was changing the climate first became prominent in 1988 when media coverage tied congressional hearings on the threat of global warming to that summer's heatwave.[25] What made the juxtaposition effective was, in the language of Chapter 3, that it paired a logical "Type 1" argument ("greenhouse effect") with a compelling "Type 2" narrative that each new weather event seemed to confirm. This was enough to persuade large swathes of the public. But that was all: While repetition maintained the pattern for believers, large fractions of the population remained unconvinced.

Thirty years later, not much has changed. We have argued that public opinion sometimes undergoes Hegelian reversals when some sufficiently large event or new political argument intrudes. But weather stories arrive so frequently that there is always plenty of evidence for each side's preferred patterns. In principle the way out of the impasse is obvious: Learn the truth from experts and deploy trusted intermediaries to teach the public. The trouble in practice is that the arguments and evidence are far more uncertain than either side likes to admit. Of course, the basic "greenhouse" physics had been known since the 1890s. But the atmosphere–oceanic system is complicated, so that even today straightforward theory calculations still predict answers that are orders of magnitude smaller than what is observed.[26] In the end, scientists changed their minds mostly for empirical reasons: Detailed statistical analysis of temperatures since the eighteenth century showed that temperatures and $CO_2$ really were rising in concert.[27] At the same time, the pattern was so faint that it had taken the scientific literature decades to sort through the ambiguities. This showed, at a minimum, that the media's constant refrain that each new weather event "proves" global warming cannot be right.[28]

Faced with these obstacles, scientists turned to computer simulations for what optimists hoped would be a "third branch" of science[29] beyond theory and observation. But these were so computationally expensive that really adequate simulations will not exist for decades. This forced researchers to insert dozens of *ad hoc* adjustments to "tune" the models so that they resembled what was seen. But even then, no single model reproduced all of the observations, and no two models agreed.[30] This left voters with a maddening assortment of possible futures to worry about ranging from benign to catastrophic. Even the blue-ribbon Intergovernmental Panel on Climate Change (IPCC) quoted the probability of climate change as lying somewhere between 66 and 90 percent – at the lower end not much better than a coin toss. As one observer put it, "waiting for a sure answer would mean waiting forever."[31]

Not surprisingly, these unknowns produced a hellish politics. In principle, of course, the idea of taking precautions against a large but uncertain risk should have been familiar. After all, Wall Street investors do it every day. But as we said in Chapter 3, voters prefer to make sharp judgments one way or the other, and just how individuals draw this line depends on life experience. Given that even scientists who had studied the evidence were uncertain, it was entirely predictable that laypeople would disagree. This led to a violent jitter as first one side and then the other held power. Knowing he could not obtain Senate ratification, President Obama agreed to the Paris Accords informally. This made it possible for President Trump to withdraw from the Accords, but also for President Biden to reinstate them. There seems to be no reason why this pattern could not go on forever, especially since evidence that the Accords are working will not arrive for decades.[32]

The politics of COVID-19 looked a lot like that of climate change, except that the drama was compressed into the space of just two years, with the threat of catastrophe (if it happened at all) never more than a few weeks away. This time the political narrative on the nightly news broadcasts mixed human interest stories about doctors and patients with daily case statistics and, especially in the beginning, computer projections. This resonated with Western audiences who were culturally predisposed to see contagious disease as a catastrophic killer with overtones of divine justice.[33] The cocktail was so unsettling that most viewers overestimated the number of COVID-19 deaths by a factor of 225.[34] At the same time, large swathes of the population, taking their cue from the continued normalcy of life around them, concluded that the risk had been overstated and was no greater than the seasonal influenza.

What made the debate so hard to resolve was that unlike, say, wartime conscription and gas rationing, the average voter had little direct knowledge of the disease. Of course, it is true that by March 2021 one-in-four Americans knew someone who had died of COVID-19, and that nearly half (43 percent) had seen a close friend infected.[35] But that was thirteen months into the pandemic, and these personal experiences were much too thin to estimate risk at any specific moment.[36] The most the average person could say with any certainty was that COVID-19 – so far – had not been nearly as bad as the pandemics described in accounts like Defoe's *Journal of the Plague Year* or America's 1918 influenza experience. As with global warming, the known facts could – and did – leave room for violently different estimates. For most people, the disease remained, in Albert Camus' words, "a smoke in the imagination." They "believed in plague only with difficulty, even when it fell on [their] head."[37] Meanwhile others, who had "gained an idea of suffering and a little more imagination" feared the worst. In Camus' story people had eventually learned which narrative was true, but for COVID-19 personal experience – mercifully – never reached these levels.

As with global warming, there was no way to break the impasse. At first, computer models helped citizens to imagine the danger. But like most epidemiology models, their predictions usually included the possibility of exponential growth within weeks. When this repeatedly did not happen, the media stopped reporting them.[38] This was, strictly speaking, unfair: The modelers had never promised that their worst-case predictions would come true, and indeed they remained a possibility. As one doctor explained, "Until we are clearly past the peak of infections we cannot know what the peak will be."[39] This meant that every wave had the potential to become a catastrophe that everyone would experience personally, and if that happened they would surely blame the politicians in charge. In the meantime, incumbents tried to protect themselves by expressing grim determination, ostentatiously spending money, and pushing previously obscure bureaucrats before the cameras to take as much responsibility as possible.

Nor was the problem limited to simulations: Most attempts to evaluate measures to combat the disease were just as vague. The result was that the formal evidence for many political "hot-button" policies like lockdowns,[40] mask mandates,[41] and restaurant closures[42] were astonishingly inconclusive. This left even responsible, well-informed voters free to believe whatever they wanted.

The last big issue of 2020 was Black Lives Matter. Unlike global warming and COVID-19, hardly any Americans doubted the problem's existence. There was, however, a very real question of how to close the gap. Despite initial optimism, 1960s-era transfer payments and affirmative action had been more palliative than cure.[43] In its own way, the Black Lives Matter organization's strident Marxism admitted this: Short of revolution, its only policy prescriptions seemed to be "Defund the Police" and making affirmative action – introduced fifty years earlier as a temporary expedient[44] – permanent.

None of this mattered, of course, if you believed that Black poverty was caused by "systemic racism." In the usual Progressive way, it would be enough to put the right people in charge. Starting with George Floyd's murder, mainstream media focused on the posterchild case where unarmed Black men were killed by police, never mentioning that the supposed pattern was statistically invalid.[45] Meanwhile, claims that the bare fact of unequal outcomes was evidence of "systemic racism" led to an impossible politics. Short of the grand experiment of abolishing capitalism, there were no reforms to try, and therefore no possibility of pragmatic politics.

The politics of all three crises unfolded along similar lines. In principle Democrats and Republicans could have taken the same side, in which case voters' choices would have shrunk to nothing. And in fact, something very like this did happen in the early stages of the BLM movement. It was only later, when the argument devolved into specific measures like teaching critical race theory in public schools, that the issue was joined. But the parties did divide over global warming and COVID-19. Here, Democrats' existing ecology and Big Government narratives made strong stands natural, after which the country's strongly polarized politics encouraged rank-and-file Republicans to oppose them. That said, Republican leaders also had more strategic reasons to oppose the Democrats' program of lockdowns and vaccine mandates for COVID-19 and high energy prices for global warming. Being directly felt, these were bound to create single-issue voters, peeling off otherwise loyal

Democrats. For the usual Downsian reasons, this could only accelerate the regular oscillation back to Republican rule in the Congress and, eventually, the White House.

The path out of these arguments is still not clear. For rational voters, the question should have required an estimate of whether Democrats' policies had produced fewer COVID-19 casualties than expected. But historical pandemics had generally lasted one to two years marked by multiple waves before becoming endemic.[46] By this standard COVID-19 was mind-numbingly average.[47] Despite this, both politicians and the press frantically insisted that each tiny change in reported casualties showed that one side or the other had been right all along. If anything, rational voters' efforts to judge success on global warming were even more at sea, since it would take decades to see the effect of current policies. In the meantime, rational voters had little choice but to go on believing whatever they thought to begin with.

The case for social voters was more nuanced. Voters who mostly cared about conformity almost certainly cared less about COVID-19 and global warming than they claimed to. Meanwhile, voters motivated by virtue signaling needed apocalyptic threats to underscore their enemies' wickedness – and despised incremental solutions that made the problem seem less urgent. Together, these tendencies predicted that social voters would continue to call for strong measures, but also balk when the time came to pay for them. The disconnect is already visible in British polling, where green voters consistently overrate the benefits of congenial activities (buying an electric vehicle, abandoning plastics) compared to painful ones (taking the bus, having fewer children, swearing off foreign vacations). This has led politicians on both sides of the Atlantic to stress feel-good measures while avoiding coercive ones.[48] The tragedy for global warming policy was that quieter responses could have done some good.[49]

It is tempting to dismiss the intractability of these debates as bad luck. But there is something more systematic at work. Western societies have become victims of their own success. On the one hand, they have solved or at least mitigated the nearer-term problems that used to monopolize voters' attention. On the other, this has let them shift their gaze to more distant problems where even world-class experts know enough to worry, but cannot agree on what should be done. Small wonder that we have more gridlock.

So, what can our institutions do? We have said that the ratio of rational to social voters changes constantly. But social voters achieve their goals the moment they agree on an issue: Having taken a position, what happens afterward – whether government tries to fix the problem, whether anything improves – is anticlimax. By comparison, the great advantage of rational voters is that they can take on new arguments and new facts, and sometimes change their minds. It might be, of course, that the press and political parties will develop the arguments they need tomorrow. The problem for now is that facts are in such short supply that rational voting is paralyzed. The aim of reform should be to make them as plentiful and accessible as the situation allows. Our final section asks what institutional reforms can do to restore the balance.

## 10.4 FIXES (2): MANAGING THE LONG DEBATE

The Framers used the frictions of a divided government to stop statutes from jittering back and forth. But their frictions also enable the gridlock that makes coercive politics possible. This lets partisans endlessly relitigate issues so that anger mounts higher and higher. We have argued that the best way to break this impasse is to give rational voters more information. One way to do this is to introduce controversial policies as limited-time experiments. This would give voters on both sides a chance to experience laws which they have so far only imagined. Alternatively, society can conduct more basic research when that is feasible.

Madison designed his institutional frictions to absorb disputes for a year or two. But beyond this they only facilitate gridlock without offering any obvious mechanism to overcome it. At least arguably, it might be better for narrow majorities to have their wish long enough to convince the minority. Sunset clauses, which provide that legislation will disappear by a certain date, provide a natural vehicle for this.

The Framers, of course, knew all about sunset clauses from Ancient Athens, the English Parliament, and their own experience in various colonial and postcolonial state legislatures.[50] Indeed, they even inserted one such clause – a prohibition on funding the US Army for more than two years at a time – into their new Constitution.[51] Hamilton thought this would deter the kinds of standing armies that had made Europe miserable.[52] In fact, the recurring debates may have *helped* the fledgling Army by forcing successive Congresses to examine alternative institutions like militias, and find them wanting. This already suggests that sunset clauses are a useful way to address issues that are simultaneously important, controversial, and poorly understood.[53]

Historically, Congress has limited itself to inserting sunset clauses in individual statutes. The question is whether a general rule would be better. This would most naturally be done in the Senate. Even if senators eventually cut back the current sixty-vote supermajority, it would make sense to retain it for *permanent* legislation. Bills that passed by narrower margins would then terminate automatically after, say, ten years. This would give even mediocre legislation time to build a constituency. If it did, reauthorization would be straightforward and might even command enough votes to make the law permanent. Given the usual "iron triangle" logic that even bad legislation is hard to undo, any statute that fails this test ought to be revisited in any case.

Sunset provisions would also help the system transition back to a more bipartisan politics. First, the idea of giving statutes a trial run is inherently pragmatic. Of course, we cannot tell politicians and voters what arguments to make or believe. What we can do, though, is conduct policy experiments that encourage pragmatic arguments by making them easier and more natural to make. Second, sunset laws might actually *accelerate* change. Even in the most optimistic circumstances, today's gridlock tends to produce a few large changes at long intervals. This makes it reasonable to think that a series of smaller but more frequent changes could be faster. Third and perhaps most importantly, sunset clauses reassure the losing side that their loss is only temporary and may yet be reversed. While this will not eliminate resentments, even a small reduction of anger and polarization could make bipartisan politics more attractive.

The question remains how effective this would be. In the past, Congress has treated sunset clauses as a kind of "snooze button," repeatedly voting to extend even highly controversial laws with little or no debate. For example, the USA PATRIOT Act sunsetted four times between 2001 and 2020, and the federal Parole Commission has now been extended six times.[54] It would be easy to criticize this as "kicking the can down the road." But one can equally argue that these issues are no longer as controversial as they once were, let alone more important than current business. This sounds like the very definition of healing.

Meanwhile, the Assault Weapons Ban (1994–2004) provides a rare example of legislation that was allowed to sunset. Probably the most interesting aspect of the experiment is that the statute included a mandated report at the end of ten years. This found that the ban's results had been practically nonexistent, and may have played a role in Congress's decision not to renew.[55] That said, more recent debate hardly ever mentions the report, suggesting that a very expensive, ten-year experiment has made almost no impression on politicians or the public mind. At least arguably, requiring the sponsors – and also opponents – of future bills to go on record saying what results they expect to see at the end of ten years would give future reports more political traction.

The second possibility for breaking long-term deadlock is to obtain new information. The idea that science can be rushed in this way might seem surprising: After all, ideas for new research take time, and so do experiments. Still, the fact remains that a surprising number of potentially important research projects currently go unfunded because they are either costly or politically controversial.[56] In the case of global warming, these notoriously include experiments to demonstrate or disprove schemes for neutralizing global greenhouse effects at perhaps one one-hundredth of the cost of conventional "carbon-zero" proposals.[57] The gap is even more obvious for COVID-19, where the best way to measure the efficacy of lockdowns and masks is to perform experiments ("challenge tests") that deliberately expose volunteers to the virus. There is nothing fanciful about this: Such tests were routinely done during World War II and the Cold War.[58] Moreover, the cost–benefit calculation for performing tests to reduce the large public health uncertainties for a disease that has cost the world $10 trillion seems obvious.[59] While COVID-19 challenge trials have been tried in a limited way in Britain, American authorities never seriously considered them because test subjects might die.[60]

The political possibilities for funding dramatic experiments seems clear. Indeed, the danger is that they might be *too* persuasive, so that one or two isolated experiments could mislead the public. But in that case the answer is to fund more experiments.

The question remains how to make debate-ending experiments more likely. One possibility would be to convene a National Academy of Science Panel of academics each year to recommend experiments that (a) have never been done, (b) are feasible on time scales significantly shorter than the problem, and (c) would produce a material advance over existing knowledge. But academia has its own sacred cows, and a panel could easily decide that it was better to continue suppressing certain experiments on grounds that their political impact was likely to exceed any evidentiary value. A better solution would change House and Senate rules to let some threshold number of congressmen put suitable research projects to an up-or-down vote. The rule could also require the bill's sponsors to specify how they expected the experiment to end, and what voters should conclude if some other outcome happened instead. That would at least limit the inevitable obfuscation on both sides.

## Notes

1 Even though Ulysses S. Grant conceded that "The Framers were wise in their generation," he immediately added that "[i]t is preposterous to suppose that the people of one generation can lay down the best and only rules of government for all who come after them, and under unforeseen contingencies." Grant [1885] at p. 312.

2 Alaska, Hawaii, Oregon, and Vermont have all passed out-of-state contribution limits, though for the moment federal appeals courts have struck down all but Hawaii's statute on First Amendment grounds; Somi (2020). The US Supreme Court has yet to address the issue; *Thompson* v. *Hebdon*, No. 19–122, 589 US ___ (2019).

3 *Rucho* v. *Common Cause*, 588 U.S. ___, 139 S. Ct. 2484, 2500 (2019).

4 The Thirty-Sixth Congress that met just before the Civil War shows what can happen when the US Constitution reverts to multiparty democracy. Members were split across four different parties, none of which commanded a majority. The chaotic sessions that followed derailed any chance to regulate slavery in the territories and, with it, the country's last, best chance of avoiding war. Catton [1961] at p. 13.

5 Catton [1961]

6 Rychter (2018).

7 Hawkins et al. (2018) at p. 6 divide the centrist 67 percent into "Traditional Liberals" (11 percent), "Passive" (15 percent), "Politically Disengaged" (26 percent), and "Moderates" (15 percent).

8 Hawkins et al. (2018) at p. 6.

9 Congress has considered proposals to exempt newspapers from antitrust laws since the 1950s. These often made sense where antitrust law had prevented newspapers from accessing scale economies through shared printing plants and the like. However, the Newspaper Preservation Act of 1970 addressed most of these cases. Recent proposals like the "Journalism Competition and Preservation Act" go further by trying to offset internet monopolies like Google by letting traditional media cartelize and fix prices themselves. Congress.gov (2022b). Even if this restored profits, it would come at the usual cost of trying to fight fire with fire: Whatever it did for newspaper profitability, increasing the number of monopolies would *also* mean higher prices and lower quality so that readers consumed less news than ever.

10 See, e.g., Williams (2019).

11 The elimination of fundamental patents in the early twentieth century did not deter massive innovation in the aviation and automobile industries.

12 47 USC §230.

13   Kessler (2021).

14   Bernie Sanders' supporters routinely claim that Democratic insiders cheated him of the party's nomination in 2016 and 2020. It is not clear that the party gained by this: Granted that Clinton and Biden were more centrist, they were also mediocre campaigners.

15   Johnson (2019).

16   Fitton (2019).

17   Problem Solvers Caucus (2018). The House's discharge petition process currently allows a majority of members to force floor votes. However, the rule has long been a dead letter because many congressmen who would like to vote on such bills fear retaliation if they defy their party's leaders. The Problem Solvers' proposed TRUST Act would create bipartisan committees armed with the right to present legislation for expedited votes in the House and Senate; See, Committee for a Responsible Federal Budget (2020).

18   This was memorably summarized in Speaker Pelosi's statement that members would have to pass Obamacare "to find out what's in it." Capehart (2012).

19   See, e.g., 18 USC § 641.

20   See Rivkin and Grossman (2022) for examples.

21   *Marsh* v. *Alabama* 326 U.S. 501 (1946).

22   Barone (2020) at pp. 55–9.

23   Antos and Cappreta (2020).

24   There were, to be sure, issues where incrementalist approaches were more or less impossible, so that politics quickly became an intractable war between rival theories. This was most obvious in wars and economic downturns, where even experts disagreed about the best way forward. But these crises were always temporary in the sense that they would almost certainly end within a few years no matter what the government did. It is true that there were also more enduring conflicts over issues like nuclear power and chemical plants, where expert opinion was deeply divided and likely to remain so for decades. These problems, however, were relatively tiny on the scale of the overall economy. This allowed politicians to muddle through knowing that whatever costs they incurred would be invisible to voters.

25   Weart (2003) at pp. 155–7.

26   Muller and MacDonald (2002). Well-informed scientists could still dismiss the possibility of human impacts "out of hand" until the 1960s and there was nothing resembling consensus before the 1990s. Weart (2003) at pp. 3 and 38.

27   Rohde et al. (2013).

28   Careful statistical analysis has yet to detect long-term trends in heat, storms, floods, wildfires, or sea level; Koonin (2021) at pp. 90–101 (heat), 102–13 (storms), 114–28 (floods and wildfires), and 129–41 (sea level).

29   "RP" (pseud.) (1992).

30   The quoted uncertainties for state-of-the-art models have changed little since 1979, and have in some cases gotten worse. Koonin (2021) at pp. 82–3 and 86. The reason is that computer calculations simulate 1,000 km grids

that are too large to represent important physical processes like cloud cover directly. So, modelers add dozens of parameters to "tune" the grids to mimic what is actually seen, adding uncertainties that swamp any possible human influence. Advances in processing power are unlikely to solve the problem for several decades. Koonin (2021) at pp. 79–81.

31 Weart (2003) at pp. 196 and 198.

32 Because it takes at least a decade to define climate, a minimum of twenty years is needed to detect change. Koonin (2021) at p. 37. Moreover, natural ebbs and flows can last up to eighty years. This makes it extremely difficult to say how much warming humans have caused since, say, 1980. Koonin (2021) at pp. 84–5. Finally, isolating human impacts would require measuring all natural sources of change to within 1 percent. Koonin (2021) at pp. 59 and 62. This is well beyond the current state of the art.

33 See generally Wald (2008).

34 KEKST-CNC (2020) at p. 24.

35 Galvin (2021). Pressure for strong COVID-19 policies was amplified by the fact that large identifiable groups, including the elderly and immunocompromised, were at substantially larger risk. Many voters were persuaded to support lockdowns less for their own sakes than because they had vulnerable friends and relations.

36 New York City was an important exception. In early 2020, COVID-19 killed one in six people over 90 and roughly 3 percent of those over 70. Rosenkranz (2020).

37 Camus [1947] at p. 74.

38 Sternberg (2021).

39 Douglas, Sugden, and Roland (2022).

40 Before COVID-19, most experts agreed that lockdowns were ineffective. The only exception was certain controversial computer simulations, which had a track record of overestimating risks. Magness and Earle (2021). After-the-fact studies suggest that lockdowns reduced the number of US and European COVID-19 deaths by just 0.2 percent. See, e.g., Herby, Jonung, and Hanke (2022).

41 The basic difficulty was that the studies had to monitor subjects for months to see whether mask-wearers, for example, got sick more often than non-wearers. But since the vast majority of both groups never got sick at all during the study period, even very large studies were only weakly predictive. For example, the leading mask study followed 6,024 persons for two months. But since only 95 of these got sick, the final statistics were based on just 42 mask wearers and 53 in the control group. The results were consistent with the proposition that masks cut infections in half – but also that they did nothing at all. Bundgard et al. (2020).

42 Even advanced Western nations could not typically trace where 70–80 percent of the cases came from. This made it impossible to say whether restaurants, say, contributed more than their share of illness. Bender and Dalton (2020). Contact tracing outside New York was even less effective. McCarthy (2020).

43 Schlaes (2019).

44  *Grutter* v. *Bollinger*, 539 U.S. 306 at 343.

45  Fryer (2019).

46  Seven of the world's eight pandemics since the eighteenth century have lasted one to two years and included two or more waves of disease. When COVID-19 first emerged, most mainstream epidemiologists predicted that it would follow a similar pattern. Osterholm et al. (2020). This was more or less what happened.

47  Not even vaccines made much of a difference: Natural immunity remained the biggest driver of transmissibility long after the pandemic had started to wane. In early 2021, 55 percent of Americans had natural immunity while only 15 percent had been vaccinated. Markary (2021).

48  The principal exception was France, where Emanuel Macron's decision to raise gasoline taxes sparked massive populist protests. Sternberg (2021).

49  Following more than a decade of intensive study, Prof. Nordhaus finds that it is far more cost-effective to invest in mitigating climate change than in trying to stop greenhouse emissions entirely. He estimates that limiting emissions to a 2½ °C temperature change by 2200 would lead to a world per capita income of just $10,000 per year. By comparison, business-as-usual growth would drive temperatures up by 6 °C with a world per capita income of $130,000. The amount of climate damage would have to be "enormous" to cancel out the benefits of growth. Nordhaus (2013) at p. 78.

50  Wikipedia (55). See also Webster [1787] at p. 558 and Plutarch [*ca.* 100 AD] at pp. 161–2. Speaking to the Constitutional Convention, Madison predicted that legislatures "in doubtful cases" would soon adopt the "policy … of limiting the duration of laws as to require renewal instead of repeal." Quoted in *INS. V. Chadha*, 462 US 919 (1983), at p. 954 and n. 18.

51  US Constitution Art. I, § 8, cl. 12.

52  *Federalist* No. 26 at p. 116 (Hamilton).

53  At the same time, sunset provisions also suppress jitter: If opponents know that Congress must revisit legislation at some definite point in the future, forcing an even earlier vote becomes less urgent.

54  Wikipedia (55); Fahrenthold (2012).

55  Wikipedia (25). The Republican-controlled House would have been loath to renew in any case.

56  Perhaps the most spectacular exception is the federal government's experimental use of a negative income tax in parts of New Jersey in the 1960s. Kershaw (1972).

57  Possible technologies including injecting aerosols into the stratosphere and pouring iron filings into the ocean to stimulate carbon-sequestering plankton have been suggested since the early 1990s. Despite this, academic scientists and government agencies managed to block serious discussion until 2015. Koonin (2021) at pp. 139–40, 203–4, and 206; Singer (2005) at p. 290. The opposition was candidly political; Keith (2019) ("Many fear, with good reason, that fossil-fuel interests will exploit solar geoengineering to oppose emissions cuts.); Lynn (2016) at pp. 2544–5 (arguing that the mere "prospect of geoengineering … may divert attention and resources away from mitigation, undermine incentives to reduce behaviors that generate

carbon emissions, or encourage political inaction"). Congress has since allocated $4 million for theoretical research and some politicians have called for
funding field experiments; Fialka (2020). Harvard briefly planned to conduct
a privately funded experiment but withdrew indefinitely in the face of protests. Fialka (2020); Kahn and Levien (2021).

58  See, e.g., Libby (1979) at pp. 331–2 (plutonium); Harris and Paxman [1982]
    at p. 170 (biological weapons).
59  Anon (2021b).
60  Strassburg (2021).

# Appendix

## A Community-Based Redistricting Algorithm

We argued in Chapter 3 that redistricting should follow two constitutional principles: Equal Population ("EP") and Community. The chapter also explained why expected interactions between voters ("Link Strength") supply a reliable proxy for the latter. This appendix addresses the practicalities of using these principles to generate detailed redistricting maps by introducing a simple computer algorithm[1] and applying it to county-level data for Texas.[2] The results display reasonable boundaries; are robust against manipulation; and provide a reliable benchmark for detecting real-world gerrymanders.

Chapter 2 described how networks influence voting in social space. Districting requires additional information about how these networks map onto physical space. The good news, as might be expected, is that neighbors in social space also tend to live and work near each other in physical space.[3] Figure A.1 presents empirical data for St. Louis, Missouri, showing the number of contacts between voters as a function of the distance (in miles) between their respective homes. The probability that a voter's interlocutor lives "d" miles away neatly approximates an inverse square law of the form $\frac{K}{d^2}$, with half of all contacts occurring within a radius of 8.4 km (fifteen minutes' drive time) for non-kin.[4] This defines an Expected Link Strength ("ELS") which can be calculated based solely on the number of citizens at each location.[5]

*Algorithm.* Our goal is to merge county-level population data[6] into congressional districts that maximize total statewide ELS subject to our EP requirement. In keeping with recent case law, we interpret EP as requiring district populations to fall within 10 percent of each other.

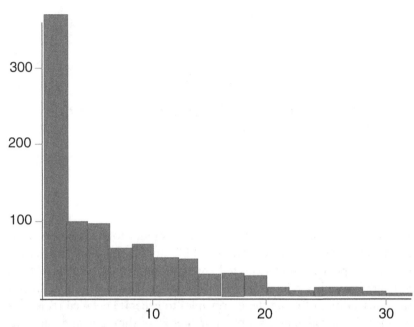

FIGURE A.1 Distance between interlocutors

Maximizing ELS would be trivial without the EP requirement: The algorithm would simply go on merging pairs until just one state-wide district remained. EP complicates this by "freezing" each district's growth when its population reaches some specified limit, so that the total number of districts stops at the constitutionally-mandated number of congressmen. An efficient algorithm should simultaneously (a) prioritize whichever mergers produce the greatest ELS, and (b) minimize the tendency of early-forming proto-districts to freeze in ways that force late-forming ones into circuitous shapes that violate compactness and, in rare instances, contiguity.

Our sample algorithm addresses the second constraint by adopting Vickrey's proposals as follows: First, it selects some point within the state at random.[7] Second, it selects whichever previously unmerged block happens to be furthest removed from that point. This implements Vickrey's insight that forming maps from the outside in minimizes our second constraint. Third, it merges the block with whichever other block produces the largest ELS. This enforces the first constraint. Fourth, the resulting proto-district uses the same criterion to find and merge with additional blocks until the merged group reaches its EP limit. Finally, the algorithm returns to the randomly selected point and repeats the process. This continues until every block has been merged into a district.

We can, of course, imagine many extensions of this procedure. For example, legislators might decide that ELS is not equally valuable to all voters, since an urban voter who already has multiple interlocutors probably values one more unit of ELS less than a rural voter who might possess no contacts at all. This can be addressed by rewriting the Vickrey rule to prioritize mergers so that low ELS blocks are the first to merge. Similarly, the algorithm can easily be extended to implement additional constraints besides EP. For example, legislators could specify how far districts could depart from compactness and/or their historical boundaries and then mandate whichever map offered the highest total ELS within that constraint.

*Example.* Texas provides a powerful real-world test of the algorithm. The state contains a wide variety of geometries ranging from neatly stacked rectangles at mid-state to outsized, irregular, and/or tilted counties in the east, south, and west. Six counties are large enough to elect one or more congressmen entirely within their borders and are ignored in what follows. This reduces the problem to allocating the remaining 244 counties across twenty-four districts.

Naively we would expect a partition that severed twenty-three out of every twenty-four links to reduce ELS by 96 percent. However, the fact that ELS follows an inverse square law means that links between close neighbors nearly always outweigh distant ones. In practice, the algorithm yields a compact map that preserves 17 percent of the state's total ELS (Figure A.2).

The map also contains two discontinuous districts. This should not matter since, as Chapter 6 argued, geometry is a poor constitutional principle in any case. Still, it would be easy to add a constraint that required contiguity everywhere with only a modest increase in total ELS.

Experiments that modify the basic algorithm, for example by changing which mergers are prioritized, produce similarly compact and continuous maps, albeit with smaller total ELS. However, district boundaries change significantly. This shows that maps featuring similar EP and ELS can look quite different and might lead to significantly different election results. This presents policymakers with a choice. On the one hand, they can follow Vickrey by automatically adopting the highest-scoring map.[8] Here the main difficulty is that our algorithm

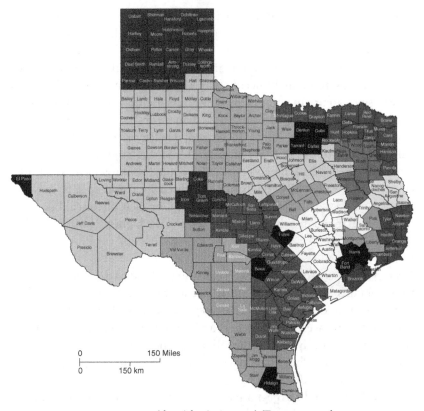

FIGURE A.2 Algorithmic maps: A Texas example

does not guarantee the most efficient map, so that researchers might later find solutions that offered still higher ELS. One practical solution would be for state officials to publicize their proposed map for a period of, say, 180 days. If members of the public can find a better map in this time, the state would adopt it. If not, the window would close, even if better maps were discovered later on. Alternatively, policymakers could let the legislature choose between all possible maps that save ELS within some fixed percent of this benchmark. That would create room to consider traditional criteria beyond EP and ELS, though it would also increase the chances of gerrymandering.

*Resistance to tampering.* Finally, even though our algorithm is neutral, the definition of census blocks might not be. We therefore ask whether partisans could manipulate the algorithm's final output by making small changes to the population, geographic size, shape, and orientation of individual blocks. Of course, it is obvious that politicians who do enough tampering can change the algorithm's results. But these interventions would also be detectible. It follows that algorithms should be designed so that small changes to inputs lead to comparably small effects.

Insensitivity to small changes seems intuitive for algorithms which randomly hop-scotch across the state, so that the next proto-district to form is almost always distant from the last one. This implies that small changes at any one location are unlikely to propagate far. The proposition can be tested by rerunning the algorithm after transferring half the population and area of one randomly selected county to its neighbor. This changed the final map in four out of ten experiments. However, the change in two of these was limited to the adjusted counties themselves. In the other two cases, seven to ten small rural counties switched districts. Given the small populations involved, this would have carried negligible weight in the final vote tallies.

Probably the best way to increase resistance to tampering would be to shrink the size of the individual "blocks" on which the algorithm operates. This is plainly true in the limit where each resident is treated as a separate "atom" because the resulting pattern is unique and hence tamper-proof. More practical implementations could easily be done at the level of the Census Bureau's census blocks or voting precincts. Numerical experiments show that rerunning calculations for counties whose physical dimensions and populations have been reduced to the size of typical US census blocks typically increases their stability.

*Modified distance laws.* Professor Huckfeldt's data (Figure A.1) were collected in just two metropolitan regions and display obvious noise. This suggests that more and bigger studies can refine our ELS law. Beyond that, the inverse square relation almost certainly breaks down at short distances. Since most of us wander freely within our immediate neighborhoods, differences of a few feet cannot possibly cause us to consult one neighbor more than another. Finally, the probability of finding nearby interlocutors depends on how easy it is to make contact in the first place. This implies that average link distances will usually be longer in rural networks than in urban ones.

*Political feasibility.* We close with a comment on practical politics. Commentators often say that gerrymandering is inevitable because incumbent legislators can always be counted on to oppose any map that reduces their chances of reelection.[9] There is something to this, but the argument needs to be examined more closely. So long as legislatures have a choice of maps, logrolling will ensure maps that benefit most legislators – always including the majority party, and sometimes incumbents more generally. By comparison, an algorithm that offers a single take-it-or-leave-it map will usually favor about half the incumbents and weaken the rest. This suggests that roughly half the chamber will benefit – enough or nearly enough to pass the measure – from the outset. Moreover, the average congressman serves for about ten years before being replaced.[10] This means that political opposition can be diluted by phasing in the algorithm over a decade or so.

## Notes

1  Available from the author under Creative Commons License 3.0, https://creativecommons.org/licenses/by/3.0.
2  Readers seeking further details should consult Karapetyan and Maurer (2021). I am grateful to Alexander Karapetyan for performing the various computer simulations described here.
3  Baybeck and Huckfeldt (2002) at p. 198.
4  Baybeck and Huckfeldt (2002) at pp. 266–7 and Table 1.
5  The existence of an inverse square law makes good intuitive sense. Before someone can become our political interlocutor, we must first meet her. But traveling away from home requires effort, implying that the probability that we will travel to a spot distance "d" from home scales like $1/d$. The chances of two people meeting is then $(1/d) \times (1/d) = 1/d^2$.
6  While we use county-level data in what follows, more granular calculations are possible. Real Census Bureau data report population down to the level of small geographic tracts called "blocks." As of the 2010 Census there were 11,155,486 blocks in the US containing an average of twenty-eight people each. See ArcGIS Hub (2020).
7  For the sake of definiteness, the calculations presented here always start from the state's centermost county.
8  See Vickrey (1961) at p. 107.
9  See *Rucho* v. *Common Cause*, 139 S. Ct. 2484 (2019) at p. 2512 (Kagan, J., dissenting).
10  Manning (2018) at pp. 5–6.

# References

2d Vote, n.d. "Company Scores," www.2ndvote.com/company-scores/.

114th Congress, 2015. "Concurrent Resolution," (Nov. 5), https://pressgallery .house.gov/adjournment-resolution.

Acevedo, D., 2021. "Tracking 'Cancel Culture' in Higher Education," *National Association of Scholars*, www.nas.org/blogs/article/tracking-cancel-culture-in-higher-education.

Achen, C. H. and L. M. Bartels, 2017. *Democracy for Realists* (Princeton University Press: Princeton, NJ).

Adams, H., 1860. "Letter to Charles Francis Adams Jr.," pp. 143–146 in Simpson, Sears & Sheehan-Dean (2011).

Adams, J., 1775. "Letter to A. Adams," pp. 32–33 in J. Rhodehamel (ed.), *The American Revolution: Writings from the War of Independence* (June) (Library of America: New York).

Adams, J., 1776. "Letter to John Penn, US National Archives," (Mar. 27), https:// perma.cc/7LNZ-DJ4L.

Adams, J., 1780. "Letter to Jonathan Jackson," (Oct. 2), https://founders.archives .gov/documents/Adams/06-10-02-0113.

Adler, L., 2016. "How Selecting U.S. Presidential Candidates Became the People's Choice," *Reuters* (Mar. 29), www.reuters.com/article/us-usa-election-selectionprocess-factbox/how-selecting-u-s-presidential-candidates-became-the-peoples-choice-idUSKCN0WW001.

Ahlin, C. and P. D. Ahlin, 2013. "Product Differentiation under Congestion: Hotelling Was Right," *Economic Inquiry* 51(3): 1750–1763.

Alcott, H. and M. Gentzkow, 2017. "Social Media and Fake News in the 2016 Election," *Journal of Economic Perspectives* 31(2): 211–236.

Alexeev, B. and D. G. Mixon, 2018. "Partisan Gerrymandering with Geographically Compact Districts," *Journal of Applied Probability* 55: 1046–59.

Allen, B., 2020. "Greece, Rome, Columbia," *Wall Street Journal* (Nov. 14).

Altman, M., 1998. "Traditional Districting Principles: Judicial Myths vs. Reality," *Social Science History* 22(2): 159–200.

*References*

AmericanForeignRelations.com, n.d. "Interwar Isolationism – Bipartisanship," www.americanforeignrelations.com/A-D/Bipartisanship-Interwar-isolationism .html.

Amy, D. J., n.d. "A Brief History of Proportional Representation in the United States," *Fair Vote*, www.fairvote.org/a_brief_history_of_proportional_ representation_in_the_united_states.

Anderson, J. A., 1995. *An Introduction to Neural Networks* (MIT University Press: Cambridge, MA).

Andrews, W., 2017. "How Each Senator Voted on Trump's Cabinet and Administration Nominees," *New York Times* (May 11).

Andriottis, A., P. Rudigeair and E. Glazer, 2021. "Stripe Stops Processing Payments for Trump Campaign Website," *Wall Street Journal* (Jan. 11).

Andronikov-Sanglade, A., 2000. "Use of the Rorschach Comprehensive System in Europe: State of the Art," pp. 338–339 in R. H. Dana (ed.), *Handbook of Cross-Cultural and Multicultural Personality Assessments* (Taylor & Francis: Abingdon, UK).

Anon, 1787. "Letters from the "Federal Farmer" to "The Republican"," pp. 245–288 in Bailyn (1993a).

Anon, 1964. "Goldwater Calls for Drive to Finish War in Vietnam," *New York Times* (Aug. 11).

Anon, 1996. "'The Era of Big Government is Over': Clinton's 1996 State of the Union," *PBS Washington Week* (Jan. 26), www.pbs.org/weta/washingtonweek/ web-video/era-big-government-over-clintons-1996-state-union.

Anon, 2010(a). "World War II: A Timeline of American Casualties," *Atlanta Journal Constitution*.

Anon, 2010(b). "National Anthem Being Nearly Ignored," *Albert Lea (Minn.) Tribune* (May 21), www.albertleatribune.com/2010/05/us-national-anthem-is- being-nearly-ignored/.

Anon, 2016(a). Partisanship and Political Animosity in 2016," *Pew Research Center* (June 21), https://perma.cc/SU9L-2Q2M.

Anon, 2016(b). "Scale of Hearst Plot to Discredit Orson Welles and *Citizen Kane* Revealed," *The Guardian* (March 28), www.theguardian.com/film/2016/ mar/28/scale-of-hearst-plot-to-discredit-orson-welles-and-citizen-kane-revealed.

Anon, 2016(c). Voice of Wilkinson: "What Aren't They Telling Us? – Chapman University Survey of American Fears," https://blogs.chapman.edu/ wilkinson/2016/10/11/what-arent-they-telling-us/.

Anon, 2016(d). "New Yorkers Run for President: History and Insights for 2016," www.gothamgazette.com/index.php/opinion/6250-new-yorkers-run-for- president-history-and-insights-for-2016-page-one.

Anon, 2019. Editorial: "A Way Out of the Shutdown," *Wall Street Journal* (Jan. 2).

Anon, 2020(a). "Why Was a Neo-Nazi Hooligan Mourned at a Football Game in Germany?" *Deutsche Welle* (March 14), www.dw.com/en/why-was-a- neo-nazi-hooligan-mourned-at-a-football-game-in-germany/a-47856332.

Anon, 2020(b). "Hartley Sawyer Fired from CW's 'The Flash' after Racist, Misogynist Tweets Surface," *NBC News* (June 8), www.nbcnews.com/pop-culture/ pop-culture-news/hartley-sawyer-fired-cw-s-flash-after-racist-misogynist- tweets-n1227701.

Anon, 2020(c). "Wendy Mesley Suspended from Hosting after Using 'Careless' Language in Discussing Racial Issue," *Canadian Broadcasting Corporation* (June 9), www.cbc.ca/news/canada/wendy-mesley-suspended-hosting-1.5604973.

Anon, 2020(d). "After Wildfire Smoke Clears, Protests Resume in Portland," *Associated Press* (Sept. 19), https://apnews.com/article/wildfires-oregon-archive-fires-portland-6e42d7a3b5b1aded2ad14d11cdf498e3.

Anon, 2020(e). Editorial: "Breaking Judicial Norms," *Wall Street Journal* (Sept. 21).

Anon, 2020(f). "Josh Hawley Grills Facebook CEO about Tool Allegedly Used to Track Users 'Across the Internet'," *Washington Examiner* (Nov. 17), www.washingtonexaminer.com/news/josh-hawley-grills-facebook-ceo-about-tool-allegedly-used-to-track-users-across-the-internet.

Anon, 2020(g). "2020 House Ratings," *The Cook Political Report*, (Sep. 18, 2020), https://cookpolitical.com/ratings/house-race-ratings.

Anon, 2020(h). Editorial: "Special Counsel John Durham," *Wall Street Journal* (2020).

Anon, 2020(i). Editorial: "Twitter's Living Censorship," *Wall Street Journal* (Nov. 2).

Anon, 2021(a). "Untitled Survey," *Generation Lab*, www.generationlab.org/_files/ugd/b2ee84_a922fc4cede84e45856dedde927d5efo.pdf.

Anon, 2021(b). "What is the Economic Cost of COVID-19?" *The Economist* (Jan. 7), www.economist.com/finance-and-economics/2021/01/09/what-is-the-economic-cost-of-covid-19.

Anon, 2021(c). Editorial: "Sheldon Whitehouse vs. the Supreme Court," *Wall Street Journal* (March 10).

Anon, 2021(d). "Rep. Mondaire Jones slams Manchin's op-ed: 'Intellectually un-serious,'" *MSNBC* (June 6), www.msn.com/en-us/news/newsenglishnews/rep-mondaire-jones-slams-manchins-op-ed-intellectually-un-serious/vp-AAKLhhX.

Anon, 2021(e). Editorial: "The 'Shadow Docket' Diversion," *Wall Street Journal* (Oct. 2).

Anon, 2022(h). Editorial: "The Beast Mode Presidency," *Wall Street Journal* (July 19).

Anon, 2022(i). Editorial: "Why Democrats are Losing the Midterms," *Wall Street Journal* (Oct. 27).

Anon, n.d.(a). "The Giolitti Era, 1900-14," *Encyclopedia Britannica*, https://perma.cc/3TM9-XSSV.

Anon, n.d.(b). "William Randolph Hearst Stops 'Citizen Kane' Ads," *History.com*, www.history.com/this-day-in-history/william-randolph-hearst-stops-citizen-kane-ads.

Anon, n.d.(c). "Reported Murder and NonNegligent Manslaughter in the US Since 1990," *Statista.com*, www.statista.com/statistics/191134/reported-murder-and-nonnegligeont-manslaughter-cases-in-the-us-since-1990/.

Anon, n.d.(d). "Combat 18," *Counter Extremism Project*, www.counterextremism.com/supremacy/combat-18

Anon, n.d.(e). "Chicks on the Right – About Us" www.chicksonright.com/about-us/

Anon, n.d.(f). "Australian Ballot," *Britannica* www.britannica.com/topic/Australian-ballot.

Anon, n.d.(g). "Expansion of the Voting Right," https://sites.google.com/site/universalmalesuffrage/expansion-of-voting-right.

Anon, n.d.(h). "The Blackford Oakes Mystery Series in Order by William F. Buckley, Jr.," *Fiction DB*, www.fictiondb.com/series/a-blackford-oakes-mystery-william-f-buckley-jr~90.htm#:~:text=Series%20List%20in%20Order%20%20%20%20Order,%20%204.5%20%208%20more%2orows%20.

Anon, n.d.(i). "Jacksonian Foreign Relations; Whig Obstructionism in the French Crisis," *University of Gronigen – Humanities Computing*," www.let.rug.nl/usa/biographies/andrew-jackson/jacksonian-foreign-relations%3b-whig-obstructionism-in-the-french-crisis.php.

Anon, n.d.(j). "Roman Patronage in Society, Politics, and Military," *Pennsylvania State University*, https://sites.psu.edu/romanpatronagegroupdcams101/what-is-patronage/.

Anon, n.d.(k). "Expansion of the Voting Right," https://sites.google.com/site/universalmalesuffrage/expansion-of-voting-right.

Anon, n.d.(l). "Primary Election," *Encylopedia Britannica*, https://perma.cc/8CBY-T4NJ.

Anon, n.d.(m). "Strikes: Labor History Encyclopedia for the Pacific Northwest," *Pacific Labor and Civil Rights Project*, https://depts.washington.edu/labhist/encyclopedia/.

Anon, n.d.(n). "Voter Turnout Rate in Presidential Primary Elections in the United States in 2020, by State," www.statista.com/statistics/1102189/voter-turnout-us-presidential-primaries-state/.

Antos, J. R. and C. C. Cappreta, 2020. "The ACA: Trillions? Yes. A Revolution? No," *Health Affairs*, www.healthaffairs.org/do/10.1377/hblog20200406.93812/full/.

ArcGIS Hub, 2020. "U.S. Census Blocks," (Sept. 3), https://hub.arcgis.com/datasets/c3f4c0d3b44f4c5f96a4bb93f1eb2106_54.

Armstrong, P. B., 2013. *How Literature Plays with the Brain: The Neuroscience of Literature and Art* (Johns Hopkins University Press: Baltimore, MD) (epub ed.)

Axelrod, T., 2022. "Jeffries Downplays Chances of 'Compromise' Speaker as McCarthy Faces Pushback," *ABC News* (Dec. 4).

Ayers, E. L., 2003. *In the Presence of Mine Enemies: The Civil War in America, 1859–1863* (Norton: New York).

Bailey, E. Jr., "Voter Turnout for Portland City Council Race between Dan Ryan, Loretta Smith at 32%" *The Oregonian* (Aug. 10, 2020).

Bailyn, B., (ed.) 1993a. *The Debate on the Constitution* (Pt. 1) (Library of America: New York).

Bailyn, B., (ed.) 1993b. *The Debate on the Constitution* (Pt. 2) (Library of America: New York).

Baker, G., 2020. "Media Watchdogs Aren't Supposed to Guard Biden," *Wall Street Journal* (Oct. 26).

Ballotpedia, 2015. "Demographics of Congressional Districts as of 2015," *Ballotpedia*, https://ballotpedia.org/Demographics_of_congressional_districts_as_of_2015.

Ballotpedia, n.d.(a). "United States Constitution," https://ballotpedia.org/United_States_Constitution.

Ballotpedia, n.d.(b). "List of Caucuses in the United States Congress," https://ballotpedia.org/List_of_caucuses_in_the_United_States_Congress.

Baracskay, D., n.d. "Political Patronage," *The First Amendment Encyclopedia*, www.mtsu.edu/first-amendment/article/1140/political-patronage.

Barbas, S., 2018. *Confidential Confidential: The Inside Story of Hollywood's Notorious Scandal Magazine* (Chicago Review: Chicago, IL) (epub ed.)

Barone, M., 2019. *How America's Political Parties Change (and How They Don't)*, (Encounter: New York) (e-pub ed.)

Barone, M., 2020. "The Normalcy of Trump's Republican Party," *Wall Street Journal* (August 23).

Barry, J. M., 2005. *The Great Influenza: The Epic Story of the Deadliest Plague in History* (Penguin: New York).

Bates, E., 1860. "Diary" (Nov. 22), p. 48 in Simpson, Sears & Sheehan-Dean (2011).

Bauerlein, M., 2011. "Nathaniel Hawthorne and the Government Worker," *The Public Discourse*, (Nov. 14), www.thepublicdiscourse.com/2011/11/4228/.

Baybeck and Huckfeldt, 2002. "Urban Contexts, Spatially Dispersed Networks, and the Diffusion of Political Information," *Political Geography* 21: 195.

Beard, C. A., 2011 [1918]. *An Economic Interpretation of the Constitution* (Barnes & Noble: New York) (epub ed.)

Benabou, R. and J. Tirole, 2006. "Incentives and Prosocial Behavior," *American Economic Review* 96(5): 1652–1678.

Bender, R. and M. Dalton, 2020. "As COVID-19 Surges, the Big Unknown is Where People are Getting Infected," *Wall Street Journal* (Nov. 15).

Berry, C. R. and A. Fowler, 2018. "Congressional Committees, Legislative Influence, and the Hegemony of Chairs," *Journal of Public Economics* 158: 1–11.

Berry, J. M. 1989. "Subgovernments, Issue Networks, and Political Conflict," in R. A. Harris and S. Miklis (eds.) *Remaking American Politics* (Westview Press: Boulder, CO).

Beschloss, M., 2018. *Presidents at War: The Epic Story from 1807 to Modern Times* (Crown: New York) (epub ed.).

Binder, S., 2014. "Polarized We Govern?" *Brookings Institution: Center for Effective Public Management* (May), www.brookings.edu/research/polarized-we-govern/.

Black, D. 1948. "On the Rationale of Group Decision Making," *Journal of Political Economy* 56(1): 23–34.

Black, E., 2019. "Gerald Ford on Impeachment: In a Practical Sense, He Nailed It," *Minnesota Post* (Dec. 9).

Blakemore, E., 2018. "After WWI, Hundreds of Politicians Were Murdered in Germany," *History* (Oct. 26), https://perma.cc/G3Q3-SCHA.

Blanning, T. 2012. *The Romantic Revolution* (Modern Library: New York) (epub ed.)

Blocker, J. S. Jr. 2006. "Did Prohibition Really Work? Alcohol Prohibition as Public Health Initiative," *American Journal of Public Health* 96(2): 233–243.

Bloom, H. 1978. *Yeats* (Oxford University Press: New York).

Bloom, H. 1998. *Shakespeare: The Invention of the Human* (Riverhead: New York).

Bobbitt, P., 1994. "War Powers: An Essay on John Hart Ely's *War and Responsibility: Constitutional Lessons of Vietnam and its Aftermath*," *Michigan Law Review* 92(6): 1364–1400.

Bobelian, M., 2016. "In Debate, Clinton and Trump Feud Over Supreme Court, Continuing a Campaign Battle Ignited by Nixon in '68," *Forbes* (Oct. 20), https://perma.cc/AW8A-LHXG.

Bokhari, A., 2020a. "Facebook, Google/YouTube, Twitter Censor Viral Video of Doctors' Capitol Hill Coronavirus Press Conference," *Breitbart News* (July 27), www.breitbart.com/tech/2020/07/27/facebook-censors-viral-video-of-doctors-capitol-hill-coronavirus-press-conference/.

Bokhari, A., 2020b. "Election Interference: Google Purges Breitbart from Search Results," *Breitbart News* (July 28), www.breitbart.com/tech/2020/07/28/election-interference-google-purges-breitbart-from-search-results/.

Bolger, D. P., 2021. *The Panzer Killers* (Caliber: New York).

Bolton, A., 2021. "Biden Risks Break with Progressives on Infrastructure," *The Hill* (June 21), https://thehill.com/policy/transportation/559220-biden-risks-break-with-progressives-on-infrastructure.

Bond, P., 2020. "Facebook's Effort to Suppress the Hunter Biden *NY Post* Story Gave it Half the Reach of Major Anti-Trump Scoops," *Newsweek* (Oct. 19).

Bond, S., 2023. "Meta Allows Donald Trump Back on Facebook and Instagram," *National Public Radio* (Jan. 25), www.npr.org/2023/01/25/1146961818/trump-meta-facebook-instagram-ban-ends.

Brands, H. W., 2018. *Heirs of the Founders: Henry Clay, John Calhoun, and Daniel Webster, The Second Generation of American Giants* (Penguin: New York).

Brann, E. T. H., 2016. *The World of the Imagination: Sum and Substance*, pp. 368–369 (Rowman and Littlefield: Louisville, CO).

Bravin, J., 2022. "Decision Marks Culmination of Long Conservative Push," *Wall Street Journal*, (June 25).

Breen, K., 2020. "Jessica Mulroney's TV Show Cancelled after Host Called Out on 'Textbook White Privilege'," *Global News* (June 11) https://globalnews.ca/news/7056919/jessica-mulroney-i-do-redo-cancelled/.

Brenan, M., 2020. "Americans Remain Distrustful of Mass Media," *Gallup Organization* (Sept. 30), https://news.gallup.com/poll/321116/americans-remain-distrustful-mass-media.aspx?version=print.

Brendon, P., 2000. *The Dark Valley: A Panorama of the 1930s* (Jonathan Cape: London, UK).

Breton, A. and R. Wintrobe, 1982. *The Logic of Bureaucratic Conduct* (Cambridge: New York).

Breyer, S., 2013. "The Authority of the Court and the Peril of Politics, (Harvard Law School Scalia Lecture)," *YouTube*, www.youtube.com/watch?v=bHxTQxDVTdU.

Brie, M., 2010. "Is Socialist Politics Possible from a Position in Government?" *Rosa Luxemburg Stiftung* (Brussels) (May 3), https://perma.cc/8XXJ-7DST.

Brinton, C. 1938. *The Anatomy of Revolution* (WW Norton: New York).

Brown, R. J., 2022. "Jon Stewart and Patriotism at the Ballgame," *Wall Street Journal* (Jan. 26).

Brownlow, W. G., 1860. "Letter to RH Appleton" (Nov. 29), pp. 49–56 in Simpson, Sears & Sheehan-Dean (2011).

Brufke, J. G., 2019. "GOP Amps Up Efforts to Recruit Women Candidates," *The Hill* (May 25) https://thehill.com/homenews/campaign/445517-gop-amps-up-efforts-to-recruit-women-candidates/?rl=1.

Bryan, G., 1787. "An Old Whig," pp. 123–26 in Bailyn (1993a).

Bryan, S., 1787 "A Most Daring Attempt to Establish a Despotic Aristocracy" (Oct. 1), pp. 52–62 in Bailyn (1993a).

Buchanan, J., 1860. "Annual Message to Congress," pp. 67–84 in Simpson, Sears & Sheehan-Dean (2011).

Bufford, W., 1993. *Among the Thugs* (Vintage: New York).

Bulla, D. W., n.d. "Party Press Era," *Britannica*, www.britannica.com/topic/party-press-era.

Bundgard, H., J. S. Bundgaard, D. E. Tadeusz et al., 2020. "Effectiveness of Adding a Mask Recommendation to Other Public Health Measures to Prevent SARS-CoV-2 Infection in Danish Mask Wearers: A Randomized Controlled Trial," *Annals of Internal Medicine* M20-6817.

Buntin, J., 2010. *LA Noir: The Struggle for the Soul of America's Most Seductive City* (Crown: New York).

Burge, R. P., 2019. "Evangelicals Show No Decline, Despite Trump and Nones," *Christianity Today*, www.christianitytoday.com/news/2019/march/evangelical-nones-mainline-us-general-social-survey-gss.html.

Burger, M. J. and E. J. Meijers, 2016. "Agglomerations and the Rise of Urban Network Externalities," *Regional Science* 95: 5.

Burgleigh, M., 2014. *Small Wars, Faraway Places: Global Insurrection and the Making of the Modern World, 1945–1965* (Penguin: New York) (epub ed.)

Burke, E., 1887 [1790]. *Reflections on the Revolution in France* (Nimmo: London, U.K.).

Burton, T. A., 2020. *Strange Rites* (Hachette: New York) (epub ed.)

Butter, M., 2020 [2018]. *The Nature of Conspiracy Theories* (trans S Howe) (Polity: Cambridge, UK and Medford, MA) (epub ed.)

Bykowicz, J., 2023. "Why Big-Money Donors Can't Reel in GOP Rebels," *Wall Street Journal* (Jan. 6).

Cabral, L. M. B., 2005. "The Economics of Trust and Reputation: A Primer," (mimeo), https://perma.cc/DJ6J-HETJ.

Camus, A., 1947. *The Plague* (eBookEden.com) (epub ed.)

Camus, A., 1991 [1942]. *The Myth of Sisyphus* (Vintage: New York) (epub ed.)

Capehart, J., 2012. Blog: "Pelosi Defends Her Infamous Healthcare Remark," *Washington Post* (June 20), www.washingtonpost.com/blogs/post-partisan/post/pelosi-defends-her-infamous-health-care-remark/2012/06/20/gJQAqch6qV_blog.html.

Caplan, B., 2007. *The Myth of the Rational Voter: Why Democracies Choose Bad Policies* (Princeton University Press: Princeton, NJ).

Captain, S., 2016. "We Don't Always Know What AI Is Thinking – And That Can Be Scary," *Fast Company* (Nov. 15), https://perma.cc/VS3B-685E.

Carey, M. P., 2012. Rpt. No. R41872, "Presidential Appointments, the Senate's Confirmation Process, and Changes Made in the 112th Congress," *Congressional Research Service* (Oct. 9), https://sgp.fas.org/crs/misc/R41872.pdf.

Carty, H., 1981. "Precedent and the Court of Appeal: Lord Denning's Views Explored," *Legal Studies: The Journal of the Society of Legal Scholars* 1(1): 68–76.

Cassel, C. A., 1982. "Predicting Party Identification, 1956–80: Who Are the Republicans and Who Are the Democrats?" *Political Behavior* 4: 265–82.

Cater, D., 1984. *Power in Washington* (Random House: New York).

Catton, B., 1976 [1961]. *The Centennial History of the Civil War. Vol. I: The Coming Fury* (Pocket Books: New York).

Cavendish, R., 2003. "The Bolshevik-Menshevik Split," *History Today* 53: 11, www.historytoday.com/archive/months-past/bolshevik-menshevik-split.

CBS News, 1960. Video: "Harvest of Shame," (Nov. 26), www.youtube.com/watch?v=yJTVF_dya7E.

CBS News, 1964. Video: "Christmas in Appalachia," *PaleyCenter.org* (Dec. 21), www.paleycenter.org/collection/item/?q=cbs+news&f=all&c=tv&advanced=1&p=1&item=T81:0213.

Chamberlain, S., 2019. "House Democrats Postpone Budget Measure Vote Amid Progressive Resistance," *Fox News* (Apr. 9), https://perma.cc/ATB6-NRWP.

Chandler, R., 1953. "*The Long Goodbye*," pp. 417–734 in F. McShane (ed.), *Chandler: Later Novels & Other Writings* (Library of America: New York).

Chang, A., 2018. "The Stories Fox News Covers Obsessively – And Those It Ignores – in Charts," *Vox*, www.vox.com/2018/5/30/17380096/fox-news-alternate-reality-charts.

Chen, D. L., J. Frankenreiter and S. Yeh, 2016. "Judicial Compliance in District Courts," (Toulouse School of Economics Working Paper No. 16–715, 2016), https://perma.cc/R67X-4PH8.

Child, I. L. and L. Siroto, 1965. "BaKwele and American Esthetic Evaluations Compared," *Ethnology* 4: 349.

Child, I. L. 1983. "The Psychological Meaning of Aesthetic Judgments," *Visual Arts Research* 9(2): 51–59.

Chowell, G., L. Sattenspiel, S. Bansal, and C. Viboud, 2016. "Mathematical Models to Characterize Early Epidemic Growth: A Review," *Physics of Life Reviews*, 18: 66–97.

Churchill, W., 2005[1956]. *History of the English Speaking Peoples, Vol. 2 – The New World* (Barnes & Noble: New York) (epub ed.)

Churchill, W., 2005 [1957]. *History of the English Speaking Peoples, Vol. 3 – The Age of Revolution* (Barnes & Noble: New York) (epub ed.)

Ciucci, F., 2017. "AI and Deep Learning, Simply Explained," *KD Nuggets*, https://perma.cc/2EAV-BSLC.

Clinton, W. J. and J. Patterson, 2018. *The President Is Missing* (Little, Brown & Co.: New York).

Clinton, W. J. and J. Patterson, 2021. *The President's Daughter* (Little, Brown & Co.: New York).

Clover, C., 2016. *Black Wind, White Snow* (Yale University Press: New Haven, CT and London) (epub ed.)

Colker, R., 2021. "The White Supremacist Constitution," *Working Paper*, https://papers.ssrn.com/sol3/papers.cfm?abstract_id=3836733.

Collins, E. 2021. "Infrastructure Package Must Win Approval of House Progressives," *Wall Street Journal* (July 31).

Committee for a Responsible Federal Budget, 2020. "Explaining the TRUST Act: Just the Facts," www.crfb.org/blogs/explaining-trust-act-just-faqs.

Committee for a Responsible Federal Budget, 2021. "The Biden Administration Has Approvd $4.8 Trillion of New Borrowing," www.crfb.org/blogs/biden-administration-has-approved-48-trillion-new-borrowing.

Committee on Licensing Geographic Data and Services, 2004. *Licensing Geographic Data and Services* (National Research Council: Washington, DC).

Congress.gov, 2022(a). "Legislation Sponsored or Cosponsored by Alexandria Ocasio-Cortez," www.congress.gov/member/alexandria-ocasio-cortez/O000172.

Congress.gov, 2022(b). "S.673 – Journalism Competition and Preservation Act of 2021," www.congress.gov/bill/117th-congress/senate-bill/673.

Congressional Research Service, 2019. Report No. R41545: "Congressional Careers: Service Tenure and Patterns of Member Service, 1789–2019," https://crsreports.congress.gov.

Congressional Research Service, 2022. In Focus: "The Major Questions Doctrine," (Nov. 22), https://crsreports.congress.gov/product/pdf/IF/IF12077.

Coogan, T. P., 1999 [1993]. *Eamon DeValera: The Man Who Was Ireland* (Barnes & Noble: New York).

Costello, J., 1982. *The Pacific War: 1941–1945* (Quill: New York).

Cotton, T. Y. C., 1986. "War and American Democracy: Electoral Costs of the Last Five Wars," *The Journal of Conflict Resolution* 30(4): 616–635.

Couch, A., T. Siegel, and B. Kit, 2021. "Hollywood Reporter, Behind Disney's Firing of 'Mandalorian' Star Gina Carano," (Feb. 16), www.hollywoodreporter.com/news/general-news/behind-disneys-firing-of-mandalorian-star-gina-carano-4133813/.

Coulter, A. 2022. "Liberal Doomsday Scenario: Free Speech on Twitter," (Apr. 27), www.breitbart.com/the-media/2022/04/27/ann-coulter-liberal-doomsday-scenario-free-speech-on-twitter/.

Covarrubias, M., G. Gutiérrez, and T. Philippon, 2019. "From Good to Bad Concentration? US Industries Over the Past 30 Years," *National Bureau of Economic Research*, Working Paper No. 25983, www.nber.org/papers/w25983.

Cox, D. A., 2021. "The State of American Friendship: Change, Challenges, and Loss," *Survey Center on American Life* (June 8), www.americansurveycenter.org/research/the-state-of-american-friendship-change-challenges-and-loss/.

Crane, E., 2022. "Dems Spend $53M to Boost Far-Right GOP Candidates Despite Rhetoric: Report," *New York Post* (Sept. 12).

Crocker, R., 2012. CRS Report No. R42831: "Congressional Redistricting: An Overview," *Congressional Research Service* (Nov. 21), https://sgp.fas.org/crs/misc/R42831.pdf.

d'Aspremont, C., J. Gabszewicz and J.-F. Thisse, 1979. "On Hotelling's 'Stability in Competition'," *Econometrica* 47(5): 1145.

Daley, E., 2021. "What is an Executive Order, and Why Don't Presidents Use Them All the Time?" *The Conversation.com* (Jan. 26), https://theconversation.com/what-is-an-executive-order-and-why-dont-presidents-use-them-all-the-time-150896.

Daly, C. B., 2017. "How Woodrow Wilson's Propaganda Machine Changed American Journalism," *Smithsonian* (Apr. 28), www.smithsonianmag.com/history/how-woodrow-wilsons-propaganda-machine-changed-american-journalism-180963082/.

Danforth, J., Ginsberg, B., Griffith, T. B., et al., "Lost, Not Stolen: The Conservative Case That Trump Lost and Biden Won the 2020 Presidential Election," *Lostnotstolen.org*, https://lostnotstolen.org/.

Dave, D. M., A. I. Friedson, K. Matsuzawa, D. McNichols and J. J. Sabia, 2020. "Did the Wisconsin Supreme Court Restart a COVID-19 Epidemic: Evidence from a Natural Experiment," *National Bureau of Economic Research*, Working Paper No. 27322.

Davis, J., 1861. "Inaugural Address," pp. 201–206 in Simpson, Sears & Sheehan-Dean (2011).

De Moustier, E. F. E., 1788. Letter to Compte de Montmorin, "On the Difficulty of Judging What the Outcome Will Be" (Mar. 16), pp. 355–356 in Bailyn (1993b).

De Tocqueville, A., 1899 [1835]. *Democracy in America* (Colonial Press: London) (H. Reeve Tr.).

Décugis, J.-M., P. Guéna and M. Leplongeon, 2021. *La Poudriere* (Grasset: Paris) (epub ed.) (in French).

Department of Defense, 1997. *Selected Manpower Statistics: Fiscal Year 1997* (US Government: Washington, DC), https://perma.cc/57Y3-A9G2.

Department of Justice/Office of Inspector General, 2019. "Report of Investigation of Former Federal Bureau of Investigation Director James Comey's Disclosure of Sensitive Investigative Information and Handling of Certain Memoranda," https://oig.justice.gov/reports/2019/01902.pdf.

Derfler, L., 2002. *The Dreyfus Affair* (Greenwood Publishing: Westport, CT).

Deschatres, F. and D. Sornette, 2005. "Dynamics of Book Sales: Endogenous versus Exogenous Shocks in Complex Networks," *Physical Review* 72: 016112-1.

DeSilver, D., 2015. "What is the House Freedom Caucus, and Who's in It?" *Pew Research Center* (Oct. 20), https://perma.cc/6CAE-HJGR.

Deutscher Bundestag, 2006. "Elections in the Weimar Republic," https://perma.cc/3W8N-9YXN.

Dickenson, J., 1768. "Letters from a Pennsylvania Farmer to the Inhabitants of the British Colonies," pp. 407–489 in Wood (2015).

Dills, A. K. & J. A. Miron, 2004. "Alcohol Prohibition and Cirrhosis," *American Law and Economics Review* 6(2): 285–318.

Dininatz, V. G., n.d. "Communist Party of the United States of America," *Britannica*, www.britannica.com/topic/Communist-Party-of-the-United-States-of-America.

Dirac, P. A. M., 1939. "The Relation between Mathematics and Physics," *Proceedings of the Royal Society of Edinburgh* 59: 122–129.

Dostoevsky, F., 2001[1864]. "Notes from the Underground," pp. 103–207 in *The Best Sort Stories of Fyodor Dostoevsky*, 2001 (Modern Library: New York) (epub ed.) at p. 114.

Douglas, J., J. Sugden, and D. Roland, 2022. "British COVID Surge is Less Severe," (Jan. 8).

Douglass, F., 1860. Essay in *Douglass's Monthly*: "The Late Election" (December), pp. 57–62 in Simpson, Sears & Sheehan-Dean (2011).

Downs, A., 1957. *An Economic Theory of Democracy* (Addison-Wesley: Boston, MA).

Drake, H. B., and Gordon, C., 2022. "Firing Civil Servants and Washington Office Politics," *Wall Street Journal* (Aug. 17).

Druckman, J. N. and K. R. Nelson, 2003. "Framing and Deliberation: How Citizens' Conversations Limit Elite Influence," *American Journal of Political Science* 47: 728–744.

DuBois, W. E. B., 1915. *The Negro*, in *The W.E.B. Du Bois Collection* 833–997, n.d. (Karpathos Collections) (epub ed.)

Dueholm, J. A., 2010. "A Bill of Lading Delivers the Goods: The Constitutionality and Effect of the Emancipation Proclamation," *Journal of the Abraham Lincoln Association*, 31(1): 22–28.

Durlauf, S. N., 1999. "How Can Statistical Mechanics Contribute to Social Science?" *Proceedings of the National Academy of Sciences* 96: 10582–10584.

Dworkin, R., 1996. *How Law Is Like Literature* (Routledge: London).

Dyck, A., D. Moss and L. Zingales, 2013. "Media versus Special Interests," *Journal of Law & Economics* 56(3): 521–553.

Ecarma, C., 2022. "New CNN Chief Wants Anchors to Say Goodbye to the 'Big Lie'," *Vanity Fair* (June 16), www.vanityfair.com/news/2022/06/cnn-chief-chris-licht-big-lie?utm_source=onsite-share&utm_medium=email&utm_campaign=onsite-share&utm_brand=vanity-fair.

Economides, N., 1993. "Hotelling's 'Main Street' with More Than Two Competitors," *Regional Science* 33(3): 303–319.

Edwards, L. P., 1927. *The Natural History of Revolution* (University of Chicago Press: Chicago, IL).

Ekins, E., 2020. "Poll: 62% of Americans Say They Have Political Views They are Afraid to Share," *Cato Institute* (June 22), www.cato.org/survey-reports/poll-62-americans-say-they-have-political-views-theyre-afraid-share#introduction.

Elber, L., 2021. "Mike Richards Out as 'Jeopardy!' Host after Past Scrutinized," (Aug. 20), https://apnews.com/article/arts-and-entertainment-abce3254b99be0348d96a7c7310d1e52.

Elberse, A., 2013. *Blockbusters: Hit-Making, Risk-Taking, and the Big Business of Entertainment* (Henry Holt & Co.: New York) (epub ed.)

Elinson, Z., 2020. "In Los Angeles, Political Leaders Press to Remove Elected Sheriff," *Wall Street Journal* (Dec. 4).

Eliot, T. S., 1957 [1944]. "What is a Classic?" in T. S. Eliot, *On Poetry and Poets* (Farrar, Straus and Giroux: New York).

Ellman, M. and F. Germano, 2009. "What Do the Papers Sell? A Model of Advertising and Media Bias," *The Economic Journal* 119(537): 680–704.

Eloise, M., 2021. "A Guide to Spotting and Avoiding 'Wokefishing' in Dating'," *Cosmopolitan* (Jan. 8), www.cosmopolitan.com/uk/love-sex/relationships/a34795394/wokefishing/.

Ely, J. H., 1973. "The Wages of Crying Wolf: A Comment on *Roe v. Wade*," *Yale Law Journal* 82: 920–949.

Engerman. S. L. and K. L. Sokoloff, 2005. "The Evolution of Suffrage Institutions in the New World," *National Bureau of Economic Research*, Working Paper, www.nber.org/papers/w8512.

Epstein, L., W. M. Landes and R. A. Posner, 2013. *The Behavior of Federal Judges: A Theoretical and Empirical Study of Rational Choice*. (Harvard University Press: Cambridge MA).

Erwin, J., 2016. "Twelve States That Considered Splitting Apart," *Mental Floss* (Sept. 5), www.mentalfloss.com/article/58789/12-us-states-considered-splitting-apart.

Etahad, M., 2020. "A Long History of Militant Activism Keeps Protests Alive in Portland," *Los Angeles Times* (Aug. 24), https://news.yahoo.com/long-history-militant-activism-keeps-100005328.html.

Fadiman, C., 1985 [1941]. "The Reviewing Business," pp. 260–272, in H Knowles (ed.) *A Treasury of American Writers from Harper's Magazine*.

Fahrenthold, D. A., 2012. "In Congress, Sunset Clauses are Commonly Passed but Rarely Followed Through," *Washington Post* (Dec. 15), www.washingtonpost.com/politics/in-congress-sunset-clauses-are-commonly-passed-but-rarely-followed-through/2012/12/15/9d8e3ee0-43b5-11e2-8e70-e1993528222d_story.html.

Fahrenthold, D. A. and K. Zezima, 2016. "For Ted Cruz, The 2013 Shutdown Was a Defining Moment," *Washington Post* (Feb. 16). https://perma.cc/VD36-77P2.

Fallows, J., 2012. "How the Modern Faux-Filibuster Came to Be," *The Atlantic* (April 2).

Farrow, R., 2017. "From Aggressive Overtures to Sexual Assault: Harvey Weinstein's Accusers Tell Their Stories," *The New Yorker* (Oct. 10).

Farrow, R., 2019. *Catch and Kill: Lies, Spies and a Conspiracy to Protect Predators* (Little, Brown & Co.: New York) (epub ed.)

Fechner, H., 2014. "Managing Political Polarization in Congress," *Utah Law Review* at pp. 757–771.

"The Federalist," [pseud: Hamilton, A, J. Jay & J. Madison]. 2018 [1787–88]. *The Federalist Papers* (Fall River Press: New York).

Feinstein, B. D., 2009. "Oversight, Despite the Odds: Assessing Congressional Committee Hearings as a Means of Control Over the Federal Bureaucracy." (PhD Thesis: Harvard School of Government).

Ferling, J., 2004. "Thomas Jefferson, Aaron Burr and the Election of 1800," *Smithsonian* (Nov. 1).

Fernández-Armesto, A., 2019. *Out of Our Minds: What We Think and How We Come to Think It* (University of California Press: Oakland, CA) (epub ed.)

Fernández del Río, A., 2010. "Coupled Ising Models and Interdependent Discrete Choices under Social Influence in Homogeneous Populations," Master's thesis, Departamento de Física Fundamental (UNED). arXiv:physics.soc-ph/1104.4887.

Fernández del Río, A., 2011. "Coupled Ising models and Interdependent Discrete Choices under Social Influence in Homogeneous Populations," (Ph.D thesis), https://arxiv.org/abs/1104.4887 (Apr. 26).

Fernández del Río, A., E. Korutcheva and J. de la Rubia, 2012. "Interdependent Binary Choices Under Social Influence: Phase Diagram for Homogeneous Unbiased Populations," *Complexity* 17(6): 31–41.

Fialka, J., 2020. "U.S. Geoengineering Research Gets a Lift with $4 Million from Congress," *E&E News* (Jan. 23), www.sciencemag.org/news/2020/01/us-geoengineering-research-gets-lift-4-million-congress.

Finneran, R. J. (ed.), 1989. *The Collected Poems of WB Yeats: A New Edition* (Macmillan: New York) (epub ed.)

Fischhoff, B., P. Slovic, S. Lichtenstein, S. Read and B. Combs, 1978. "How Safe is Safe Enough? A Psychoactive Study of Attitudes Toward Technological Risks and Benefits," pp. 80–103 in Slovic (2000).

Fish, S. 1989. *Doing What Comes Naturally: Change, Rhetoric, and the Practice of Theory in Literary and Legal Studies* (Oxford University Press, 1989).

Fischer, S., 2022. "Scoop: CNN Evaluating Partisan Talent as Part of Push to Make Coverage More Neutral," *Axios* (June 7), www.axios.com/2022/06/07/cnn-evaluating-partisan-talent-chris-licht.

Fitton, T., 2019. "'Air Pelosi' – What You Don't Know About the Lucrative Travel Our Leaders Enjoy on Your Dime," *Fox News* (Jan. 24), https://perma.cc/MJ4M-RRQD.

Fitzpatrick, M., 2013. "Why Ted Cruz Read Green Eggs and Ham in the U.S. Senate," *CBC News* (Sept. 25), https://perma.cc/HZN3-ABMC.

Fitzpatrick, S., 1996. "Signals from Below: Soviet Letters of Denunciation of the 1930s," *Journal of Modern History* 68 (4): 831–866.

Fitzpatrick, S. and R. Gellately, 1996. "Introduction to the Practices of Denunciation in Modern European History," *Journal of Modern History* 68(4): 747–767.

Flint, J., 2020. "A&E Has Lost Half Its Viewers Since Dropping 'Live PD'," *Wall Street Journal* (July 24).

FOIA Project Staff, 2019a. "FOIA Suits Rise Because Agencies Don't Respond Even as Requesters Wait Longer to File Suit," *The FOIA Project* (Dec. 15), http://foiaproject.org/2019/12/15/foia-suits-rise-because-agencies-dont-respond-even-as-requesters-wait-longer-to-file-suit/.

FOIA Project Staff, 2019b. "Scrutinizing Attorney Fee Awards in FOIA Legislation," *The FOIA Project* (Dec. 19), http://foiaproject.org/2018/12/19/attorney-fee-awards-foia-litigation/.

Ford, C. S., E. T. Prothro and I. L. Child, 1966. "Some Transcultural Comparisons of Esthetic Judgment," *Journal of Social Psychology* 68: 19.

Foreman, C. H. 1988. *Signals from the Hill: Congressional Oversight and the Challenge of Social Regulation* (Yale University Press: New Haven, CT).

van Frank, M. 2015. "'This Is the Right Place': Mormon Migration to Utah," *The Spectrum*, www.thespectrum.com/story/life/faith/2015/02/20/right-place-mormon-migration-utah/23771155.

Frazee, G. and Desjardins, L., 2018. "How the Government Shutdown Compared to Every Other Since 1976," *PBS* (Dec. 26), https://perma.cc/PL66-BEW7.

Freeman, 2020. "Can Bernie Standers Find Happiness?" *Wall Street Journal On-Line* (Dec. 29), www.wsj.com/articles/can-bernie-sanders-find-happiness-11609193851.

Fryer, R. G. Jr. 2019. "An Empirical Analysis of Racial Differences in Police Use of Force," *Journal of Political Economy* 127(3): 1210–1261.

Fudenberg, D. and E. Maskin, 1986. "The Folk Theorem in Repeated Games with Discounting or Incomplete Information," *Econometrica* 54 (3): 533–554.

Fuller, T., 2022. "In Landslide, San Francisco Forces Out 3 Board of Education Members," *New York Times* (Feb. 16) www.nytimes.com/2022/02/16/us/san-francisco-school-board-recall.html.

Furr, A., 2021. "Connecticut Democrat Proposes Bill to Fine Those Who Do Not Vote in State Elections," *Breitbart News* (Jan. 29), www.breitbart.com/local/2021/01/28/connecticut-democrat-proposes-bill-to-fine-those-who-do-not-vote-state-elections/.

Gage, B. 2022. *G-Man: J. Edgar Hoover and the Making of the American Century* (Viking: New York).

Galam, S., and S. Moscovici, 1991. "Towards a Theory of Collective Phenomena: Consensus and Attitude Changes in Groups," *European Journal of Social Psychology* 21: 49–74.

Gallup Organization, n.d. "Congress and the Public," https://news.gallup.com/poll/1600/congress-public.aspx.

Galston, W. A. 2019. "Biden Exits Abortion's Wide Middle Lane," *Wall Street Journal* (June 11).

Galvin, G. 2021. "As White House Warns of Fourth Wave, 1 in 4 Adults Say They Know Someone Who's Died of COVID-19," *Morning Consult* (Mar. 31), https://morningconsult.com/2021/03/31/how-many-us-adults-know-someone-who-died-of-covid/.

Gammerman, E., 2021. "Goodnight Ninja? Knuffle Blobfish? Children's Books Get the Algorithm Treatment," *Wall Street Journal* (Mar. 24).

Gangel, J., J. Herb, M. Cohen, E. Stewart, and B. Starr, 2021. "'They're Not Going to F**king Succeed': Top Generals Feared Trump Would Attempt a Coup After Election, According to New Book," *CNN Politics* (July 14), www.cnn.com/2021/07/14/politics/donald-trump-election-coup-new-book-excerpt/index.html.

Gans, D. J. 1985. "Persistence of Party Success in American Presidential Elections," *Journal of Interdisciplinary Studies* 16(2): 221–237.

Gehlbach, S., 2022. *Formal Models of Domestic Politics* (Cambridge University Press: New York and Cambridge).

Gellman, I., 2021. "Nixon's Noble Pass on a 1960 Recount," *Wall Street Journal* (Jan. 5).

Gentzkow, M., E. L. Glaeser, and C. Goldin, 2006. "The Rise of the Fourth Estate: How Newspapers Became Informative and Why It Mattered," pp. 187–230 in E. L. Glaeser and C. Goldin (eds.), *Corruption and Reform: Lessons from America's Economic History* (University of Chicago Press: Chicago, IL).

George, D. A., 2012. Blog: "What Is a Fan Page of Facebook? You Need to Know This!" *Heyo Blog* (Aug. 9), https://blog.heyo.com/what-is-a-fan-page/.

Gill, N. S. 2019. "Patrons and Clients in Roman Society," *ThoughtCo.*, www.thoughtco.com/patrons-the-roman-social-structure-117908#:~:text=The%20people%20of%20ancient%20Rome,and%20loyalty%20to%20their%20patrons.

Giridharas, A., 2019. "Once More, with Feelings," *Time* (June 17).

Gittleson, B., 2021. "Biden Tells Muir on Filibuster Exception for Voting Rights: 'Whatever It Takes'," *ABC News* (Dec. 23), https://abcnews.go.com/Politics/biden-tells-muir-filibuster-exception-voting-rights-takes/story?id=81919381.

Goetzmann, W. N., S. A. Ravid and R. Sverdlove, 2013. "The Pricing of Soft and Hard Information: Economic Lessons from Screenplay Sales," *Journal of Cultural Economics* 23: 271.

Golding, B., 2023. "Schiff Wanted Journalist Paul Sperry's Account Suspended Over Reporting on Trump Whistleblower, Twitter Files Reveals," *New York Post* (Jan. 3).

Goldsmith, J., 2019. *In Hoffa's Shadow: A Stepfather, a Disappearance in Detroit, and My Search for the Truth* (Farrar, Straus and Giroux: New York) (epub ed.)

Goldstein, A., 2016. "How the Demise of Her Health-Care Plan Led to the Politician Clinton is Today," *Washington Post* (Aug. 25) https://perma.cc/CLL6-2FYP.

Gonyea, D., 2019. "The Longest Government Shutdown in History, No Longer – How 1995 Changed Everything," *National Public Radio* (Jan. 12) https://perma.cc/9S54-NPVU.

Goodwin, M., 2018. "Hillary's Calling for a 'Civil' War – Where's the Outrage?" *Fox News* (Oct. 10) https://perma.cc/K6EV-3UYK.

Gordon-Reed, A., 2011. "'Uncle Tom's Cabin' and the Art of Persuasion," *The New Yorker* (June 13–20).

Grant, U. S., 2009 [1885]. *The Complete Personal Memoirs of Ulysses S. Grant* (Seven Treasures Publications: n.p.) (epub ed.)

Gray, M., 2020. "Maven Media Staffers Call for Shutdown of Blue Lives Matter Website," (June 6), https://nypost.com/2020/06/06/maven-staffers-call-for-shutdown-of-blue-lives-matter-website/.

Greeley, H. 1860. Editorial: "Going to Go," *New York Tribune* (Nov. 9), pp. 8–10 in Simpson, Sears & Sheehan-Dean (2011).

Green, D., 2021. Exclusive: "New York Times Quashed COVID Origins Inquiry," *The Spectator* (Aug. 2).

Green, D. P. and A. S. Gerber, 2015. *Get Out the Vote: How to Increase Voter Turnout* (Brookings Foundation).

Green, M. N., 2015. *Underdog Politics: The Minority in the US House of Representatives* (Yale University Press: New Haven and London).

Greenberg, D. 2016. *Republic of Spin: An Inside History of the American Presidency* (WW Norton: New York) (epub ed.)

Grinspan, J., 2016. *The Virgin Vote: How Young Americans Made Democracy Social, Politics Personal, and Voting Popular in the Nineteenth Century* (University of North Carolina Press: Chapel Hill) (epub ed.)

Grinspan, J., 2021. *The Age of Acrimony: How Americans Fought to Fix Their Democracy, 1860–1913* (Bloomsbury: New York) (epub ed.)

Grofman, B., 1985. "Criteria for Districting: A Social Science Perspective," *UCLA Law Review* 33: 77.

Grofman, B., 1991. "What Happens After One Person-One Vote? Implications of the United States Experience for Canada," p. 156 in J. C. Courtney, P. MacKinnon and D. E. Smith (eds.) *Drawing Boundaries: Legislatures, Courts, and Electoral Values*.

Guelzo, A. C., 2013. *Gettysburg: The Last Invasion* (Knopf: New York) (epub ed.)

Guelzo, A. C., 2015. "What Did Lincoln Really Think of Jefferson?" *New York Times* (July 4).

Guelzo, A. C., 2021a. "Lee, Robert E. and Slavery," *Virginia Humanities* (Feb. 9), https://encyclopediavirginia.org/entries/lee-robert-e-and-slavery/.

Guelzo. A. C., 2021b. *Robert E Lee: A Life* (Knopf: New York) (e-pub ed.)

Guess, A., B. Nyhan and J. Reifler, 2018. "Selective Exposure to Misinformation: Evidence from the Consumption of Fake News in the 2016 US Presidential Campaign," *Working Paper, (Princeton Center for the Study of Democratic Politics)* https://csdp.princeton.edu/publications/selective-exposure-misinformation-evidence-consumption-fake-news-during-2016-us.

Guevara, E., 1961. *Guerilla Warfare* (University of Nebraska Press: Lincoln, NE).

Guriev, S., N. Melnikov and E. Zhuravskaya, 2021. "3G Internet and Confidence in Government," *Quarterly Journal of Economics* 136(4): 2533–2613.

Gwynne, S. C., 2014. *Rebel Yell: The Violence, Passion, and Redemption of Stonewall Jackson* (Scribners: New York).

Hamburger, P., 2021. "Court Packing is a Dangerous Game," *Wall Street Journal* (Apr. 16).

Hanson, P. C., 2015. Report: "Restoring Regular Order in Congressional Appropriations," (Brookings Institution: Washington, DC) https://perma.cc/VR8S-TH68.

Hargett, K., 2020. "Tuskegee Experiment History Leads to Coronavirus Mistrust: Some African Americans Say They Are Against the Coronavirus Vaccine," *KSLA12 (Shreveport LA) News* (Dec. 10), www.ksla.com/2020/12/10/tuskegee-experiment-history-leads-coronavirus-mistrust/.

Harris, R., and J. Paxman, 2002 [1982]. *A Higher Form of Killing* (Random House: New York).

Harris, W. C., 2011. *Lincoln and the Border States* (Kansas University Press: Lawrence KS).

Hawes, J., 2019. *The Shortest History of Germany* (The Experiment: New York) (epub ed.)

Hawkins, S., D. Yudkin, M. Juan-Torres and T. Dixon, 2018. "Hidden Tribes: A Study of America's Polarized Landscape," *More in Common*, www.immigrationresearch.org/system/files/Hidden_Tribes.pdf.

Hawthorne, N., 1994 [1850]. *The Scarlet Letter* (Dover: New York) (e-pub ed.)

Hay, J., 1861. "Diary" (May 10), pp. 350–354 in Simpson, Sears & Sheehan-Dean (2011).

Heller J., 2015. "Rumors and Realities: Making Sense of HIV/AIDS Conspiracy Narratives and Contemporary Legends," *American Journal of Public Health* 105: 43–50.

Helmore, E., 2020. "Can Anna Wintour Survive Fashion's Reckoning with Racism?" *The Guardian* (June 20), www.theguardian.com/fashion/2020/jun/13/anna-wintour-vogue-diversity-racism-debate.

Henkel, J., 2004. "The Jukebox Model of Innovation: A Model of Commercial Open Source Development," *Center for Economic Policy Research Working Paper* https://papers.ssrn.com/sol3/papers.cfm?abstract_id=578142.

Henninger, D., 2018. "What is Elizabeth Warren?" *Wall Street Journal* (Oct. 17).

Herby, J., L. Jonung, and S. H. Hanke, 2022. "A Literature Review and Meta-Analysis of the Effects of Lockdowns on COVID-19 Mortality," *Journal of Applied Economics* 200: 1–61, https://sites.krieger.jhu.edu/iae/

files/2022/01/A-Literature-Review-and-Meta-Analysis-of-the-Effects-of-Lockdowns-on-COVID-19-Mortality.pdf.

Heshmat, S., 2015. "Why Do We Remember Certain Things, But Forget Others?" *Psychology Today*, www.psychologytoday.com/us/blog/science-choice/201510/why-do-we-remember-certain-things-forget-others.

Hill, B. 1860. "Speech at Milledgeville," pp. 14–33 in Simpson, Sears & Sheehan-Dean (2011).

Von Hippel, 2020. "Romney's Not Really Alone. Republican Senators Were Ready to Impeach Nixon in 1974," *Washington Post* (Feb. 12).

Hofstadter, R. 1952. "Cuba, the Philippines, and Manifest Destiny," pp. 623–658 in Hofstadter (2020).

Hofstadter, R., 1955. *The Age of Reform: From Bryan to FDR* (Vintage: New York) (epub ed.)

Hofstadter, R., 1959(a). "The Political Philosophy of the Framers of the Constitution," pp. 800–814 in Hofstadter (2020).

Hofstadter, R., 1959(b). FDR's Economic and Social Philosophy," pp. 815–836 in Hofstadter (2020).

Hofstadter, R., 1964(a). "What Happened to the Antitrust Movement," pp. 659–700 in Hofstadter (2020).

Hofstadter, R., 1964(b). "Goldwater and Pseudo-Conservative Politics," pp. 579–619 in Hofstadter (2020).

Hofstadter, R., 1964(c). "Goldwater and His Party," pp. 896–918 in Hofstadter (2020)

Hofstadter, R., 1969. *The Idea of a Party System: The Rise of Legitimate Opposition in the United States, 1780–1840* (University of California Press: Berkeley and London).

Hofstadter, R., 2020. *Hofstadter* (S. Willenz, ed.) (Library of America: New York).

Holmes, O. W. Sr., 1858. "The Deacon's Masterpiece: Or the Wonderful 'One-Hoss Shay. A Logical Story," in O. W. Holmes Sr., *The Wonderful 'One Hoss' Shay and Other Poems*, 1897 (Frederick A. Stokes: New York).

Holmes, T., 2020. "38% of Americans Are Currently Boycotting a Company, and Many Cite Political and Coronavirus Pandemic-Related Reasons," *CompareCards News and Advice*, www.comparecards.com/blog/38-percent-boycotting-companies-political-pandemic-reasons/.

Hoppe, D., 2021. "The Filibuster Made the Civil Rights Act Possible," *Wall Street Journal* (April 11).

Horwitz, J. and J. Scheck, 2021. "Facebook Increasingly Suppresses Political Movements It Deems Dangerous," *Wall Street Journal* (Oct. 22).

Hotelling, H., 1929. "Stability in Competition," *The Economic Journal* 39 (153): 41–57.

House Budget Committee, 2021. "Budget Reconciliation: The Basics," (Aug. 11), https://budget.house.gov/publications/fact-sheet/budget-reconciliation-basics.

Houston, S. 1860. "Letter to HM Watkins and Others," (Nov. 20), pp. 37–42 in Simpson, Sears & Sheehan-Dean (2011).

Huckfeldt, R., 1986. *Politics in Context: Assimilation and Conflict in Urban Neighborhoods* (Agathon Press: New York).

Huckfeldt, R., 2014. "Networks, Contexts, and the Combinatorial Dynamics of Democratic Politics," *Political Psychology* 35 (Supp.): 43–68.

Huckfeldt, R., 2017. Ithiel de Sola Pool Lecture: "Interdependence, Communication, and Aggregation: Transforming Voters into Electorates," *PS: Political Science and Politics* 50(1).

Huckfeldt, R., J. J. Mondak, M. Hayes, M. T. Pietryka, and J. Reilly 2013. "Networks, Interdependence, and Social Influence in Politics," pp. 662–698 in L. Huddy, D. O. Sears, and J. Levy, eds., *Oxford Handbook of Political Psychology* (Oxford University Press: New York).

Hughes, S. and L. Wise, 2020. "Filibuster Rule Changes Weighed," *Wall Street Journal* (Sept. 2).

Iwao, S. and I. L. Child, 1966. "Comparison of Esthetic Judgments by American Experts and by Japanese Potters," *Journal of Social Psychology* 68: 27.

Jackson, M. O. 2008. *Social and Economic Networks* (Princeton University Press: Princeton, NJ).

Jefferson, T., 1787(a). "Letter to WS Smith" (Nov. 13), in Bailyn (1993a) at pp. 309–310.

Jefferson, T., 1787(b). "Letter to John Madison" (Dec. 20), pp. 209–213 in Bailyn (1993a).

Jefferson, T., 2018 [1785]. "Notes on the State of Virginia," pp. 69040–7139 in *The Complete Works of Thomas Jefferson* (Madison & Adams Press: Praha: Czech Republic) (epub ed.)

Jenkins, H. W. Jr., 2019. "Who Will Turn Over the 2016 Rocks?" *Wall Street Journal* (Nov. 27).

Jenkins, H. W. Jr., 2021(a). "Google and Facebook on the Barbie," *Wall Street Journal* (Feb. 24).

Jenkins, H. W. Jr., 2021(b). "Jan. 6 and DC's Political Death Inquests," *Wall Street Journal* (Mar. 6–7).

Jenkins, H. W. Jr., 2021(c). "Delta's Gift is Hybrid Immunity," *Wall Street Journal* (Aug. 21).

Jenkins, H. W. Jr., 2021(d). "The Hunter Biden Laptop is Real," *Wall Street Journal* (July 9).

Jenkins, H. W. Jr., 2022(a). "Why the 'Big Lie' Narrative Will Fail," *Wall Street Journal* (Jan. 8).

Jenkins, H. W. Jr., 2022(b). "Media Bias and Hunter's Laptop," *Wall Street Journal* (Apr. 13).

Jervis, R., 2010. *Why Intelligence Fails: Lessons from the Iranian Revolution and the Iraq War* (Cornell University Press: Ithaca, NY).

Johnson, D., 1962. "Wilson, Burleson, and Censorship in the First World War," *The Journal of Southern History* 28(1).

Johnson, P. E. and R. Huckfeldt, 2005. "Agent-Based Explanations for the Survival of Disagreement in Social Networks," in A. Zuckerman (ed.), *The Social Logic of Politics* (Temple University Press: Philadelphia, PA).

Johnson, R., 2019. "Close the Book on Shutdowns," *Wall Street Journal* (Sept. 22), https://perma.cc/7Q5R-VVM3.

Johnson, T., 2021. "ABC News' 'World News Tonight' Tops First Quarter, But Viewership of Evening News Falls across Broadcast Networks," *Deadline*

(Mar. 30), https://deadline.com/2021/03/abc-news-world-news-tonight-ratings-first-quarter-evening-newscasts-1234724520/.

Johnston, R. J., and C. J. Pattie, 2011. "Social Networks, Geography, and Neighbourhood Effects," pp. 307ff. in J. Scott and P. J. Carrington (eds.) *The Sage Handbook of Social Network Analysis* (Sage Publishing: Thousand Oaks, CA).

Johnston, R. J., K. Jones, R. Sarker, C. Propper, S. Burgess, and A. Bolster, 2004. "Party Support and the Neighbourhood Effect: Spatial Polarisation of the British Electorate, 1991–2001," *Political Geography* 23: 367–402.

Kahn, N. L. and S. J. Levien, 2021. "SEAS Researchers Postpone Test Flight for Controversial Geoengineering Project to Block Sun," *Harvard Crimson* (Apr. 5), www.thecrimson.com/article/2021/4/5/seas-sun-blocking-test-flight-postponed/.

Kahneman, D., 2011. *Thinking Fast and Slow* (Farrar, Strauss and Giroux: New York).

Kane, T., 2019. "Trump Base Wants Immigration Compromise," *Wall Street Journal* (Feb. 27) https://perma.cc/UW3N-NFCY.

Kantor, J. and M. Twohey, 2017. "Harvey Weinstein Paid Off Sexual Harassment Accusers for Decades," *New York Times* (Oct. 5).

Karapetyan, A. and S. M. Maurer, 2021. "Picking Up the Pieces: Options for Federal Anti-Gerrymandering Law after Rucho," *Wake Forest Journal of Law & Policy* 11(2): 237–295.

Kavanaugh, S. D., 2021. "Amid Calls to 'Defund the Police,' Most Portland Residents Want Police Presence Maintained or Increased, Poll Finds," (May 18), www.oregonlive.com/news/2021/05/amid-calls-to-defund-the-police-most-portland-residents-want-police-presence-maintained-or-increased-poll-finds.html.

Keith, D., 2019. Blog: "Let's Talk About Geoengineering," (Harvard University: Keith Group) (Mar. 21), www.project-syndicate.org/commentary/solar-geoengineering-global-climate-debate-by-david-keith-2019-03.

Keith, T., 2014. "Wielding a Pen and a Phone, Obama Goes It Alone," *National Public Radio* (Jan. 20), www.npr.org/2014/01/20/263766043/wielding-a-pen-and-a-phone-obama-goes-it-alone.

KEKST-CNC, 2020. Report: "COVID-19 Opinion Tracker (Fourth Edition)," (July 10–15), www.kekstcnc.com/media/2793/kekstcnc_research_covid-19_opinion_tracker_wave-4.pdf.

Kendall, B. and M. Hackman, 2021. "DACA Immigration Program Invalidated by Federal Judge," *Wall Street Journal* (July 17).

Kennedy, D. M. 1986. "Reverence, Ignorance and Blazing Apathy," *New York Times* (Sept. 14).

Kennedy, D. M., 1999. *Freedom from Fear: The American People in Depression and War, 1929–1945* (Oxford University Press: New York).

Kerns, K. and L. S. Locklear, 2019. "Three New Census Bureau Products Show Domestic Migration at Regional, State, and County Levels," *US Census Bureau* (Apr. 29), www.census.gov/library/stories/2019/04/moves-from-south-west-dominate-recent-migration-flows.html.

Kershaw, D. N., 1972. "A Negative-Income-Tax Experiment," *Scientific American* 227(4): 19–25 (Oct.).

Kessler, A., 2017. "Bad Intelligence Behind the Wheel," *Wall Street Journal* (Apr. 24).

Kessler, A., 2021. "Online Speech Wars are Here to Stay," *Wall Street Journal* (Jan. 25).

Key, P., 2020. "Obama: Not Easy to 'Unwind' Fox News, Rush Limbaugh Falsely Claiming 'White Males Are Victims,'" *Breitbart News* (Nov. 25), www.breitbart.com/clips/2020/11/25/obama-not-easy-to-unwind-fox-news-rush-limbaugh-falsely-claiming-white-males-are-victims/.

Kiefer, H., 2020. "Second City CEO Andrew Alexander Resigns Following Accusations of Institutional Racism," *Vulture* (June 5), www.vulture.com/2020/06/second-city-andrew-alexander-resigns-after-claims-of-racism.html.

Kiley, J., 2017. "In Polarized Era, Fewer Americans Hold a Mix of Conservative and Liberal Views," *Pew Research Center* https://perma.cc/FWG6-LPHB.

Kilgore, E., 2019. "Yes, a 'Glass of Water' Could Win AOC's Seat. That's Why Progressives Demand More from It," *New York Magazine* (Apr. 16) at https://nymag.com/intelligencer/2019/04/safe-districts-exist-to-produce-insurgents-like-aoc.html.

King, M. T., 2020. "Amy Klobuchar, Insurgent," *Wall Street Journal* (Feb. 18).

Klein, E., 2021. "Barack Obama on How Joe Biden Is 'Finishing the Job,'" *New York Times* (June 1).

Koh, Y., 2020. "Neighbors Resort to Online Shaming," *Wall Street Journal* (Apr. 14).

Kolhatkar, S., 2019. "How Elizabeth Warren Came Up with a Plan to Break Up Big Tech," *The New Yorker* (Aug. 20).

Koonin, S. E., 2021. *Unsettled: What Climate Science Tells Us, What It Doesn't, and Why It Matters* (BenBella: Dallas, TX) (epub ed.)

Kosinski, M., D. Stillwell and T. Graepel, 2013. "Private Traits and Attributes Are Predictable from Digital Records of Human Behavior," *Proceedings of the National Academy of Sciences* 110: 5802.

Kreiter, M., 2017. "Is Health Care Reform Dead? Effort to Bring Ultra-Right on Board Could Alienate Centrists," *International Business Times* (Apr. 4), https://perma.cc/UW4N-L4LZ.

Kruzel, J., 2018. "Why Trump Appointments Have Lagged Behind Other Presidents," *Politifact* (Mar. 16), https://perma.cc/T4EN-ZBED.

Labaree, B. W., 1962. "New England Town Meeting," *The American Archivist* 25(2): 165.

Lamond, G., 2006. "Precedent and Analogy in Legal Reasoning," *Stanford Encyclopedia of Philosophy*, https://plato.stanford.edu/entries/legal-reas-prec/.

Lange, J., G. Slattery and D. Morgan, 2023. "Insight: Why Republican Hardliners Can Afford to Say No to U.S. Debt Ceiling Increase," *Reuters* (Feb. 14) www.reuters.com/world/us/why-republican-hardliners-can-afford-push-us-brink-default-2023-02-14/.

LBJ Library, 2012. Video: "The Poverty Tours (Apr.–May 1964)" www.youtube.com/watch?v=oVyZ_vKuY-M.

Lee, E., 2020. "At Wall Street Journal, News Staff and Opinion Side Clash," *New York Times* (July 24).

Leighley, J. E. and J. Nagler, 2013. *Who Votes Now? Demographics, Issues, Inequality, and Turnout in the United States* (Princeton University Press: Princeton, NJ).

Lessig, L., 2006. *Code* (Basic Books: New York) (2nd ed.)

Letwin, W. L., 1956. "Congress and the Sherman Antitrust Law: 1887–1890," *University of Chicago Law Review* 23(2): 221–258.

Levenson, A., 2018. "Coin Flips, Poker Hands and Other Crazy Ways America Settles Tied Elections," *CNN* (Jan. 4), www.cnn.com/2018/01/04/us/tie-elections-history-lots-coins-draws-trnd/index.html.

Levenson, S., 1982. "Law as Literature," *Texas Law Review* 60: 373–406.

Levine, A. J. and M. Funakoshi, 2020. "Financial Sinkholes: Campaign Spending in the 2020 U.S. Election," *Reuters* (Nov. 24) https://graphics.reuters.com/USA-ELECTION/SENATE-FUNDRAISING/yxmvjeyjkpr/.

Levine, R. S., 2021. *The Failed Promise: Reconstruction, Frederick Douglass, and the Impeachment of Andrew Johnson* (Norton: New York) (epub ed.)

Libby, L. M., 1979. *The Uranium People* (Scribners: New York).

Library of Congress, n.d. "Constitution Annotated: Offices Eligible for Impeachment," https://constitution.congress.gov/browse/essay/artII_S4_1_2_1/.

Lincoln, A., 1858. Speech: "A House Divided," https://d1lexzaozk46za.cloudfront.net/history/am-docs/the-house-divided-speech.pdf.

Lincoln, A., 1861(a). "First Inaugural Address" (Mar. 4), pp. 210–219 in Simpson, Sears & Sheehan-Dean (2011).

Lincoln, A., 1861(b). "Message to Congress in Special Session" (July 4), pp. 427–442 in Simpson, Sears & Sheehan-Dean (2011).

Lipsitz, K. and J. M. Teigen, 2010. "Orphan Counties and the Effect of Irrelevant Information on Turnout in Statewide Races," *Political Communication* 27: 178.

List, C., 2013. "Social Choice Theory," *Stanford Encyclopedia of Philosophy* https://perma.cc/NEY2-MPYE.

Loewen, J. W., 2011. "Five Myths about Why the South Seceded," *Washington Post* (Feb. 26).

Lorenz, T., 2022. "Meet the Woman Behind Libs of Tik Tok, Secretly Fueling the Right's Outrage Machine," *Washington Post* (Apr. 19) www.washingtonpost.com/technology/2022/04/19/libs-of-tiktok-right-wing-media/.

Lowell, A. L., 1888. *Essays in Government* (Houghton Mifflin: Boston, MA).

Lowell, J. R., 1861. "The Pickens-and-Stealin's Rebellion," *The Atlantic* (June), pp. 415–426 in Simpson, Sears & Sheehan-Dean (2011).

Luttwak, E. N., 1976. *The Grand Strategy of the Roman Empire: From First Century AD to the Third* (Johns Hopkins: Baltimore, MD).

Lynn, A. C., 2016. "The Missing Pieces of Geoengineering Research Governance," *Minnesota Law Review* 100: 2509–257.

Lysiak, M., 2020. *The Drudge Revolution: The Untold Story of How Talk Radio, Fox News, and a Gift Shop Clerk with an Internet Connection Took Down the Mainstream Media* (BenBella Books: Dallas, TX) (epub ed.)

Maatman, G. L. Jr., 1981. "Protest Boycotts and Federal Labor Laws: The Russian Trade Boycott," *Northwestern Journal of International Law & Business* 3: 211.

Madison, J., 1787a. "Letter to Thomas Jefferson" (Oct. 24), pp. 192–208 in B. Bailyn (1993a).

Madison, n.d. 1787b, "Constitutional Convention Debates," (Aug. 25) *The Avalon Project*, https://avalon.law.yale.edu/18th_century/debates_825.asp#1.

Madison, J., 1788. "Patrick Henry's Objections to a National Army and James Madison's Reply," pp. 695–700 in Bailyn (1993a).

Madison, J., 1798. "Letter to T. Jefferson" (2 April) https://founders.archives.gov/documents/Madison/01-17-02-0070.

Magness, P. W. and P. C. Earle, 2021. "The Fickle 'Science' of Lockdowns," *Wall Street Journal* (Dec. 19).

Maguill, D., 2017. "Did Nancy Pelosi Say Obamacare Must be Passed to 'Find Out What Is in It'?" *Snopes* (June 22), www.snopes.com/fact-check/pelosi-healthcare-pass-the-bill-to-see-what-is-in-it/.

Mahdawi, A., 2021. "The President and Senate are the Oldest in US History," *The Guardian* (Nov. 9), www.theguardian.com/commentisfree/2021/nov/09/biden-and-his-senators-are-oldest-in-us-history-what-is-stopping-younger-generation-breaking-through.

Maier, F. X., 2022. "How Marxism 'Won' the War of Ideas," *Wall Street Journal* (Jan. 7).

Makary, M. 2021. "We'll Have Herd Immunity by April," *Wall Street Journal* (Feb. 18).

Malenga, S., 2021. "Capitalist Havens of Free Speech," *City Journal* (Spring) www.city-journal.org/capitalist-havens-of-free-speech.

Malone, S. J., 1997. "Recognizing Communities of Interest in a Legislative Apportionment Plan," *Virginia Law Review* 83: 461.

Mankiw, G. N., 2020. "A Skeptic's Guide to Modern Monetary Theory," *National Bureau of Economic Research*, Working Paper No. 26650 www.nber.org/papers/w26650.

Manning, J. E., 2018. Report No. R44762: "Membership of the 115th Congress: A Profile," *Congressional Research Service* www.senate.gov/CRSpubs/b8f6293e-c235-40fd-b895-6474d0f8e809.pdf.

Martinez, A., 2017. "Americans Have Seen the Last Four Presidents as Illegitimate: Here's Why," *Washington Post* (Jan. 20) https://perma.cc/CS3N-V32Y.

Maurer, S. M. 2012. "The Penguin and the Cartel: Rethinking Antitrust and Innovation Policy for the Age of Commercial Open Source," *Utah Law Review* 1: 269–318.

Maurer, S. M., 2014a. "From Bards to Search Engines," *South Carolina Law Review* 66(2): 495–541.

Maurer, S. M. 2014b. "Public Problems, Private Answers: Reforming Industry Self-Governance Law for the 21st Century," *DePaul Business & Commercial Law Journal* 12(3): 297–360.

Maurer, S. M. (ed.), 2017a. *On the Shoulders of Giants: Colleagues Remember Suzanne Scotchmer's Contributions to Economics* (Cambridge: New York).

Maurer, S. M., 2017b. *Self-Governance in Science* (Cambridge University Press: New York).

Maurer, S. M., 2018. "Digital Publishing: Three Futures (and How to Get There)," *Cardozo Arts & Entertainment Law Journal* 36(3): 675–733.

Maurer, S. M. and M. O'Hare, 2007. "Fear Itself: Predicting and Managing Public Response to a WMD Attack," in S. M. Maurer (ed.) *WMD Terrorism* (MIT Press: Cambridge, MA).

Maurer, S. M. and G. Rutherford, 2007. "The New Bioweapons: Infectious and Engineered Diseases," pp. 111–138 in S. M. Maurer (ed.) *WMD Terrorism: Science and Policy Choices* (MIT Press: Cambridge, MA).

Maurer, S. M. and S. Scotchmer, 2006. "Open Source Software: The New Intellectual Property Paradigm," in T. Hendershott (ed.), *Handbook on Information Systems* (Elsevier: Amsterdam, Holland).

Maurer, S. M. and S. Scotchmer, 2015. "The Lost Message of Terminal Railroad," *California Law Review Circuit* 5: 296–334, www.californialawreview.org/the-essential-facilities-doctrine-the-lost-message-of-terminal-railroad/.

Mayhew, D. R., 2002. *Electoral Realignments: A Critique of an American Genre* (Yale University Press: New Haven, CT).

Mayhew, D. R., 2003. "Supermajority Rule in the U.S. Senate," *PS: Political Science and Politics* 35(1): 31–36.

Mazmanian, A., 2018. "OPM Puts Agencies on Notice About Hiring Politicals for Civil Service Jobs," *Federal Computer Week* (Mar. 8), https://fcw.com/articles/2018/03/08/burrowing-opm-congress.aspx?m=1.

McCarthy, W., 2020. "The State of US Contact Tracing: Is it Working?" *PolitiFact* (Oct. 13), www.tampabay.com/news/health/2020/10/13/the-state-of-us-contact-tracing-is-it-working-politifact/.

McCaskill, N. D., 2021. "Progressive Democrats Test-Drive New Hardball Tactics, *Los Angeles Times* (Nov. 17), www.latimes.com/politics/story/2021-11-17/progressives-test-drive-some-new-hardball-tactics-in-democratic-party.

McCubbins, M. D., R. G. Noll and B. R. Weingast, 1984. "Congressional Oversight Overlooked: Police Patrols Versus Fire Alarms." *American Journal of Political Science* 28: 165–179.

McCubbins, M. D., R. G. Noll and B. R. Weingast. 1987. "Administrative Procedures as Instruments of Political Control," *Journal of Law, Economics, and Organization* 3: 243–276.

McDonald, M., 2019. "The Predominance Test: A Judicially Manageable Compactness Standard for Redistricting," *Yale Law Journal* 129: 18.

McDonough, J., 1994. "The Longest Night: Broadcasting's First Invasion," *The American Scholar* 63(2): 193–211.

McGinnis, J. O. and M. Rappaport, 2008. "The Condorcet Case for Supermajority Rules," *Supreme Court Economic Review* 16: 67–71.

McGurn, W., 2020. "AOC's Hill of Beans," *Wall Street Journal* (July 13).

McIntee, T., 2018. "Electing Presidents the Way the Founding Fathers Expected Us To," *Electoral University Press* https://medium.com/electoral-university-press/electing-presidents-the-way-the-founding-fathers-expected-us-to-6259acb7d4ef.

McKinley, J., 2022. "India Walton Says She's Unlikely to Beat the Write-in Incumbent, Byron Brown, in the Buffalo Mayor's Race," *New York Times* (Nov. 3).

McMaster, H. R., 2011. *Dereliction of Duty: Lyndon Johnson, Robert McNamara, The Joint Chiefs of Staff, and the Lies That Led to Vietnam* (HarperCollins: New York) (epub ed.)

McWhirter, C., 2021. "Atlanta's Crime Wave Makes Some Residents Look to the Suburbs," *Wall Street Journal* (Mar. 11).

McWhorter, D., 2001. *Carry Me Home: Birmingham, Alabama: The Climactic Battle of the Civil Rights Revolution* (Simon & Schuster: New York).

Meacham, J., 2008. *American Lion: Andrew Jackson in the White House* (Random House: New York) (epub ed.)

Mead, J. W., 2012. "*Stare Decisis* in the Inferior Courts of the United States," *Nevada Law Journal* 12: 787–830.

Melendez, L. 2021. "Are Acronyms a Symptom of 'White Supremacy Culture?'" (Feb. 1), https://abc7news.com/amp/sfusd-renaming-schools-board-meeting-san-francisco-school-sf/10229093/.

Meltzoff, A. N., 2002. "Imitation as a Mechanism of Social Cognition: Origins of Empathy, Theory of Mind, and the Representation of Action," pp. 6–25 in U. Guswami, *Blackwell Handbook of Childhood Cognitive Development* (Blackwell Publishing: Hoboken, NJ).

Mencken, H. L. 2010 [1920]. *Prejudices (Second Series)* (Library of America: New York).

Mencken, H. L. 2010 [1927]. *Prejudices (Sixth Series)* (Library of America: New York).

Mendolsohn, D. 2018. "Is *The Aeneid* a Celebration of Empire – or a Critique?" *The New Yorker* (Oct. 8).

Meyer, R. J. 2023. "There's a Precedent for Kevin McCarthy's Conundrum," *Wall Street Journal* (Jan. 6).

Michigan Senate Oversight Committee, 2021. "Report on the November 2020 Election in Michigan," (June 23), https://misenategopcdn.s3.us-east-1.amazonaws.com/99/doccuments/20210623/SMPO_2020ElectionReport.pdf.

Mitchell, A., M. Jurkowitz, J. B. Oliphant and E. Shearer, 2020. "Americans Who Mainly Get Their News on Social Media are Less Engaged, Less Knowledgeable," www.journalism.org/2020/07/30/americans-who-mainly-get-their-news-on-social-media-are-less-engaged-less-knowledgeable/.

Mixon, F. G. Jr, 2019. "The Modern Theory of Bureaucracy," pp. 17–35 in *A Terrible Efficiency: Entrepreneurial Bureaucrats and the Nazi Holocaust* (Springer: Berlin).

Moe, T. M., 1998. "The Presidency and the Bureaucracy: The Presidential Advantage," in M. Nelson (ed.), *The Presidency and the Political System* (CQ Press: 5th ed.)

Mommsen, H., 1996. *The Rise and Fall of Weimar Democracy* (University of North Carolina Press: Chapel Hill).

Montgomery, J., 2020. "Poland to Pass Law Protecting Online Free Speech Against Big Tech," *Breitbart News* (Dec. 26) www.breitbart.com/europe/2020/12/26/poland-to-pass-law-protecting-online-free-speech-against-big-tech-censorship/.

Monmouth University Polling Institute, 2021. "Public Supports Both Early Voting And Requiring Photo ID to Vote," www.monmouth.edu/polling-institute/reports/monmouthpoll_us_062121/.

Morci, P., 2021. "Democrats Will Never Let a Good Crisis Go to Waste," *Washington Times* (July 20), www.washingtontimes.com/news/2021/jul/20/democrats-will-never-let-a-good-crisis-go-to-waste/.

Morrison, K., 1980. Book Review: "Holding Fast the Inner Lines," *Annals of the American Academy of Political and Social Science* 451: 189–190.

Motyl, Prims & Iyer, 2020. "How Ambient Cues Facilitate Political Segregation," *Personality and Social Psychology Bulletin* 46(5): 723–737.

Moulton, C. (ed.), 1998. "Population" in *Ancient Greece and Rome: An Encyclopedia for Students* (Scribners: New York) at p. 366.

Muller, R. and G. J. MacDonald, 2002. *Ice Ages and Astronomical Causes: Data, Spectral Analysis, and Mechanisms* (Springer Praxis: Berlin).

Mullin, B., J. Chung, K. Hagey, and R. Ballhaus, 2020. "Trump Allies Explored Buyout of Newsmax TV as Fox News Alternative," *Wall Street Journal* (Nov. 15).

Murphy, M., 2020. "One in 20 Staff at Tech Company Coinbase Leave After Boss Makes 'No Politics at Work' Pledge," *The Telegraph (UK)* (Oct. 20).

Nag, O. S. 2017. "Largest Landslide Victories in US Presidential Election History," *World Atlas* https://perma.cc/97DS-CJ8A.

National Conference of State Legislatures, n.d. "State Quarantine and Isolation Statutes," www.ncsl.org/research/health/state-quarantine-and-isolation-statutes.aspx#State%20Laws.

NBC News, 2018. "NBC News Exit Poll: Majority of Voters Don't Think Trump Should Be Impeached," (Nov. 6) https://perma.cc/Z3KK-Q6HH.

Nelson, M., 1982. "A Short, Ironic History of American National Bureaucracy," *The Journal of Politics* 44(3): 747–778.

Nelson, S. 2021. "White House 'Flagging' Posts for Facebook to Censor Over COVID Misinformation," *New York Post* (July 15)

Newkirk, V. R., 2017. "How Redistricting Became a Technological Arms Race," *The Atlantic* (Oct. 28) www.theatlantic.com/politics/archive/2017/10/gerrymandering-technology-redmap-2020/543888.

Newton, C., 2021. "What Really Happened at Basecamp," *Platformer* (April 27), www.platformer.news/p/-what-really-happened-at-basecamp.

Nichols, D. A., 2017. *Ike and McCarthy: Dwight Eisenhower's Secret Campaign Against Joseph McCarthy* (Simon & Schuster: New York) (epub ed.)

Nicolay, J. G., 1861. "Memorandum Regarding Abraham Lincoln" (Nov. 5–6), pp. 5–7 in Simpson, Sears & Sheehan-Dean (2011).

Niemöller, M., 1946. "First They Came," *Holocaust Memorial Day Trust*, https://perma.cc/9SKZ-LDMS.

Niskanen, W. A., 1968. "The Peculiar Economics of Bureaucracy," *American Economic Review* 58(2): 293–395.

Nolte, J., 2021. "Blacklisting Campaign Launched Against Mommy Blogger for Trump Donations," *Breitbart News* (Jan. 29), www.breitbart.com/politics/2021/01/28/nolte-blacklisting-campaign-launched-against-mommy-blogger-trump-donations/.

Noonan, P., 2021. "Covid Anxiety and Fear of the Base," *Wall Street Journal* (Aug. 14–15).

Noonan, P., 2022. "Nixon's Example of Sanity in Washington," *Wall Street Journal* (Apr. 2–3).

Nordhaus, W. 2013. *The Climate Casino: Risk, Uncertainty, and Economics for a Warming World* (Yale University Press: 2013) (epub ed.)

Norman, J., n.d. "William Clowes Introduces High Speed Printing in Large Scale Book Production," *History of Information* www.historyofinformation.com/detail.php?id=4370.

Nowrasteh, A., 2016. "Proposition 186 Turned California Blue," *Cato at Liberty* (July 20) (Cato Institute: Washington, DC) www.cato.org/blog/proposition-187-turned-california-blue.

Nye, I., 1946. "The Slave Power Conspiracy: 1830–1860," *Science and Society* 10(3): 262–274.

O'Hara, J., 2016. *Short Stories* (C. McGrath, ed.) (Library of America: New York).

O'Kane, C., 2020. "Four "Vanderpump Rules" Cast Members Won't Return to Show after Past Racist Actions Resurface," *CBS News* (June 10).

O'Neil, T., 2018. "Lindsey Graham to Democrats: 'Boy, You All Want Power. God, I Hope You Never Get It'," *PJ Media* (Sept. 27) https://perma.cc/K5W9-76HF.

Ollman, B., 2017. "Toward a Marxist Interpretation of the US Constitution," *Jacobin* (July) https://jacobinmag.com/2017/07/founding-fathers-constitutional-convention.

Orwell, G. [EA Blair], [1942]. "Rudyard Kipling," https://orwell.ru/library/reviews/kipling/english/e_rkip.

Osterholm, M. T., K. A. Moore, J. Ostrowsky, et al., 2020, "COVID-19: The CIDRAP Viewpoint" (Part 1: Apr. 30), *Center for Infectious Disease Research and Policy*, www.cidrap.umn.edu/sites/default/files/public/downloads/cidrap-covid19-viewpoint-part1_0.pdf.

Otis, J., 1764. "The Rights of the British Colonies Asserted and Proved," pp. 43–122 in Wood (2015).

Ottley, R., 1995 [1942]. "Negroes are Saying...," pp. 434–452 in S. Hynes, A. Matthews, N. C. Sorel and R. J. Spiller, *Reporting World War II* (Vol. 1) (Library of America: New York).

Page, B. I. and R. Y. Shapiro, 1992. *The Rational Public: Fifty Years of Trends in American Policy Preferences* (Chicago University Press: Chicago IL).

Paletta, D., 2019. "By Pursuing Shutdown, Trump Revealed How Much America Depends on Government," *Washington Post* (Jan. 26) https://perma.cc/6D5U-RXB7.

Palmer, A., 2021. "Amazon Employees Call for Company to Cut Ties with Parler After Deadly U.S. Capitol Riot," *CNBC* (Jan. 9) www.cnbc.com/2021/01/09/amazon-employees-demand-company-drop-parler-after-capitol-riot.html.

Palmer, D., 2020. "Bernie's Millions Beat Mike's Millions," *Wall Street Journal* (Feb. 19).

Parry, A., 1969. "Power Was Lying in the Street: We Picked it Up," *New York Times* (Sept. 28).

Pasley, J., 2019. "Fox News and CNN are 2 of America's Biggest News Sources – But They Couldn't Be More Different," *Business Insider* (Dec 31) www.businessinsider.com/fox-news-cnn-change-evolution-2010-2019-11#it-was-zucker-who-brought-back-the-tagline-this-is-cnn-as-he-tried-to-strengthen-the-networks-identity-20.

Pauly, M., 2016. "Why Libertarians Are (Still) Plotting to Take Over New Hampshire," *Mother Jones* (Feb. 1) www.motherjones.com/politics/2016/02/libertarians-new-hampshire-free-state.

Pear, R. 2017. "13 Men, and No Women, are Writing New G.O.P. Health Bill in Senate," *New York Times* (May 8) https://perma.cc/VU98-8XQ3.

Pehme, M., 2021 "Cuomo's Office Terrorized Me for Doing My Job as a Journalist," *NY Post* (Feb. 22) https://nypost.com/2021/02/22/cuomos-office-terrorized-me-for-doing-my-job-as-a-journalist/.

Perez, C. E., 2018. *Artificial Intuition: The Improbable Deep Learning Revolution* (self-published: n.p.)

Petrova, M., 2011. "Newspapers and Parties: How Advertising Revenues Created an Independent Press," *American Political Science Review* 105(4): 790–808.

Petrova, M., 2012. "Mass Media and Special Interest Groups," *Journal of Economic Behavior and Organization* 84: 17–38.

Pielkalkiewic, J. and A. W. Penn, 1995. *Politics of Ideocracy* (SUNY University Press: New York).

Pietryka, M. T., J. L. Reilly, D. M. Maliniak, P. R. Miller, R. Huckfeldt and R. B. Rapoport, 2018. "From Respondents to Networks: Bridging between Individuals, Discussants, and the Network in the Study of Political Discussion," *Political Behavior* 40: 711–735.

Pinckney, C. C., 1788. "Charles Cotesworth Pinckney Explains America's Unique Structure of Freedom" (May 14), pp. 577–591 in B. Bailyn (ed.) *The Debate on the Constitution* (Pt. 2) (Library of America: New York).

Plokhy, S. 2021. *Nuclear Folly: A History of the Cuban Missile Crisis* (Norton: New York) (epub ed.)

Plutarch, 1914 [*ca.* 100 AD]. *Plutarch's Lives* (B. Perrin trans.), (Harvard University Press: Cambridge, MA).

Pollack, N. 2021. "American Publishing in Censorship Mode," *Book & Film Globe* (May 7), https://bookandfilmglobe.com/politics/american-publishing-in-censorship-mode/.

Polsby, D. D. and R. D. Popper, 1991. "The Third Criterion: Compactness as a Procedural Safeguard Against Partisan Gerrymandering," *Yale Law & Policy Review* 9: 301.

Popper, K., 1963. "Science as Falsification," pp. 33–39 in K. Popper, *Conjectures and Refutations: The Growth of Scientific Knowledge,* (Routledge: London).

Posner, R. A., 1989. *Law and Literature: A Misunderstood Relationship* (Harvard University Press: Cambridge, MA).

Posner, R. A., 2008. *How Judges Think* (Harvard University Press: Cambridge, MA) (epub ed.)

Problem Solvers Caucus, 2018. "Break the Gridlock: A Package of Reforms to Make the House Work Again for the American People," https://perma.cc/DJP9-K9RJ.

Pruitt, S., 2018. "Trump Holds Some JFK Assassination Files Back, Sets New 3-Year Deadline," *History Channel* (Apr. 26), www.history.com/news/final-jfk-files-assassination-documents-release.

Public Policy Institute of California, (2021). "California Voter and Party Profiles," (Sept.), www.ppic.org/publication/california-voter-and-party-profiles/.

Pulitzer, R. and C. H. Grasty, 1919. "Forces at War in Peace Conclave," *New York Times* (Jan. 18).

Quitt, M. H., 2008. "Congressional (Partisan) Constitutionalism: The Apportionment Act Debates of 1842 and 1844," *Journal of the Early Republic* 28: 629.

Rahilly, J., 2006. "Questions of 'h' in Northern Ireland: Breathing New Life on the Aspiration Theory," *Etudes Irlandaises* 31(2): 47–61.

Raleigh, K. E., 2017. "Limiting Mail and Wire Fraud's Scope," *Criminal Justice* 31: 30.

Rall, T., 2019. "Progressives Who Prefer Trump to Biden," *Wall Street Journal* (June 5).

Rall, T., 2021. "Free Speech Has Consequences," *Wall Street Journal* (Sept. 30).

Ramaswamy, V. and J. Rubenfeld, 2022. "Twitter Becomes a Tool of Government Censorship," *Wall Street Journal* (Aug. 17).

Randolph, E., 1787. "Governor Edmund Randolph's Reasons for Not Signing the Constitution" (Dec. 27), in Bailyn (1993a).

Rehnquist, W. H., 2004. *Centennial Crisis: The Disputed Election of 1876* (Vintage: New York) (epub ed.)

Reilly, K., 2016. "Read Hillary Clinton's 'Basket of Deplorables' Remarks About Donald Trump Supporters," *Time* (Sept. 10) https://perma.cc/YX77-UHMA.

Renoult, J. P., 2016. "The Evolution of Aesthetics: A Review of Models," in Z. Kapoula and M. Vernet (eds.), *Aesthetics and Neuroscience: Scientific and Artistic Perspectives* (Springer: Berlin) at pp. 271–299.

Restuccia, A., R. Bade, J. Bresnahan, and B. Everett, 2019. "Both Parties Aim to Woo Defectors as Shutdown Drags On," *Politico* (Jan. 14) https://perma.cc/FGX9-8T62.

Revision World, n.d. "Types of Socialism," https://revisionworld.com/a2-level-level-revision/politics/types-socialism.

Richie, A., 1998. *Faust's Metropolis: A History of Berlin* (Caroll & Graf: New York).

Ricks, T. E., 2020. *First Principles: What America's Founders Learned from the Greeks and Romans and How That Shaped Our Country* (Harper & Row: New York) (epub ed).

Riley, J., 2020. "What's So Great About High Voter Turnout?" *Wall Street Journal* (Nov. 4).

Ripley, R. B., and G. A. Franklin, 1976. *Congress, the Bureaucracy, and Public Policy* (Dorset Press: New York).

Risen, C. 2014. *The Bill of the Century: The Epic Battle for the Civil Rights Act* (Bloomsbury: New York).

Rivkin, D. B. and A. M. Grossman, 2022. "The End of the Work-Around Era," *Wall Street Journal* (Jan. 7).

Roberts, A., 2014. *Napoleon: A Life* (Penguin: New York) (epub ed.)

Roemer, T., 2015. "Why Do Congressmen Spend Only Half Their Time Serving Us?," *Newsweek* (July 29) www.newsweek.com/why-do-congressmen-spend-only-half-their-time-serving-us-357995.

Rohde, R., R. A. Muller, R. Jacobsen, E. Muller, S. Perlmutter, A. Rosenfeld, J. Wurtele, D. Groom and C. Wickha, 2013. "New Estimate of the Average Earth Surface Land Temperature Spanning 1753 to 2011," *Geoinformatics and Geostatistics: An Overview* 1(1): 1–7.

Romero, D. and B. Goggin, 2022. "FBI Responds to Mark Zuckerberg Claims in Joe Rogan Show," *NBC News* (Aug. 26) www.nbcnews.com/politics/politics-news/fbi-responds-mark-zuckerberg-claims-joe-rogan-show-rcna45082.

Rose, L. A., 2007. *Power at Sea: The Breaking Storm, 1919–1945* (University of Missouri Press: Columbia).

Rosen, D., 2011. "Two Centuries of Presidential Sex Scandals," *Counterpunch* (Feb. 21), www.counterpunch.org/2011/02/21/two-centuries-of-presidential-sex-scandals/.

Rosenkranz, R., 2020. "The Measure of New York's Covid Devastation," *Wall Street Journal* (June 3).

Rosenthiel, T. 2010. "How a Different America Responded to the Great Depression," *Pew Research Center* www.pewresearch.org/2010/12/14/how-a-different-america-responded-to-the-great-depression/.

Roskin, M. G., 2005. "19th-Century Roots of Contemporary Political Science," *Encyclopedia Britannica*, www.britannica.com/topic/political-science/19th-century-roots-of-contemporary-political-science

Rossiter, K. M., D. W. S. Wong, and P. L. Delamater, 2018. "Congressional Redistricting: Keeping Communities Together?" *The Professional Geographer* 70: 609.

Rothenberg, S., 2007. "For the Thousandth Time, Don't Call Them Push Polls," *Inside Elections* (March 12), https://insideelections.com/news/article/for-the-thousandth-time-dont-call-them-push-polls.

Rove, K., 2021(a). "Pelosi Might Steal an Iowa House Seat," *Wall Street Journal* (March 8).

Rove, K., 2021(b). "The White House's Week of Unforced Errors," *Wall Street Journal* (June 30).

Rove, K., 2023. "The House GOP's Immaturity Caucus," *Wall Street Journal* (Jan. 12).

Roy, A., 2012. "The Inside Story on How Roberts Changed His Supreme Court Vote on Obamacare," *Forbes.com* (July 1), www.forbes.com/sites/theapothecary/2012/07/01/the-supreme-courts-john-roberts-changed-his-obamacare-vote-in-may/?sh=77979d2bd701.

"RP" (pseud.), 1992. "The Third Branch of Science Debuts," *Science* 256(5053): 44–47.

Rude, E., 2016. "The 'Beefsteak Election': When Meat Changed the Course of American Politics," *Time* (Aug. 30), https://time.com/4471656/the-beefsteak-election/.

Russell, B., 1910. "The Study of Mathematics," pp. 58–73 in *Mysticism and Logic and Other Essays* (Taylor, Garnett, Evans & Co.: Watford, UK).

Rychter, T., 2018. "How Compulsory Voting Works: Australians Explain," *New York Times* (Nov. 5), https://perma.cc/X2MJ-UV54.

Salam, R., 2022. "The HIdden Consensus on Immigration," *Wall Street Journal* (Nov. 18).

Sale, R., 1977. "Fairy Tales," *The Hudson Review* 30: 372.

Salganik, M. J., P. S. Dodds and D. J. Watts, 2006. "Experimental Study of Inequality and Unpredictability in an Artificial Cultural Market," *Science* 311: 854–856.

Sasse, B., 2020. "Make the Senate Great Again," *Wall Street Journal* (Sept. 9).

Savage, L., 2019. "The Anatomy of MSNBC: An Interview with Michael Arria," *Jacobin* (Oct. 6), www.jacobinmag.com/2019/10/medium-blue-the-politics-of-msnbc-liberal-media.

Schankerman, M., and S. Scotchmer, 1999. "Damages and Injunctions in Protecting Intellectual Property," pp. 167–195 in S. Maurer (2017a).

Schlaes, A., 2019. *Great Society: A New History* (Harper: New York).

Schlesinger, A. M., 1962. "The Aristocracy in Colonial America," *Proceedings of the Massachusetts Historical Society* (Third Series) 74: 3–21.

Scotchmer, S. 2006. *Innovation and Incentives* (MIT Press: Cambridge, MA).

Seib, G. F., 2020. "Senate, Presidential Races More Often Move in Tandem," *Wall Street Journal* (Aug. 1).

Seib, G. F., 2021. "Why the Political Center Has Eroded," *Wall Street Journal* (Oct. 5).

Selan, H., 1987. "Interpreting RICO's 'Pattern of Racketeering Activity' Requirement After *Sedima*: Separate Schemes, Episodes or Related Acts?" *California Western Law Review* 24: 1.

Severi, M., 2022. "Bill Clinton says 'Fair Chance' US Could Lose Constitutional Democracy," *Washington Examiner* (June 16), www.washingtonexaminer.com/news/bill-clinton-concerned-about-us-democracy-future.

Severino, C. (2019). "Yes, the ABA Is Still a Left-Wing Advocacy Group," *National Review* (Sept. 27) www.nationalreview.com/bench-memos/yes-the-aba-is-still-a-left-wing-advocacy-group/.

Shearer, E. and A. Mitchell, 2021. "News Use across Social Media Platforms in 2020," *Pew Research Center*, www.journalism.org/2021/01/12/news-use-across-social-media-platforms-in-2020/.

Shelley, P. B. 1821. "A Defence of Poetry or Remarks Suggested by an Essay Entitled 'The Four Ages of Poetry'," pp. 478–510 in D. H. Reiman and S. B. Powers (eds.), *Shelley's Poetry and Prose* (1977) (Norton: New York).

Sherrod, R., 1944. "I Didn't Know Whether We Had the Heart to Fight a War," pp. 683–712 in S. Hynes, A. Matthews, N. C. Sorel, and R. J. Spiller, *Reporting World War II Part One: American Journalism 1938–1944* (1995) (Library of America: New York).

Shiels, B., 2015. *WB Yeats and World Literature: The Subject of Poetry* (Routledge: Abington, UK).

Showah, R., 2022. "How Democrats Lost Their Majorities," *Wall Street Journal* (July 6).

Simon, H. A., 1992. "Altruism and Economics," *Eastern Economic Journal* 18(1): 73–83.

Simpson, B. D., S. W. Sears and A. Sheehan-Dean, 2011. *The Civil War: The First Year Told by Those Who Lived It* (Library of America: New York).

Singer, S. F., 2005. "The Revelle-Gore Story: Attempted Suppression of Science," pp. 283–297 in M. Gough (ed.), *Politicizing Science: The Alchemy of Policymaking* (Hoover Institution: Palo Alto, CA).

Skoning, G. D., 2015. "How Congress Puts Itself Above the Law," *Wall Street Journal* (Apr. 15).

Slovic, P., 2000. *The Perception of Risk* (Earthscan: London & Sterling, VA).

Slovic, P., B. Fischhoff and S. Licthenstein, 1979. "Rating the Risks," pp. 104–120 in Slovic (2000).

Small, S. A., 2020. *Forgetting: The Benefits of Not Remembering* (Crown: New York).

Smart, C., 2018. "The Differences in How CNN, CNBC, and Fox Cover the News," *The Pudding* https://pudding.cool/2018/01/chyrons/.

Smith, D., 2021(b). "Actually, Blue States Still Fare Better on COVID," *Minneapolis Star Tribune* (Dec. 6), www.startribune.com/counterpoint-actually-blue-states-still-fare-better-on-covid/600124468/.

Smith, M. and Hamilton, A. 1788. "Melancton Smith and Alexander Hamilton Debate Representation, Aristocracy, and Interests," pp. 757–775 in Bailyn (1993b).

Smith, R. N., 2021(a). Review: "'The First Inauguration:' A Pledge to Serve," *Wall Street Journal* (Jan. 20).

Solender, A., 2020. "House Democrat Calls to Exclude 126 Republicans From Next Congress for Supporting Texas Lawsuit," *Forbes* (Dec. 20), www.forbes.com/sites/andrewsolender/2020/12/11/house-democrat-calls-to-exclude-126-republicans-from-next-congress-for-supporting-texas-lawsuit/?sh=75e790681fd9.

Somi, G. J., 2020. "The Death of Non-Resident Contribution Limit Bans and the Birth of the New Small, Swing State," *William & Mary Bill of Rights Journal* 28(4): 995–1024, https://scholarship.law.wm.edu/wmborj/vol28/iss4/4.

Speer, N. K., J. R. Reynolds, K. M. Swallow, and J. M. Zacks, 2009. "Reading Stories Activates Neural Representations of Visual and Motor Experiences," *Psychological Science* 20: 989.

Spuford, F., 2010. *Red Plenty* (Faber & Faber: New York) (epub ed.)

Starr, G. G., 2013. *Feeling Beauty: The Neuroscience of Aesthetic Experience* (MIT Press: Cambridge, MA).

Starr, P., 2001. "What Happened to Health Care Reform?" *American Prospect* (Nov. 19) https://perma.cc/2S62-9MY2.

Steinberg, B. and J. Moreau, 2020. "ABC News Exec Barbara Fedida Placed on Administrative Leave after Report of Insensitive Comments," *Variety* (June 20), https://variety.com/2020/tv/news/barbara-fedida-abc-news-administrative-leave-1234634091/.

Sternberg, J. C., 2021. "Oops, Boris Johnson Told the Truth about Climate," *Wall Street Journal* (Oct. 21).

Stevens, J. Jr., 1787. "On the Errors of 'Cato' and of Celebrated Writers," (Dec. 5–6), pp. 457–564 in B. Bailyn (ed.) *The Debate on the Constitution* (Pt. 1) (Library of America: New York).

Strassburg, J., 2021. "Researchers Infect Volunteers with Coronavirus, Hoping to Conquer Covid-19," *Wall Street Journal* (Sept. 4).

Strassel, K. A., 2021. "Pelosi's Cannon Fodder," *Wall Street Journal* (Aug. 26).

Strauss, P. L., 2019. "The Trump Administration and the Rule of Law," *Revue Francaise d' Administration Publique* 170: 433–446.

Strong, G. T., 1860. "Diary (Nov. 26–Dec. 1)," pp. 43–47 in Simpson, Sears & Sheehan-Dean (2011).

Swaim, B., 2019. Review: "Prognosticators, Take it Easy," *Wall Street Journal* (Nov. 8).

Swaine, J., 2018. "National Enquirer Owner Admits to 'Catch and Kill' Payment to Ex-Playmate," (Dec. 12), www.theguardian.com/us-news/2018/dec/12/national-enquirer-trump-payments-david-pecker-catch-and-kill.

Swasey, B. and C. H. Jin, 2020. "Biden Won by Narrow Margins in Arizona, Georgia, Wisconsin," *National Public Radio* (Dec. 2) www.npr .org/2020/12/02/940689086/narrow-wins-in-these-key-states-powered-biden-to-the-presidency.

Syrett, D., 1964. "Town-Meeting Politics in Massachusetts, 1776–1786," *William & Mary Quarterly* 21: 352.

Tadelis, S., 2013. *Game Theory: An Introduction*, https://perma.cc/Y6QG-Z826.

Takala, R., 2020. "Twitter Justifies Allowing Iran to Threaten Genocide: 'Commentary on Political Issues of the Day'" *Mediaite* (July 30) www.mediaite.com/news/twitter-justifies-allowing-iran-to-threaten-genocide-commentary-on-political-issues-of-the-day/.

Tap, B., 2002. "Amateurs at War: Abraham Lincoln and the Committee on the Conduct of the War," *Journal of the Abraham Lincoln Association* 23(2): 1–18 http://hdl.handle.net/2027/spo.2629860.0023.203.

Tau, B., and A. Viswanatha, 2018. "Justice Department Watchdog Probes Comey Memos Over Classified Information," *Wall Street Journal* (Apr. 20).

Taubman, W., 2003. *Khrushchev: The Man and His Era* (WW Norton: New York).

Terzian, P., 2019. "The Boy Who Cried Coup," *Wall Street Journal* (Mar. 3).

Thomas Yeo, B. T., F. M. Krienen, S. B. Eickhoff, et al., 2015. "Functional Specialization and Flexibility in Human Association," *Cerebral Cortex* 25: 3654–3672.

Thompson, A., 2007. "The New Powers in College Football Carry Old Baggage," *Wall Street Journal* (Nov. 20).

Thompson, C., 2008. "If You Liked This, You're Sure to Love That," *New York Times Magazine* (Nov. 21).

Tisdale, E., 2017 [1815]. "The Gerry-mander," *Smithsonian Magazine* (July 20), www.smithsonianmag.com/history/where-did-term-gerrymander-come-180964118.

Tobias, C., 2018. "Senate Blue Slips and Senate Regular Order," *Yale Law & Policy Review* (Nov. 20) https://perma.cc/JV6T-MJV2.

Tolan, C., 2018. "How a Battle Over Same-Sex Marriage 14 Years Ago Sparked Gavin Newsom's Political Rise," *San Jose Mercury News* (Feb. 11) www .mercurynews.com/2018/02/11/gavin-newsom-san-francisco-same-sex-marriage-licenses/.

Topaz, J., 2014. "Poll: One-Third Say Impeach Obama," *Politico* (July 25) https://perma.cc/FQ84-ARG5.

Trachtenberg, J., 2020(a). "Simon & Schuster Employees Submit Petition Demanding No Deals with Trump Administration Authors," *Wall Street Journal* (Apr. 26).

Trachtenberg, J., 2020(b). "Barnes & Noble's New Boss Tries to Save the Chain – and Traditional Bookselling," *Wall Street Journal* (Dec. 5).

Trevor-Roper, H. R., 1969. "History and Sociology," *Past & Present* 42(1): 3–17.

Tribe, L. and J. Matz, 2018. *To End a Presidency: The Power of Impeachment* (Basic Books: New York) (epub ed.)

Trickey, E., 2018. "When America's Most Prominent Socialist Was Jailed for Speaking Out Against World War I," *Smithsonian* (June 15), www.smithsonianmag.com/history/fiery-socialist-challenged-nations-role-wwi-180969386/.

Truman, H. S., 2016 [1973]. *Oxford Essential Quotations* (4th ed.), www.oxfordreference.com/view/10.1093/acref/9780191826719.001.0001/q-oro-ed4-00011019.

Tullos, A., 2004. "The Carolina Piedmont," https://southernspaces.org/2004/carolina-piedmont/.

U.S. Census Bureau, 2020. "QuickFacts," (Feb. 5), https://perma.cc/5VUJ-H9DB.

Uhrmacher, K. and K. Schaul, 2017. "Three Months in and Trump's Cabinet Already Has More 'No' Votes than Any Other," *Washington Post* (Apr. 27).

United States Courts, n.d. "About the Supreme Court," www.uscourts.gov/about-federal-courts/educational-resources/about-educational-outreach/activity-resources/about.

US Dept. of Justice, 2010. "Horizontal Merger Guidelines," www.justice.gov/atr/horizontal-merger-guidelines-08192010.

US Dept. of Justice, 2018. "A Review of Various Actions by the Federal Bureau of Investigation and Department of Justice in Advance of the 2016 Election," https://oig.justice.gov/reports/2018/o1804.pdf.

US House Dept. of History, Art & Archives, n.d.(a). "List of Individuals Expelled, Censured, or Reprimanded in the US House of Representatives," https://perma.cc/X46M-6T5Y.

US House Dept. of History, Art & Archives, n.d. (b). "Discipline & Punishment," https://perma.cc/2H6F-FXD7.

US National Archives, 2016. "9/11 Commission Records," www.archives.gov/research/9-11.

US Senate, n.d. "United States Senate Expulsion Cases," https://perma.cc/W9D8-4NR4.

Varian, H. and C. Shapiro, 1999. *Information Rules: A Strategic Guide to the Network Economy* (Harvard Business School Press: Boston, MA).

Varon, E. R. 2014. *Appomattox: Victory, Defeat, and Freedom at the End of the Civil War* (Oxford University Press: New York) (epub ed.)

Vaughn, S. 1980. *Holding Fast the Inner Lines: Democracy, Nationalism, and the Committee on Public Information* (University of North Carolina Press: Chapel Hill) (epub ed.)

Vickrey, W. 1961. "On the Prevention of Gerrymandering," *Political Science Quarterly* 76(1): 105–110.

Vincent, I., 2021. "How George Soros Funded Progressive 'Legal Arsonist' DAs Behind US Crime Surge," (Dec. 16), https://nypost.com/2021/12/16/how-george-soros-funded-progressive-das-behind-us-crime-surge/.

Vinet, E. V., 2000(a). "The Rorschach Comprehensive System in Iberoamerica," pp. 347–352 in R. H. Dana (ed.) *Handbook of Cross-Cultural and Multicultural Personality Assessments* (Taylor & Francis: Abingdon, UK).

Viscusi, W. K. and R. J. Zeckhauser, 2005. "The Perception and Valuation of the Risks of Climate Change: A Rational and Behavioral Blend," *National Bureau of Economic Research*, Working Paper No. 11863.

Voigtlander, N. and H.-J. Voth. 2012. "Persecution Perpetuated: The Medieval Origins of Anti-Semitic Violence in Nazi Germany," *Quarterly Journal of Economics* 1339–1392.

Wade, N. 2022. "Cleaning Twitter's Augean Stables," *City Journal* (Dec. 21), www.city-journal.org/cleaning-up-twitter.

Wade, N., J. Mecklin and R. Bronson, 2021. Video: "The Origin of COVID: Did People or Nature Open Pandora's Box at Wuhan?" (June 10) http://info.thebulletin.org/e/878782/watch-now-the-origin-of-covid-/wjjn/304374893?h=J6sv_tyVH9Fg9kWl-VZHbvmoPt66M8bIWoy4WmFpsVY.

Wald, P. 2009. *Contagious: Cultures, Carriers, and the Outbreak Narrative* (Duke University Press: Durham, NC).

Waldvogel, J., 2017. "The Random Long Tail and the Golden Age of Television," in S. Greenstein, J. Lerner & S Stern (eds.), *Innovation Policy and the Economy*.

Waldvogel J., and I. Reimers, 2015. "Storming the Gatekeepers: Disintermediation in the Market for Books," *Informational Economics and Policy* 31: 47–58.

Wallace, M., 1968. "Changing Concepts of Party in the United States: New York, 1815–1828," *The American Historical Review* 74(2): 453–491.

Wallison, P. J., 2018. *Judicial Fortitude: The Last Chance to Rein in the Administrative State* (Encounter: New York).

Wallner, J., 2020. Blog: "A Brief History of Legislative Quorums," *Legislative Procedure*, www.legislativeprocedure.com/blog/2020/6/1/a-brief-history-of-legislative-quorums.

Walsh, D., 2020. "McConnell condemns Schumer's Comments targeting Supreme Court Justices," *National Public Radio* (Mar. 5) www.npr.org/2020/03/05/812465786/mcconnell-condemns-schumers-comments-targeting-supreme-court-justices.

Walsh, K. C., 2004. *Talking about Politics: Informal Groups and Social Identity in American Life* (University of Chicago Press: Chicago, IL).

Ward, J. J., 1981. "'Smash the Fascists...': German Communist Efforts to Counter the Nazis, 1930–31," *Central European History* 14: 30.

Washington, G. 1787. "Letter to Charles Carter" (Dec. 27), p. 612 in Bailyn (1993a).

Washington, G. 1796. "Farewell Address," https://web.archive.org/web/20090612002306/www.access.gpo.gov/congress/senate/farewell/sd106-21.pdf.

Watt, R. M. 2001 [1962]. *Dare Call it Treason: The True Story of the French Army Mutinies of 1917* (Dorset Press: New York).

Watt, R. M. 2001 [1968]. *Kings Depart: Versailles and the German Revolution* (Dorset Press: New York).

Watts, D. J. 2003. *Six Degrees: The Science of a Connected Age* (W.W. Norton: New York).

Watts, D. J., 2011. *Everything is Obvious (Once You Know the Answer)* (Crown: New York) (epub ed.)

Watts, D. J. and P. S. Dodds, 2007. "Influentials, Networks, and Public Opinion Formation," *Journal of Consumer Research* 34: 441–58.

Weart, S. R., 1988. *Nuclear Fear: A History of Images* (Harvard University Press: Cambridge, MA).

Weart, S. R., 2003. *The Discovery of Global Warming* (Harvard University Press: Cambridge and London)

Weber, M., 2015. *Weber's Rationalism and Modern Society: New Translations on Politics, Bureaucracy, and Social Stratification*, (T. Waters and D. Waters eds.) (Palgrave Macmillan: London).

Webster, N. H., 1787. "Reply to the Pennsylvania Minority" (Dec. 31), pp. 553–562 in Bailyn (1993a).

Webster, N. H., 1919. *The French Revolution: A Study in Democracy* (2d ed.) (Constable & Co: London).

Weiner, E., 2008. "The Long, Colorful History of the Mann Act," *National Public Radio* (Mar. 11) www.npr.org/templates/story/story.php?storyId=88104308.

Weiner, I. B., 2003. *Principles of Rorschach Interpretation* (Taylor & Francis: Milton Park, UK) (2nd ed.)

Weinschel, A. J., 2000. *Antitrust-Intellectual Property Handbook* (Glasser Legalworks: Little Falls, NJ).

Weissert, W., 2021. "Veterans are Prized Recruits as Congressional Candidates," *Associated Press News* https://apnews.com/article/veterans-9cad3c4211a0e15 852c44c8d75681254.

Wells, G, and I. Lovett, 2018. "The Toxic Online World Where Mass Shooters Thrive," *Wall Street Journal* (Sept. 5).

White, I. K. and C. N. Laird, 2020. Blog: "Why are Blacks Democrats?" *Ideas* (Feb. 25) *Princeton University Press*, https://press.princeton.edu/ideas/why-are-blacks-democrats.

Whitener, K., 2021. "Senate Rules and Budget Reconciliation Explained," *Georgetown University Health Policy Institute* (Jan. 25) https://ccf.george town.edu/2021/01/25/senate-voting-rules-and-budget-reconciliation-explained/.

Whittington, K. 2007. *Political Foundations of Judicial Supremacy: The Presidency, the Supreme Court, and Constitutional Leadership in U.S. History* (Princeton University Press: Princeton NJ).

Wikipedia (1). "1916 United States Presidential Election," https://en.wikipedia .org/wiki/1916_United_States_presidential_election.

Wikipedia (2). "2010 United States Senate Election in Alaska," https:// en.wikipedia.org/wiki/2010_United_States_Senate_election_in_Alaska.

Wikipedia (3). "2013 New York CIty Mayoral Election," https://en.wikipedia .org/wiki/2013_New_York_City_mayoral_election.

Wikipedia (4). "2017 New York CIty Mayoral Election," https://en.wikipedia .org/wiki/2017_New_York_City_mayoral_election.

Wikipedia (5). "Advocacy Journalism," https://en.wikipedia.org/wiki/Advocacy_ journalism.

Wikipedia (6). "Article 48 (Weimar Constitution)," https://en.wikipedia.org/ wiki/Article_48_(Weimar_Constitution).

Wikipedia (7). "Astroturfing," https://en.wikipedia.org/wiki/Astroturfing.

Wikipedia (8). "At Large," https://en.wikipedia.org/wiki/At-large.

Wikipedia (9). "Authorization for Use of Military Force Against Iraq Resolution of 2002," https://en.wikipedia.org/wiki/Authorization_for_Use_of_Military_ Force_Against_Iraq_Resolution_of_2002.

Wikipedia (10). "Authorization for Use of Military Force Against Iraq Resolution of 1991," https://en.wikipedia.org/wiki/Authorization_for_Use_of_ Military_Force_Against_Iraq_Resolution_of_1991.

Wikipedia (11). "Ballot Selfie," https://en.wikipedia.org/wiki/Ballot_selfie.

Wikipedia (12). "Bans on Nazi Symbols," https://en.wikipedia.org/wiki/Bans_ on_Nazi_symbols.

Wikipedia (13). "Benjamin Disraeli," https://en.wikipedia.org/wiki/Benjamin_ Disraeli.

Wikipedia (14). "Blackstone's Ratio," https://en.wikipedia.org/wiki/Blackstone% 27s_ratio.

Wikipedia (15). "Blue Network," https://en.wikipedia.org/wiki/Blue_Network.

Wikipedia (16). "CBS," https://en.wikipedia.org/wiki/CBS.

Wikipedia (17). "Charles Stewart Parnell," https://en.wikipedia.org/wiki/ Charles_Stewart_Parnell.

Wikipedia (18). "Compensated Emancipation," https://en.wikipedia.org/wiki/ Compensated_emancipation.

Wikipedia (19). "Continental Congress," https://en.wikipedia.org/wiki/ Continental_Congress.

Wikipedia (20). "Deep Throat (Watergate)," https://en.wikipedia.org/wiki/Deep_ Throat_(Watergate).

Wikipedia (21). "Democratic Peace Theory," https://en.wikipedia.org/wiki/ Democratic_peace_theory.

Wikipedia (22). "Emotion and Memory," https://en.wikipedia.org/wiki/ Emotion_and_memory.

Wikipedia (23). "Ernst Ising," https://en.wikipedia.org/wiki/Ernst_Ising.

Wikipedia (24). "False Consciousness," https://en.wikipedia.org/wiki/False_ consciousness.

Wikipedia (25). "Federal Assault Weapons Ban," https://en.wikipedia.org/wiki/ Federal_Assault_Weapons_Ban.

Wikipedia (26). "Filibuster in the United States Senate," https://en.wikipedia.org/ wiki/Filibuster_in_the_United_States_Senate.

Wikipedia (27). "Hyphenated American," https://en.wikipedia.org/wiki/ Hyphenated_American#Nativism_and_hyphenated_Americanism,_189 0%E2%80%931920.

Wikipedia (28). "Independent Agencies of the United States Government," https://en.wikipedia.org/wiki/Independent_agencies_of_the_United_States_ government.

Wikipedia (29). "Iron Triangle (US Politics)," https://en.wikipedia.org/wiki/Iron_ triangle_(US_politics).

Wikipedia (30). "Jerusalem Embassy Act," https://en.wikipedia.org/wiki/ Jerusalem_Embassy_Act.

Wikipedia (31). "Johann Gottfried Herder," https://en.wikipedia.org/wiki/ Johann_Gottfried_Herder.

Wikipedia (32). "John Tyler," https://en.wikipedia.org/wiki/John_Tyler.

Wikipedia (33). "Journalistic Objectivity," https://en.wikipedia.org/wiki/ Journalistic_objectivity#:~:text=Objectivity%20in%20journalism%20 aims%20to,or%20agree%20with%20those%20facts.

Wikipedia (34). "Let's Go Brandon," https://en.wikipedia.org/wiki/Let%27s_ Go_Brandon.

Wikipedia (35). "List of Wars Involving the United States," https://en.wikipedia.org/wiki/List_of_wars_involving_the_United_States.

Wikipedia (36). "Mass Media in the US," https://en.wikipedia.org/wiki/Mass_media_in_the_United_States#Newspapers.

Wikipedia (37). "Median Voter Theorem," https://en.wikipedia.org/wiki/Median_voter_theorem.

Wikipedia (38). "Miscellany for Deletion," https://en.wikipedia.org/wiki/Wikipedia:Miscellany_for_deletion/User:UBX/onemanonewoman_4th_nomination.

Wikipedia (39). "Mutual Broadcasting System," https://en.wikipedia.org/wiki/Mutual_Broadcasting_System.

Wikipedia (40). "Partition and Secession in California," https://en.wikipedia.org/wiki/Partition_and_secession_in_California.

Wikipedia (41). "Paul Broca," https://en.wikipedia.org/wiki/Paul_Broca.

Wikipedia (42). "Pendleton Civil Service Reform Act," https://en.wikipedia.org/wiki/Pendleton_Civil_Service_Reform_Act.

Wikipedia (43). "Pennsyltucky," https://en.wikipedia.org/wiki/Pennsyltucky.

Wikipedia (44). "Penny Press," https://en.wikipedia.org/wiki/Penny_press#:~:text=The%20emergence%20of%20the%20penny,not%20supported%20by%20political%20parties.

Wikipedia (46). "Progressive Party (United States 1912)," https://en.wikipedia.org/wiki/Progressive_Party_(United_States,_1912).

Wikipedia (47). "Propaganda of the Deed," https://en.wikipedia.org/wiki/Propaganda_of_the_deed?msclkid=951ccc15daac911eca605c7fc0393a737.

Wikipedia (48). "Propaganda of the Spanish-American War," https://en.wikipedia.org/wiki/Propaganda_of_the_Spanish%E2%80%93American_War.

Wikipedia (49). "Reconciliation (United States Congress)," https://en.wikipedia.org/wiki/Reconciliation_(United_States_Congress)#Origins.

Wikipedia (50). "Rotten and Pocket Boroughs," https://en.wikipedia.org/wiki/Rotten_and_pocket_boroughs."

Wikipedia (51). "Russian Revolution," https://en.wikipedia.org/wiki/Russian_Revolution#:~:text=The%20Bolsheviks%20had%20undergone%20a,leading%20cities%20of%20Russia%E2%80%94St

Wikipedia (52). "Saturday Night Massacre," https://en.wikipedia.org/wiki/Saturday_Night_Massacre#:~:text=The%20Saturday%20Night%20Massacre%20marked,see%20policy%20regarding%20Nixon%27s%20role.

Wikipedia (53). "Sedition Act of 1918," https://en.wikipedia.org/wiki/Sedition_Act_of_1918.

Wikipedia (54). "Standing (Law)," https://en.wikipedia.org/wiki/Standing_%28law%29#:~:text=Standing%20%28law%29%20From%20Wikipedia%2C%20the%20free%20encyclopedia%20In,case.%20Standing%20exists%20from%20one%20of%20three%20causes%3A.

Wikipedia (55). "Sunset Provision," https://en.wikipedia.org/wiki/Sunset_provision.

Wikipedia (56). "Temperance Movement," https://en.wikipedia.org/wiki/Temperance_movement.

Wikipedia (57). "The Day After," https://en.wikipedia.org/wiki/The_Day_After/.

Wikipedia (58). "Triangulation (Politics)," https://en.wikipedia.org/wiki/Triangulation_(politics)#:~:text=In%20politics%2C%20triangulation%20is%20a,ideas%20of%20one%27s%20political%20opponent.

Wikipedia (59). "Turing Machine," https://en.wikipedia.org/wiki/Turing_machine.

Wikipedia (60). "United States Presidential Primary," https://en.wikipedia.org/wiki/United_States_presidential_primary.

Wikipedia (61). "Voter Turnout in United States Presidential Elections," https://en.wikipedia.org/wiki/Voter_turnout_in_United_States_presidential_elections.

Wikipedia (62). "Arrow's Impossibility Theorem," https://en.wikipedia.org/wiki/Arrow%27s_impossibility_theorem.

Wilentz, A., 2020. "Kamala Harris is the Latest Product of San Francisco's Long-Running Political Machine," *Town & Country* (Oct. 6), www.townandcountrymag.com/society/politics/a34252538/kamala-harris-san-francisco-politics/.

Williams, A., 2004. "The Alchemy of a Political Slogan," *New York Times* (Aug. 22).

Williams, R. P., 2019. "Our Brush with Google Censorship," *Wall Street Journal* (May 8).

Williamson, O. E., 1975. *Markets and Hierarchies: Analysis and Antitrust Implications* (Free Press: New York).

Willsher, K., 2020. "Albert Camus Novel *The Plague* Leads Surge of Pestilence Fiction," *The Guardian* (Mar. 28), www.theguardian.com/books/2020/mar/28/albert-camus-novel-the-plague-la-peste-pestilence-fiction-coronavirus-lockdown.

Wilson, J. Q., 2000 [1989]. *Bureaucracy: What Government Agencies Do and Why They Do It* (Basic Books: New York).

Winik, J. 2001. *April 1865: The Month That Saved America* (Harper Collins: NY).

Winthrop, J., 1788. "Cherish the Old Confederation Like the Apple of Our Eye" (Jan. 11–18), pp. 762–773 in Bailyn (1993a).

Wolfinger, R. E. and S. J. Rosenstone, 1980. *Who Votes?* (Yale University Press: New Haven, CT).

Wollaston, S., 2018. "Growing up in the Wild Wild Country Cult," *The Guardian* (Apr. 24) www.theguardian.com/tv-and-radio/2018/apr/24/wild-wild-country-netflix-cult-sex-noa-maxwell-bhagwan-shree-rajneesh-commune-childhood.

Wood, G. S. (ed.), 2015. *The American Revolution: Writings from the Pamphlet Debate 1764–1772* (Library of America: New York).

Wood, P. W. and D. J. Pierre, 2019. *Neosegregation at Yale* (National Association of Scholars: New York), www.nas.org/storage/app/media/Reports/NeoSeg%20at%20Yale/NeoSegregation_at_Yale.pdf.

Wood, T., 2021. "Moving Industry Statistics," *MoveBuddha.com* (Oct. 30), www.movebuddha.com/blog/moving-industry-statistics/.

Woolley, J. and G. Peters, n.d. "Presidential Signing Statements," *The American Presidency Project*, www.presidency.ucsb.edu/documents/presidential-documents-archive-guidebook/presidential-signing-statements-hoover-1929.

Yeats, W. B. 1989 [1919 (b)], "The Second Coming," p. 119 in Finnernan (1989).

Yeats, W. B., [1919 (a)]. "Ego Dominus Tuus," p. 102 in Finneran (1989).

Yeats, W. B., 1932. "Remorse for Intemperate Speech," pp. 156–157 in Finneran (1989).

Yoo, J. C., 2002. "War and the Constitutional Text," *University of Chicago Law Review* 69: 1639–1684.

Yoo, J. C., 2004. "War, Responsibility, and the Age of Terrorism," *Stanford Law Review* 57(3): 793–823.

# Index

civil disobedience. *See* riots and
assassinations
Civil War. *See* war and armed conflicts
climate change. *See* global warming
Clinton, Hillary, 54, 112, 164, 166, 243,
317, 342
Clinton, William Jefferson ("Bill"), xiv, 82,
91, 109, 145, 244, 285
CNN. *See* Cable News Network ("CNN")
coercive politics, xii, 16, 169, *See also*,
Congress, Coercive politics
in the American political system, 160–1
and centrist voters, 161
costs and inefficiencies of, 163–4, 169,
239, 240
elections, 152
European examples of, 158–60
fragility of, 160–1, 169–70, 240
theory of, 160–3
voter support for, 161, 177
recent trends, 323
stability of, 1
Columbia Broadcasting System ("CBS"),
93, 102, 114
Congress, 19
bipartisan politics in, 216, 217, 223–6,
239, 242
caucuses, 227–8
coercive politics, xii, 4, 217, 229–31, 239
destabilizing effects of, 230–1
effect of political parties on, 24, 216,
218, 227, 229
ejection of members, 221, 241
filibusters and government shutdowns,
19, 156, 231, 245
advantages and limitations, 237–8
history of, 235–6, 238, 246
possible reforms, 328
as vehicles for measuring intensity,
235–7, 246, 247
as vehicles for suppressing jitter,
235, 239
Framers' expectations, 24, 216, 217, 221–3
gridlock in, 19, 229
history of, 181, 254–5
impeachment. *See* president and
executive branch
incumbency
advantages of, 226–8, 242
leadership and committees, 219, 223–4,
226, 227, 242, 247
seniority, 227–8

members electoral incentives, 223, 239
and presidential vetoes. *See* president
and executive branch
Problem Solvers Caucus, 328
rules and self-governance, 218–21
incentives and stability of,
218–20, 226
possible reforms, 328, 329
conspiracy theories. *See* political reasoning
and rhetoric
Constitution, U.S., 1–4, 7, 10, 14, 17, 87,
137, 139, 151, 181, 188, 193,
*See also* Congress; Judges and
Courts; president and executive
branch; voting and elections
Amendments to
1st Amendment (protecting free
speech), 327, 331
10th Amendment (reserving power to
the states), 197
13th Amendment (ending slavery), 21
14th Amendment (civil rights), 202
15th Amendment (equal protection),
203
Bill of Rights, 152
checks and balances, 9, 19
deliberate frictions, 10, 11, 231, 245
and jitter, 10, 11
Commerce Clause, 198–9, 203
Declaration of War clause, 271–2,
288, 290
Electoral College and Senate
bias toward small states, 193, 194,
210, 326
in early Republic, 249, 279
English precedents for, 7
expansive interpretation of federal
powers, 199, 203–5, 211, *See
also* federalism, expansive
interpretation of federal powers
federal structure, 189, 192, 201
Non-Delegation Doctrine. *See* separation
of powers
one-man-one-vote, 14, 182–3,
205, 208
goals of, 16–17
possible future amendments, 328
limited government, principle of, 11,
18, 196
secession and nullification, 201–2,
214, 215
separation of powers, 3, 8–10, 137